MW01617113

Black Religion / W
Series Editors Dwight N. Hopkins and Linda E. Thomas
Published by Palgrave Macmillan

"How Long This Road": Race, Religion, and the Legacy of C. Eric Lincoln
Edited by Alton B. Pollard, III and Love Henry Whelchel, Jr.

African American Humanist Principles: Living and Thinking Like the Children of Nimrod
By Anthony B. Pinn

White Theology: Outing Supremacy in Modernity
By James W. Perkinson

The Myth of Ham in Nineteenth-Century American Christianity: Race, Heathens, and the People of God
By Sylvester Johnson

Loving the Body: Black Religious Studies and the Erotic
Edited by Anthony B. Pinn and Dwight N. Hopkins

Transformative Pastoral Leadership in the Black Church
By Jeffery L. Tribble, Sr.

Shamanism, Racism, and Hip Hop Culture: Essays on White Supremacy and Black Subversion
By James W. Perkinson

Women, Ethics, and Inequality in U.S. Healthcare: "To Count Among the Living"
By Aana Marie Vigen

Black Theology in Transatlantic Dialogue: Inside Looking Out, Outside Looking In
By Anthony G. Reddie

Womanist Ethics and the Cultural Production of Evil
By Emilie M. Townes

Whiteness and Morality: Pursuing Racial Justice through Reparations and Sovereignty
By Jennifer Harvey

The Theology of Martin Luther King, Jr. and Desmond Mpilo Tutu
By Johnny B. Hill

Conceptions of God, Freedom, and Ethics in African American and Jewish Theology
By Kurt Buhring

Black Theology and Pedagogy
By Noel Leo Erskine

The Origins of Black Humanism in America: Reverend Ethelred Brown and the Unitarian Church
By Juan M. Floyd-Thomas

Black Religion and the Imagination of Matter in the Atlantic World
By James A. Noel

Bible Witness in Black Churches
By Garth Kasimu Baker-Fletcher

Enslaved Women and the Art of Resistance in Antebellum America
By Renee K. Harrison

Ethical Complications of Lynching: Ida B. Wells's Interrogation of American Terror
By Angela D. Sims

Representations of Homosexuality: Black Liberation Theology and Cultural Criticism
By Roger A. Sneed

The Tragic Vision of African American Religion
By Matthew V. Johnson

Beyond Slavery: Overcoming Its Religious and Sexual Legacies
Edited by Bernadette J. Brooten with the editorial assistance of Jacqueline L. Hazelton

Gifts of Virtue, Alice Walker, and Womanist Ethics
By Melanie Harris

Racism and the Image of God
By Karen Teel

Self, Culture, and Others in Womanist Practical Theology
By Phillis Isabella Sheppard

Sherman's March and the Emergence of the Independent Black Church Movement
By Love Henry Whelchel

Black Men Worshipping: Intersecting Anxieties of Race, Gender, and Christian Embodiment
By Stacy C. Boyd

Womanism Against Socially-Constructed Matriarchal Images: A Theoretical Model Towards a Therapeutic Goal
By MarKeva Gwendolyn Hill

Indigenous Black Theology: Toward an African-Centered Theology of the African-American Religious
By Jawanza Eric Clark

Black Bodies and the Black Church: A Blues Slant
By Kelly Brown Douglas

A Theological Account of Nat Turner: Christianity, Violence, and Theology
By Karl Lampley

African American Female Mysticism: Nineteenth-Century Religious Activism
By Joy R. Bostic

A Queering of Black Theology: James Baldwin's Blues Project and Gospel Prose
By EL Kornegay Jr.

Formation of the African Methodist Episcopal Church in the Nineteenth Century: Rhetoric of Identification
A. Nevell Owens

Toward a Womanist Ethic of Incarnation: Black Bodies, the Black Church, and the Council of Chalcedon
Eboni Marshall Turman

Religio-Political Narratives: From Martin Luther King Jr. to Jeremiah Wright
Angela D. Sims, F. Douglas Powe Jr., and Johnny Bernard Hill

Churches, Blackness, and Contested Multiculturalism : Europe, Africa, and North America
Edited by R. Drew Smith, William Ackah, and Anthony G. Reddie

Womanist and Black Feminist Responses to Tyler Perry's Productions
LeRhonda S. Manigault-Bryant, Tamura A. Lomax, and Carol B. Duncan

James Baldwin's Understanding of God: Overwhelming Desire and Joy
By Josiah Ulysses Young III

A Womanist Pastoral Theology Against Intimate and Cultural Violence: A Narrative Approach to Self-Recovery
By Stephanie M. Crumpton

Kairos, Crisis, and Global Apartheid: The Challenge to Prophetic Resistance
By Allan Aubrey Boesak

Kairos, Crisis, and Global Apartheid

The Challenge to Prophetic Resistance

Allan Aubrey Boesak

palgrave
macmillan

KAIROS, CRISIS, AND GLOBAL APARTHEID

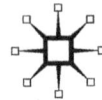

Softcover reprint of the hardcover 1st edition 2015 978-1-137-50308-4

First published in 2015 by
PALGRAVE MACMILLAN®
in the United States—a division of St. Martin's Press LLC,
175 Fifth Avenue, New York, NY 10010.

Where this book is distributed in the UK, Europe and the rest of the world, this is by Palgrave Macmillan, a division of Macmillan Publishers Limited, registered in England, company number 785998, of Houndmills, Basingstoke, Hampshire RG21 6XS.

Palgrave Macmillan is the global academic imprint of the above companies and has companies and representatives throughout the world.

ISBN 978-1-137-50309-1   ISBN 978-1-137-49531-0 (eBook)
DOI 10.1057/9781137495310

Library of Congress Cataloging-in-Publication Data is available from the Library of Congress.

A catalogue record of the book is available from the British Library.

Design by Newgen Knowledge Works (P) Ltd., Chennai, India.

First edition: June 2015

10 9 8 7 6 5 4 3 2 1

For Gayraud Wilmore, elder statesman of the black church, friend and mentor, and, Nicholas Wolterstorff, matchless thinker and scholar, and undaunted friend.

In both of whom the priceless gift of friendship has found such glorious expression With respect and gratitude

Contents

Introduction 1

1 Hearing the Cry and Reading the Signs of the Times: A Humanity with a Kairos Consciousness 9

2 At the Heart of It All: Kairos, Apartheid, and the Calvinist Tradition 39

3 The Time for Pious Words Is Over: Kairos, Decision, and Righteous Choices 69

4 The Inclusiveness of God's Embrace: Kairos, Justice, the Dignity of Human Sexuality, and the Confession of Belhar 93

5 The End of Words? Kairos, Challenge, and the Rhetoric of the Barricades 119

6 Speaking Truth to the Tower: Kairos, Dissent, and Prophetic Speech 141

7 Combative Love and Revolutionary Neighborliness: Kairos, Solidarity, and the Jericho Road 169

8 That Which Avails Much: Kairos, Public Prayer, and Political Piety 199

Notes 213

Bibliography 255

Index 267

Introduction

It took the compelling and inescapable moral authority of the Palestinian cry for justice—a cry from within the authenticity of Christian witness in the midst of unnamable, unremitting suffering and courageous struggle, of unbearable contradictions and deep complexities—to reconnect the remnants of the prophetic movements in the churches worldwide to their prophetic tradition, and reawaken the sense of *kairos* in communities where the prophetic voice has long been silent. Not since 1985, with the publication of the first *Kairos Document* in South Africa, in the midst of apartheid's darkest decade—and the publication of subsequent *Kairos Documents* in different countries—has the word kairos commanded such concentrated theological, political, and ecumenical discussion.[1]

Since its publication the Palestinian *Kairos Document* of 2009 has been receiving wide attention and thoughtful, encouraging responses from concerned circles within different faith communities across the world, and has given rise to a new and challenging ecumenical and interfaith conversation.[2] It has also caused considerable soul searching, leading many in diverse faith communities to ask serious questions about their lack of prophetic witness, their silence in the face of glaring injustices, their complicity in at best tolerating, and at worst perpetuating, rather than challenging and transforming, systems of domination and oppression.

It brought to the fore questions around the meaning of a "kairos consciousness" as well as a "kairos theology," and the possibility of an ecumenical, interfaith, "global kairos movement" that is being explored even as I write. How does such a kairos consciousness contribute to the renewed debates on "kairos" and how does it impact our biblical interpretation and the prophetic witness and praxis that flow from it? In the Christian community, those of us who have been practitioners of the prophetic theology that forms and informs the tradition within which the South African *Kairos Document* (1985) was born, are now once again compelled to raise new questions about the relevance and efficacy of such a prophetic tradition for the times in which we live, and whether the Scriptures can speak as clearly, reveal as relentlessly, inspire as powerfully as they did for us when we discovered God's challenge, God's kairos, in the crises of our times then.

It raises, especially, questions about our prophetic faithfulness, now that the seats of power in our countries are no longer occupied by an "enemy" but by "our own" and yet the demands for justice are as unrelenting as they were then; now that so much of the violence that is devastating communities and countries across the globe seeks to find justification in the faith we profess; and now that global imperial powers and their demands are as real, and as ruthless, as in the times of the ancient Hebrew prophets and Jesus. Since the challenges from the Palestinian struggles for justice, freedom, and peace are ongoing, urgent, and presently commanding attention throughout the world as never before, every response to the Palestinian *Kairos Document* seems compelled to include a "call for action." These are all issues the present book seeks to grapple with in an effort to contribute to this global, ecumenical, theological conversation.

The first *Kairos Document* was published in response to the political perversity and theological heresy of apartheid in South Africa. Today, the new discussions around kairos take place within a situation of what has been called "global apartheid."

In our thinking and thus in the strategies for resistance against apartheid, we discerned that the struggle was not just against an evil system and its consequences, but that it should be aimed at the very pillars on which such systems are built. We then started to define the fundamentals of the apartheid system in South Africa and it is remarkable how those fundamentals are found in global systems of oppression and domination today.

- Colonialism and its vile legacy, which included slavery, subjugation, dehumanization, dispossession, and generational trauma;
- Social Darwinism, expressed in customs, laws, and attitudes enshrining white superiority and black inferiority, which provided the basis for South Africa's peculiar racist, pigmentocratic societal structures;
- Socioeconomic, capitalist exploitation, not exclusively based on race, but also, for example, on gender injustice;
- Cultural domination resting on cultural annihilation on the one hand and cultural assimilation on the other, the key being that the culture of the subjugated peoples and groups is always deemed worthless compared to the culture of the dominant groups, and therefore unworthy of consideration and contribution;
- Psychological, ideological, political, and economic power; as well as the power derived from international (white) solidarity and global systems of domination;

- A belief in white innocence based on a powerful ideology of white, and in many ways, particularly Afrikaner victimhood;
- Violence in all its forms: systemic, structural, ideological, and pervasive, and physical violence, guaranteeing and solidifying control;
- Finally, and in South Africa absolutely crucial, ideologized religion (sometimes called civil religion), its belief systems, central to which was the belief in white exceptionalism in general and Afrikaner chosenness in particular with its unique and exclusive covenant with God, and its power in the justification of domination and subjugation.

In understanding these fundamentals, we understand better why our global struggles today can be defined as struggles against a new global apartheid, and why for so many, especially South Africans, the identification of "Israeli apartheid": its attitudinal as well as systematic aspects, its pervasive violence, the oppression and domination by a minority is so immediately recognizable.[3] This book argues that the manifestations of global apartheid, like South African apartheid 30 years ago, constitute a life-and-death crisis for God's most vulnerable and defenseless children.[4] Of course, what is true of global inequalities on a massive scale between North and South is distressingly, and increasingly, true of societies within countries all over the world.[5] This crisis, in turn, constitutes a kairos, a moment of discernment, conversion, and commitment, a challenge to people of faith from God and from the suffering people.

Chapter 1 is an effort to define and understand the meaning of a "kairos consciousness" and a "kairos theology," which is a concept introduced in this new round of the discourse on kairos. In the process we are asking the question whether, and where, God might be at work in the upheavals, struggles, and moments (and movements) of resistance of our times and whether in those crises there is a kairos moment for people of faith to discern and respond to. This is a question that was raised from the global South in the period (1960s and 1970s) just before the crises in South Africa specifically called forth the debate on kairos in the 1980s. In light of the present waves of domination, destruction, and oppression; of resistance, revolutions, and upheavals across the global South as well as in the heart of global empire such as the protests against police brutality and for human rights so poignantly represented by the name "Ferguson" in the United States I am persuaded that this question has become pertinent again. It also, in reflecting on a theme that runs throughout this book, asks what it means when someone is called a "prophet." Are they always the steadfast, rock solid, courageous women and men of God who inspire us so much? Those fearless speakers of truth whom we try to emulate with a strange mixture of admiration, trepidation, and envy, fearing sometimes that the chasm between us and the likes of Elijah, Rizpah, Amos, and Jesus; Sojourner Truth, Lilian Ngoyi, and Fannie Lou Hamer; Dietrich Bonhoeffer, Albert Luthuli, and Martin Luther King Jr., is so huge that we will never find the courage that forms the bridge so we can cross it and just get closer to their spirit, let alone being clothed with a "double portion" of it, as Elisha begs from Elijah. And are we, as a result, as Jesus speaks of the prophetic vulnerability of John the Baptist in Matthew's gospel, more "like a reed shaking in the wind"?

As from chapter 2 the issues become more sharply focused. Where do we discern crises that are in fact kairos moments? To try and answer this question we turn first to apartheid South Africa, the birthplace of the first *Kairos Document*, and probe the meaning of kairos and the struggle for the relevance of the Calvinist tradition. This is the tradition that was presented by the powerful white Dutch Reformed Churches with their inordinate influence on government and the white Afrikaans-speaking community, as the mainstay of the theological and moral justification of apartheid. At the same time however, this same Reformed tradition, in the way it was received, reinterpreted, and applied by the black Reformed Churches, became foundational and singularly inspirational for black Reformed Christians, as well as for Christians from other traditions in their participation in the struggle for freedom. This chapter seeks to illustrate how a theological tradition, used as a tool of abuse and oppression by powerful interests, can be reclaimed as inspiration for struggles for freedom by the powerless and the oppressed. It raises a further interesting question: Can a radical Reformed theology make a meaningful contribution to the ecumenical involvement in struggles for justice and peace and freedom today, also in those places and situations where one's first theological thoughts do not turn to John Calvin and the legacy he left behind?

This question becomes even more pertinent as we discover, at least in my view, how much of a precursor to modern liberation theology Calvin's theology of social justice actually was.[6] Taking the form of a somewhat personal theological reflection while simultaneously tracing the development of a theological countertradition, the chapter asks what in that tradition remains relevant and inspiring for the local and global justice struggles we are engaged in today. We now know that for many South Africa's reconciliation process has become something of a model to be emulated by other nations and communities in situations of conflict. But is there something to learn from the dangers of providing religious, theological, and biblical justification for systems of oppression? Can we learn from the prophetic tradition and the theological struggle against the apartheid heresy that made that reconciliation process possible?

Chapter 3 looks at the life and work of two figures whose decision to follow Christ in costly discipleship would bring painful consequences for themselves but simultaneously would have transformational impact on the life of the church and the struggles of their day: Dietrich Bonhoeffer, theologian, pastor, and resister in Hitler's Germany and Christiaan Frederick Beyers Naudé, Afrikaner, pastor, and resister in apartheid South Africa. Every situation of conflict and struggle presents persons of faith with serious and profound decisions to make as regards to their own participation in such struggles, and to consider the impact those decisions are sure to have on their ministry, their political witness as well as on their personal lives.

We seek to discover the relationship between an abiding kairos consciousness as we understand it and the courage to make life-transforming decisions in the difficult, risk-laden but liberating choices Bonhoeffer and Naudé had made, and the difference those choices made in the struggles they joined, and in the process in the witness of the church in the world. What is there to learn from such legacies of prophetic faithfulness as contemporary crises are turned into kairos moments today, and what difference, if any, does it make when Bonhoeffer and Naudé are examined, not through analyses from the rich, global North, but, as Bonhoeffer himself sought to do, "from below," from the viewpoints and experiences of oppressed communities, which is also the lens of the kairos prophetic tradition?

Chapter 4 relates to one of the greatest challenges for the church today, but in Africa and the global South especially, now more of a kairos call than ever in light of the utterly shocking draconian legislation aimed against LGBTI persons, adopted by Uganda's parliament and signed into law by President Yoweri Museveni in the very week this manuscript is completed, and the disastrous consequences this holds for African societies, the African church, and the church of Christ world-wide. The chapter engages my own denomination, the Uniting Reformed Church in Southern Africa, its decisions regarding this matter and the significant ramifications, in my view, for that denomination's greatest achievement, the Confession of Belhar, and consequently also for that church's prophetic witness in South Africa and the world.

Since I believe that no prophetic ministry, preaching or action is authentic or effective unless it is rooted in the prophetic, covenantal tradition in Scripture, as it is rooted in the hopeful witness of the people as they seek to remain true to that covenant—from Moses and Elijah to Isaiah and Micah to John the Baptist and Jesus of Nazareth—chapters 4, 5, 6, and 7 are all efforts to understand the necessity of biblical interpretation for faith-bound prophetic action in the world. These chapters endeavor to develop what one might call a theology of prophetic preaching. I seek to explore what it might mean when we take prophetic preaching, as words *and* actions, to its most concrete, vivid, and public conclusion, as Preaching scholar Richard Lischer urges us to do.[7] Together with New Testament scholar Richard Horsley, South African Hebrew Bible scholars Gunther Wittenberg and Gerald West, and growing numbers in scholarly circles, I read the Bible as "a history of faithful resistance" against imperial powers for the sake of freedom and justice,[8] a book that seeks to celebrate God's liberating work in history on behalf of God's people. Seeking to remain true to the tenets of liberation theology, I employ a hermeneutics of suspicion, liberation, and inclusion and I am heartened by how these have remained relevant, indeed have gained renewed applicability and urgency in the current struggles against imperial globalism.

Throughout my life I have approached the Bible not just as a book to study and critically reflect on, but also as one inspired by it, overwhelmed by the power of its message, its good news for the enslaved, the poor, the downtrodden, and the afflicted and its insistence on God as a God of compassionate justice and freedom in whom our hope is anchored. I remain fascinated by the unremitting struggles captured in the pages of the Bible between the representatives of the covenantal, prophetic tradition on the one hand, and the forces of imperial domination and oppression on the other. At the same time, within ancient Israel, there are struggles between the faithful prophets who seek God's justice for the poor and downtrodden and those powerful and privileged elites, their religious sycophants and justifiers, whose imitation of the ways of empire in the oppression and domination of the poor and vulnerable within Israel has caused such misery and devastation and called forth such righteous anger and persistent resistance. I remain as fascinated by the longings for hope, liberation, and redemption these struggles, as we find them within in those pages, represent in their ancient contexts and continue to inspire within the hearts of oppressed communities of faith even today.

Chapter 8 is a reflection on kairos, prayer, and public piety and here I return to what noted South African theologian Charles Villa-Vicencio called "among the most significant and prophetic events in the history of the theological struggle against apartheid in the turbulent 1980s by the church in resistance to apartheid,"[9] namely the highly controversial call to pray for the downfall of the apartheid regime in 1985. I reintroduce the *Call for the End to Unjust Rule* to reflect on an open letter to a minister in President Thabo Mbeki's cabinet 15 years later. This chapter probes the meaning of prayer, politics, and public piety for us today in the current climate of heightened, and yes, treacherous civil religiosity in the service of empire, historically so decisively present in the United States, but relatively new and growing in the global South.

In the writing of this book my debt to friends, colleagues, and diverse audiences is such that I find it hard to express my gratitude. Some of these chapters have been inspired by the life and work of departed heroes of the faith such as Dietrich Bonhoeffer to whom I was first introduced almost 40 years ago by my now sadly departed friend and teacher at the Protestant Theological University in Kampen, the Netherlands, Gerard Rothuizen, and the late Beyers Naudé, a white Afrikaner and rebel against apartheid who, I feel now, I have met just in time to fundamentally affect my life and who became a mentor and friend. Bonhoeffer's influence on my theology and my life is huge, and the older I get the more I discover aspects of his thinking and facets of his life that enlighten and inspire me in ways that I find constantly surprising. This much will be evident throughout this book. Chapter 7 is inspired by the ministry of a remarkable pastor and friend, Dr. J. Alfred Smith Sr., pastor emeritus of Allen Temple Baptist Church in Oakland California.

I am deeply grateful to those, at churches and academic institutions, before whom I have had the honor of speaking on some of the subjects which have now become chapters in this book. Their critical responses have been of enormous help in my rethinking of the material they have so graciously listened to. A few of the chapters here have been published before but all have been thoroughly revised for inclusion in this work. There are of course those friends and colleagues who have read portions of this book and have done me the honor to respond with correction, suggestions, friendly agreement to disagree but always encouragement: Nicholas Wolterstorff, Vuyani Vellem, Charles Villa-Vicencio, Leonora Tubbs Tisdale, John De Gruchy, Curtiss Paul DeYoung, and Simangaliso R. Kumalo. Those who over many months have engaged me in discussion on some or all of this material deserve my deepest gratitude. My students and colleagues at Butler University and Christian Theological Seminary are a pleasant and uplifting constant in my sojourn here in a place of seemingly unending winters.

Of course, and as always, I am amazed at the infinite patience, steadfast support, and tireless encouragement of my family. That my wife Elna and our children not only put up with my busyness and preoccupations in these endeavors, but actually loved and encouraged me through it all is a grace I do not deserve, but nonetheless eagerly embrace and gratefully hold onto.

Allan Aubrey Boesak,
Indianapolis,
Ash Wednesday, 2014

1

Hearing the Cry and Reading the Signs of the Times: A Humanity with a Kairos Consciousness

Kairos Consciousness

South Africans who stand in the prophetic tradition of the *Kairos Document* that came out of South Africa in the dark days of the anti-apartheid struggle and the first state of emergency in 1985, are the first to admit that the Palestinian Kairos called them to a moment of awareness of that prophetic tradition they seemed by and large to have forgotten. It was a reawakening of kairos in a community where the prophetic voice has not only been scarce, but even when hesitantly raised, also not gladly heard since the birth of a democratic South Africa in 1994. This holds true, I suggest, for the church in the United States as well, and perhaps elsewhere.[1] It seems that every response to *Kairos Palestine* begins with some confession of guilt.

In December 2009 the *Palestine Kairos Document* was published. It could easily have been one more kairos document in addition to all those other kairos documents that followed the original kairos document from South Africa.[2] But this time it was different. It set in motion what some are calling a "global kairos movement" and through the responses from the United States and South Africa to begin with, triggered serious attention for what has been named "the rebirth of kairos theology."[3] It also raised a question that indicated that the response to the *Palestinian Kairos Document* was considering something much more profound, and which will prove to be much more durable, namely the question of a kairos consciousness.

"Is there such a thing as a kairos consciousness?" was the question I was asked by Rev. Edwin Arrison, one of the leaders of Kairos Southern Africa in 2011. It was one year after a series of conversations in circles of progressive, concerned persons in faith communities; the year, essentially in response to the *Palestinian Kairos Document*, "Kairos Southern Africa" was launched stating its sweeping vision: "A Humanity with a Kairos Consciousness." I then responded with some preliminary thoughts on what I thought was an important and intriguing question, now more so than ever.[4] In light of the reemergence since then of a "kairos theology" and the concomitant establishment of not just a Southern African, but, as the bold vision statement of Kairos Southern Africa makes clear, a global kairos movement,[5] we should reflect more carefully on what such a kairos consciousness might be.

Kairos is not so much a "time" or a "season" but a *moment*, unique, for people of faith to see, understand, and act upon. But speaking of a "kairos consciousness" already indicates that what is meant here is more than just the realization of some matter of mere momentary import. It suggests an abiding awareness, what one could call a prophetic alertness, a readiness for when such a moment might arrive. The phrasing of the vision statement also suggests more than an individualized consciousness, indeed, a consciousness that stirs, embraces, and inspires "humanity." The understanding is clear: in 1985, a group of prophetic Christians were overwhelmed by a moment of truth for the situation in South Africa, and the *Kairos Document* spoke specifically to the South African context of racist domination, political oppression, socioeconomic exploitation, and the silence of the church in regard to all these. Almost to our surprise we discovered how others, in their specific contexts across the globe—and not only in the global South—understood their situations of political, social, and theological crises as a kairos moment for themselves. Hence the birth of several kairos documents across the world since 1985.[6] Now, however, there is a deliberateness to the call not merely for new kairos documents, but for an abiding kairos consciousness *for humanity*. The crisis we are facing now is a *global* crisis, the call to understand this moment as a kairos moment is for *all* humanity.

It is, moreover, a moment of truth, revealing the falsehoods without which an unjust status quo cannot exist, but which blind, beguile, and disable us. Without seeing, discerning, and acting the moment passes us by. Hence the kairos moment is decisive. A kairos consciousness is a consciousness awake and open to the discovering of, and responding to the decisiveness and uniqueness of that moment. Such a kairos moment also reveals the truth about ourselves, strips us of all pseudo-innocence,[7] and as such it is a moment of discernment, repentance, conversion, and commitment. In that moment we discover the truth: about the situation with which we are faced, about ourselves and the Other; about the realities of pain and suffering, about the demands of love and justice, and about the God-given possibilities for real and fundamental change. It is also the truth that sets us free. It is simultaneously a shocking and a liberating moment.

Crucially, however, a kairos consciousness knows that the discovery of that moment of truth is not a moment of triumphalist gloating, confirming and celebrating our own spiritual superiority, but rather of profound and humble joy for the gift of discernment, discontentment, and dissent. Discernment of what is wrong in a situation and the crisis it creates for the most vulnerable, discontent with that situation of injustice, and a refusal to leave things as they are; and dissent from the dominant judgment that the status quo is acceptable, unchangeable, or irreversible.

The discovery of a moment of truth in history is not the result of our intelligence and extraordinary cleverness. It is revelation, the gift of the Holy Spirit. We are not the truth: the truth has found, recovered, and reclaimed us. We are not the light: the light illumines and leads us. We are not *the* voice: we speak and act because we heard the Voice that calls us to do justice, love mercy, and walk humbly with our God. The voice we hear and respond to is the voice of the voiceless, the poor, and oppressed, those who are the faces at the bottom of the well. In those voices, is the forceful argument of John Calvin, we hear the very voice of God:

> Tyrants and their cruelty cannot be endured without great weariness and sorrow...Hence almost the whole world sounds forth these words, "How long?" When anyone disturbs the whole world by his ambition and avarice, or everywhere commits plunders, or oppresses miserable nations, when he distresses the innocent, all cry out, "How long?" And this cry, proceeding as it does from the feeling of nature and the dictates of justice, is at length heard by the Lord...[The oppressed] know that this confusion of order and justice is not to be endured. And this feeling, is it not implanted by the Lord? *It is then the same as though God heard Himself, when he hears the cries and groaning of those who cannot bear injustice.*[8]

This is an insight from Calvin I have had cause to return to and reflect upon again and again,[9] and in this context it is most helpful in understanding what I mean by a kairos consciousness. This is how I understand Calvin on this issue. Notice first how such a consciousness understands the indivisibility of justice. Martin Luther King Jr., was right: injustice anywhere is a threat to justice everywhere. Calvin's repeated "the whole world" is not just rhetorical hyperbole or a manner of speaking. It is a keen awareness of the impact of injustice on humanity as a whole, to quote yet another famous word of Martin Luther King Jr., of the "inescapable network of mutuality" and the "single garment of destiny," of our common yearning for justice and of the need for human solidarity in resisting injustice and striving for justice. It understands the workings of power and the destruction wrought by power "divorced from the fear of God" as Calvin states elsewhere. It is remarkable how relevant this insight has become in our globalized political and economic power realities and in the deadly stranglehold of a few—the now universally recognized 1 percent!—on the rest of humanity and on creation as a whole.

Second, still engaging Calvin, a kairos consciousness understands the difference between "order" and "justice" and refuses to accept that tyranny, injustice, and oppression should be tolerated as necessary for "order," or more precisely, *mistaken* for order. Calvin calls this a "confusion." For Calvin—despite his grave concern for order in society and his fear of chaos, or perhaps better put, *because of* his concern for proper order in society—"order," or in its other, often used, and always lethal combination, "law and order," in our global reality more and more parading as "national security"—is not the enforced state of confusion when the law, violence, and the abuse of power are used to protect the position of the powerful and privileged and to keep the poor impoverished and the subjugated silent. Order prevails when compassionate justice is done and there is no confusion about right and wrong in society. A kairos consciousness, in reading the signs of the times, making political judgments and calling upon the church to act will, I think, embrace Paul Lehmann's contention about what he calls "the proper priorities of politics," namely that "Freedom is the presupposition and the condition of order: order is not the presupposition and condition of freedom. Justice is the foundation and criterion of law; law is not the foundation and criterion of justice. These are the proper priorities of politics."[10]

Third, the cry for justice is not only implanted *by* the Lord; it is as though God hears Godself when the oppressed cry "How long?" Their cry is God's cry, emanating from the heart of a God wounded by the injustices inflicted upon the poor and defenseless.[11] If a renewed Kairos movement is "now conceived and established to nurture the prophetic voice that recognizes the face of God in the face of the poor and most marginalized people" as Kairos Southern Africa proclaims in its constitution,[12] then a kairos consciousness that understands injustice and injury inflicted upon God's children as wounds inflicted *upon God* is absolutely vital.[13]

It is the "poor and oppressed" of whom Calvin speaks, who form "the people" in the language of the *Kairos Document*. Their cries are not the plaintive cries of helpless resignation and desolate hopelessness. These are cries of pain *in protest to their suffering*. These cries are constituted by their pain *and* their resistance to injustice. These are cries of struggle: the oppressed are not sitting idly by, waiting for some miracle to be performed in their behalf. They are the active, hopeful *sizwe*, who refuse to be silenced by the opium of post-apartheid civil religiosity (in other words, state theology) employed by politicians who speak blandly of South Africa as a "Lord-fearing nation, a God-fearing country," where Christians are called to "raise the moral consciousness of the nation" while leaving politics and economics to the politicians and experts. This dichotomy is called for because the ANC already has a chaplain-general "to ensure that the ANC stays close to God's light," and that it does "everything in accordance with what God requires" as Deputy President Cyril Ramaphosa assures them.[14] The people reject these post-1994 state theological heresies and continue to challenge both church and state in the name of a prophetic theology that arises out of the cries of the people which are indeed "heard by the Lord."

But Calvin is quite radical in this and we must not miss it: if it is true that God is not just hearing the poor and oppressed when they cry out against injustice, but God is hearing *God's own self* in their cries, it means that God is not just the God of the poor; God presents Godself *as* the poor and oppressed. Their cries *are* God's cries. Those cries may be the cries of the powerless, but they make their appeal upon us with inescapable authority. Furthermore, Calvin speaks of all those "who cannot bear injustice." He means not only those upon whom injustice is inflicted, but also those who cry out *on their behalf*, and therefore do what is right and just. In their cry as well God hears Godself, and in their doing of justice the wounds of God are healed.[15]

A kairos consciousness will observe, experience, and judge the world as seen through the eyes of the suffering, the poor, and the marginalized, in so doing seeing the world through the eyes of Jesus.[16] This means, besides much else, that one is no longer blinded by the propaganda of the powerful, by the pressures of contemporary society or global imperial powers to conform to what those powers may deem normal or acceptable. One will, instead, resist being dictated to by one's own fears or desires to be part of a world that scandalizes Jesus because that world lures us with privileges and the comfort of protection against the powerful or against the appeal (or the wrath?) of those brothers and sisters we are leaving behind. For the Palestinians who produced the *Palestinian Kairos Document* and living under Israeli occupation, witnessing the relentless destruction and the weeks of civilian deaths in Gaza, "seeing through the eyes of Jesus" has existential, and extraordinarily poignant significance, as Palestinian liberation theologian Naim Stifan Ateek makes clear:

> Like many Palestinians today, Jesus was born under occupation and throughout his life knew only a life under occupation. All his travels, his eating and drinking, his teaching and healing ministry, his relationships with others—every aspect of his life—were carried out under the

> oppressive domination of the Romans. Finally, he was executed by the occupation forces in collusion with the religious leaders of first-century Jerusalem.[17]

It also means that one can no longer avoid making choices, and those choices will reflect God's choices: for the poor, the wronged, the destitute, and the vulnerable. This depicts an engaging consciousness, an understanding that because one is no longer blind to injustice, one can no longer be neutral. One cannot but join the struggle for the sake of justice and righteousness. A kairos consciousness becomes an engaging, liberation-oriented consciousness, intent on the humanizing of God's world.

A kairos consciousness is a critical and simultaneously self-critical consciousness. It is critical because it discerns and critiques the situation in which we live, understanding that it is a situation of life and death, and seeing through the eyes of those who suffer and are most vulnerable, it offers prophetic critique of that situation, and calls for prophetic resistance in that situation. Such a consciousness understands that there is a conflict, a struggle going on for the sake of those whose lives are precious in God's sight and that the moment calls for the church to take sides. Because it is a matter of life and death neutrality is not possible. It is a conflict between rich and poor, oppressor and oppressed, powerful and powerless, beneficiaries and victims, those who are included in the circles of power and privilege and those who are excluded, denied flourishing and a meaningful life.

From India habil James Massey tells us where, for Indian Christians with a kairos consciousness, that critique will lead us: "The final call of Kairos that comes to social activists (including the church) is: they should move from an 'ambulance ministry' to a 'ministry of involvement and participation' in the struggle of the Dalit-Bahujan for their liberation (including their own), so that a 'just society' may get established, in which peace will reign with justice, and all will live with fuller redeemed dignity and recovered humanity."[18]

In that critique there is no room for sentiment and romanticism—peoples' lives are at stake. That critique will be wary of notions of "critical solidarity" with governing powers that in our recent South African history has so quickly, and disastrously, replaced solidarity with the poor and prophetic faithfulness to God. A kairos consciousness is aware that the crisis we are facing is not just economic, social, and political; it is at the deepest level a moral crisis.

By the same token though, a kairos consciousness is a *self-critical* consciousness. This works on at least two levels. There is indeed a conflict, but there are Christians on both sides of that conflict. There are those Christians, and sometimes whole hierarchies within churche who seek to use the Bible, the tradition, and theology to serve and protect the status quo, those who uphold and sustain it, and those who benefit from it to the detriment of the poor, the weak, and the vulnerable. On the other side of the conflict are those Christians with a kairos consciousness who understand God's call in that moment as a call to repentance and conversion, to commitment to justice and the liberation of the oppressed.[19] Hence the very important distinction of the 1985 *Kairos Document* between what it identified as three theologies: state theology, church theology, and prophetic theology.[20] A kairos consciousness is critical vis-à-vis the church that takes sides with the oppressors, but does not try to deny the fact that we ourselves are part of the church. The call of the kairos moment is therefore a call to repentance. That is why the *Kairos Document* was called "A challenge to the church."

It understood, correctly, that "The time has come...[1985] is the KAIROS moment of truth not only for apartheid but also for the church." It understood that the "crisis in South Africa" constituted not just a crisis in society; it was a crisis within the church. In this crisis "there will be no place to hide." What the crisis reveals is that the church, tragically but not at all surprisingly, is deeply divided. Here however, an important issue arises. In discerning the kairos moment in the crisis the prophetic theology of the *Kairos Document* did more than recognize that such a crisis exists. Prophetic theology stood, and acted, in tension, and in contention with "church theology" and "state theology." It contested the willingness of the church to make alliances with "state theology" for whatever reason. It recognized the role of the church in creating the crisis and then acting as if the crisis did not exist. As a consequence, it called the church to repentance and conversion, to the unmasking and undoing of injustice and the doing of justice; to say "no" to compliance with the oppressive powers and "yes" to solidarity with the poor and oppressed. It called on the church to exchange its fear of state power for the fear of the Lord. It challenged the church to turn its back on the rewards of expediency and to choose instead the risks of obedience; to shun the comforts of complicity and embrace instead the uncertainties of the struggle for justice.

It called the church to a different kind of witness, to a life truer and more faithful to its confession that Jesus Christ is Lord, not the imperial powers to which the church has made itself beholden. In challenging the church with the call to stand with the oppressed and challenge the oppressor, prophetic theology, in engaging the crisis in society and confronting it with the justice Yahweh requires, did not simply find itself in a situation of crisis as if by accident. It *provoked* the crisis—albeit a different kind of crisis—within the church and in society. That moment of truth is not just the truth about society; it is the truth about the church—its faithfulness to Christ, its choices, its witness, its relationship with God, in other words, its life. Hence the intensity of the crisis.

Walter Brueggemann makes this even clearer. "The task of prophetic ministry is," he says, "to nurture, nourish, and evoke a consciousness and perception alternative to the consciousness and perception of the dominant culture around us."[21] Brueggemann makes the point that the public crises Christians are facing are not isolated, incidental, and temporary. They are, he insists, the result of "the dominant crisis that is enduring and resilient, of having our alternative vocation coopted and domesticated."[22] So in following Brueggemann and applying his superb understanding of the prophetic imagination to my understanding of a kairos consciousness, we should say that a kairos consciousness is also an *evocative* consciousness. It evokes the crisis by evoking in us a consciousness *alternative* to the dominant consciousness, a consciousness that *resists* the cooptation and the domestication of our prophetic imagination and our prophetic ministry.

At another level, however, the self-critical consciousness knows, as South Africa's Steve Biko insisted, that the strongest ally of the oppressor is the mind of the oppressed; that oppressors of all sorts and all eras cannot be successful without the cooperation or submission of the oppressed; that through the pressures of fear or the desires for reward or a distorted theology we ourselves might become complicit in our own oppression or that of others. A kairos consciousness knows that throughout all times in history God has raised up faithful women and men who heard God's voice in the cries of the oppressed, who took refuge in the love of God and from within that place of refuge found courage and stepped into the world to challenge the powers of evil—so when for us that time comes we recognize it, acknowledge it, and are called to embrace it. Their prophetic courage stirs, disturbs, and unsettles us even as it moves, inspires, and emboldens us—from the Hebrew midwives denying the Pharaoh the right to deny them their right to do justice to Moses and Elijah and Jeremiah and Amos; to Mary in the Magnificat and the women who followed Jesus in defiance of patriarchal power to the martyrs of the church of all ages. All of them faced a kairos moment of discernment, repentance, and of discontent; of conversion, decision, and dissent; of commitment and resistance. Hence there are choices to be made here: a kairos consciousness is one that urges us to make righteous choices.

Certainly choices are made on empirical evidence, as a result of painstaking and correct social, political, and economic analysis, and a proper understanding of the ways in which power and powerlessness work, a thorough grasp of the insidiousness of systemic inju... their generational tenacity. This is what the *Kairos Document* calls "reading the signs of the times." Our struggle, in the famous line from Ephesians 6:12, is not just against enemies of flesh and blood, "but against the rulers, the authorities, against the cosmic powers of this present darkness, against the spiritual forces of evil in heavenly places." If this is true, we would do well to remember that for these "cosmic powers and rulers" imperial power on earth is never enough; they *will* seek to occupy the heavenly places as they do the earth, not resting until *their* will is done in heaven as it is on earth. But then we cannot afford to be led by a blind pseudo-innocence that leaves no room for the combatant love—of which I speak below—that is necessary to change the world so that it more faithfully reflects the theater of God's glory.

As such, a kairos consciousness will do yet another thing. It will, Cornel West, speaking of prophetic witness, reminds us, highlight the reality of evil, both personal and institutional evil, "including the evil of being indifferent to personal and institutional evil." As prophetic consciousness, its aim is to shatter deliberate ignorance and willful blindness to the suffering of others and to expose the clever forms of evasion and escape we devise in order to hide and conceal injustice."[23]

Just as certain, however, a kairos consciousness makes these choices on the basis of faith. Much more than the liberation of the oppressed is at stake here. Because Christians participate in and benefit from the oppression of others while claiming faith in the God of Jesus Christ who came to establish justice in the earth, that faith, the integrity of that Gospel, and the credibility of the witness of the church are at stake. The moment of truth is a moment to act for the sake of justice and humanity, but also for the sake of the integrity of the Gospel. These are the deepest issues in the "apartheid is a heresy" debate of the late 1970s and early 1980s which preceded the writing of the *Kairos Document*.[24] It is for this reason that the Dutch Reformed Mission Church in South Africa, in first formulating the Belhar Confession in 1982 and naming the theology that has undergirded and justified apartheid a heresy, already spoke of "a moment of truth."[25] This calls for critical judgment and acts of prophetic faithfulness and prophetic courage; hence the emphasis on humility, truthfulness, and integrity. This is another reason why the stakes are so very high.

In sum then, I would say that a kairos consciousness is therefore a critical, self-critical, and engaging consciousness. It is also a liberating, empowering, evocative, and humanizing consciousness and allows, no, *urges* us to respond to the discernment of the moment of truth, in resistance to the powers of evil, for the sake of the wronged and powerless, and for the sake of the Gospel.

For this reason the call to conversion is so crucial in our thinking on kairos. It is not, to be sure, the emotional conversion experience so many of us have grown up with, that leads us to a spiritualized, individualized, inner experience of the love of God with no understanding of the love of God in Christ for the cosmos (Jn 3:16). Neither is it the "conversion experience" the Roman emperor Constantine was supposed to have had, when he had a vision of the cross emblazoned in the sky inscribed with the words *In hoc signo vinces!—In this sign conquer!* Some translate, *Conquer by This!* The church has not yet recovered from that vision's deadly consequences for the church and the world. Neither has the world. Pastor/activist Brian McClaren has written beautiful words on this. "Imagine a different conversion," he says, one that never happened but could have:

> Instead of a gold-plated, bejeweled spear-cross with the words "Threaten and kill by this", imagine that Constantine had seen a vision of a basin and a towel with the words "Serve by this", or a vision of a simple table of bread and wine with "Reconcile by this", or a vision of Christ's outstretched arms with "Embrace by this", or a vision of the birds of the air and flowers of the field with "Trust like this", or a vision of a mother hen gathering her chicks with "Love like this", or a vision of a dove descending from heaven with the words, "Be as kind as this." But it was not so.[26]

Indeed. I would add just one thing. Imagine that Constantine, having seen all of the above, had a vision of Jesus on the cross, overcoming the power of violence and domination and death with the power and of love and servanthood and sacrifice, with the words, "Resist by this."

"This is the KAIROS," the *Kairos Document* declared in 1985, "the moment of grace and opportunity, the favorable time in which God issues a challenge to decisive action." This crucial sentence tells us two more things. First: in reality it is not so much the cadre of prophetic Christians who are making the call to conversion, action, commitment, and change. The challenge comes from God, in the cries of the oppressed and the defenseless. To hear and respond to that call is not so much an act of extraordinary power or courage for which we pat ourselves on the back, as an obedient response to grace.

Second: it is the grace of God that calls us from our sinful apathy to commitment and acts of justice, and it is grace that offers the church and the world the opportunity for repentance, conversion, and change. It is grace that makes of the challenge also an invitation. If you can only see what I see, Yahweh seems to be saying, then together we can change this world and make it into a dwelling place for all God's children. This makes of a kairos consciousness, besides all else, a hope-filled, life-giving consciousness. Precisely for these reasons, kairos consciousness is not a consciousness that we naturally possess, but one that is awakened in us by the Spirit of God, by the promises of God, and it calls on those promises for God's sake, for the sake of creation, and for the sake of the oppressed whose sufferings are the cause of the wounds of God. In the healing of those wounds is the redemption of humanity.

Where God Is at Work

In 1961, that remarkable and influential lay theologian from India, M. M. Thomas, created an intense ecumenical debate, especially in Europe, with his assertion that Christians should discern the hand of God at work in history, specifically in the revolutions and upheavals in Asia and Africa at that time.[27] We should keep in mind that the most recent kairos document is a challenge to the world from Palestine—a document that in no small measure should take the credit for the revival of the global kairos movement.[28] In this first half of the twenty-first century *Kairos Palestine* puts the struggle for justice for Palestinians and peace in the Middle East front and center as a call upon the world and a challenge to the ecumenical church as much as the 1985 *Kairos Document* intended to do (and did) for the struggle in South Africa. It is also a reminder that the emergence of a global kairos movement brings together the struggles of peoples from across the world. In light of this it is perhaps not out of place to revisit M. M. Thomas' words.

A global kairos movement today with the purpose of engendering a kairos consciousness for "all humanity" will not only be concerned with struggles for racial and socioeconomic justice as was the focus of the first *Kairos Document*. It will have to be concerned with worldwide struggles today, struggles for ecological justice, the rights of indigenous peoples which are so closely related to the well-being of the earth; with movements for economic justice in the face of the devastation wrought by globalized neoliberal economics such as the Occupy Movement as a movement mainly of the rich North but which echoed, and joined forces with, the struggles for social justice of the global South. It will be concerned with the endless devastation of perpetual war, with the broad issue of global resistance to the scourge of war, and with the specifically focused issue of rape as weapon of war as we are seeing in the Democratic Republic of the Congo and elsewhere as women's bodies become occupied territory; with the growing, and utterly alarming trends of patriarchal domination with its concomitant devastating consequences in the worldwide, deeply embedded culture of violence against women, in too many instances justified by what the 1985 *Kairos Document* identified as "church theology." It will be confronted with the challenges of choices between the forces of violence and the forces of nonviolence in struggles for freedom and democracy today raging across the world.

Within these struggles falls the struggle for the dignity and rights of lesbian, gay, bi-sexual, transgender and intersex persons who by all indications are under renewed onslaught in frightening, and far too often deadly ways in different parts of the world and to whom in so many places the church has so scandalously closed its doors, so that they find themselves cast by the wayside and left to die at the hands of self-appointed, self-righteous avengers of God. It shall also have to take account of the fearsome uncertainties of the Palestinian struggle, the Arab Spring in North Africa and the Middle East, the promise, the temptations, and the hard lessons; the battles between the forces of violence and the forces of nonviolent transformation for ownership of those revolutions. It cannot ignore the battles against predatory imperial powers whose desires for global domination seemingly dare not allow a single peoples' revolution remain the *peoples*' revolution, and the painful and vexing paradoxes and contradictions these are producing even as I write.[29]

A kairos consciousness will, in a word, have to take serious cognizance of what Elizabeth Schüssler Fiorenza has called "kyriarchy" or "kyriocentrism," an ideology of "lordship" and domination which she defines as "a complex pyramidal system of intersecting multiplicative social structures of supremacy and subordination, of ruling and oppression."[30] The term is all the more compelling, since Fiorenza points to the perverse inversion of the Lordship of Christ, which is the exact opposite of the kind of "kyriarchy" she is exposing. The early Christians called Christ "Kyrios," appropriating for Jesus of Nazareth the same title that Caesar claimed for himself. But Caesar's title spells domination, oppression, threat, fear, and death. In Jesus, the title is rejection of and resistance to the very meaning of kyrios as Rome understood it: love, justice, compassion, mercy, servanthood, liberation, inclusion, peace. To call Jesus "Lord" therefore, was to join God's resistance against the forces of domination and death.[31]

Our present imperial realities pose the same challenges, present the same divine pretensions, claim the same ultimate loyalties, expect the same fearful obedience, and wreak death and destruction upon those who dare to challenge it. Quite apart from the civil religious elements essential to all imperial rule, journalist Tom Engelhardt offers this insight: "Imagine," writes Engelhardt, "what we call 'national security' as, at heart, a proselytizing warrior religion."

> It has its holy orders. It has its sacred texts (classified). It has its dogma and its warrior priests. It has its sanctified promised land, known as

> the "homeland". It has its seminaries, which we call think tanks. It is a holy monotheistic faith in that it broaches no alternatives to itself. It is Manichaean in its view of the world. As with so many religions, its god is an eye in the sky, an all-seeing Being who knows your secrets... [It] is an implacable warrior religion, calling down retribution on people often seen only poorly by video feed, thousands of miles distant from Washington, D.C., Langley, or Fort Meade, Maryland. It's no mistake that the weapons fired by their fleet of drone craft are called Hellfire missiles, since it is indeed hellfire and brimstone that they believe they are delivering to the politically sinful of the world. Nor is it happenstance that the planes which fire those missiles have been dubbed Predators and Reapers (as in "Grim"), for they do see themselves as the anointed deliverers of Death to their enemies... Put all this together and what you have is a description of a militant organization whose purpose is to carry out a Washington version of global jihad, a perpetual war in the name of the true faith... It has pumped fear into the American soul. It is a religion of state power.[32]

A kairos consciousness shall have to be alert to these heresies, identify them, expose them, and take them head on, remembering, and proclaiming, in the face of empire, that God chose the foolish, the weak, the low, and despised in order to shame the wise and the strong, and to "reduce to nothing things that are" (1 Cor. 1:27–28), and that "none of the rulers of this age" understood God's wisdom (1 Cor. 2:8). The goal is, after all, not simply the production of new kairos documents, but the birth of a "global kairos movement," that seeks "to bring down the mighty (and systems) from their thrones and lift up the lowly," inspired and carried by the call for "a humanity with a kairos consciousness." Not only our inescapable global realities, but also, and especially our kairos consciousness, disallow us ignorance of and innocence regarding these struggles: in our global situation the only road that leads to Jerusalem is the Jericho Road.

But let us return to M. M. Thomas. Taking the Lordship of Christ as central to Christian understanding, Thomas argued that Christ, as Lord of history, is at work in all nations of the world in spite of, and indeed *through* the ambiguous political, economic, and social actions in any given country. These upheavals, insofar as they represent the search for what he called "the new humanity," for freedom and a new dimension of humane life, fulfill the promises of Christ and must be seen as commensurate with the work of God in Christ.

This does not mean that these revolutions determine the work of God, or represent *all* of what God is doing in history; much less that the gospel can be identified with all that happens in such revolutions. It means, rather, that God is in control of the revolutions of history; not that the divine power is subordinate to the revolutionary purposes of human beings, but that the "pressures of God are at work in them" says Thomas. In other words, wherever human beings rise above themselves, find the courage to work for genuine justice and humanity, resist the forces of evil by overcoming evil with good, and seek to create room for the flourishing of justice and humanity, there God is at work, for that is the will of God for humanity.

Some Western theologians took immediate umbrage, but Thomas' arguments resonated powerfully in the global South. James Cone for example would cause the same kind of controversy with his conviction that "Christianity is not alien to Black Power; it is Black Power… [F]or the gospel proclaims that God is at work with us now, actively fighting the forces which would make man captive. And it is the task of theology and the Church to know where God is at work so that we can join (God) in this fight against evil."[33] And again,

> Black theology is the religious explication of black people's need to redefine the scope and meaning of black existence in white racist society. Black power focuses on the political, social and economic condition of black people, seeking to define concretely the meaning of black self-determination…Black theology puts black identity in a theological context, showing that black power is not only consistent with the gospel of Jesus Christ: it is the gospel of Jesus Christ.[34]

Cone has been challenged on this issue and has indeed found different ways of making the argument but the point essentially remains, strengthened by a crucial caveat.[35] Those of us who claimed God's love and compassionate justice for our struggles for racial and economic justice, believing that our struggles for justice are "consistent with the gospel of Jesus Christ" cannot but embrace the call for engagement in the justice struggles now engulfing the world. The God whom we called upon is the same God whose hand is at work in history, in the efforts of women and men who are seeking a better, more just, more humane world and who are fighting for the integrity of creation, despite, and indeed *against* the onslaught of evil forces who are desperate to claim violent ownership of every revolution toward justice, dignity, and shalom.

But Thomas makes two further points. First, we must not make the mistake of limiting the work of God's Holy Spirit to the church. The church and the world both center around Christ and history is not easily divided into "salvation history" and "secular history." Christians can see, through faith, that the promises of Christ are fulfilled in revolutionary action. "Under the creative providence of God the revolutionary ferment in Africa and Asia has within it the promise of Christ for a fuller and richer life for Man and society." These promises include the new discovery of selfhood, freedom, dignity, new forms of society, and the search for the meaning of life. Second, it is our faith *in Christ*, not in human endeavor that makes us discern the work of Christ in contemporary history.

Dietrich Bonhoeffer raises the same issue but from a different perspective, namely that of suffering.[36] Discipleship, Bonhoeffer argues, is to "stand with God in the hour of God's grieving"—that is "to be caught up in the way of Christ." It is not our religion that makes us believers and followers of Christ; rather it is participation in the sufferings of God. We are called to share the suffering of God at the hands of a hostile world. We are disciples of Christ when we stand by God in the hour of God's grieving. In other words, if we stand by those who suffer in the world, wherever and whoever they may be, we are standing by God. It is for their sake that God is at work in the world, so that creation as a whole may be redeemed.

I believe Bonhoeffer, Thomas, and Cone are right. In the incredible human drama that is unfolding before our eyes, in the seemingly hopeless struggles against the forces of destruction and evil, even in the vortex of painful and bewildering contradictions, Christians can see the work of God toward freedom and justice, dignity and meaningful life and the search for a new humanity. Why should we see this in Martin Luther King Jr., but not in Malcolm X; in South Africa but not in Palestine; in Nelson Mandela's work for reconciliation but not in the women's fight for dignity and the protection and assertion of their rights; in the brave men and women fighting for eco-justice but not in the equally brave women and men who are claiming their God-given humanity as LGBTI persons; in the masses following Gandhi but not in the masses of the Arab Spring uprisings?

The issue is not whether Christians should first baptize those actions, Christianizing them into acceptability as it were. I am arguing, like Bonhoeffer, Thomas, and Cone, that our faith in Jesus Christ allows us, no, *compels* us to recognize where God is at work in our history. Simultaneously it helps us to discern where the name of God is falsely claimed to legitimize destructive and oppressive ideologies. But it also allows us to see where God stands, namely with the poor and oppressed, the destitute and the wronged, with those deprived of justice and dignity, who are now in the name of God rising up to claim that God-given dignity; and hence to stand where God stands, alongside those who suffer for righteousness sake, see through their eyes and hope with their hearts.

Our loyalty to Christ does not distance us from our brothers and sisters in Palestine, in North Africa and the Middle East, or from the indigenous communities of Canada in their fight against fracking and the further dispossession of their lands for instance. This loyalty ties us specifically to those who, in the midst of unnamable temptations, against frightening odds and corrosive onslaughts, remain determined to represent the redemptive possibilities of nonviolent resistance, what Mary Elizabeth King has called the "quiet revolution."[37] We recognize in their struggle for freedom and justice, in their courage and commitment, in their willingness to sacrifice even their very lives for justice and the creation of "a new humanity" a kairos moment and the call of discipleship, and we support them in obedience to Christ. I agree with Paul Lehmann:

> The difference between believers and unbelievers is not defined by church membership, or even, in the last analysis, baptism. The difference is defined by imaginative and behavioural sensitivity to what God is doing in the world to make and keep human life human, to achieve...the new humanity.[38]

Inspired by their courage, we must this time make the right choices. We must trust the people directly involved in those struggles, laying their lives on the line every day, to work out their destiny according to the promises of God. In making these choices, we must be careful to discern the immense pressures emanating from the powers of empire and their lackeys in these situations of turmoil and upheaval, who know that the more violent the revolution, and the stronger the grip of hopelessness and helplessness on the oppressed, the more likely they will achieve their own goals of control of the revolution and of permanent domination. Hence the consistency with which they act as if more effective forms of violence are in fact the way to freedom and peace. We must, in these ongoing struggles, not give up hope but choose for the good and gentle powers so that the powers of evil and injustice might be challenged and overcome.

Are these situations not fraught with danger? Will we not err in the decisions we have to make? That is always possible. But when we were fighting apartheid and asked the ecumenical movement and the world to take a strong stand against apartheid and the churches who provided that system with moral, biblical, and theological justification, we recalled Bonhoeffer's plea to the ecumenical movement in 1933. It was a time when there was much prevarication in the church and the political world on the question of Nazi Germany's racism, its lethal tendencies, and its challenge to the church in Germany and the world.[39] We, like the ecumenical church then, have to make up our minds knowing that we are subject to error, like everything human, Bonhoeffer argued, once again emphasizing the Christian call to faithfulness and love:

> But to put off acting and taking a position simply because you are afraid of erring, while others have to reach infinitely more difficult decisions

> daily, seems to me to almost go against love. To delay or fail to make decisions may be more sinful than to make wrong decisions out of faith and love...and in this case it is really now or never. "Too late" means "never"...Let us shake off our fear of this world—the cause of Christ is at stake; are we to be found sleeping?[40]

The call for courage and to stand up for justice by standing with those who are fighting for justice in the Middle East and North Africa today as well as those engaged in the constant struggles for justice and dignity and the well-being of the Earth is as clear as was the call for justice and solidarity during South Africa's freedom struggle. A kairos consciousness that seeks to engage humanity for the sake of redemption of the cosmos as a whole cannot ignore the call.

A Kairos Theology?

As the title of his reflections on the matter of a kairos theology makes clear, Clint Le Bruyns raises the issue as a question rather than as an assertion: are we now talking about the "rebirth" of a kairos theology?

Le Bruyns takes issue with John De Gruchy, who has described kairos theology as one of the (prophetic) theologies of the antiapartheid struggle: "One of the key theologies of the struggle for liberation."[41] Le Bruyns argues against such a view, on two grounds. First, it means that kairos theology, despite its enduring prophetic character, should be relegated to the apartheid era. As was the case with liberation theology in the view of so many (white) liberal theologians, the argument would be that now that apartheid as we have known it no longer exists and the antiapartheid struggle, in its strict sense, has come to an end, there would no longer be any need for such a theology. Second, the liberational orientation of the theology expressed in the kairos documents cannot be limited to the South African struggle against apartheid only.

Le Bruyns' reasoning is correct, but he seems not to have taken note of the fact that since then De Gruchy has not only reaffirmed liberation theology, but confirmed the prophetic, liberation tradition as the tradition from which the 1985 *Kairos Document* was birthed.[42] The theology of the kairos documents has, Le Bruyns contends, become a "theological tradition" that has exerted a "tremendous impact" on various other settings and situations in the world. True to its prophetic nature, it has "facilitated prophetic praxis in relation to different spheres of public life—politics, economic, civil society, and public opinion formation."[43]

But it is easy to gain the impression that Le Bruyns is speaking of a theological tradition created by the 1985 *Kairos Document* which is best reflected in "public theology." We must pause here to reaffirm that there indeed is a theological tradition in which the *Kairos Document* is embedded. However, the theological tradition of the South African *Kairos Document* is not a tradition created by the *Kairos Document* in and of itself, *ex nihilo,* so to speak. In truth, the *Kairos Document* was *born into* the tradition of prophetic theology in South Africa. I am speaking of the tradition represented by the theology of prophetic resistance which early on in struggle history had broken with the theology of accommodation to existing situations of oppression.[44] I mean a theology convinced that a theology of protest would never be enough, understanding that protest is always a form of begging, and that only a theology of resistance could respond adequately to the call to costly discipleship.

This is the theology that inspired Christian participation in slave revolts and resistance against colonial oppression. It is the theology so well understood and represented by the hopeful politics of Sol Plaatjie who in 1916 declared to his people and the world that the "one thing that stood between us and despair is the thought that Heaven has not yet deserted us;"[45] the theology that undergirded the Christian obedience of Albert Luthuli and the oppressed masses of the Defiance Campaign that led to disobedience to the unjust laws of the apartheid government; the Luthuli who reminded us that "the road to freedom is via the Cross."[46] By Z. K. Matthews and his idea of "a Peoples' Congress" which gave birth to the people's gathering at Kliptown and the Freedom Charter, and the astonishing faith and courage of the women when they marched on Pretoria and declared the death of apartheid in their songs of faith and defiance. It is the tradition carried by black liberation theology, radicalized black Christianity and the struggle for a hermeneutic of liberation and by the children of Soweto who set the country alight with their vision of justice.

I am speaking of the prophetic tradition embraced by the *Kairos Document* as the theology represented by the "apartheid is a heresy" debates, the ABRECSA Charter of 1981, and the Belhar Confession of 1986, first drafted and presented to the church in 1982.[47] By the call for prayer for the downfall of the apartheid regime in 1979, the theology of the theological rationale for the day of prayer and the prayer services of 1985. This tradition is encapsulated by the sheer, stunning courage of those Christians involved in the struggle for liberation and justice throughout these years based on their conviction that God is a God of justice, that freedom is our God-given right, and that we are called to be more obedient to God than to human authorities. This is the prophetic tradition which birthed the *Kairos Document* and that is the tradition the new kairos movement should seek to recapture.

If kairos theology is the theology embedded in a "theological tradition" as it has expressed itself in the theological praxis and reflection on that praxis in different contexts of the world, it is indeed a theology alongside other expressions of liberation theology. Moreover, kairos theology is experiencing a "rebirth" in my view, precisely because of its specific emphasis on the importance of the discernment of a kairos moment, its prophetic nature and its ecumenical appeal which in the present global situation is understood as indispensable for the life of the church and the redemption of God's creation by those engaged in prophetic praxis. Second, because of its rootedness in liberation theology as it found voice in its various expressions over the last 40 years or so. Quite appropriately, its rebirth is located, as was its birth, in the global South—in 1985 in South Africa and presently in Palestine and Southern Africa—from within the womb of the liberation theological tradition. Le Bruyns, entirely properly, notes the view of his colleague from Pretoria University, Vuyani Vellem, who states,

> Black Theology in South Africa, Kairos Theology, Black Theology in America, Latin American Liberation Theology, Minjung, Dalit, Feminist Theology, African Theology, Contextual Theology and Womanist Theology—all use the category of liberation to define their task, purpose and methodology. All of them, originating from different contexts, symbolize a global, "worldly" expression of the liberation motif for another possible world.[48]

In a remarkably perceptive essay, Charles Villa-Vicencio speaks of the prophetic tradition as it took shape in the New Testament church and the Constantinian turn that transformed a persecuted and impoverished social minority into a church led by a hierarchy of wealthy and powerful bishops, princes, and emperors that assigned the poor to the margins of the church. In doing so, Villa-Vicencio, from an entirely different perspective, confirms both the prophetic tradition of the church and the tradition in which kairos theology stands:

> Since this dramatic imperial feat, Christianity, with some notable exceptions, has grown accustomed to bolstering the powerful and neglecting the poor and vulnerable. Among the exceptions can be counted the confessing church in Nazi Germany, the church of the poor in Latin America that gave birth to liberation theology, the black theology genre that emerged from the civil rights movement in the U.S., the feminist and womanist theology movements in different parts of the world, and the signers of the three Kairos documents in South Africa (1985), Palestine (2009), and the United States (2011).[49]

We must, however, within this context, take this discussion one step further. Like all liberation theologies, kairos theology is not about a "theme" or a "cause" that is transient and random—a fad, in other words—that fades as soon as that cause is reckoned by some to be over, or the fad is no longer fashionable or useable. In this regard, feminist theologian Letty M. Russell speaks for all expressions of liberation theology when she states simply but powerfully, "Feminist theology is *not* about women. It is about God."[50] It is about God and God's liberating acts of justice in history for the sake of the oppressed and the downtrodden. Kairos theology can be properly understood only when one keeps in mind the salient elements of liberation theology, so perhaps we should briefly remind ourselves of what these might be. Keeping in mind our discussion on a kairos consciousness might also be helpful.[51]

1. Liberation theology is always done from the perspective of those who have traditionally been rendered powerless and voiceless in society and in the church; those who suffer as a result of domination and oppression, whose opinion does not matter, nor is it asked for, because from them no wisdom is expected. Liberation theology is unthinkable without its rootedness in the struggles and intuitive theological responses of the people.
2. In doing so, liberation theology took seriously the issues of power and powerlessness, raised questions not only regarding individual attitudes or behavior, but pertinent to societal and ecclesial structures and systems of domination and subjugation.
3. Liberation theology not only sought to *describe* these situations of oppression and domination, but also to *empower* the powerless with the power of the Gospel and this not merely in an inner sense but in the sense that it enables and compels them to become agents in history, to strive for liberation and justice in their own context and the context of humanity.
4. Liberation theology rejects the traditional interpretation of the biblical message, refusing to leave the gospel in the hands of the powerful and privileged to be used for their purposes of subjugation and oppression, insisting that a proper interpretation of scripture is liberational, rather than oppressive.
5. This is important when we remember the pernicious use of the Bible in the justification of the calamities that have struck oppressed people: land theft, genocide, colonialism and slavery; how easily the church accepted the justification of war and all forms of violence, and how the Bible has been, and is still being used to keep women in a subservient role and for the exclusion of those children of God who do not conform to the rules of heteronormativity. Equally important is to remember how the Bible has been used to keep oppressed and subjugated people of all kinds in subservience, teaching them that any form of resistance and any demand for the respect and protection of their rights was unchristian.

6. Liberation theology is keenly aware of the fact that traditionally the Bible has been interpreted from the view point of the powerful: white, privileged, male. Hence liberation theology in all its expressions constantly raises the question whether or not the manner in which the Bible has been read and interpreted by the powerful is accurate; not only accurate in regard to contemporary situation but also in regard to the biblical contexts themselves. This is what we have called the ideological and hermeneutical "suspicion" that has become so crucial in biblical interpretation and theological reflection.
7. Therefore, reading the Bible "from below," as liberation theology has wisely learned from Dietrich Bonhoeffer, as well as reading our socio-economic and political situations "from below" are key to the praxis of liberation theology. Liberation theology holds that the perspective in the Bible itself is one from below—that the Bible itself is essentially a history of resistance against forces of domination and oppression. This becomes clear not only in the biblical story as a story against imperial domination and enslavement from outside ancient Israel, but as well in the prophetic tradition against the tendencies within the covenant community itself to imitate the imperial ways of the powers around them. Hence the Bible's insistence on God's preferential option for the poor, the persistent calls for justice for the oppressed, the widow, the orphan, and the stranger.
8. Since liberation theology speaks of a God active in history on behalf of humanity and the cosmos, to bring the cosmos under the reign of God's compassionate justice and freedom, an activity of God which we are invited to join, theology itself is reflection on action transforming the world. It is therefore faith active in the world, and faith is, in the words of Latin American theologian Hugo Assmann, the action of love within history.[52]
9. As liberation theology views it, it is striking how much emphasis the Bible places on what we have called the "inverted order of the reign of God." The God we meet in the Bible is, unlike the gods of the nations surrounding ancient Israel, not a God whose special relationship is with the elites, the rulers, the powerful and the privileged, associated with the images of a pharaoh, a king, or an emperor who themselves become gods. The God of Israel is first and foremost a God of slaves who is keenly aware of their plight, and graciously and powerfully responds to their longings for freedom. This God "hears" the cry of the oppressed, "sees" their sufferings, and is determined to "come down and rescue" them from the hand of their oppressor. This God loves and desires justice, *is* entirely justice and compassion, hates injustice and is the defender of the poor, the weak, the vulnerable and defenseless.
10. The powerful kings and the ruling elites of Israel who, in defiance of God's covenant with the people subject the people to oppression, exploitation, and humiliation are confronted by prophets who are politically powerless and socially insignificant, but whose source of inspiration and courage is an entirely different kind of power.
11. The New Testament proclaims Jesus of Nazareth "Lord," "king," and "Son of God," yet he is a king like no other and confounds, no, *nullifies* all

expectations of what it means to be a "king" in worldly terms. He is born in a stable, in all respects the opposite of the palace, the child of a peasant girl and a poor carpenter, and whose legitimacy is seen as suspect. He is from Galilee, despised and looked down upon by others, from a region from which nothing good is expected.[53] Yet he is the incarnation of God's majesty as lives and work among the poor and the oppressed, God's chosen One upon whom the Spirit of the Lord rests. He is the incarnation of God's resistance against the powers of evil, domination, and oppression in all their forms, as he is the incarnation of God's inclusive love and mercy, and God's desire for compassionate justice for all humanity.

12. Jesus is the complete reverse of the imperial powers who claim the titles of "lord," "king," and "god." Theirs is the power of oppression and domination, of threat, intimidation, and violent destruction. His is the power of love, liberation, justice, and *shalom*. He contrasts the power of domination with the power of redemptive and empowering love. Every naming of Jesus as "Lord" is an act of defiance and resistance against the powers of domination who in their boundless arrogance and hubris claim the power of a god over the lives of God's children.
13. This Jesus is crucified by the empire and its abusive power, but rises from the grave, nullifying the power of violence—the essence of imperial domination—denying violence and death any power over him, since the grave "cannot hold him" just as violence and death have no hold over those who follow him. For those who follow him, the resurrection is Jesus' *apanastasia*, rebellion (the New Testament word for "resurrection"), Jesus' rebellion against death and its power, against evil and its hold, against fear and its paralyzing grip on our lives. It is the call to join God in God's revolution, in God's work in history for the sake of God's children and God's creation.
14. Liberation theology does not claim to represent something completely new. It has always known that it simply is a renewed understanding of what is at the heart of the covenant tradition in the Bible, from Moses through the eight-century prophets to Jesus of Nazareth, hence its celebration of the exodus, the persistent calls for justice of the prophets, and Jesus' proclamation of liberation, his life of resistance and sacrifice for the sake of the little people of God.
15. Liberation theology does not claim universality as do, from their confident, secure positions of power and privilege, most expressions of Western theology, but rejoices in its contextuality, in the specificity of the situations in which it comes to life in the liberational interpretation of the biblical message and the faithful praxis of God's people everywhere, through which "the powerless gird on strength." When black liberation theology, for instance, lost sight of the interconnectedness of issues of justice and dignity, and failed to be self-critical regarding its own sexism, its complicity with patriarchy and male domination, the women were completely justified in their critique as well as in the insistence upon Womanist and feminist theologies that spoke to their situations far more eloquently and effectively than a male-dominated or male-oriented liberation theology

ever could. The same is true of those adherents of queer theology who remind liberation theology of its failure to have, in its biblical interpretation a hermeneutic of liberation, but also a hermeneutic of inclusion.[54] Hence my emphasis on a kairos consciousness that is critical as well as self-critical.

If such specificity and uniqueness could be ascribed to kairos theology, South African theologian Dirk J. Smit has discerned it well in the various kairos documents. Kairos documents, he says,

> [A]lways begin with a sense of extreme urgency, irrespective of the deep differences between contexts and the diverse foci of the analysis of causes and consequences. It is always described as an either/or situation. The moment is decisive. The stakes are immeasurably high. They concern matters of life and death. Neutrality is no longer possible. One must be for or against. Everyone should be challenged to make this choice, to take an option. Prophetic action is called for...They take the role of the churches in these historical struggles very seriously...calling them to conversion and radical change. They are self-critical, aware of their own complicity in the historical development of the evils, injustices, and spirals of violence. They prophetically dare to name a concrete historical enemy and to locate the major causes of destruction in their respective contexts. Attempts to unmask contemporary forms of idolatry are common. They all affirm hope, historical and social hope for those often without hope...[55]

It is in these characteristics that the unique contribution of kairos theology, as an expression of liberation theology, is celebrated.

It is true that the attempts to silence the voice of the prophetic theological tradition in South Africa and pressures from the ruling elites on the church to conform since 1994 have had a decidedly negative impact on the call to prophetic faithfulness. I have pointed this out before.[56] There were, moreover, Le Bruyns reminds us, also attempts to formulate theologies more in line with the expectations of a "post-apartheid," "post-liberation" society.[57] That is also true.

There were those of us who insisted early on after the euphoria of 1994 that in South Africa we are nowhere near a "post-apartheid" society, that political liberation must be followed by socioeconomic liberation and that this liberation is not to be found by plunging blindly into the abyss of neoliberal capitalism in unthinking imitation of the rich North. We argued that the shift of power into black hands is not *ipso facto* a shift toward the kind of justice that defines freedom, and that the people having the vote is not the same as the people finding their voice. We pointed out that our reconciliation process would remain incomplete, unfulfilled, unsustainable, and cheap if it is de-linked from the costly demands of the systemic *undoing* of injustice and the equally systemic *doing* of justice, of personal and political repentance, restitution, and the restoration of human dignity. We warned that an incomplete revolution is the same as a postponed revolution, and that if we could not find the courage to face the sins of our past we would not gain the integrity to face the challenges of our future. We were largely ignored, marginalized, and in some ways targeted because our expression of liberation theology within the context of post-1994 South Africa did not fall in with the demands of the new national, official narrative of a post-apartheid, de-racialized, reconciled rainbow nation.[58]

The attempts to declare liberation theology passé and to create theologies more acceptable to the "new" South Africa did not, however, fill the void. Le Bruyns, as a theologian of the younger generation, makes this clear:

> The post-apartheid theological discourse in South Africa alerts us to the possibility (at least), or the reality (more frankly-speaking), that our theologies in the new South Africa may not necessarily be as appropriate and responsive as we would like for the kind of public impact and critical participation that the times demand... We do not appear to be fully confident that we have a public theology evidencing these much-needed dimensions of contextuality, criticality and change.[59]

When Le Bruyns then states that "this is why in various quarters in more recent years we are revisiting the South African Kairos Document and our kairos theological tradition,"[60] he is in fact expressing a desire for the prophetic theological tradition as represented by liberation theology which is the prophetic theology of the *Kairos Document*. Curiously though, Le Bruyns himself does not refer to the prophetic tradition as the tradition of liberation theology, and thus of the kairos documents.[61] But in reality *Kairos Palestine*, which Le Bruyns credits with the reawakening of a kairos consciousness in South Africa, is itself not conceivable without Palestinian liberation theology. Before the work of Sabeel—"an ecumenical center that applies a theological approach and nonviolence to address the Palestinian/Israeli conflict"—as Palestinian liberation theologian Naim Ateek testifies, Palestinian Christianity was dominated by a theology that "did not have a vision of the liberator Christ," while the very real need was for a theology that "helps liberate our theologies and, at the same time, helps us understand what it means to walk with God and do God's work in the world today."[62] Instead, the church was captivated by an "incarcerated theology" which led to the "silence of many church hierarchies in the face of the political powers that oppress and enslave people."[63] Such silence, Ateek writes, "is deadly." Ateek is right: it *is* deadly, for the church as well as for the people. To break that deadly hold Sabeel embraced liberation theology, found a Christian voice in the struggle for justice, freedom and peace, created room for an authentic

Christian presence in the Intifada, and paved the way for the *Palestinian Kairos Document.*

I am suggesting that without liberation theology which is also the liberation of theology, as Naim Ateek repeatedly makes clear, and so courageously embraced by Sabeel,[64] without whose prophetic witness, in turn, the hold of "incarcerated theology" would never have been broken, the climate for the birth of the *Palestinian Kairos* in the Palestinian Christian Church would not have been created. If a kairos theology distances itself from this liberational, prophetic tradition, it will loosen itself from its roots, and like those other theologies Le Bruyns laments, wither and die.

Le Bruyns knows and tacitly acknowledges this when he speaks of his participation in theological discussions since the *Kairos Palestine Document* and the responses to it. "These individual and collective initiatives have convinced me about the emerging rebirth not so much of a kairos theology, but of a kairos theological tradition with its kairos consciousness marked by contextuality, criticality, and change."[65] These, however, are precisely the prophetic tradition of liberation theology in all its expressions and it is within this prophetic tradition, I suggest, that a kairos theology must find its rightful place.

Like a Reed in the Wind?

The mere mention of the word "prophetic" evokes the word "courage," and with it come images of "fearlessness," "strength," "solidity," "resilience." These images may be inspiring; they are also terrifying. A prophet is never a prophet by choice, but always by calling. And it does take courage to stand before powers and principalities and speak God's word of truth, correction, and judgment, and to articulate a vision so fundamentally different from what those in power find comfort and legitimization in. But the Bible is careful to remind us that we are to take nothing for granted here.

In Matthew's gospel (11:7–11) Jesus turns to the crowds following him and asks three questions to which he apparently does not expect any response from his listeners. In fact, the passage makes clear that he does not intend to leave any room for any response whatsoever. He answers his questions himself. "What did you go out into the wilderness to see?" he asks, and then answers with another question, "A reed shaken by the wind?" Before anyone in the crowd has a chance to respond, Jesus asks again, "What did you go out to see?" followed by, "Someone dressed in soft robes?" Immediately Jesus asks a third time, "What did you go out to see? A prophet? Yes, I tell you, and more than a prophet."

There is a detectably impatient, I dare say aggressive rush in Jesus' speech here. One detects a palpable, and rising, tension in the passages that make up Matthew 11 which begins with the question, via his disciples, from the imprisoned John the Baptist—"Are you the one who is to come, or shall we wait for another?"—to the intriguing remarks about the kingdom of God and violence to the three-fold woes to the cities Chorazin, Bethsaida, and Capernaum. It ends with the invitation to take on Jesus' "easy" yoke and "light" burden through which action those who follow him will find "rest for their souls."

There is undoubtedly much to say about Matthew 11 as a whole, fascinating as it is, but it is those first rapid-fire questions and answers, Jesus verbally crowding out the crowd to make space for his own answers to his own questions, that arrest our attention here—the thrice-repeated "What did you go out to see?" The anxiousness in John's question—"Are you the one who is to come, or shall we wait for another?"—seems contagious. John is in prison because of his prophetic witness and he will not come out of there alive. Jesus knows this. This is, after all, what every prophet must, however fearfully, learn to acknowledge: the life-threatening risks of speaking truth to power, the ruthlessness of the empire as it responds to threats, perceived or real, against imperial power and privilege, and the deeply disturbing presence of the question that never completely leaves the mind: "Is it worth it?"

When John is indeed beheaded by Herod because Herod recognizes a power greater than his own at work in John—powers that he will also recognize in Jesus (Matt. 14:1)—Jesus, upon hearing this, got into a boat by himself, withdrew from the crowd and his disciples to a "deserted place to be with himself" (Matt. 14:13). By Chapter 11 Jesus knew two things: that the time for him to step forward and assume his public role as prophet had come; and that he himself would not escape the ultimate fate of the true prophet that was now threatening John. So, the Jesus speaking here is not the rabbi asking a question and then patiently, perhaps indulgingly, waiting for his pupils to absorb it, think about it, and then giving their response. Jesus has an urgent point to make here.

Some scholars see in Jesus' questions a distinction he draws between John the Baptist and Herod.[66] Whereas Herod lived in palaces—Herod did have a palace at Machaerus on the edge of the wilderness, east of the Dead Sea—and wore the fine robes of royalty, John wore a coat of camel's hair, ate not the rich foods and delectable delicacies of the spoiled and privileged but locusts and wild honey. Herod, a conscienceless despot and murderous tyrant to those below him, nonetheless scraped and bowed and fawned before those above him: the Roman elite around him and the emperor in Rome. A true coward, he would do nothing to displease his colonial masters, and do anything to gain their favor. He was, in Jesus' words, "like a reed in the wind," easily swayed by his passions, fears, and instincts for survival. In stark contrast, John was the true prophet, solid as a rock, truthful in his witness, faithful to his God and his calling, fearless in bringing his message, not disturbed if he caused offense to the powerful. There is much merit in this argument.

But perhaps there might be more to this. Jesus was indeed holding John up as an admirable example of prophetic faithfulness. Hence Jesus was careful to tell John's disciples— "Go and tell John what you hear and see"—that in his own work for the kingdom of God he would continue to do the work John began, and more, and in more radical fashion. By this I mean that whereas John witnessed in the wilderness and drew the crowds to him there to be baptized, Jesus took himself and the crowds to the seats of power in Jerusalem, to the Temple and the palace, and confronted the powers at the heart of the beast so to speak. Then he added, "Blessed is anyone who takes no offense at me" (v. 6). Those last words are not a display of throw-away bravado I think, nor an attempt to play the preemptive dispenser of blessings in order to bar anyone from taking offense. They are uttered to show Jesus' deep respect for this greatest of prophets "born of women" whose faithfulness has indeed caused offense to the powerful, and for which he would now pay the ultimate price. The prophet in the wilderness would be an example to the prophet from Galilee.

But I think there are at least two more things we could learn from this important passage. First, Jesus spoke in response to what he knew was John's deepest struggle at that point: the crisis prophetic witness and the "is-it-worth-it?" question inevitably create for the faithful prophet. I will die before my work is finished, John seems to say, and I am not sure just how much I have achieved. So much remains undone: was it all in vain, or are you the one who will somehow take this up and finish it, despite the terrible wrath of the powers against whom we are set to speak the offensive truth of God's kingdom? Is the empire forever to have the last word? Every prophet has faced such a moment: from Moses and Elijah to Isaiah and Jeremiah. So would Jesus, and that intensely.

So on my reading, secondly, Jesus was not so much contrasting John with Herod as holding up the real crisis every prophet of God will in some way or another come to face. And it is therefore good to remember that the true prophet never ends up *in* the palace, dressed up in the finery of royalty's favorite spokesperson and comforter, sitting at the table with kings and emperors, partaking of the food of the privileged and the pampered, as reward for their loyalty. That is the reward of the court prophet, the bought and packaged puppets of the empire. No, the true prophet will always be *against* the palace, outside the camp of comfort and complacency, outside the circles where power resides, excluded from the vestiges of patronage, protection, and profit. And in those crises caused by confrontation and offense, by inner doubts and the sense of inadequateness, the prophet is indeed "like a reed in the wind." Not swayed by temptations from the palace but assailed by doubt, fear, and uncertainty, following the call to obedience but not having the faintest clue where that might lead, nor, truthfully speaking, having any desire to go where that might lead.

Perhaps turning again to Dietrich Bonhoeffer might shed more light on this sensitive, uncomfortable, but nonetheless crucial issue. One of Bonhoeffer's most truthful moments, in my view, dawned upon him in prison, when he wrote that utterly moving poem, "Who Am I?"[67] It is not about the fact that he is in prison, nor whether he has been put there unjustly. It is, rather, a question about the core of his being, about an entirely different kind of struggle: about the heart of his calling, between faithfulness to it and his vulnerability because of it. It reveals the struggle between what he manages to present to the world and the truth of his inner knowledge about himself. It begins:

> Am I then really all that other men tell of?
> Or am I only what I know of myself?

He struggles with the way he is perceived: strong and grounded in his faith, rooted in his knowledge about the justness of his cause, and heroic in the face of certain death. His fellow inmates and the wardens see him as rock steady and secure in his faith. Instead he is "restless and longing and sick," and he knows it is the sickness of fear and doubt. He longs for life as he knew it, filled with the songs of birds, the colors and the smells of flowers. Outside are the sounds of the futility of war, the all-consuming hatreds, the *Sieg, Heil* cries of Nazi obsessiveness, the empty braggadocio in the face of self-created horrors. Inside is the clang of prison cell doors, the shouts of prison guards and the muted despair of fellow prisoners who share space with your body but have no understanding of the longings of your soul. He is "powerlessly trembling" for words of kindness from friends whose distance from him is unbearably infinite—he cannot bridge it.

He is not the calm, self-possessed prophet of God they admire and envy. He is—again that word—"trembling." But this time it is not the trembling of longing but the trembling of anger: at despotisms, not just one, but many, at every level of life, not sparing anyone, young or old, devouring whatever stands in their way; and at the humiliations God's people outside are subjected to and he himself here in prison, "petty" but insistent and insidious and everywhere. So away from the well-meaning admiration and the desperate praise he is on his knees before God, but his prayers empty him, drain him, exhaust him. He is as "weary" of praying as he is of thinking as he is of wrestling with God and, like Elijah, he is "ready to say farewell to all."

As one who has experienced the desolateness of isolation in prison, assailed by doubts and battered by uncertainties too many to count, too persistent to ignore, and too voracious to fend off, feeling the pain because of the conviction that one is called by God to speak truth to power; or who felt almost like a fraud, showing the face of courage on the outside while being mauled by the fangs of fear on the inside, ready more than once "to say farewell to it all," I can only say, "how true!"[68] It is no wonder that the prophet Jeremiah, in his matchless, audacious, ferocious struggles with God and with his calling has become such a refuge, such a sanctuary for those whose lives have been turned into multiple contradictions, whose souls have never learned to deal with the turmoil of being called by a God who, insisting on radical obedience, is determined not to let go. Is it indescribable grace or unspeakable terror? "Why," Bonhoeffer would ask somewhere else, "are you so terrifyingly near us?" It is better not to speak too easily, or too glowingly, of "the prophetic calling." It is even better, though, to ask with Bonhoeffer, "Who am I?" and to discover the only answer worth knowing:

> Whoever I am, thou knowest, O God, I am thine.

The prophet is not a rock of brave, stoic solidity. We are, as Jesus would come to know and experience in Gethsemane, more often like a reed in the wind. We do not rush to the cross, trembling with scarcely contained excitement of eagerly anticipated, triumphant martyrdom. We fight with God, through sweat turned into blood, to take the cup away from us. Nevertheless, the prophet stands against the power of the powerful, not because the prophet is so strong, but because the prophet is overcome by that other power, and by that alternative vision that contradicts the present, and that holds out such an irresistible promise. And it is holding on to that vision, seeing not what is before us but seeing what God sees that gives strength to do what Yahweh requires.

Many find that hard, Bonhoeffer admonishes us, because they have come to believe that "the meaning of present events is chaos, disorder, and catastrophe; and in resignation or pious escapism they surrender all responsibility for reconstruction and for future generations. It may be that the day of judgment will dawn tomorrow; in that case, we shall gladly stop working for a better future. *But not before.*"[69]

2

At the Heart of It All: Kairos, Apartheid, and the Calvinist Tradition

At the Heart of the Reformed Tradition: Making Choices

"It is not enough," says John Calvin in his commentary on Isaiah 58:6–7, "to *abstain* from acts of injustice, if you refuse your assistance to the needy." In other words, it is not just about *not* doing injustice as if that is the fulfillment of God's commandment, Calvin says. It is about two things: the *undoing* of injustice *and* the doing of justice. Moreover, it is not about those we find acceptable for some reason; it is about *all* God's children, created in God's image and therefore our flesh and blood:

> By commanding them to "break bread to the hungry," God intended to take away every excuse from covetous and greedy men, who allege that they have a right to keep possession of that which is their own... And indeed, this is the dictate of common sense, that the hungry are deprived of their just right, if their hunger is not relieved... At length he concludes—*And that you hide not yourself from your own flesh.* Here we ought to observe the term *flesh,* by which he means all men universally, not a single one of whom we can behold, without seeing as in a mirror, "our own flesh". It is therefore proof of the greatest inhumanity, to despise those in whom we are constrained to recognize our own flesh.[1]

It is a compelling insight, and for apartheid South Africa, driven as it was by a racist, oppressive, and utterly exclusivist ideology that claimed to be Christian and, more specifically, Reformed in the tradition of John Calvin, entirely indispensable. These are words my heart could sing to, and a Reformed theology I could aspire to, but I did not meet or come to know this Calvin in the Dutch Reformed Church theology I was taught in South Africa. It would be years before I could claim this Reformed tradition as truly mine.[2]

My first conscious realization of the impact, meaning, and legacy of John Calvin and the Reformed tradition on my life and ministry came in the 1960s, in 1964 to be precise, in my first proper conversation with that courageous Dutch Reformed minister and rebel Afrikaner, Beyers Naudé.[3] It was the decade of the Sharpeville massacre, of the Rivonia trial in the wake of the Treason trial and the imprisonment of Nelson Mandela; of my study of theology and entry into the ministry, of Cottesloe[4] and the response of the white Dutch Reformed Church (DRC) to the momentous events of the time. It was the decade of my introduction to Beyers Naudé and the Christian Institute, to Koot Vorster, ultra conservative Dutch Reformed Church leader, stalwart of apartheid and unapologetic proponent of the theology that undergirded that evil system.

While Beyers Naudé confronted us, the younger generation in the black Dutch Reformed churches, with the concepts of "ecumenism," "the confessing church," and "divine obedience," Koot Vorster confronted us with "the dangers of liberalism," the biblical justification of apartheid, and his visceral fear of and distaste for *"verbastering"*—the mixing of the races—(the Afrikaans equivalent of what the American South used to call "mongrelization") of both the *volk* (the Afrikaner people) the church, and the faith.

Toward the end of that decade I was also introduced to Steve Biko and his devastating critique of the black church and to Aunt Maria Arendse of Immanuel Dutch Reformed Mission Church, a stalwart of the congregation, and her quite merciless though completely justified exposure of the inadequacies of my theological training in the face of apartheid injustices when she challenged me to preach on the particular injustice of the Group Areas Act,[5] then in the process of being inflicted upon the black communities of Paarl, the town where I, at age 22, was ordained into the ministry.

It was the first time I had heard of the "Boer-Calvinism" espoused by Dr. Vorster and the vast majority of the DRC,[6] of how apartheid was a true reflection of the Reformed belief in *sola Scriptura*, a biblical and Christian policy, and a "consistent Calvinism" that did not succumb to the weakness of "integration and the intermingling of blood"; that apartheid was not only the purest expression of Reformed faith, but precisely the obedience to the "law of love," and the "only solution to South Africa's race problem."[7]

Contrary to this, Beyers Naudé introduced me to the whole array of apartheid theology designers and defenders, but importantly, also to the dissidents, few though they were, and more crucially, held up the challenge to discover for myself the authentic Calvinist Reformed tradition he knew the white Afrikaans churches had lost. Even then Beyers Naudé was also convinced, and in turn convinced me, that apartheid could only be effectively challenged if it is understood not merely as a fascist political, socioeconomic system, maintained by ruthless violence in all its forms but also, and crucially, as a (pseudo) theological, moral construct, the last being absolutely indispensable to the first.

Time and space does not allow for a discussion on the impact of Dr. Vorster's *verbastering* ideas on the mind and psyche of a young South African person of mixed descent, and to ponder the impact of my "mongrelization" on my humanity and on my being Christian even though the resurgence of racism in South Africa at this point in time does merit such a conversation.[8] I would understand that better when I was later introduced to the philosophy of Black Consciousness. What we must make some time for, however, is the impact of the concept of apartheid as a biblical, Christian and especially Reformed expression of faith and life in South Africa and the response of black Reformed Christians. This response would make of it a challenge to the global church.

Even then we,—I believe I may in this regard speak for a whole generation of black Christians—began to feel the pressures of a serious dilemma. These were *kairos* moments, for us, surely, but as certainly for the Reformed tradition as such in South and Southern Africa.[9] The first question was whether we could remain Christian in a situation where Christians were so unashamedly the oppressor and Christianity was so confidently used to justify that oppression. But the second question was more specific and vexing, and raised the problem I would not be ready to deal with till more than a decade later: was the Calvinist Reformed tradition so burdened, so contaminated by contradictions that we should deny it, or a challenge so full of promise that we should claim it?[10]

The justification of our oppression as a Christian, but especially *Reformed* expression of faith and a *Reformed* reading and interpretation of Scripture, with the theology of apartheid as a *Reformed* theological construct constituted the uniqueness of apartheid racism, and we, black Reformed Christians, were stung by this reality. Apartheid was born out of the Reformed tradition. It was, in a very real sense, the brainchild, the logical political consequence, of the white Dutch Reformed Church mission policy which has its roots in the fateful decision of 1857.[11] Now this Reformed tradition has been fatally merged with the ideals of Afrikaner nationalism and German *Volksromantik* and this policy was presented as a pseudo-gospel that offered salvation for all South Africans.[12] The God of the Reformed tradition, it became clear to us then, was the God of slavery, fear, persecution, and death. How could this God then also be the God of our salvation, our rock, the stronghold of the oppressed in times of trouble (Ps. 9:9), the One who gives justice to the weak and orphan, maintains the right of the lowly and destitute, rescues the weak and needy and delivers them from the hand of the wicked? (Ps. 82). We began to understand early what we finally articulated in 1981: Apartheid had become the grave of the dignity, the true identity and the credibility of the Reformed tradition.[13]

For the black spiritual children of John Calvin this became an acute, painful crisis. The choice facing us was no less pain-filled. Did we have to swear off our Christian identity in order to stand and struggle for justice and freedom? More pertinently, did we have to deny our Reformed heritage, write it off completely and seek our inspiration from ideologies seemingly better suited to the struggle? Was the voice of Marx and Lenin, and were the teachings of Frantz Fanon and the example of Ché Guevara stronger, more alluring, more enduring?

Was the Calvinism of the white South African Reformed churches, responsible for political oppression, economic exploitation, unbridled capitalism, social discrimination, and the total disregard for our human dignity the authentic expression of our inherited faith? By the same token, being Reformed was equated with total, uncritical acceptance of the status quo, sinful silence in the face of human suffering and manipulation of the Word of God in order to justify oppression. Being Reformed was to support the intransigence of the rulers of the day and the offering of the unconditional submission of the oppressed. This was presented as Christian obedience, but was this the obedience that Yahweh required?

For black Reformed Christians suffering under the tyranny of apartheid the anomaly was almost unbearable, the question fundamental and decisive. Was the Afrikaner version of the Reformed tradition, the equation between being Reformed and being oppressive and racist, justified? What, ultimately, lies at the heart of the Reformed tradition?

Besides our political and social realities there were these persistent voices that goaded and challenged us. We heard Steve Biko who reminded us that in a country "teeming with injustice and fanatically committed to the practice of oppression, intolerance and blatant cruelty because of racial bigotry…," where black people "are made to feel the unwanted stepchildren of a God whose presence they cannot feel," black Christians not just suffered Christianity as "the ideal tool for the maintenance of the subjugation of people"; we also "connived" at it.[14]

We owed him a response.

We also heard Helmut Gollwitzer:

> Whether Rome won or Wittenberg or Geneva; whether it was to be justification through good works or by faith; whether the Decrees of Dordt

> or the Statements of the Remonstrants were to become the o
> doctrine; whether Cromwell or Charles I would be the victor
> yellow, and black people of the world this was all irrelevant.
> bearing whatsoever on their situation... Nothing of all this would stop the capitalistic revolution as the revolution of the white, Christian, Protestant peoples that would spread all over the world to open the era of slavery which even today (albeit not in the same form), is not yet ended.[15]

We had heard Koot Vorster:

> Our only guide is the Bible. Our policy and outlook on life are based on the Bible. We firmly believe the way we interpret it is right. We will not budge one inch from our interpretation [in order] to satisfy anyone in South Africa or abroad... We are right and will continue to follow the way the Bible teaches.[16]

We also heard Aunt Maria Arendse, an extraordinary woman of faith, a member of my first congregation, who, when she confronted me directly with the effects of the Group Areas Act and the horrors it inflicted upon her and her family, simultaneously confronted me with the greatest problem constituted by the Reformed theology I was taught in seminary, namely that it *was* the problem. We owed them all a response. South African theologian John De Gruchy saw it well: speaking of the legitimacy of being a Reformed theologian of liberation, he makes the point that much Reformed theology, not least as articulated by John Calvin, "is in critical solidarity with contemporary forms of liberation theology and in some respects is their prototype."[17] However, precisely as we realized and made our life's work, De Gruchy adds, "Reformed theology needs to be liberated from various captivities, not least that of dominating social groups and ideologies, in order to be a truly liberating theology today."[18]

All of these realities reenforced the question we had to answer: What is the true Reformed identity? Does the Reformed tradition have a future in South Africa?[19] It is as pertinent a question now as it was in 1981. It was then, as it is now, a *kairos* moment, a time for critical and self-critical appraisal, a time for making choices.

At the Heart of the Reformed Tradition: Giving Voice to the Voiceless

Since then black Reformed Christians have been trying to respond to that question, and it is a quest that still has not ended. In important ways, as we shall see, it was John Calvin himself who answered the question, but we had to find different ways to hear him, discern his voice among the clamor of the powerful that claimed him for themselves; discover within ourselves the belief and courage to articulate it and act upon it. For centuries the Calvinism that had become Calvin's voice had dominated our lives through the bitter realities of colonialism, land dispossession, slavery, oppression, exploitation, genocide, and apartheid. It spoke always from within the centers of power, security, certitude, and exclusion. How could dispossessed, disenfranchised, dehumanized, and disempowered people hear that voice?

What would almost immediately become evident is the resistance from the powerful to the possibility that we should hear Calvin at all, let alone articulate him for ourselves and claim him as our own. Early on in South Africa's colonial history Khoi-Khoi evangelists, who preached the Gospel despite persistent persecution by white settlers, found it necessary to proclaim to both white colonists and their own people that white people "did not own the Gospel"[20] even though they now owned the land as well as the people whom they have made their slaves. Resistance to colonization and slavery grew in the Cape. It was inevitable that these tensions would be felt in the church which increasingly sought to manifest itself as a settler church, a church of slave owners. In at least one recorded instance, Khoi Christians turned to the singing of the Genevan Psalms as source of inspiration and comfort, and as expression of resistance.

The steady racialization of the church, so historian Richard Elphick tells us, was cause for growing tensions within the Dutch Reformed Church.[21] London Missionary Society missionary Johannes Theodorus van der Kemp "faced a mixed and volatile congregation as he entered the Graaff-Reinet church on June 1, 1801."[22] Besides the white church members, Elphick quotes from van der Kemp's report, he encountered a "greater number of Heathen of the Hottentot and other nations." It was a curious scene. The group of Khoi-Khoi Christians was singing from Psalm 134,

> Come bless the Lord, all you
>   servants of the Lord,
> who minister by night in
>   the house of the Lord.
> Lift up your hands in the sanctuary,
>   And praise the Lord.
> May the Lord, Maker of heaven
>   and earth
>   bless you from heaven.

Outraged that the "heathen" were claiming the church as their own, clearly praising God for their being blessed to be "servants" of God, the white congregants tried to drown them out by singing Psalm 74, specifically the stanzas 4–10:

> Your foes have roared within your holy place…
> They desecrated the dwelling place of your name…
> How long, o Lord, is the foe to scoff,
> Is the enemy to revile your name forever?[23]

The rhymed version (stanza 9) turns the question of verse 11 into an invocation:

> Stretch out your hand, your strong right hand
> Destroy them Lord, the violators of your dwelling![24]

The "outrage" of the white colonizers was partly fueled by the serious resistance against colonial occupation the Khoi-Khoi and other colonized people were engaged in at the time.[25] Note here how the Khoi-Khoi were not considered fellow worshippers, children of the same God, or fellow Christians. They were the "enemy," the "desecrators of God's holy dwelling place," the "violators of holiness" who needed to be "destroyed." White Christians were making clear that there was no room for them in the "consecrated place"; that in their resistance against white colonialist oppression and in the struggle against slavery they were, *ipso facto*, the "enemies of God."

But from another, but crucial perspective it is noteworthy how these Khoi Christians found in the Psalms a language of resistance and strength, a counter-language to the language of oppression, subjugation, rejection, and resignation that was the language of white, settler Christendom. They discovered, in the words of Hebrew Bible scholar Walter Brueggemann, their "prophetic imagination," an alternative consciousness to the dominant consciousness of the slave society that held them captive.[26] They responded politically, through resistance and slave revolts, but also theologically, by an imaginative embrace, and in many ways reinterpretation of the Psalms.

But secondly, note that Psalm 134, the psalm they chose to sing that day, is not a psalm of resistance, calling for justice such as Psalm 146 for example, or Psalm 82, about which John Calvin wrote such powerful, inspiring words. Psalm 134 is a song of praise. It does not protest against anything; it simply claims the joy of being servants of the Lord. It claims the blessings that come from the Maker of heaven and earth. It does not protest; it simply gives thanks for the blessings that come to those who are servants of Yahweh. It is a song that celebrates the liberating truth that God has chosen to make them, the lowly and despised in South Africa's colonial slave society, God's servants.

But that is a chosenness the white "chosen people" could not abide. For in truth, it was a claim that challenged the claim at the core of white, Christian Afrikanerdom. They, *exclusively,* were the chosen people of God, the servants of God called to do God's will in "darkest Africa among the heathen," where God had predetermined their destiny and given them overlordship. That was the most precious claim at the heart of white, colonialist Calvinism. The simple but audacious confidence exhibited by the Khoi Christians that day, rooted not in power but in faith, is more revolutionary than protest. It is the revolutionary and utterly offensive claim Jesus makes in Luke 4:25–27 in his sermon in the synagogue in Nazareth. When Jesus was speaking of God's good news to the poor and afflicted and the year of the Lord's favor, the crowd was "amazed at the gracious words." However, the moment he went on to include the gentiles in the promises of God, stressing the radical inclusion of God's mercy and grace, they were "filled with rage," drove him out of town, and attempted to throw him off the cliff (vv. 28–29).

The struggle of the Khoi and San was not only for their land, freedom, and dignity; it was also for an authentic understanding of the Bible which they could not read but *knew* instinctively was not what they heard from Dutch Reformed preachers. That struggle was also for the Reformed tradition, which they did not fully understand, but nonetheless *intuited* to be something else entirely from what had been made of it.

So the question arose quite early on: do black Christians baptized into the Reformed faith have claim on the Reformed tradition the same as whites? Were they inheritors of the Calvinist legacy on equal footing with whites? More importantly, have they the right to interpret this tradition and Calvin's theology *for themselves*? These early tensions set the tone for future relations with white Reformed Christians. The same question would arise with even more intensity in the 1970s and 1980s as the black Reformed churches of South Africa lay claim to their Reformed heritage and the legacy of John Calvin and as heirs to that tradition joined the struggle for liberation and humanity in South Africa and for the authenticity of the Gospel and the Reformed tradition in the life of the church.[27]

By the end of the 1970s, we no longer asked the question. We simply claimed both our Reformed heritage and our right to it. We also claimed the right "to redeem (the tradition) from the quagmire of political ideology and nationalistic propaganda to which (it) had fallen victim in South

Africa."[28] In an address to the South African Council of Churches annual conference in 1979 I raised the issues one by one:[29]

- "The supremacy of the Word of God" over against the "manipulation of the Word of God to suit culture, prejudice, or ideology" which is "alien to the Reformed tradition";
- The Word of God, we said, is the word that "gives life. It cannot at the same time be the justification of the death that comes through oppression and inhumanity."
- It "speaks to our total human condition and offers salvation that is total, complete." It is not a handbook for politics or economics, but it does "provide us with the fundamental principles of justice, love and peace that we, in the making of our societies, ignore at our peril";
- It is the "critique of all human actions" and "holds before us the norms of the kingdom of God."
- As another "precious principle" we emphasized the Lordship of Jesus Christ over "every single inch of life." Over against the pietistic compartmentalization of life as we were taught, we held that life is indivisible, as God is indivisible.
- We believed, with Nicholas Wolterstorff, that the Reformed faith is a "world-formative," transformative faith, which makes the transformation of the world toward justice, peace, and reconciliation part of our discipleship of Jesus Christ.
- If the world should indeed be the "theatre of God's glory," it called for the rejection of "acceptance, idealization, and institutionalization" of the so-called brokenness of the world; of the notion of "divine ordination" in the structures of injustice in the world.
- We began to understand the heart-beat of the Gospel: justice, love, reconciliation, unity, prophetic faithfulness—and just how lost we as individuals, church, and society would be without them. We needed to understand just how close to the heart of the Gospel were these realities, and ask whether they lay at the heart of the Reformed tradition as well.
- This understanding led to a concerned engagement with the world and its kingdoms, "visible and invisible" (Abraham Kuyper), and is probably best expressed by Brazilian Reformed theologian Rubem Alves, when he states: "What drives us is not the belief in the possibility of a perfect society, but rather the belief in the non-necessity of this imperfect order."[30]

In my view, this struggle to give form, shape, identity, and content to our understanding of the Reformed faith is epitomized sublimely in the Confession of Belhar, whose prophetic truth, ecumenical appeal, and theological power have inspired and carried us through times of unspeakable horrors but which, with equal power, so quickly became a critical and enduring challenge to our own spiritual and theological integrity.

At the Heart of the Reformed Tradition: "The Wounds of God"

In the process of understanding what this claim to the Calvinist tradition meant, black Reformed Christians discovered how much at the heart of the Reformed tradition are what Nicholas Wolterstorff calls "the wounds of God" which by the same token, he argues convincingly, lies at the heart of understanding Calvin's theology of social justice. These are the issues of compassionate justice, God's preferential option for the poor, the oppressed and the wronged; the protection of the rights of the vulnerable, marginalized, and needy, the equitable distribution of wealth, power, privileges, and responsibilities. We learned to read Calvin differently, and discovered, through the inspiring work of Nicholas Wolterstorff, perhaps more than any other, who taught us that understanding John Calvin's "exceptionally bold" theology of social justice was to understand the woundedness of God: that Calvin teaches us that God deems God's own self violated in the wounds inflicted upon human beings created in God's image.[31]

> To inflict injury on a fellow human being is to wound God; it is to cause God to suffer. Behind and beneath the social misery of our world is the suffering of God. If we truly believed that, says Calvin, we would be much more reluctant than we are to participate in victimizing the poor, the oppressed, and the assaulted of the world. To pursue justice is to relieve God's suffering.[32]

We heard John Calvin as he insisted that "the name 'neighbor' extends indiscriminately to every person, because the whole human race is united by a sacred bond of fellowship...To make any person our neighbor it is enough that they be human" and we claimed it for ourselves in the struggle against all forms of racism and exclusion of all kinds.[33]

In reading Calvin's language on the sacraments, we understood better the sinfulness of our South African church history, the absolute affront to Christ in the fact that historically it was precisely the sacraments, Baptism and Holy Communion that became the source and justification for the division of the Reformed churches in South Africa on the basis of race and skin color. After Calvin's insistence that the Table of the Lord brings about the essential unity of the church, since it brings unity with Christ, he turns to the social effects of the sacrament which sharing Communion brings as an obligation:

> Now since he has only one body, of which he makes us all partakers, it is necessary that all of us also be made one body by such participation... We shall benefit very much from the sacrament if this thought is impressed and engraved upon our minds: that none of the brothers and sisters can be injured, despised, rejected, abused, or in any kind offended by us, without at the same time injuring, despising, and abusing Christ by the wrongs we do; that we cannot disagree with the brothers and sisters without at the same time disagreeing with Christ; that we cannot love Christ without loving him in the brothers and sisters; that we ought to take the same care of our brother's and sister's bodies as we take care of our own; for they are members of our body; and that, as no part of our body is touched by any feeling of pain which is not spread among all the rest, so we ought not to allow a brother or sister to be affected by any evil, without being touched with compassion for them.[34]

There is nothing ambiguous about this. We *heard* John Calvin and understood how much the white Dutch Reformed Church in insisting upon it, as well as we ourselves, in resigning ourselves to it, have come to the Table without discerning the body of the Lord, "ate and drank judgment against ourselves" (1 Cor. 11:29). We *heard* Calvin and for us racism in society and in the church became a sin, an assault upon the holiness of God, a wounding of God, a denial of the reconciling work of Jesus Christ, a heresy and a blasphemy.[35]

However, Calvin's view extended far beyond the church. His insights on the oneness of the human race insisted that God has "joined us together and united us in one body," urging us to employ ourselves for the sake of the neighbor, "so that no one is addicted to his own person, but that we serve all in common."[36] These are lessons in human solidarity, inclusivity, and servanthood without which the church cannot be the church, and without which we cannot exist humanly in the world. These were lessons that were not only theologically indispensable; politically as well, a truly humane society is unthinkable without them. They did not simply point to racism in whites; they critiqued and corrected racist and exclusivist tendencies in all of us.

We also heard Calvin's fiery sermons against wealth, selfishness, and the mindless pursuit of profits:

> There will be those who would rather that the wheat spoil in the granary so that it will be eaten by vermin, so that it can be sold when there is want...(for they only wish to starve the poor...) How true is it that our Lord is mocked by those who want to have much profit.[37]

We heard and understood that Calvin was here not speaking of charity, but of justice. "A just and well-regulated government," Calvin said in a sermon on Psalm 82:3, "will be distinguished for maintaining the rights of the poor and afflicted." Again the call is not for "Christian charity" that would leave systemic injustices untouched. So for Calvin, as it must be for us, what is at stake here are the *rights* of the poor. [38]

So we have come to understand that as the irreducible criterion for *all* governments and *all* times. It is not *who* is in government that determines our judgment, but *how* they govern. It is not whether the government pleases "the market" or the whims of the wealthy that counts; neither does ethnicity or skin color; but whether, Calvin says, "the poor person is content." [39]

It is this radical Reformed understanding of the choices God makes that makes Abraham Kuyper say, and he is doing no more than following Calvin in this:

> When rich and poor stand opposed to each other, Jesus never takes his place with the wealthier, but always with the poorer. He is born in a stable; and while foxes have holes and birds have nests, the Son of Man has nowhere to lay his head... Both the Christ, and also just as much his disciples after him as the prophets before him invariably took sides *against* those who were powerful and living in luxury, and *for* the suffering and the oppressed.[40]

This is the character of the radical Calvinism that black Reformed Christians made the corner stone of our theological and political understanding of justice and which ultimately decimated the spurious blend of *Volk* romanticism, pietism, racism, and nationalism that made up the "Boer Calvinism" of white South Africa. Their pretenses of Reformed theology were not durable, nor sustainable.

At the Heart of the Reformed Tradition: Divine Obedience

Our hearing and listening to Calvin differently did not just take us on a different path from that of the power structures in the white Reformed churches, the dominant theology that governed their thinking and praxis, and the policies of their government; it set us on a collision course.

This much was already clear in the choices Beyers Naudé had made in the early 1960s but it was also true of the choices we had to make. When the 100 ministers from the Dutch Reformed Church in Africa took a cautious but prophetic stance against apartheid in 1973 the course was set. Followed by the formation of the *Broederkring*—the "Circle of

Brothers"—(later called the *Belydende Kring,—the Confessing Circle*), the number of decisions by the Dutch Reformed Mission Church synod in 1978 calling apartheid a sin and a pseudo-gospel, and the condemnation of a whole range of apartheid laws, confrontation would no longer be avoided.

The somber note struck in the Dutch Reformed Mission Church synod decision in 1978 would become increasingly true: "If a Christian is bound by their conscience to follow the way of criticism which brings them in conflict with the state, then they should obey God more than humans. In this case, however, they should be prepared to accept suffering in the spirit of Christ and his apostles." It was synod's clear understanding that resistance to the oppression of apartheid was the way of Christ and his disciples, hence the encouragement to accept suffering "in the spirit of Christ and his disciples." Here again, we were following Calvin.[41]

My own call for massive civil disobedience to the South African Council of Churches and for direct involvement of the churches in the struggle for liberation in 1979 was directly informed by the radical Calvinism I had come to embrace, and blended with black liberation theology, and my response to the threats uttered toward the churches by the then minister for Justice Alwyn Schlebusch was likewise a testimony based on my understanding of the Reformed tradition.[42] We were convinced that we were the true heirs of the Reformed tradition in South Africa:

> So when Beyers Naudé sides with the poor and the oppressed in South Africa, [we said], "*he* is the true representative of the Reformed tradition, not those who banned him and sought to bring dishonour to his name.
>
> When the Presbyterian Church of Southern Africa decided to challenge the government on as fundamental an issue as Christian marriage, it is closer to the Reformed tradition than are those who vindicate an unjust law.
>
> It is not the perpetrators of injustice, but those who resist it, who are the true representatives of the Reformed tradition. "[43]

The response from the defenders of apartheid, in government but especially in the white church, was immediate and severe, not merely because their power and privileges were threatened—even though that was true—but even more, I submit, because we raised and pushed the existential and theological question: who were, in South Africa, the true representatives of the Reformed tradition? Who, in South Africa, were the legitimate spiritual heirs of John Calvin? Hence the sustained attacks not just on our politics, but also on our theology.[44] In defense of apartheid, they too, claimed the Reformed tradition; in fact presented themselves as the only legitimate spiritual children of John Calvin. The debates about the limits of governmental power, all the more fierce because we turned theory into praxis in the streets of protest, might serve as example.

At first, it seemed that in our resistance to the apartheid regime we were wrong and the apartheid theologians were right. After all, did not Calvin himself repeatedly make the point that "all governmental authority" came from God and that they ought to be obeyed, for they bear the sword not in vain?[45] Did Calvin not say that to govern was a divine calling, "holy and lawful before God," as he wrote to King Francis I of France in the dedication of his *Institutes,* whom he urged to see himself as a "minister of God?"[46] As a result, we are called to submit to their authority, "not only to those princes who discharge their duty to us with becoming integrity and fidelity, but of all who possess the sovereignty even though they perform none of the duties of their function."[47] Indeed, we should obey them even if they rule in unjust and tyrannical manner...(since) "They all *equally* possess that sacred majesty with which (God) has invested legitimate authority."[48] power of public authority is "noble and divine"; it is given by God to "the ministers of his justice and judgment." Accordingly,

> he should be held in the same reverence and esteem by his subjects, in so far as public obedience is concerned, in which they would hold the best of kings if he were given to them.[49]

Calvin also deals extensively with Romans 13 where Paul describes government as "servant of God" who does not "bear the sword in vain," (Rom. 13:4),[50] and this is where conservative Calvinists find refuge. I have dealt with this famous and contentious text earlier,[51] but it is clear that the argument remains highly relevant in post-1994 South Africa as president Jacob Zuma's statement before the 2013 Presbyterian Synod in Giyani, faultlessly echoing the apartheid regime's theological convictions, makes clear: "Whether we like it or not, God has made a connection between the government and the church...[E]veryone must submit himself to the governing authorities, for there is no authority except that which God has established."[52] Suffice it here, however, to simply make five points:

1. To use Paul's description of governmental authority without taking into account the context of empire and resistance to empire within which he worked and wrote, together with the context of the church in Rome as well as the political import of all of his writings within the context of empire, is to enhance the possibility of misunderstanding Paul from the outset.[53]
2. The key to understanding the Romans 13 passage is not, as traditional interpretation holds, in verse 1, but rather verse 4: government is nothing, if it is not "God's servant (*leitourgos!)* for your good." I made this

point in 1985 in the heat of the debate surrounding our call to pray for the downfall of the apartheid regime, but it is gratifying to note that Nicholas Wolterstorff, in a very recent work, comes to the same conclusion.[54] Wolterstorff argues, correctly, that government is a servant of God also in executing wrath on wrongdoers—the "sword." My point is, however, that even that execution of wrath cannot be a willful, random act of vengeance, retribution, or oppression. It too, will be an act "for your good" in *protection* of the rights of the poor, the defenseless and the downtrodden, the outcasts and the despised.

3. Calvin's expectation of government is not in the first place that it be a "terror" to those who do wrong. In the first place Calvin, as did Paul, expected government to be worthy of the authority granted it by God: "A magistrate who truly answers to his title; who is the father of his country, and, as the poet calls him, the pastor of his people, the guardian of peace, the protector of justice, the avenger of innocence…"[55] In my view, this is not mere obeisance to earthly power, it is rather, a critical standard to which governmental authority is being held.
4. Using the description "servant of God," jumping, as it were, over the first crucially important words to "bearing the sword not in vain," without in the same breath emphasizing, as Paul does, the words that immediately follow, "*for your good*," is to omit a crucial referential framework for the whole text.
5. In light of Paul's own theological and political stance within the wider scopus of his epistles, it is wrong to interpret "submission" here as blind, unquestioning obedience to civil authority.

On this last point Calvin himself disproves his conservative followers, even though we have to wrestle with him through a dilemma he himself creates.[56]

Allow me to pinpoint the issues that make up my argument here regarding this famous *Institutes* passage that still causes so much debate:

> In the *Institutes*, Calvin presents us with a view that first extols the virtues and unquestionable authority of even an evil government that we have to obey. But then he introduces a critical hesitation with two crucial provisos. First, that when tyranny becomes unbearable, (as it invariably does), God "raises up servants as public avengers and arms them with a commission to punish unrighteous dominion, and to deliver a people who have been unjustly oppressed"; persons who by their "fury" sometimes "meditate and attempt something altogether different." Second, in the obedience upon which Calvin seems to insist, Calvin calls for one—only one—exception. But that is precisely the exception that Calvin not only allows to dominate the whole passage; he makes it the very last words of his *Institutes*.
>
> But in the obedience which we have shown to be due to the authority of governors, it is always necessary to make one exception, *and that is entitled to our first attention*—that it do not seduce us from obedience to him,

> to whose will the desires of all kings ought to be subject, to whose decrees all their commands ought to yield, to whose majesty all the sceptres ought to submit. And indeed, how preposterous it would be for us, with a view to satisfy men, to incur the displeasure of him on whose account we yield obedience to men! The Lord, therefore, is King of kings...[57]

Read as a whole, this is an immensely impressive paragraph of sustained argument, with masterful rhetorical repetition and skillful rephrasing of Calvin's central argument. It is one of the most brilliant examples of Calvin's powerful rhetorical theology[58] and we were entirely persuaded.

We understood this to mean, first, that the sovereignty of God supersedes the sovereignty of any earthly ruler. The God who desires and loves justice comes first. Second, we owe this God our unconditional obedience, our deepest loyalty, no matter the claims of loyalty foisted upon us by earthly powers, no matter the cost. Third, the recognition that tyranny is in its essence unbearable, not just for human beings, but for God. Fourth, that there are limits to both the acceptance of tyranny and our obedience to tyrants. Fifth, this obedience is costly, for "the wrath of a king is as messengers of death," as Calvin, quoting Proverbs 16:14, confirms. Divine obedience comes with a price. Nonetheless we should not be afraid, since genuine authority is "not diminished" when it is subordinated to God "before whom even the principalities of heaven tremble with awe."

Then Calvin ends with words that reverberate with a power that can transform any situation and strengthen those who dare stand up for justice, dignity, and freedom. They have rung like a bell in the public witness of generations of Christians fighting for justice and liberation in South Africa, from Sol Plaatjie and James Calata to Albert Luthuli; from Albertina Sisulu to Francis Baartman and Beyers Naudé to my generation. I have made these words my own and cannot even recall how many times I have meditated upon them in the frightening silence of prison cells, clung to them in those lonely places of spiritual and political desolation, preached them or used them in public witness to inspire in others the courage and faith always necessary in struggles for justice everywhere:

> But since this edict has been proclaimed by that celestial herald, Peter, "We must obey God rather than men", let us console ourselves with this thought, that we truly perform the obedience which God requires of us, when we suffer any thing rather than deviate from piety. And that our hearts may not fail us, Paul stimulates us with another consideration—*that Christ has redeemed us at the immense price which our redemption cost him, that we may not be submissive to the corrupt desires of men, much less be slaves to their impiety.*[59]

At the Heart of the Reformed Tradition: Costly Discipleship

For black Reformed Christians all of this came to mean that resistance to tyranny is not only possible but necessary, indeed a "commission" from God. But already dilemma upon dilemma is piling up. Calvin gives the right to resistance to "magistrates" it seems, public officials clothed with some "authority" presumably recognized by the tyrant within the contemporary system of government. But do these officials themselves form the resistance movement or do they in fact *lead* the people in it? Is their "calling" vicarious on behalf of the people or do the people whom they lead in rebellion also, and simultaneously, receive this "commission" from God? And is the "fury" Calvin speaks of limited to the "officials" and how does that fury manifest itself? That "fury" surely means resistance out of righteous anger for the injustices inflicted and the pain the innocent must endure, but does it include violent resistance as well? According to Calvin under certain circumstances, it does, but in our situation, where would that take us? Furthermore, would such a limitation (to the magistrates only) be consistent for Calvin, who in everything else is set against hierarchies, preferred some form of direct political representation for the people, and virtually created the theology of the "priesthood of all believers"?

These were questions black South Africans had to come to terms with. But our dilemma in apartheid South Africa was not unique. It was faced also by the French Huguenots in their struggle against the French monarchy and the Roman Catholic hierarchy. Calvin's admonitions based on Romans 13 the Huguenots found too easy and simplistic: Calvin should understand their situation better: "The enemy violates every godly and human right every day," they let Calvin know.[60]

The legitimate authority, who according to Calvin, should rise up in fury against oppression and in protection of the people, Prince Antoinne of Navarre, refuses to move a finger. Frustrated by the dichotomy in Calvin's thinking, the resistance in France now takes on two forms, vio lent and nonviolent. Through it all though, they hold onto the key Calvin himself recognizes, indeed sets as standard: "We have to obey God more than humans."

Then a crucially important development follows. First, the Huguenots, seeking a consistency in Calvin they can follow, began to read wider than just the *Institutes*, and in this regard they discovered the consistent radical Calvin especially in the *Commentaries* and in the *Sermons*. Second, Theodore Beza, friend of Calvin and Reformed thinker and leader in his own right, helps them by making the distinction between a tyrant that had no right to rule to begin with, and a rightful ruler who later abuses his power and so becomes tyrannical.[61]

The importance of Beza's contribution in my view lies in his emphasis on understanding the term "legitimacy" as applied to rulers and authorities. When Beza asked the question: Are *all* rulers legitimate, and what does it mean? he also brought back to the center of the discussion Calvin's criterion for legitimate rule, namely justice to the poor, the vulnerable, and the oppressed, those who in their suffering of injustice, represent the wounds of God. It was these two issues that made the Huguenots develop the radical reading of John Calvin which led to the development of the first, full, modern theory of the lawfulness of political resistance.[62]

In South Africa too, the challenge was to find the radical Calvin the Huguenots have discovered, and whether that Calvin was the consistent one. We followed the Huguenots. But we also tried to follow Calvin's argument itself in the *Institutes* more closely.

- Calvin demands obedience to earthly rulers. But then Calvin makes clear: obedience to God is above all. He calls obedience to rulers who go against God's Word (that we read as God's unchangeable desire for justice and protection of the poor and defenseless) as "seduction" and "absurd."
- It would be "preposterous" if we, in order "to satisfy men," would incur the displeasure of God.
- Earthly authorities are all subject to God. God is "the King of kings," who "is to be heard alone, above all, for all, and before all."
- Rulers preside over us, but "only in God," and should they command anything against God, "we should not pay the least attention."
- Neither should we "pay any regard to all that dignity," namely all that dignity Calvin himself has bestowed upon the rulers as "invested [in their office] by God," for their acts of oppression and injustice nullify that dignity. Their tyranny means that they "rise up against God" and therefore "degrade their own dignity." In their rule of oppression they "wish to spoil God of his rights, and, as it were, to seize upon his throne and draw him down from heaven." At stake here then, is not only the injustice that wounds God. God, Calvin says, has *rights*: namely the right to do justice and undo injustice and the demand that those who are given authority in God's name do the same; to desire the full flourishing of shalom in the lives of God's children, especially the poor, despised, and the downtrodden. God also has the right to be obeyed—above all and before all. This is as strongly put as one could imagine. At issue here, I believe, is the matter of legitimacy. Is a government that in Calvin's view is a "tyranny," still a "legitimate" government?

- In God's "goodness and providence," Calvin argues further, God "arouses" "avengers" such as Moses, Othniël, and Daniel were for ancient Israel, to "deliver" the people from injustice and "dominion."

The conclusion, in my view, is inescapable: divine obedience overrides all obedience to unjust rulers. Injustice is not to be borne, because injustice itself not only injures God, it is rebellion against God. Christians ought not to participate in that rebellion through their silence or their complicity. Calvin makes that crystal clear in his commentaries and sermons. In Calvin's thinking most immediately related to the "exception" he makes in the *Institutes*, his commentary on the Book of Acts Chapters 4 and 5, he is not ambiguous at all. In his comments on the scene where Peter and John appear before the Sanhedrin, he starts off with a sober, and devastating, assessment of the abuse of power. "Here we may see the deadly evil of power divorced from the fear of God."[63] Calvin does not ever begrudge civil authority the power to rule. That power is a gift from God, meant for good, that is, the doing of justice and the undoing of injustice, the protection of the weak and vulnerable, all this to the glory of God. It is when that power is "divorced from the fear of God" that it becomes abusive, oppressive, and illegitimate, in other words, a "deadly evil." And as such it has to be resisted.

On 4:19 he begins, "Let us remember to whom they make this answer." The answer Peter and John gave was, of course, almost rhetorical: "Whether it is right, *in God's sight,* to listen to you rather than to God, you must judge..." But clearly there was nothing for the Sanhedrin to judge: "For we cannot keep from speaking about what we have seen and heard." Peter and John have put them in an impossible position. There was really no choice, and the Sanhedrin, not ignorant of the covenantal claims of Yahweh's absolute sovereignty—no other gods!—knew this. For Calvin the Council "did rightly represent the church." But the Sanhedrin was much more than a "religious" body. It was "the high priests' political council, made up from the aristocracy in Jerusalem, the highest legislative body in Jewish Palestine, the supreme judicial court, the grand jury for important cases, the council of the Pharisaic school, and the final court of appeals in deciding halakic questions."[64] The power this council wielded was power over all matters of life, religious and political, and it was this power that was being abused. It is to this body that Peter and John are saying, "Whether it is right in the sight of God to listen to you rather than to God..." The question of obedience to unjust rulers or to God is not just religious, it is profoundly political. And as political act it is profoundly religious.

Calvin knows this too, as he seamlessly moves from religious to civil powers in the next paragraph: "Whatever title then men may hold, they are to be listened to only on the condition that they do not lead us away from obeying God." And one sentence on he leaves no doubt: "We must obey princes and others who are in authority, but only in so far as they do not deny to God His rightful authority as supreme King, Father and Lord." These are "the limits of civil government." In paragraph after paragraph Calvin makes this point so that by the time he gets to the classic text in the clash between the duty of Christians and the will of the state, 5:29, he simply states, "God sets men over us in such a way that He keeps His own authority unimpaired."[65]

If a magistrate is carrying out his function properly, Calvin argues, there is no need for tension. Rather, in order to obey God we must submit to them. "But as soon as governors lead us away from obedience to God, seeing that they enter into conflict with God impiously and boldly, they must be put in their place…Then all the fumes of their offices will vanish."

Tyranny is a "violation of human dignity," Calvin says, "For full humanity *requires* liberty…"[66] Notice how Calvin conflates the "degradation" of the dignity of authority with the "violation of human dignity" [of their subjects], as he conflates that with their "spoiling God of God's rights." Tyrants, Calvin says, are "hated by the whole world," for tyranny is "a perversion of order, its overthrow can thus be called a *restitutio,*" a restitution "to its original order," which can only be a "restitution" of the justice which lends dignity and legitimacy to authority and to which the oppressed have a right. God self "cannot endure tyrants and He listens in empathy to the secret groans of those who live under them."[67]

Resistance to tyranny does indeed bring risks and unforeseen changes, but, says Calvin, "Only a degraded people could prefer the yoke of tyranny to the inconveniences of change."[68]

Calvin is quite harsh on those who for some reason or another are afraid to resist tyranny. "There is no doubt that God has struck with a spirit of cowardice those who, like asses, willingly offer their shoulders for burdens."[69] Since tyrants do not "rest their injuries until the wretched people have altogether given up," resistance is inevitable and Calvin finds inspiration for that resistance in the example of the Hebrew midwives who stood up against the Pharaoh.

Speaking of the Pharaoh's ever more harsh oppression of the people of Israel, Calvin makes sure that there is no misunderstanding about the intentions of tyrants. First, he teaches us, they want the people to become inured to their own oppression, to meekly accept that there is no alternative to slavery. Tyranny invariably loses "all regard for justice." There are "no bounds" to its harshness [because it knows] "that this is the best receipt for governing them, so to oppress them that they dare not open their mouths...till they grow hardened, and, as it were, callous to their own bondage."[70] Or put differently, in the words of Steve Biko, until their minds become their oppressor's best ally. But this, Calvin says, is nothing but "tyrannical insolence."

This tyranny must be resisted because—and this is Calvin's second lesson to oppressed people in search of freedom as he ponders this story from Exodus—it serves the purpose of all tyrants, designed "in order that they [the people] may turn away from Moses, and renounce the hope presented to them from on high."[71] In other words, not just helplessly give up, but willfully *renounce* all hope for freedom and all faith in God and in God's justice. These are grave matters; it is the worst thing oppressed people could do. To renounce hope is not only to be resigned to one's oppression, it is to invite death. Whereas elsewhere for Calvin it is the tyrant who denies God's rights to do justice by doing injustice and oppressing God's people, here it is the people who deny God by renouncing all hope in God's liberating power. Elsewhere Calvin makes the point that tyrants, in their boundless arrogance and insistence on oppression denies God God's right to free the people from that oppression, now that onus is on the people. Renouncing all hope in God is the same as depriving God of God's right to secure justice in love and freedom. The tyrant will not stop until he has "destroyed in them all recollection of God," that is, erased from their memory all the promises of God, and all recollection of the truth that God is a God who loves and desires justice; that God's own freedom to be a just and liberating God is the guarantee for the freedom of God's people. Tyrants seek to erase all recollection of the hope-giving, life-saving truth that against that love for justice and freedom no tyrant shall prevail.

In his book *The Mighty and the Almighty*,[72] Nicholas Wolterstorff engages these matters at length. On the question of obedience to civil authorities and what Calvin could have meant to include under his single "exception," Wolterstorff, in engaging John Witte,[73] remarks on Witte's point that "the examples (Calvin) mentions are all cases of the magistrate ordering citizens to violate the so-called First Table of the Decalogue."[74]

The so-called First Table has to do with commandments directly related to God, the Second Table relates to "the neighbor," the commandments that seek to regulate just human relationships. But Wolterstorff quickly cuts to the core: "So if a magistrate does not order me to worship an idol, but instead orders me to treat my neighbor in a way God forbids," Wolterstorff asks, "am I to disobey?"[75]

I have two problems with the way Witte argues. First, dealing with the issue in this way does not help us to dissolve the dilemma Calvin creates for himself as well as for us with the contrast between that last sentence and the foregoing argument on obedience to political authorities. I have already made the point that I believe the last words in the *Institutes* on divine obedience should be read as the framework for all Calvin has to say on this matter. It seems to me also that Calvin, in the Commentaries and Sermons, while referring to our obedience to civil authorities every now and then, is much more consistent in his condemnation of tyrants, and our resistance to them in our obedience to God's call for justice. When and if tensions arise between civil authorities and Christians struggling for justice as God's desire for God's people in the world, there is no claim higher than the claim of God on our obedience. Then, as far as earthly powers are concerned, we should, as Calvin advises, utterly ignore them.

Furthermore, in terms of their intention and demands, there is no dichotomy between the so-called First and Second Tables. I am not sure why the question arises at all. If it denotes a dilemma, it is a false dilemma derived from the (modern, Western) cultural and theological assumption of a dichotomy between commandments regarding God and commandments regarding the neighbor, or differently put, between "religious" life (vertically, toward God) and "secular" life, (horizontally) regarding human relationships. But the Bible knows no such dichotomy. There is no separation of faith and life, or faith and politics. Ancient Israel would have regarded that as entirely artificial. Ritual, civil, and criminal law, moral imperative and social mores were inextricably intertwined. Besides, governing the "Ten Commandments," New Testament scholar Richard Horsley reminds us,[76] was the faith in God's great acts of deliverance, particularly the liberation from bondage in Egypt. At the core of the covenant were the commandments of exclusive loyalty to the force of freedom as their transcendent ruler and further commandments prohibiting exploitative socioeconomic practices in the people's relations with one another. The first commandment, "You shall have no other gods before me" has immediate and wide-ranging political implications. Israel was to have "no other god." "That meant also, since YHWH was the king giving the covenant, that Israel was to have no king apart from YHWH, including no human king. Israelites were not to 'bow down' and 'serve' any other gods."[77]

Corresponding with, and inextricably bound to the exclusive loyalty in the first few commandments were the prohibitions of exploitative social-economic relations between Israelite families and the rest of the commandments.[78] That is why, when asked about the Law, Jesus spoke of the Law as undivided and inseparable: love for God, and love for the neighbor, as oneself. What Calvin says about obedience is true for faith and for politics. Obedience to God above all is our obligation for every situation in life. It is for this reason that the Reformed tradition speaks of the Lordship of Christ over every area of life. There is not a single inch that is not touched by it. It is for this reason too, that Calvin, in his commentary on Acts as we have seen, moves so easily from the church to civil authorities, maintaining the same demand for obedience to God above all. The violations of abusive power have to be resisted and corrected, in church as well as in political and civil life. I do not think that Calvin allows for such obfuscation on this point. Thus, when Wolterstorff asks, "if a magistrate orders me to treat my neighbor in a way that God forbids, do I obey?" we can safely respond, "No." The injustice done to the defenseless is "wounding God." And it begins with the sin of "bowing down" to a god other than God.

Black South African Reformed Christians were therefore not just presented with a *kairos* by our people already committed to struggle, the youth and the members of our congregations who could not take their unjust suffering anymore. We were also confronted by Calvin himself. In the *Institutes* Calvin apparently counsels patience, even extreme patience under oppression, but in the *Commentaries* he returns to the "cowardice" of those who meekly accept their oppression: "Disobedience to impious and wicked edicts of kings" is permissible to all—and here Calvin refers to the Hebrew midwives who disobeyed Pharaoh's command to kill the Hebrew male children—for those who "obey the wicked commands of men display in their cowardice an inexcusable contempt for God."[79] So now it is not just "renouncing all hope." It is showing "contempt for God." Calvin really raises the stakes in this matter. And on the famous words of Peter to the Sanhedrin Calvin comments, "A ruler must be brought to order who exalts himself to the point that he diminishes the honour and right of God" and goes "beyond the limits of his office."[80] Again we hear the bold assertion of the *rights* of God. In South Africa we had no doubt that the apartheid regime had gone beyond these limits and decided that we would rather suffer apartheid's wrath than show contempt for God and for the rights of God.

Besides, the "patience" Calvin counsels us on is the patience to endure for the sake of justice, *in the struggle for justice* which Calvin places on the same plain as the struggle for the truth of God's Word:

> To suffer persecution for righteousness' sake is a singular comfort. For it ought to occur to us how much honour God bestows upon us thus furnishing us with the special badge of his soldiery. *I say that not only they who labor for the defense of the gospel but they who in any way maintain the cause of righteousness suffer persecution for righteousness.*[81]

So Wolterstorff concludes quite correctly: "In short, Calvinist patience is not the patience of passive acceptance but the patience of one who suffers as she struggles against the world's evils."[82]

Just to be clear though, Wolterstorff reiterates:

> Calvinist patience then, is the paradoxical, unstable combination of grieving over the pain and deprivation that come one's way as one lives a life incorporating struggle for the gospel and for justice, of thankfully allowing one's suffering to contribute to the "making" of one's soul, and of taking joy from being united through one's suffering more firmly with Christ who cried out upon the cross and the God who is wounded by the world's wounds.[83]

This is exactly the spirituality of struggle we have talked about before. In South Africa, our people were disenfranchised, disempowered, and dehumanized in every way thinkable and unthinkable. It was clear to us that the apartheid regime and those who supported them had gone "beyond the limits" of their office, and those who had benefited from their oppression of the people had "degraded" not just their own dignity but also the worthiness of the God whose authority they claimed. They, even in claiming the name of God, *precisely in claiming the name of God*, had "spoiled God of God's rights," seeking to "draw God down from heaven."

Calvin often states the view that tyrants and "wicked rulers" are God's instruments for punishing the sins of the people.[84] In our situation, however, our oppression was based purely on racism. Would Calvin, in light of his views on our common humanity and the image of God in every person, have argued that the color of our skin was so offensive to God that it constituted our "sin" and invited the cruelty of apartheid? Would he have concurred with white South Africans that their whiteness proved that they were God's elect, more worthy, more deserving, more iconic, less sinful before God? When, during the struggle, we sang that song of mourning, *senzenina, "What have we done?"* that was precisely the wrenching question we asked of God. Was God *punishing* us for being black? Had Calvin known the depths of the depravity of racism, would he not most vehemently have protested? If Calvin had known that American "manifest destiny" would lead to the devastation of genocide relentlessly and systematically inflicted upon Native American people, would he still hold this view, blaming them for their "sins," forgetting the sins of those who inflicted misery, oppression, and murder upon them? The very thought is preposterous. As we have seen, Calvin also knows that the people can be "unjustly oppressed," in other words, not because of *their* sins, but because of the greed and avarice of their oppressors.

In South Africa practically every avenue to redress had been systematically closed off. Brutal, violent repression was the invariable response to every nonviolent effort toward change and had been for decades. How could we not see in Albert Luthuli, Nelson Mandela, Oliver Tambo, and Steve Biko the "servants of God" raised up "to punish unrighteous dominion and injustice"? Apartheid was tyranny. How could we not see the "fury" and the "attempt to (do) something altogether different," in the fury of the children in 1976, and in the uprising of the masses after 1983 who went on to indeed do "something altogether different"? And is "meditating" on something different not the same as "dreaming a different world," which so strongly underlay our struggle for something not yet seen, but dreamed of, prayed and hoped for?

Calvin preached that since cruelty "and the confusion of order and justice" cannot be endured, the oppressed cry out "How long?", and it "is then the same as though God heard himself, when he hears the cries and groaning of those who cannot bear injustice."[85] How then, could we not hear the voice of God in the tears of our mothers and the cries of the poor, or see in apartheid's "law and order" the "utter confusion of order and justice" that Calvin so angrily denounced? How could we not see the wounds of God in the unbearable injustices of apartheid, in the wounds of the tortured body of Steve Biko, in the humiliation of our fathers and mothers; in the mutilated and massacred children of Soweto and Elsies River, of Athlone and Lingelihle?

Calvin allowed for magistrates "appointed to restrain the willfulness of kings," to resist evil rulers. Having had no public representatives as decreed by apartheid law, we had no public defenders with official authority, causing us to rethink Calvin's argument about public officials and private persons. Who were our "magistrates"? Not the white government, and certainly not the black vassals of apartheid in the homelands and dummy political bodies set up and paid for by the regime, who, like Herod under the Romans, so cravenly did their master's bidding, or in Calvin's words, "connived at kings in their oppression"? These "representatives," instead of standing up for the rights and freedom of the people, involved themselves in the "most nefarious perfidy, because they fraudulently betray the liberty of the people..."[86]

Under apartheid's racist dispensation *all* black people were relegated to noncitizens without any claim to rights. We had no right to vote; we were not represented in any form in the chambers of parliament, where in a genuine, responsive democracy, the willfulness of governments can be "restrained." In apartheid South Africa's whites-only parliament, in its army and police forces and in its courts, the oppressed people had no defenders or protectors. Our defenders came from among the oppressed, the same as Moses, Othniel, and Daniel whom Calvin praises as shining examples of resistance. How could we, in the face of apartheid, not rise in defense of the dignity of the oppressed in whom God sees Godself "as in a mirror?" How could we not be stung by Calvin's exposure of our cowardice if we, like "asses bending to the yoke," should meekly accept our oppression? Since we were excluded from "restraining" tyranny in the chambers of political decision-making, were we to be judged for seeking to restrain tyranny in the streets of resistance? It is in that spirit that black Reformed Christians chose for the struggle for justice in South Africa. When we understood Bonhoeffer's insight that "the virtue of obedience could be misused in the service of evil,"[87] Calvin's "one exception" became the rule for our life, and a call to obedience we dared not disobey.

At the Heart of the Reformed Tradition: The Tenderness of Conscience

In South Africa today, we remain confronted by the obstinacy of racism, the arrogance of power, the perniciousness of poverty, the growing gap in equality, and the dangerous seduction of violence; by the continued struggle to make the world a safe place for children, the dignity, worthiness, and equality of women and the rights of persons other than heterosexual. Globally too the challenges are frightening: global economic injustice and ecological destruction; global war, violence, peace, and the destructive role of religion; food and water security, human trafficking and modern slavery; the new idolatries in the worship of money and things and the gospel of consumerism. While 3 billion people worldwide suffer increasing hunger and impoverishment, the assets of the world's 3 richest billionaires are more than the combined wealth of the 600 million inhabitants of the least-developed countries.[88]

Through the *Accra Confession* of 2004 and its scathing critique of empire and global capitalism, the World Alliance of Reformed Churches, (now the World Communion of Reformed Churches) has brought not only a new sensitivity to global justice and ecological responsibility to the ecumenical movement, but by initiating a *processus confessionis* in this all-important issue, lent to it a uniquely Reformed theological gravitas, simultaneously reminding its member churches at a crucial historical juncture of what it means to be Reformed. As enduring was the insight that the *Accra Confession* discovered this truth by seeing the world of domination and suffering, of new tyrannies and idolatries not through the lens of power, privilege, and entitlement, but "through the eyes of those who suffer," a classic Reformed way of reading the Bible, the situation in the world, and discerning the signs of the times.[89] That remains a unique contribution to ecumenical witness in the world.

Calling to mind the challenge left us by Helmut Gollwitzer, what is the relevance of the Reformed tradition in the face of these realities? What difference does it make to the new situation of global apartheid? I am convinced that we are called again and again by the enduring promise of the radical Reformed tradition. And much of it rests with our ability, our responsibility, indeed our courage, to take those steps Calvin in his time took, even those steps he could not see and could not take and yet would be the inescapable logic of his own theological convictions and biblical hermeneutics.

With Calvin we shall have to continue to seek a world which shall be the theater of God's glory, where justice and peace shall reign and the integrity of God's creation be upheld and defended. We shall have to uphold the dignity with which God has endowed governmental authority, understanding that the honor Calvin speaks of lies in their response to the plight of the poor, the weak, and vulnerable as Calvin insisted. They are, after all, "servants of God for your good," and to that standard we shall hold them accountable. With Calvin we shall measure government by the justice they do to the downtrodden, and we shall honor our iconicity (Wolterstorff) in being endowed with the image of God, reflected in ourselves and in the Other. We shall constantly remind them that our highest loyalty and obedience are due to God who is "King of kings" and whose word is heard "above all, before all, for all."

In our ongoing struggles for the sake of the other, all God's children and God's creation, we shall recall Calvin's words on our expectations of civil government, in my view not uttered as an exhortation to glorify powers and principalities, nor as a call to blind obedience and unquestioning submissiveness but as sublime and prophetic critique of governmental power in reminding it where that power originates and how it should be judged. Writing with powerful rhetorical persuasion, insisting that politics is not a game of heartless power, ruthless expediency, or self-serving piousness but a "righteous calling" toward compassionate justice, Calvin sets the bar high indeed:

> How will they dare to admit iniquity to their tribunal, when they are told that it is the throne of the living God? How will they venture to pronounce an unjust sentence with that mouth which they understand to be an ordained organ of divine truth? With what conscience will they subscribe impious decrees with that hand which they know has been appointed to write the acts of God? In a word, if they remember that they are the vice regents of God, it behooves them to watch with all care, diligence and industry that they may in themselves exhibit a kind of image of the Divine Providence,

> guardianship, goodness, benevolence, and justice. But let them constantly keep the additional thought in view, that if a curse is pronounced on him that "doeth the work of the Lord deceitfully" a much heavier curse must lie on him who deals deceitfully in a righteous calling.[90]

We shall have to remember also, that Calvin's extreme reticence in the matter of civil resistance was not simply fueled by a blind conservatism or his justified fear of anarchy and chaos, but by his desire to preserve what he fervently hoped would be an instrument in God's hand to dispense justice, protect the weak, and uphold the rights of the powerless. He certainly was not driven by a desire to maintain the status quo at all costs. Hence his "one exception" that overrides all else, displaying as it does, precisely in its resistance through obedience, "the wonderful goodness and power and providence" of God.

And if it be necessary to follow the road of confrontation and resistance, we shall honor this reticence, understanding the dangerous allure of violence today better than John Calvin did in his time, even as we tried to do in the darkest days of the struggle when in the middle of the state of emergency in 1985 we called upon the wisdom of Paul Lehmann from who we learned that:

> A politics of confrontation in Jesus' sense is neither submission to, nor legitimation of, existing governments. It is a much more subtle practice of love of neighbour that recognizes in existing authorities the great divide between self-justifying legitimacy that ends in the tyranny of order and a self-justifying rebellion that ends in the tyranny of anarchy.[91]

That discernment is as necessary today as it was then. It is today as true for our global realities. What is crucial here is what Abraham Kuyper found in Calvin and the Reformed tradition and helped us to discover, namely what Kuyper called the "tenderness of conscience."[92] Kuyper understands this not as an inner sense of privatized right or wrong, but as right or wrong "within the universal character of religion" in its "complete universal application."[93] It is not an inner-worldly theology at work here; it is a *public* theology, with a *public prophetic* witness.[94] I have interpreted that to be a tenderness that is entirely devoid of narcissistic romanticism but instead bent on compassionate justice; the tenderness that means allowing ourselves to be disturbed by the wounds of God, wounded by the things that wound God, seduced by the dream of God for the world: of justice, peace, humanity, solidarity, so that we seek the sovereignty of God "in all spheres and kingdoms, visible and invisible."[95]

This tenderness of conscience brings us face to face with the Other in whom we discover the face of God, and in so doing bringing us "face to face with the living God, so that the heart trembles before God's holy majesty,"[96] and that is the spirituality that brings us the gift of human righteousness. Above all, it brings us face to face with the wounds of a grieving God at the injustices inflicted upon God's little ones. This is not the escapism which is the self-absorbed, paralyzing result of our common, sinful helplessness at the "brokenness of the world" leaving us with either despair and hopeless anger, or cynicism and hypocrisy. It is, rather, the righteousness of hopeful resistance to our sinful estrangement from God and the Other and our tendencies to self-possessed selfishness which holds our prophetic imagination captive and keeps us from dreaming a different world. It is to walk in the light of understanding instructed by this tenderness which is, in its essence, a response to God's vulnerable love:

> To perpetrate injustice on a fellow human being is to wound God; the cries of the victims are the expression of divine suffering. Thus the call to justice is rooted ultimately in the pathos of God, in God's vulnerable love. The call to eliminate injustice is the call to alleviate divine suffering. If we believed that, and believed it firmly, we would be far more reluctant than we are to participate in the acts and the structures of injustice. If we believed that and believed it firmly, we would ceaselessly struggle for justice and against injustice, bearing with thankful, joyful, patience the suffering which that struggle will bring upon us.[97]

Ordinarily, writes William Stacy Johnson, "we might expect a work in Christian theology to conclude with the resurrection and eternal life...But [Calvin] chose to bring his major work to a climax with reflections *not* on the world to come but on our political responsibility for *this* world."[98] Our faith has political consequences and calls for righteous choices. Also, Reformed Christians understand that for this tradition the dominating principle was not, soteriologically, justification by faith, as it is for Lutheranism, for example. It is, rather, in the widest sense of the word, cosmological, seeking the Lordship of Christ in all of life, not for the sake of exclusivist domination and triumphalist exploitation, but rather for the sake of compassionate justice and truthful servanthood.

Reformed spirituality is not a closeted or disembodied piety; it is a worldly holiness, a world-engaging and world-transforming faith. It insists that the Earth is not a conquerable source for the instant gratification of the rich, but that it is the Lord's and that we are accountable stewards of this precious gift; that the people of the world are not pawns made for profit while considered less than profits, but bearers of the image of the living God. That the cosmos is not a stage for the hubristic arrogance of the powerful, but that it is the theater of God's glory, and that that glory is best seen in our doing what Yahweh requires: the undoing of injustice and the doing of justice, loving mercy, and walking humbly with our God.

3

The Time for Pious Words Is Over: Kairos, Decision, and Righteous Choices

Kairos and Decision

It is Dietrich Bonhoeffer who in so many ways illustrates and helps us understand the power and meaning of a kairos consciousness—the consciousness that helps us to discern and act upon a kairos moment. I had always thought that such a kairos consciousness in Bonhoeffer became clearest when he made those momentous decisions that have so marked his theology and his life. The decision about grabbing the spokes of the wheel, in the famous essay on the "Jewish Question" for example; or his decision that commitment to social justice and peace is at heart a commitment about and to Christ himself, as he writes to his brother.[1]

But lately I have come to think more and more that all these crucial decisions have their foundation in the one decision he had made very early on and which now seems to me to be key to understanding his life and work. In a letter of January 1, 1935, not paid much attention, Bonhoeffer writes from Finkenwalde to "a woman to whom (he) had been engaged."[2] He speaks of his discovery of the Bible and how his now different reading of that book had changed his life, led him to "become a Christian." This was a transformational experience; one that challenged Bonhoeffer in ways he had not known before. He had theological knowledge but did not know Jesus Christ; he had religion but no faith; he prayed "very little," had "turned the gospel of Jesus Christ into something of personal advantage for myself... " Then, he writes, the Bible, and particularly the Sermon on the Mount, "freed me from all that." Suddenly the Bible was not simply a book to be studied and critically dissected. It became a book that inspires and liberates, and brought Bonhoeffer to a decision that would change his life. It made him, he says, "a Christian." By that he did not mean some religious person who knew *about* Christ. He meant that he became *a follower of Christ.* A disciple.

This decision, to know and follow Christ, led to a further decision: to set aside his desires for the academy and become committed to the church. It was a moment of discernment, conversion, and commitment; a decision which caused, Eberhard Bethge would later write, "a momentous, inner revolution."[3] It was a shift away from the distanced, noninvolved, intellectualized theologizing of the academy to an understanding of the Christian faith that called for following Christ in one's personal life as well as one's life in the world. Knowing and following Christ means that understanding those kairos moments that call for acts of justice and peace are moments that call for discernment and decision; for conversion and commitment and righteous, risk-filled choices. It is the kind of conversion and commitment that would lead to a better understanding of the cost of true discipleship. I contend that without this profound personal experience that led to an equally profound decision, Bonhoeffer would not have been able to write those intensely moving and powerful words about costly discipleship, cheap grace, and costly grace. And neither would he have been able to engage in those courageous acts of justice and solidarity in church and in society.

For Bonhoeffer the repercussions were immense. "It was a great liberation," he writes. "It became clear to me that the life of a servant of Jesus Christ must belong to the church, and step by step it became plainer to me how far that must go." The decision to follow Christ was a "great liberation." It freed him from the safe, but spiritless study of theology as discipline without personal commitment to Christ and service to the church. It also freed him from the stranglehold of that peculiar patriotic, political pietism that comes with all nationalistic forms of Christianity, as rife in the Germany of his time as it was in apartheid South Africa and rampant still in the United States.

He now understood better that the life of a servant of Christ "must belong to the church." But Bonhoeffer did not mean a church disconnected from Christ in its disconnect from the world, a church turned into itself, trapped in the rituals of a meaningless religiosity without a commitment to the transformation of the world. He meant a church "for others," one that understood and believed its confession that Jesus Christ is Lord, and that it was to Christ, not to church authorities, patriotic sentiments, or a culture that provides political and economic privilege that the church owed ultimate loyalty and obedience. A church that even while living in Hitler's shadow,[4] would walk in the light of Jesus Christ. It was an insight of faith with enormous political consequences.

Simultaneously, it became clear to him, "step by step," how far this must go. I read these words in two ways. First, that his decision took him on a path that one can follow only step by step. One cannot calculate the whole journey, nor control what happens on the way. For every step the disciple of Christ follows in obedience, trusting in Christ. Second, in following Jesus, the disciple of Christ must know that for Jesus that path led to the places where God is to be found. This was a thought that would captivate Bonhoeffer all his life. Those are not the places one might want to go, but in deciding to follow Christ one has no choice but to go. In a letter a few months later, April 1936, Bonhoeffer speaks of his decision—because of that first decision to follow Christ— to go not where he chooses, but where God is to be found:

> If I am the one who says where God shall be, so I will always find a God there who corresponds in some way to me, is pleasing to me, who belongs to my nature. If it is, however, God who speaks where [God] chooses to be, than that will probably be a place which is not at all pleasing to me. But this place is the cross of Christ. And he who will find him there must be with him under this cross...This is no place which is pleasing or *a priori* sensible to us, but a place strange to us in every way and which is entirely contrary to us. But it is the very place God has chosen to encounter us.[5]

It is a decision and commitment one makes in faith and complete trust—once made one has no control over where the path may lead. And here is where decision becomes a calling, but it is a calling to do God's will no matter what: "My calling is quite clear to me. What God will make of it I do not know...I must follow the path." As far as the decision itself is concerned, "I believe its nobility will become plain to us only in coming times and events. If only we can hold out."[6] Bonhoeffer is not referring to some mystical or eschatological revelation. It is in the real, historical events of the "coming times," in the struggles *against* Hitler and *within* the church, *against* the Nazi's and *for* those considered "less worthy," *against* the *Deutsche Christen* and *for* the gospel of Jesus Christ that the decision will be tested and its "nobility"—its validity and its righteousness—will be proved if the followers of Jesus Christ can endure to the end. Where, and when it would end, one did not know. One's calling was to "endure."

It is this discernment, and this kind of uncompromising commitment to Jesus Christ both personal and in the struggles for peace and social justice that had drawn me to Dietrich Bonhoeffer and Beyers Naudé, and it helps explain why both of them have had such a formative influence in their historical contexts and why that influence is still so pervasive today.

It is remarkable how significant is the role of decision in the life and theology of both Dietrich Bonhoeffer and Beyers Naudé. It is foundational to both in their development as theologians and ecumenical leaders from the first time they understood and responded to the call to a different life, and, I believe, the framework within which to interpret their life and work.

As I have argued elsewhere and as has become clear in Bonhoeffer's words cited above, I speak of "decision" not linguistically, as a word, but theologically, as an act of faith, a fundamental and transformational choice with consequences for oneself certainly, but far beyond oneself. It is an act taken not in certitude or pride but in fear and trembling, walking not by sight but by faith. It is an act the consequences of which one cannot foresee nor be completely prepared for, but it is nonetheless taken in what one is convinced is obedience to Jesus Christ.[7]

It is at this foundational level that Beyers Naudé finds convergence with Dietrich Bonhoeffer. Already during his work with the German expatriate congregation in Barcelona, Bonhoeffer discovered the life-changing significance of decision for the life of the Christian. "The question before us," Bonhoeffer told his congregation in 1928,

> [I]s whether in our own day Christ still stands in the place where decisions are made concerning the most profound matters we are facing, namely concerning our own lives and the life of our people [the *Volk*]...whether the Spirit of Christ can still speak to us of the ultimate, final, decisive matters.[8]

In truth, Bonhoeffer says, it is not us, but Christ who is at the center of this decision, for Christ himself "represents an all-or-nothing decision."[9] In his life and ministry Jesus of Nazareth purposefully went to all the places of forsakenness and rejection where the poor and the weak, the powerless and the fearful, those considered as nothing by the privileged and the powerful, cowered in the shadows. On the cross, he took upon himself all the arrogance and violence of earthly powers as they avenged themselves upon the powerless and their audacity to hope. On the cross he made the "all or nothing" decision by giving his life for them, turning the scandal of a death on the cross into a moment of transformation and resistance to the powers of death.

Hence, our decisions must lead us to the place "where Christ stands." Above, Bonhoeffer knows that place to be "under the cross." As he followed the path of costly discipleship "step by step," Bonhoeffer understood more and more that that place—"under the cross"—is to be found with "the children, and the morally and socially 'least of these', those viewed as less worthy."[10] These were the ones who were being crucified, the ones who represent Christ "in our midst."

Increasingly too, the desire to find the place where Christ stands—with the "least of these"—would lead Bonhoeffer beyond his concerns for his "own people"—the *Volk*—to all those found "unworthy" by the

Nazi's, rejected, despised, persecuted: the Jews, the gays, the disabled, the Roma, the communists, and finally the true patriots of the resistance. He understood that it would "concern our own lives." No longer would his life be his own, it would be owned by Christ and Christ's love for the "less worthy." It would be a life of struggle and sacrifice. It touched his decisions about his "own people" and it would involve judgment, and alienation. His love for Christ and for those regarded as Other would bring accusations of betrayal and defeatism. Where Christ was calling him to stand would not at all be easy.

The decisions we take, so Bonhoeffer reads and interprets Colossians 3:1–3, will determine

> whether we Christians have enough strength to witness before the world that we are not dreamers with our heads in the clouds...that our faith really is not opium that keeps us content within an unjust world. Instead, and precisely because our minds are set on things above, we are that much more stubborn and purposeful in protesting here on earth...[11]

Bonhoeffer speaks of the "strength," the courage, to witness before the world. But first, the "world" he speaks of is a hostile world, a world in the grip of evil, quite specifically the world of Adolf Hitler, of the Nazi's, of challenge and risk of persecution, of the ultimate limits of horror and death. Second, he has, *by decision*, left the safe and comfortable world of New York, Union Seminary, and Abyssinian Baptist Church behind. But it was also his decision to return to Germany that made that comforting world ultimately unbearable for Bonhoeffer: how could he be safe while "the brethren" of the Confessing Church were facing such agonizing decisions every day?[12] The "witness" Bonhoeffer thinks of can no longer be words, however thoughtful and eloquent those might be. From now on witness can only be the act of taking a stand where Christ is to be found: in the places where the plagues fall, where death casts its shadow. The strength for this kind of witness comes not of earthly power, of connections with those in high places, or of the guarantees of protective privilege. This is a strength that comes from faith in the empowering Spirit of God.

Third, Bonhoeffer consciously takes us back to the New Testament: our witness before the world is *martyria:* standing with Christ and suffering with Christ for the sake of righteousness and peace, amidst and against the harsh realities of pain and suffering, humiliation, hunger, and death. That is what he means with the phrase "our heads (not) in the clouds." This is not the so-called realism of cynicism or of political expedience. It is the prophetic realism of faith. We are driven, moreover, not by what the world thinks or expects of us, but by "the things above." When we are seeing and contemplating "the things above," in other words, the desire of God for love, compassionate justice and peace, we cannot be content with living in this unjust world.

When we understand how much the Other is our sister and brother, our kinfolk, and that their call upon us is a call from our flesh and blood—that is when we will face the injustices of the world with strength and courage and determination, "much more stubborn and purposeful," not vague and vacillating, "in protesting here on earth." "On earth": our dreams are not the dreams of wishful thinkers. We dream the dreams of God: namely of justice and peace, of mercy and compassion; of a different, more humane world we work to make possible through our acts of *martyria*. *Martyria* is resistance.

For Beyers Naudé as well this would be the issue that would prove to be life-changing. Would he be willing to witness to the world, his world of apartheid and Afrikaner exceptionalism, of white privilege and power, of adoration and a bright, shining future which would turn into a world of hatred, bitter rejection, and violence because of that witness and what would be seen as his "betrayal" of the *Volk* and the Afrikaner Cause? For Beyers too, it was a matter of leaving that first, comfortable world behind, to consciously and purposefully turn his back on it, choosing instead the world of blackness, of suffering and pain, of protest and struggle. This would be a decidedly different kind of witness than his preaching from the wealthy and influential pulpit of Aasvoëlkop DRC congregation in the northern suburbs of Johannesburg.

For Beyers, too, as much as for Bonhoeffer the first, final, and compelling question was Christ: "Is your first obedience and highest loyalty to Christ?" he asked his church in that first sermon after he made his decision to accept the position of editor of the progressive, critical magazine *Pro Veritate*, foreshadowing his becoming Director of the Christian Institute. This is crucial, for in following Christ to that place of final and ultimate decisions one would have to be "disobedient yet at the deepest level obedient, unfaithful yet faithful at the deepest level."[13] For Beyers, as for Bonhoeffer, this decision would take him beyond the concerns for his own people —the *Volk*—to solidarity with the oppressed, the downtrodden, the wronged; those considered "less worthy" by white supremacy in South Africa.

So Beyers Naudé's decision led him from the isolationist comfort of privileged white Afrikanerdom to the exposed identification with South Africa's oppressed; from the protection of power to the vulnerability of solidarity and powerlessness; from ensconced neutrality to passionate engagement; from a theology of apartheid to an intuitively critical theology, simultaneously Reformed and ecumenical, and open to the inspiring revelations of God in faiths other than his own; from unquestioning resignation to sustained resistance, from the certainties of entitlement to the risks of struggle. In doing so, it brought him to the "place where Christ stands," and is always to be found.

Like Bonhoeffer, he would discover that in those places the Spirit of Christ would speak to him of "ultimate, final, decisive matters."

"The Parting of the Ways"

However, decisions that concern ultimate, final, and decisive matters always lead to a parting of the ways. The title of this chapter, "The time for pious words is over," is a key sentence in an article written by Beyers Naudé in October 1970 which, significantly, bore the title "The Parting of the Ways."[14] In that article, Naudé defends his decision to publicly support the World Council of Churches' Programme to Combat Racism (PCR) started in 1969, and more specifically the decision of the PCR in 1970 to launch its "Special Fund," meant to provide financial support for the humanitarian programmes of the Southern African liberation movements. It was, without a doubt, the most controversial, but for Southern Africa's black people, the most courageous and decisive decision of the WCC, because it was the clearest sign yet of active, meaningful ecumenical solidarity.

Already the PCR itself had cost the WCC dearly, but that initial indignation was now multiplied. Churches in the rich North were scandalized: the WCC was targeting white racism in South Africa and by implication their tolerance of, perhaps support for it. The WCC had, in their eyes, already been making common cause with "godless Communists," and now it was giving church money to "terrorists." The outrage was instant, visceral, and sustained. The World Council was not just vilified, it was punished: many churches withdrew their financial support and instead joined forces with the most conservative elements in their countries in their condemnation of the WCC. In South Africa the reaction was hysterical.[15]

The broader context of the WCC decision, and subsequently that of Beyers Naudé, was the situation in South Africa at the time. On March 21, 1960, the Pan Africanist Congress staged peaceful demonstrations against the hated Pass laws in Johannesburg and Cape Town. As the march neared Sharpeville police station near Johannesburg, police opened fire with live ammunition, killing 69 persons and wounding over 186 others, most of them shot in the back. In Evaton the protest was broken up by low-flying fighter jets and in Langa near Cape Town 3 people were killed and 27 injured in a baton charge by police.[16] Other protest actions followed. The costs of these actions would be high for all involved, as Sharpeville, against all expectations, suddenly became the iconic turning point for the struggle for freedom in South Africa. Government reaction was immediate and harsh and a series of even more draconian laws were put in place. Liberation movements were banned, as were many activists. The Rivonia trial followed the Treason trial of 1956–1961, leaders were convicted and sent to Robben Island, others were forced into exile; all political activity was driven underground. In December 1961 the African National Congress made its decision to turn from nonviolent resistance to military action and formed Umkhonto we Sizwe, the armed wing of the ANC.

At his trial, Nelson Mandela explained why:

> We of the ANC had always stood for a non-racial democracy, and we shrank from any action which would drive the races further apart. But the hard facts were that 50 years of nonviolence had brought the African people nothing but more and more repressive legislation, and fewer and fewer rights...I came to the conclusion that as violence in this country was inevitable it would be unrealistic to continue preaching peace and nonviolence.[17]

Mandela was referring to the decades-long struggle of black people which had ultimately led to the "Defiance Campaign" of the 1950s, the extraordinary and persistent nonviolent campaign of mass defiance and protests, the courageous response of South Africa's oppressed people to the historic changes in 1948 which placed political power in the hands of the National Party and the Afrikaner and brought in apartheid, with its harrowing consequences, as official policy of the land. The fifties was also the decade of the Kliptown gathering where the Freedom Charter was adopted in 1955 and of the Women's March on Pretoria (1956)—all extremely effective expressions of nonviolent resistance. But he was also referring to the intransigence of the white minority regime, its ever more violent responses to peaceful protest, and its refusal to reconsider its policies of racial supremacy and apartheid.

But Sharpeville confronted especially the churches with new, fundamental challenges. Under the leadership of the WCC the Cottesloe Consultation was called where the South African member churches debated the political situation and the response of the church. The Cottesloe Declaration was issued.[18] It called for an end to discrimination and for the granting of citizenship of all who "permanently" lived in South Africa. It declared that there were no scriptural grounds for the prohibition of mixed marriages, spoke out against exclusion "from any church on the grounds of colour or race," and it strongly encouraged the churches to take up their prophetic responsibility toward government.

Beyers Naudé was part of the Dutch Reformed Church delegation to that Consultation and when Prime Minister Hendrik Verwoerd applied severe public and private pressure on the church and the leadership buckled under that pressure, Naudé refused to distance himself from the Cottesloe Declaration even when, ominously, his church began to turn against him. Basing his stand on the biblical text in the book of Acts 5:29, just as before him the Confessing Church in Germany and Albert John Luthuli in South Africa had done, Naudé declared,

> It is a choice between religious conviction and submission to ecclesiastical authority. By obeying the latter unconditionally I would save face, but lose my soul.[19]

Already then, in 1963, Naudé discerned a crisis, a kairos which called for decision, conversion, and commitment. He knew that this was a matter of Christian obedience, of conscience and courage, of making dangerous, but righteous and liberating choices, and he discerned that the choice was between "saving face" and "losing (his) soul." Naudé also had been involved in the formulation of that other important document of the 1960s, the "Message to the people of South Africa."[20] It too was a strong theological statement, emphasizing the unity of humankind and the church and calling apartheid and separation "sinful," a "novel gospel," and a "false faith."

It could be argued that these documents could be considered quite bold for their time, and certainly it did call for a certain amount of courage to speak critically of apartheid in the 1960s. I acknowledge that fully. But that argument is almost always made from a white point of view. True also is the fact that one should not make judgments on these documents with perfect hindsight, in the light of our later, radicalized views. But that is not my intention. If one places these documents not within the framework of the white South African perspective, but within the black context, it is clear just how far they fall short of articulating the black realities and black aspirations of the time. One only has to look at the writings of Chief Albert Luthuli at the time to see the point.[21]

On a more critical, black reading therefore, the Cottesloe Declaration fails to utter an unequivocal condemnation of the Bantustan policy, the 1913 and 1936 Land Acts, or even of apartheid—not in a generalized way—but as a *system of institutionalized racial oppression and systemic economic exploitation*. There is no clear vision of a nonracial, democratic society and for the need for a radical shift of power relations as essential for fundamental political change as articulated so clearly by black leaders for decades. So when the Declaration states that black people (the Declaration speaks of "these groups") "have an equal right to make their contributions to society," one is entitled to ask: what *kind* of society and what *kind* of government; in fact, *whose* government are black people expected to make their contributions to?

The Declaration has "no objection in principle to the direct representation of coloured people in parliament." But what does this mean? Are they speaking of the "white parliament" of South Africa? Does this mean tacit approval of the Bantustans? What about the black majority who according to the apartheid dispensation, did not permanently reside in South Africa and therefore had no rights in the land of their birth, including the right to be represented "in parliament?"

It is exactly this kind of enlightened apartheid logic that would eventually lead to President P. W. Botha's 1983 constitution with its Tri-cameral parliamentary system which, despite its apartheid-advantages offered to "coloureds" and "Indians" and which won such wide support among the white electorate who hailed it as "reform" but nonetheless could not convince those communities. It was roundly, and rightly, totally rejected by those communities in the formation of and their participation in the United Democratic Front, and the boycott of those apartheid elections on both political and moral grounds.[22] It shows also just how out of touch with both reality and black aspirations the white church leadership were, despite their good intentions. After all, how difficult could it have been for the white church leadership to travel from Johannesburg to Groutville in the province of KwaZulu-Natal, to consult with Luthuli, the liberation movement's leader, respected across the world for his nonviolent leadership and a fellow Christian, on the true feelings and political aspirations of black people?

There is another serious matter we should consider here. Cottesloe declares that "the present tension [i.e. after Sharpeville] is the result of a long historical development *and all groups bear responsibility for it*."[23] This is a most remarkable sentence. On whose behalf, one wonders, does the Declaration speak? How is such a-historical analysis possible? Even a superficial glance at history shows the long, and amazingly patient engagement by black people in their struggle to make sure white South Africa understood "the things that make for peace," and the contempt with which this was treated by successive white minority regimes. Leaders such as Albert Luthuli went out of their way to make sure there were no misunderstandings around the legitimate desires of black people.[24] Why then put the blame for the violent response of the apartheid regime to the nonviolent protests of March 21 on the black protesters instead of where blame belongs, namely at the door of the white government, their police, and their army? And, lest we forget, on the white voters who gave the government its mandate, benefited from its policies, and accepted the protection offered by its violence?

Why is there such a lack of understanding of the root causes of the conflict? The Sharpeville massacre, the violence that preceded it, and its immediate aftermath, is not something black people should take responsibility for, as Albert Luthuli made very clear.[25] It should be the white representatives of the churches, as direct beneficiaries of apartheid, if not as its direct perpetrators, who should at least have acknowledged, if not taken vicarious responsibility for the intransigence of the white minority government, its resolute resistance to calls for justice and equality; its relentless violent reactions to calls for peaceful change, and for the utter failure of the church to unequivocally stand up for justice while the people were dying in the streets. So, instead of praising the oppressed for their persistent nonviolent resistance and searching for ways to support them in their struggles for justice and freedom, the Declaration seeks to apportion blame on an equal basis to the perpetrators and victims alike, without any understanding of the need for resistance against oppression whatsoever.

One should ask why the Declaration forces the victims to share responsibility for "the present tension" after Sharpeville with the apartheid government and its supporters? It is the same as demanding of them to share the responsibility *for* their oppression, the denial of their rights and the fact of their death *with* the perpetrators and beneficiaries *of* their oppression. Black Consciousness did make such a call upon South Africa's oppressed masses, but that was a call made within the context of a call to resistance to oppression, not a call to take responsibility for the oppressor's intransigence and to accept the situation as it was. Why should the protesters be made to feel guilt at their legitimate protest, at the audacity of their hope, at the display of their courage to demand rights, justice, and equity in the land of their birth? This is perhaps one salient reason why one finds no hint of acknowledgment of white guilt, of collective responsibility, remorse or repentance in any of the two documents. Theologically as well as politically this is a serious omission.

Upon reflection therefore, ultimately these documents were not adequate for the times they were produced, and in the challenging times that would follow they would prove to be treacherously soft ground for the churches to stand on. The inadequacy is not because they were not well-intentioned. Rather, it is because of the failure to read the signs of the times, and to read those signs through the eyes of the suffering; a failure to yield to the greater experiential wisdom of black people; and above all a failure to open themselves to the sagacity of black political leadership. They failed for a lack of kairos consciousness which would have offered a much different perspective on reading both the South African situation and the Scriptures. They did not understand that the time for pious words was over.

As I have been arguing, a kairos consciousness compels one to see the situation no longer through the eyes of the privileged and comfortable, but instead through the eyes of those who suffer. Now, in 1970, Naudé, discerning the situation in his country, decided that those words were not enough. Statements, however well-intentioned, would no longer suffice. The time for pious words was truly over. The ecumenical church challenged him, and his kairos consciousness left him no choice but to turn the deepest of his convictions into action. He chose for solidarity with black people, not on the basis of charity or some vague notion of liberal politics, but in their struggles for justice and on the basis of his faith.

Beyers Naudé did not choose for violence, and neither was that the intention and choice of the World Council of Churches as both he and the WCC were accused of. But now he knew three things: First, he recognized apartheid as an inherently violent system, and not just the physical aspects of it. Note also his use of the term "counter-violence," denoting a violent response to a violent situation, not the initiation of violence. Second, one could not condemn the counter-violence of the oppressed if one did not condemn the fundamental causes for the violence, namely the persistent, violent oppression of the oppressor and the unrelenting refusal to come to terms with political and social justice. Third, one needed to actively join the struggles of the oppressed in the ways that one could, and while not condoning, then at least understanding the choices the oppressed had to make under extraordinarily difficult circumstances and historical duress as Mandela's statement from the dock makes clear.[26] Naudé argues,

> One is constantly reminded of the fact that long existing systems of oppression and violence called into being struggles where counter-violence was seen to be the inevitable answer to meet and overcome such existing forms of violence, and I do not think that Christ gives us the right to judge or condemn those who, in finding themselves in such situations of tyranny and oppression, have come to the conclusion that, having tried all else, there is no option left to procure liberation but through violence.[27]

But such solidarity does not make one give up one's own deep convictions, or the responsibility to continue to engage the oppressor in nonviolent resistance, and through sacrificial commitment try to influence what Albert Luthuli called "the character of the resistance." So with the credibility conferred upon him by his righteous choices, Naudé goes on to say,

> But I hold the conviction that this is not, and cannot be, and will never be the truly satisfying answer which God has made available to his children

> on earth. I sense—and I admit my inadequacy or failure to grasping this more clearly—that there is a dimension of divine power and moral force available to us as human beings which we as a church or as a Christian community have not yet been able to grasp and act upon…I implicitly believe that once this divine power of moral force is understood and effectively utilised, it will in turn create a human initiative presently lacking in our society to resolve situations and systems of conflict through other means than those of violence.[28]

One can almost hear the echoes of Bonhoeffer's struggles on this crucial issue, as he confronted the church and his own conscience, with the so-called Jewish Question:

> There are thus three possibilities for action the church can take vis-à-vis the state: *first,* questioning the state as to the legitimate state character of its actions, that is, making the state responsible for what it does. *Second,* is service to the victims of the state's actions. The church has an unconditional obligation towards the victims of any societal order, even if they do not belong to the Christian community. "Let us work for the good of all…" The church may under no circumstances neglect either of these duties. The *third* possibility is not just to bound up the wounds of the victims beneath the wheel, but to seize the wheel itself.[29]

This is the decision, "to seize the wheel itself," putting oneself at the highest risk by grabbing its spokes and forcing to a halt the machinery that grinds humanity to a pulp that led to Bonhoeffer's active participation in the resistance and the plot to kill Hitler. In this context, and with the situation in apartheid South Africa taking on ever grimmer proportions, Naudé knew what it meant to take sides with the oppressed, and that "taking sides" would have to be more than just words, however radical those words may sound. For both men, the time for pious talk was over; the time for faithful, risk-filled *martyria* was upon them. The kairos moment had come.

Naudé's decision was greeted "with shock and horror by his own community" recalls theologian Denise Ackermann.[30] Naudé himself noted the virulent reactions, correctly read the signs of the times, and knew this decision to be "the parting of the ways," as he titled the article in which he explained himself.

In my view, however, the "shock and horror" Ackermann speaks of pertained not only to the Afrikaner community as she suggests. It was certainly not just Naudé's own Afrikaner community that was horrified at the WCC's action and Naudé's decision to support it. The whole white community, Afrikaans and English speaking, and the white church, Afrikaans and English speaking, shared the indignation, outrage, and fear. "What becomes clear," writes Charles Villa-Vicencio in his very pertinent critique of white English-speaking churches' questionable position after Sharpeville "is that these churches were not prepared to cross the divide from protest to resistance in 1960 anymore than they were in 1953."[31] The situation in 1970 would prove to be no different.

Naudé had already in 1963 broken away from the Dutch Reformed Church and already then Afrikanerdom had cut him off when they forced him to choose between his membership of the church and his ordination, and the Christian Institute. So by 1970 this particular "parting of the ways" had already occurred. What Naudé now knew was that the liberal English community and so-called antiapartheid churches who supported and iconized him because he was so critical of, and therefore ostracized and denied by the Afrikaner community, would now also turn against him. He was going farther than liberal English politics and liberal English theology in South Africa would allow. Those churches, like the Afrikaans churches, were, in the formulation of Charles Villa-Vicencio, equally "trapped in apartheid."[32] The prophet to the Afrikaner had suddenly become the prophet to the *whole* white community. Now, that Word of God he had held up to the white DRC, as mirror to see themselves as they are, as "fire of flame and sledge hammer"[33] was held up to the whole white community; and the ringing call to obedience he made to the DRC and the Afrikaner people was now a call directed to all whites:

> [T]here is only one way for me: to be obedient to God... You also are called upon to choose, to decide. You cannot escape it. And please note: the decision has nothing to do with my person or convictions, with my remaining or leaving... fundamentally it concerns Christ. If so, obey his word. Do you live by his word? God will not let you go until you have chosen![34]

The Serpent Question

For Bonhoeffer, at heart, the "peace question" was the same as the "Jewish question," for in the first and most important instance both were decisions not just *about* Christ, but *for* or *against* Christ. This is a political decision, to be sure, but one driven by faith and in obedience to Christ. The challenge is to political authority, but the command comes from Christ. Hence the stark and uncompromising language, not because Bonhoeffer demanded some fictitious or hypocritical moral high ground, but because he understood what was at stake: truthful prophetic witness to earthly powers, the life of the church, the authenticity of our faith in Jesus Christ, and the very lives of the victims. Note also that for Bonhoeffer the "problem" was not peace or justice, but in fact the church and the choices the church refused to make.

In a sermon preached on August 28, 1934, Bonhoeffer returns to the questions of peace and justice and the responsibility of the church to make the right choices. The language is strong, unambiguous, and gripping as Bonhoeffer weaves into his argument the story from Genesis 3:

> Nationalism and internationalism have to do with political necessities and possibilities. The ecumenical church movement, however, does not concern itself with these things, but with the commandments of God, and regardless of consequences it transmits these commandments to the world...Peace on earth is not a problem, but a commandment given at Christ's coming. There are two ways of reacting to this command from God: the unconditional, blind obedience of action or the hypocritical question of the Serpent: "Did God not say...?" This question is the mortal enemy of all real peace...Has God not understood human nature well enough to know that wars must occur in this world, like laws of nature? Must God not have meant that we should talk about peace, to be sure, but that it is not to be literally translated into action? Must God not really have said that we should work for peace, of course, but also make ready tanks and poison gas for security? And then perhaps the most serious question: Did God not say you should protect your own people? Did God say you should leave your own prey to the enemy? No, God did not say all that. What God said is that there shall be peace among all people—that we shall obey God without further question; that is what God means. Anyone who questions the commandment of God before obeying has already denied God...[35]

Here Bonhoeffer reminds his listeners of what I would call "the serpent question." I do not mean the serpent's question as in the question of the serpent, but that the question itself becomes like a serpent, as it would in an African parable. It is "the most serious" question. We should let the power of the image settle in our minds: A snake, writhing and slithering through the mind, raising its head at an unexpected moment, coiled, lying in wait, ready to strike at the first sign of a misstep by us. If it strikes, it poisons, hurts, paralyzes; leaves us fearful of every step we take. In its insidiousness, its innocent perniciousness, this very first question in the Bible is perhaps the deepest source of every other pain-filled question human beings cry out to God, and Bonhoeffer understood its power perfectly. That is why all the questions Bonhoeffer confronts his audience with are all perfectly reasonable questions, posed as evident truths.

The serpent comes not as a frightful apparition or a nightmare; it comes as "one of the creatures the Lord God has made," though the Bible is quick—with good reason—to name it the "most cunning" of all God's creatures.[36] Among the ancients the serpent symbolized wisdom, fertility, and immortality. Here, though, the emphasis is on its "craftiness." In this Genesis story wisdom is not used to perceive truth or gain the right knowledge but to deceive and mislead. It does not open the door to immortality, it leads to death. For that reason Bonhoeffer calls it "hypocritical." The serpent question might be directed at the woman, but in fact it is about God. The question, "Did God (really) say?" was not about whether the human couple had misunderstood or misinterpreted God. It is about whether God was trustworthy, about who has the final say in our lives; about the question to whom we owe ultimate allegiance, loyalty, and obedience. Bonhoeffer understood this clearly. Hence his application of the serpent question to the challenging situations the church of his day was facing: the questions of war and peace, of obedience to God or obedience to human beings, loyalty to the demands of God's kingdom, or to one's own people and one's own interests? The serpent question is indeed "the mortal enemy" of all real peace and justice. The issue now, as it was then, is whether in these life-and-death matters we shall resist the serpent and obey God "without question."

So in the context of the ongoing struggles for freedom, justice, and peace—in North Africa and the Middle East; of LGBTI persons and women under serious physical and spiritual attack; of indigenous communities to preserve or regain a way of life that will be life-giving to all of creation, or Palestinians who in their struggles for justice, freedom, and dignity have become the measure of our sense of moral and political responsibility at this point in our history; of those peacemakers who have the courage to stand up against the greed and callousness of warmongers, whether in corporate board rooms or political chambers, scientific laboratories or presidential offices—our mortal enemy is still the serpent question: "Did God really say"? Are they really all God's children, with a right to genuine freedom, peace, justice, and dignity? Did God really say we should fight for their rights and freedom, against our own entrenched interests, for their right to determine their own future against our sinful desire to control it so as to better exploit what they have inherited for the sake of profit? Did God really say that we should shout out on their behalf and not hold back, stand with them in their struggles to loose the bonds of injustice, to undo the thongs of the yoke, to let the oppressed go free, and to break every yoke; that we should not hide ourselves from them because they are, as children of the one God, our flesh and blood? (Is. 58). Yes, God did, Bonhoeffer reminds us, and "anyone who questions the commandment of God before obeying has already denied God."

In his address at the Fanø conference Bonhoeffer asks the startling question that makes the political profoundly theological, and determines whether our choices are righteous: "Why do we fear the fury of world powers? Why don't we take the power from them and give it back to Christ?"[37] Here again, the issue is not to imitate the violence of earthly power, but to challenge earthly power with an entirely different kind of power. For it is precisely in embracing the gentle powers of love, peace, faith, courage, and inclusion that we are able "to take power away" from earthly powers because it exposes them for what they really are: brute force, violent domination, pure greed, relentless exploitation, and ruthless manipulation but without moral authority. In doing this, we surrender not to fear or threat or intimidation, nor to our own desires but to Christ, following Christ in his outrage at injustice and in his love of justice, doing not only *what* God desires but, as Paula M. Cooey phrases it as she speaks of "desire as the language of dissent": *as* God desires it: "[to] yearn, hunger, thirst, and ache for righteousness, justice, peace on earth, and restoration for the whole of creation."[38] This, I think, is what Bonhoeffer means by saying that we are to give the power back to Christ. Giving it back to Christ disempowers the evil forces that threaten life, but it empowers us to the doing of hope-giving and life-affirming deeds of power, as Christ has promised. Yielding to Christ sets us free to make this choice and to challenge the powers of domination and evil at an entirely different level.

I suggest that for Beyers Naudé "the parting of the ways" here is a parting with South Africa's white communities in their support for apartheid, for Bonhoeffer with the choices of his people for Nazism, and for both with the official church, its theological hypocrisy, its political indecisiveness, its feigned neutrality, and above all its inability to resist the lure of the Serpent Question: "Did God really say . . . "?

Loyalty and Lesser Loyalties

There is, of course, more to this. While this decision may have seriously alienated Beyers Naudé from the larger white community, it placed him irrevocably on the side of the black majority. *This* was where his obedience to Christ had ultimately led him: not away from the whites into political and theological limbo, but into political and theological solidarity with the oppressed and into a new community of struggle and faithfulness. By choosing to stand so firmly with South Africa's black oppressed people, even in the sensitive matter of the liberation movements, Naudé chose resolutely for the struggle against white supremacy and apartheid, and for justice and liberation and human rights for all.

In the process, he explicitly also chose against the capitalist system "which is basically exploitative, unjust and discriminatory," and for a system of equality more "in accordance with the biblical criteria of justice, freedom and human dignity than the present capitalist system of free enterprise which is operating in South Africa today."[39] So in reality the parting of the ways represented something much more radical than just church politics, and as with Bonhoeffer, it led him to difficult and risky places. But he knew that those were the places where Christ is still to be found.

In the ten years since the Sharpeville massacre and in the years following the "Cottesloe Declaration" and the "Message to the People of South Africa," Beyers Naudé had not only moved away from the DRC, he had moved far beyond the political stance and theological argumentation of the whole white community and their churches.

Much is always made of Naude's "abiding loyalty" to the Afrikaner people. Despite remaining "an Afrikaner in body, mind and soul," Denise Ackermann writes, "Beyers Naudé became a fearless critic of his people, and precisely because he cared for them and remained deeply connected to them."[40] I am not contending here that Naudé did not love or care for the Afrikaner, and that he did not know them to be his people. Indeed he did. Hence his agony on their behalf for their apartheid crimes and his love in his willingness to take vicarious responsibility for what they were doing to black people.[41]

But I do contest the statement that he remained an Afrikaner in "mind and soul," just as by the mid-1930s Bonhoeffer could no longer be a German "in mind and soul." The "German mind and soul," taken captive, and mesmerized by the grandiosity of the Nazi ideal were no longer the mind and soul of Dietrich Bonhoeffer. By 1970, the collective mind of the Afrikaner was no longer the mind of Beyers Naudé. That Afrikaner mind was the mind of white supremacy, of cold self-interest, harsh, racist, violent oppression, and ruthless self-preservation. All this had become deeply alien to *his* mind and soul. By the seventies his soul no longer resonated with the cheap grace of charity, missionary sympathy, and "good neighbourliness" that were the fig leaves of the apartheid religiosity.[42] Instead it was touched by a rebellious, combatant love; the longing for compassionate justice which knows that solidarity with apartheid white South Africa could not abide solidarity with South Africa's oppressed people. By 1970, Naudé's renewed, converted, committed kairos-conscious mind understood three crucial things: one, that there were oppressed people in South Africa; second, there was an oppressor, his own people; and third, that there was a struggle for justice and freedom. Neutrality in these matters was no longer possible:

> There is no neutrality possible, or no true neutrality in a situation of crisis and I think one of the major problems of the church is that it was in a certain sense educated to see itself as a neutral body (liberal theology at its height!) We have…misunderstood the concept of reconciliation so that the church, or many parts of the church leadership, believes that you can only be a reconciling agent if you remain neutral, and that's not possible.[43]

As Bonhoeffer got drawn deeper into the struggle for justice by the power of his obedience to God, he would see the church's efforts at neutrality as almost unforgivable: "In reality, there are no 'neutrals'. They actually belong to the other side."[44] Bonhoeffer went further:

> The church confesses that it has witnessed the arbitrary use of brutal force, the suffering in body and soul of countless innocent people, that it has witnessed oppression, hatred and murder without raising its voice for the victims and without finding ways of rushing to help them. It has become guilty of the lives of the Weakest and most Defenceless Brothers and Sisters of Jesus Christ.[45]

Here Bonhoeffer offers a contrast with the "witness" he spoke of earlier. Now, "witness" has the function of "seeing," and in seeing becoming a witness to the atrocities before our eyes and in our midst. But Bonhoeffer does not reduce all that has happened to one word, as I have just done. With the rhythm and force of prophetic condemnation he stacks one atrocity upon another and names them separately: *the arbitrary use of brutal force, suffering in body and soul, oppression, hatred,* and *murder*, and this was done to *countless innocent people.* But in witnessing all this, the church has "not [even] raised its voice." It has failed to witness, that is, to speak for those who cannot speak, to suffer with those who suffer, to stand with them in their suffering, and to act against the wrongdoer. The church is a witness to evil, but is not able to offer *martyria,* cannot find the courage to name, condemn, and resist this evil. The sins of the church are grave indeed. In that it has become guilty: it has failed the "most defenceless brothers and sisters of Jesus Christ" and as a consequence it has failed Christ. For Bonhoeffer as well as for Beyers Naudé, in the deeper, higher loyalty to Christ, which called for loyalty to the Other in whose suffering Christ was suffering and in whose face they saw the face of Christ, the loyalty to "their people" became a "lesser loyalty."[46]

Beyers understood better than most what kind of loyalty the Afrikaner community expected:

> In the Afrikaner society there is such a deep sense of loyalty...Loyalty to your people, loyalty to your country, loyalty and patriotism have in a certain sense become deeply religious values...So that anybody who is seen to be disloyal to his nation, to his people, is not only deemed to be a traitor, but in the deeper sense of the word, he is seen as betraying God.[47]

It is because he understood the totalitarian nature of that loyalty and its demands that he understood so well its consequences, and the choices it presented. A choice for those loyalties would be in direct opposition to the choices for Christ he had made. For that very reason he was always so clear on the demand for Christian obedience and loyalty to Christ above all, and the extent to which loyalty to Christ alone would make one understand the place of "lesser loyalties," and how these lesser loyalties not just competed with one's loyalty to Christ, but in fact displaced it.

It was especially dangerous since the "lesser loyalties" claimed to be of God, and resisting them was presented as tantamount to resisting God. Then "lesser loyalties" actually become "false loyalties."[48] It is this combination of courage and consciousness that enabled Beyers Naudé to see earlier and more clearly than others the deep and complex roots of the heresy of apartheid. It was not just the formal theological and biblical justification. It was as well, and dangerously so, the informal, insidious and all-pervasive cultural embodiment of a false, deceitful, carefully inculcated consciousness that presented itself as Christian. It takes a kairos consciousness to make that discernment.

In light of this, and judging by the curiously mild tone of its public utterances regarding the ANC government considering the seriousness of the ongoing political, social, and economic injustices facing the country on the one hand and the hesitant witness of the church since 1994 on the other, one should ask whether Kairos Southern Africa has not tripped up itself in its undeclared, or even unconscious, loyalties to the ANC, or has not been able to make the distinction, like Beyers Naudé, between loyalty to Christ and the "lesser loyalties" that become an entrapment in one's prophetic ministry. Certainly the documents issued so far have not been able to match the prophetic tone and content of the *Kairos Document* of 1985, or the documents of the time in general.[49]

In fact, that greater obedience and deeper loyalty led Naudé to ever deeper solidarity with the oppressed, and helped him, in the words of the *Belhar Confession*, to "stand where God stands—namely against injustice and with the wronged..."[50] What Beyers Naudé was looking for, indeed yearning and pleading for, was a different Afrikaner than those he called "in control and in power" at the time. He was convinced that that different Afrikaner did exist and he sought to give support and encouragement to those "enlightened" Afrikaners who tried to take a stand within Afrikanerdom even though he knew those efforts not to be adequate.[51] It is not that he did not understand the fears they had to overcome:

> The fear that if they speak, the Church will be harmed, the fear that our members are not yet ready to accept these truths; the possible repercussions in our congregations.[52]

Of course he also knew that "in such a situation we are called to act with the utmost responsibility;" but, he insisted, "[we] certainly should not remain silent. The proclamation of the truth of the Gospel cannot harm the Church of Jesus Christ!...Why then do we fear? Has the time not come for us to proclaim clearly and with joy: Thus saith the Lord?"[53] For these enlightened Afrikaners too, the time for pious words was over.

He chose to stand with Steve Biko and the Black Consciousness movement and by doing that he had taken upon himself the "condition of blackness,"[54] had become one with us in struggle, in rejection and exclusion, in suffering and in hope; in anticipation of freedom. Here Naudé's kairos consciousness became, as it must, a liberating, engaging, and humanizing consciousness. Liberated from the condition of whiteness because he willingly and deliberately stepped away from white power and privilege, he was free to speak prophetically about blackness and whiteness. It was from within this condition of blackness that he spoke so clearly to all of white South Africa, endeavoring to transmit to them Steve Biko's prophetic concerns: "You are building your future existence on a false security," he said. "Break away from the illusion that this road will bring you the safety and security you are so anxiously seeking..." And then, fully aware of the decisions he himself had to make, he continued, speaking to white English liberals,

> It is no longer good enough to voice your opposition to apartheid or separate development only through motions and resolutions. You should go further: you should become truly committed to the cause of freedom by your willingness to relinquish illegitimate privilege and power and to share it with all the people of the land. You should participate more actively and meaningfully in a radical programme of non-violent action to bring about fundamental social and political change.[55]

The message to the Afrikaner community was equally clear:

> Break free from the prison of your subservience to an ideology that is leading our country towards disaster and that can destroy the Afrikaner as well...Do not seek security in weapons, in an exclusive identity or in

> clinging to false loyalties... Grab the hand of friendship that is still being extended, even at this late hour... *Steve Biko's death has helped me to wake up to my life, my true liberation...*[56]

The last sentence, quite startling in its consequences, is the result of the working of that engaging, evocative, liberating kairos consciousness; of seeking, and finding the place where Christ stands, of rising above the lesser loyalties. It is the fruit of the condition of blackness, of embracing and sharing the contagious courage that comes from solidarity in struggle. It is the epiphany of humanness. It is the ubuntufication of the human spirit. And that is what Naudé wanted white people to experience. But he knew, as Dietrich Bonhoeffer had learned in the 1930s from Adam Clayton Powell Sr. of Abyssinian Baptist Church in Harlem New York, that there is no such thing as cheap grace;[57] that there is a price to pay for solidarity, combative love and sacrificial discipleship, that when we are called by Christ we are called to die even as we are called to live in a completely new, liberated way. They could experience that "true liberation" only if they were ready to take upon themselves the condition of blackness so that they could be open to the humanization of their spirit. Hence Naude's testimony:

> Steve Biko challenges me to not keep quiet anymore but to voice my deepest convictions about what is right and true, to stand up for them and to suffer for them if necessary—even if this should mean that I have to endure condemnation and rejection by my own people...[58]

For Beyers Naudé this process, this discovery of his life, his true liberation, meant the embracing not just of the condition of blackness but the rendering of himself to the vulnerability of powerlessness by giving up white power and privilege, sharing the condemnation and suffering of those who struggle against oppression, but also allowing himself to be woven into the tapestry of hope and freedom; exchanging the desperation of white survival for the life-giving birthing of true humanity, the opening of the hand to let go of the power that abuses and oppresses in order to grasp the extended hand for the sake of the power that serves and heals and liberates.

No More "Cheap Talk": Turning Words into Deeds

Reflecting on the life and work of Dietrich Bonhoeffer and Beyers Naudé for the kairos moment that is upon us today means being confronted with prophetic clarity with our past, our present realities, the pain and unfulfilled longings of the poor. It means being confronted with our political and theological complicity in the painful truth that we have created what the Accra Confession calls "a scandalous world" of harsh, utterly shocking inequalities among and within nations, resource-driven wars, poverty and disease of which the most vulnerable victims are women and children; a world of intolerable global economic injustices and unconscionable ecological plundering and destruction of the earth for the sake of profits.[59]

When we see the suffering of people and of nature caused by rapaciousness, neglect, and sheer greed; testing our "lesser loyalties" and our loyalty to Christ and Christ's desire for justice, we are challenged to understand that our pious sermonizing becomes what Beyers Naudé called "nothing but cheap talk, yes, an act of hypocrisy." Like Bonhoeffer's, his language becomes more challenging, confrontational even as he insists that "all talk of reconciliation remains meaningless, and even becomes dangerous if words are not transformed into deeds."[60]

With the violence of perpetual war engulfing our world, making more victims of innocent men, women, and children than ever before despite our smart bombs and precision weapons and computer-driven drones (or perhaps precisely because of these!) while so many hide behind a Christian patriotism that is willing to destroy the world for the sake of brute power but in the name of God, we need Bonhoeffer's passion for peace, Bonhoeffer's courage to name the Serpent question, "Did God really say?", as "the mortal enemy of obedience, and therefore the mortal enemy of real peace... Anyone who questions the commandment of God before obeying has already denied God."[61]

We stand idly by as party-political interests are persistently deemed more important than the interests of the nation; as loyalty to ethnic demands and group interests outweigh loyalty to the principles of justice, freedom, and democracy, the needs of the people, or our ultimate loyalty to Christ. We feign neutrality as fear and mindless sycophancy replace prophetic courage in the pulpit and political integrity in parliamentary chambers; as naked greed replaces selfless service; as sacrifice becomes a plague devoutly spared the rich but relentlessly inflicted upon the poor.

In our churches, while facing life and death issues such as the LGBTI issue has become for Africa, spurred on by fundamentalist, neocolonialist, money-driven theologies from the United States, we wallow in sentimental pietism and get lost in a maze of political indecisiveness; we engage in what Beyers Naudé called "opposition by evasion" because our lack of conviction and our theological un-rootedness make us "dodge the Word" that challenges us to acts of decision, obedience, conscience, and courage.[62]

In the global community today we are facing serious challenges across the world in terms of our constitutional democracies, political integrity, spiritual authenticity, political moral authority, and our prophetic faithfulness. In our day, in our presence, struggles for justice, freedom, human dignity, and the integrity of creation are sweeping across the globe. And in the church of Jesus Christ we must face the question whether we have the courage to be on the right side of those struggles, ready to make the decisions that will take us to the places where Christ is to be found. Now, more than ever, the challenge still stands: "It is time to transform words into deeds. The time for pious talk is over."

4

The Inclusiveness of God's Embrace: Kairos, Justice, the Dignity of Human Sexuality, and the Confession of Belhar*

Understanding Kairos, Understanding Liberation

In its 2008 General Synod the Uniting Reformed Church in Southern Africa considered a report on "homosexuality."[1] That was a moment, in my view, in which this church, who had declared apartheid, its biblical and theological justification a heresy, and led the ecumenical movement in doing the same; who in formulating in 1982, and adopting in 1986 the Belhar Confession as a new standard of faith, was confronted with yet another kairos moment in South Africa.[2]

I was the convenor of that task team and presenter of the report at the synod. It was one of those utterly shattering, fundamentally life-changing experiences. After a hostile, and theologically disturbingly crude, debate, the synod rejected the report, its contents, its conclusions, and its recommendations calling for justice for LGBTI persons and referred the report for reconsideration.[3] These reflections were inspired not so much by the rejection of the report and the decision of synod to call for another report. Synods and church assemblies do that all the time and in my experience church politics holds few surprises. Even though the words, "another, more anti-gay report" were deleted from the amended version of the original proposal, the intention could not have been clearer.[4]

What was striking and shocking, even though hardly unknown in debates on this matter it seems, was the stridently hostile tone of the debate, the blatant homophobic and intentionally hurtful language that dominated the discussion all through the afternoon. Speakers who took the floor did not even attempt to disguise their contempt. Some spoke openly of LBGTI persons as "animals," "not created by God"; of bestiality and of LBGTI persons as being a "scandal" and "stain" upon the church. As painful was the silence that not only tolerated but in truth legitimized the condemnations.

It was an experience that had left me shaken and disoriented. How could the same church that took such a strong stand against apartheid and racial oppression, gave such inspired leadership from its understanding of the Bible and the radical Reformed tradition; that had, in the middle of the state of emergency of the 1980s with its unprecedented oppression, its desperate violence, and nameless fear given birth to the Belhar Confession that spoke of reconciliation, justice, unity, and the Lordship of Jesus Christ, now display such blatant hatred and bigotry, deny so vehemently for God's LGBTI children the solidarity we craved for ourselves in our struggle for racial justice, bow down so easily at the altar of prejudice and homophobic hypocrisy? We who had rescued the Reformed tradition from the heresy and blasphemy of the theology of apartheid and forged a new identity for that tradition in struggles for justice and compassion, were now the ones embracing that heresy in our howling condemnation of our own flesh because of their different sexual orientation.

In the entire debate, I detected no awareness of our Reformed roots. In the scorching insults toward LGBTI persons and the few who stepped into the breach for them, the Calvin who helped us understand so much during the struggle against apartheid was not even vaguely recognizable. Of the John Calvin who insists that "Scripture helps us in the best way when it teaches that we are not to consider what [people] merit of themselves but look upon the image of God in all [people], to which we owe honour and love...by virtue of the fact that he forbids you to despise your own flesh,"[5] there was no sign. Striking in Calvin is the degree to which he begins from the claims of the Other; how that claim is grounded in the fact that we are kinfolk, members of the one family of God; how each of us in our "iconicity" is grounded in our imaging of God.[6] The Calvin who told us that in insulting or despising the brother or sister we despise Christ, and that in inflicting injustice upon the other we wound God, was a rejected, excluded embarrassment.

What called forth the most ire by far, however, was the fact that the report interpreted the Belhar Confession in a way that called for solidarity with, embrace, and inclusion of LGBTI persons, in the same way that the Confession calls for justice and dignity for people of color in a racist dispensation. Probably the best-known words of the Belhar Confession are the words that echoed in the church's conviction that "the church should stand where God stands": namely with the wronged, the poor, the destitute, and powerless against the powerful. The report took the view that these categories included those despised, rejected, and marginalized as a result of their sexual orientation. What the report, in view of the church's stand in the struggle for racial justice took for granted, the synod rejected with a vehemence I find incomprehensible to this day.[7]

That synod was, in more than one way, one of the most devastating experiences of my life. And this is not just about my personal experiences. The issue has much wider implications. In July 2008, the very year the synod debated this issue, well-known South African journalist Jon Qwelane, writing in his regular column, likened being gay to bestiality. "I do pray," a Cape Town newspaper editorial recalls Qwelane's words, "that some day a bunch of politicians with their heads firmly connected to their necks will muster the balls to rewrite the constitution of this country, to excise those sections which give license to men marrying other men, and ditto women. Otherwise, at this rate, how soon before some idiot demands to 'marry' an animal, and argues that this constitution 'allows' it"?[8]

"Astonishingly," the editorial goes on to say, "more than a year after Qwelane spewed forth his vitriol," the South African government appointed Qwelane ambassador to Uganda "officially one of the most homophobic countries on earth." The editorial pointed out that in this "rabid anti-homosexual atmosphere" Ugandan gay activist David Kato was bludgeoned to death in his home in January 2011. That same year the Equality Court returned a verdict, finding Qwelane guilty of hate speech for his "particularly vile piece of homophobia." The newspaper, because of its consistent defense of the Constitution and the rights of LGBTI persons, could publicly take a prophetic stance against this misguided appointment: "A man found guilty of hate speech of the sort cannot be the official face of South Africa anywhere, and especially not in a country where gays and lesbians are actively persecuted." The *Cape Times* was joined by many—individuals and civil organizations—across the country.

The Uniting Reformed Church was not one of those who protested this grotesque appointment and the betrayal to the Constitution it represents. The reason is as painful as it is obvious: how could the URCSA, seeing the stand of its synod right in the middle of these dramatic events, authentically speak a word of prophetic truth on behalf of human dignity and compassionate justice? How could it step into the breach for God's LGBTI children at home or in Uganda; how could it join the call upon the South African government to recall Mr. Qwelane, reaffirm the values enshrined in our Constitution, come to the aid of the LGBTI community and their families in Uganda and seek justice for those walking in the shadow of death simply, and only, because of their sexual orientation? In this matter, so urgent for the truthful witness of the church in Africa today, members of the URCSA cannot look to their church for prophetic truth and faithfulness. They would have to turn to a secular court of law and a newspaper to find that word.

:hapter addresses three questions:

(a) Whether the Belhar Confession, having being birthed during the time of the church's struggle against the system of apartheid in South Africa, could and should be restricted to that context of apartheid and racial injustice, to that time and that particular situation, and made applicable only to similar contexts of racism elsewhere in the world.
(b) Whether one should expect from black people who themselves have experienced the pain of discrimination, humiliation, rejection, and exclusion because of the color of their skin, to be more open to solidarity with LBGTI persons in *their* quest and call upon us for justice and the recognition of their human dignity and their rights.
(c) And whether justice, since it is grounded in the justice, compassion, and mercy of God toward shalom, is in fact indivisible.

In her lucid study arguing for a hermeneutic of inclusion, Cheryl B. Anderson quotes a pastor from Los Angeles who puts the matter succinctly:

> Oppression is oppression is oppression...Just because we're not the ones who are being oppressed now, do we not stand with those oppressed now? This is the biblical mandate. That's what Jesus is all about.[9]

Should we expect from those who, in their own struggles against racist oppression, leaned so heavily on the exodus metaphor as inspirational in the struggle, to take that paradigm one step further? In other words, will those who stood so firmly on Exodus 3:7, "I have observed the misery of my people who are in Egypt; I have heard their cry...and I have come down to deliver them," now also "know the heart of an alien, for you were aliens in the land of Egypt?" (Ex. 23:9). Will they understand that LGBTI persons are made into aliens in their own land, strangers in the church, exiled from our love and consideration? Will they understand that all outsiders, like they once were in the country of their birth, are worthy of inclusion, and that that inclusion is God's intention?

For the black church in South Africa it is crucial to understand that any ethic derived from the faith in the God of liberation, that wishes to remain faithful to that liberation tradition must also remain rooted in the praxis of that liberation. Miguel De La Torre is correct:

> The act of solidarity becomes the litmus test of biblical fidelity and the paradigm used to analyse and judge how social structures contribute to or efface the exploitation of the marginalized. To be apart from the marginalized community of faith is to exile oneself from the possibility of hearing and discerning the gospel message of salvation—a salvation from the

> ideologies that mask power and privilege and the social structures responsible for their maintenance.[10]

Moreover, these questions are raised within a context of great urgency and against the background of growing homophobia[11] or more properly put, bigotry, and an exacerbating climate of murderous violence aimed at LGBTI persons in Africa in general, but increasingly in South Africa as well.

Uganda now holds the dubious distinction of arguably being the most openly anti-LBGTI country on the African continent, with its legislation severely criminalizing "homosexuality." Kampala's *Rolling Stone* newspaper has captured the attention of the world with its "exposure" of especially gay men and its banner headline call to "Hang Them!" Giles Muhambe, the publisher, is clear: "Whatever happens to gays is a result of their own misdeeds." Meanwhile, at least one gay person has already been brutally beaten to death in Kampala.[12] Muhambe's response indicates the extent to which the victims of his violent campaign have to shoulder the blame for their suffering at the hands of those incited by the newspaper's incendiary writing: "Kato brought death to himself...," and in a chilling reminder of the language from the synod floor, Muhambe continues, "Kato was a shame to this country." Muhambe has no sense of guilt or responsibility: "I did not call for him to be killed in cold blood like he was..."[13] In South Africa, LGBTI persons are victims of all kinds of abuse and violence, including murder and so-called corrective rape by gangs of thugs, especially of lesbian women, a perverse kind of "therapy" to make her change her "deviant" ways now that she knows what "real" sex with "real" men is like. This is on the increase despite South Africa's constitutional protection of the rights of LGBTI persons, including their right to marriage.

For us this constitutes an immediate crisis, since it is, for God's LGBTI children, literally a matter of life and death.[14] Behind the fierce Ugandan legislation is born-again parliamentarian David Mahati, backed by the powerful and influential, but shadowy US right-wing Christian group, "The Family," organizers of the "National Prayer Breakfasts," an event that no US president since Eisenhower has dared miss. Mahati believes he is chosen by God to "deliver humanity from this calamity."[15] The guilt of the Christian church in this matter is grave.

Kairos and the Consequences of Confession

In G. D. Cloete's and D. J. Smit's anthology on the Belhar Confession, *A Moment of Truth*,[16] South African theologian J. J. F Durand, a member of the drafting committee of the Belhar Confession and in every respect standing in the prophetic tradition of Beyers Naudé, made two telling contributions. In both those contributions Durand, understanding the essential nature of a confession in general and of the Belhar Confession in particular, held up a challenge to the then Dutch Reformed Mission Church which turned out to be prophetic both in its far-sightedness and in its truthfulness.

In 1994, the DRMC united with the larger part of the Dutch Reformed Church in Africa to become the Uniting Reformed Church in Southern Africa, a predominantly black church with a few white members. Following the earlier Dutch Reformed Mission Church, the united church embraced the Belhar Confession as a fourth confession alongside the three older Reformed standards of faith.[17] For the new church, as for the DRMC earlier, Belhar more and more came to express the theological self-understanding of the church, especially in the emotional and pitched battles with the white Dutch Reformed Church (DRC) in the drawn-out and seemingly unending struggle over church unification.

In many ways, those increasingly bitter battles which centered on the standing and character of Belhar, were about the question persistently put by the white church: how necessary is Belhar now, post-1994, for the unity of the churches of the DRC family? How relevant is Belhar "now that apartheid is over?" What else can be said about Belhar except that it serves as perpetual accusation aimed at the white church; a painful reminder of the oppression of apartheid, the betrayal of the gospel and the Reformed faith by the white church, and of the struggle against both? In the ill-fated and disastrous debates on URCSA's position on sexual justice and dignity these questions, quite separate from the issues with the DRC, once again took center-stage.

Crucially, the prophetic insights of Jaap Durand came to haunt the church in ways not many of us had foreseen or imagined. In 1984, in that first contribution, *Is a Confession Really Necessary?*, this is what Durand said:

> A confession dare not engage with mere trivialities. It can only be an extension of the church's ancient confession that Jesus is Lord. This is the guarantee of the continued relevance of the confession... For this reason I am convinced that the Confession of Belhar will outlive apartheid and the heresy that led to it and will retain its message. The three core issues at stake here, unity, reconciliation and justice, are close to the heart of the gospel. [18]

He went on, "a true confession rises above the circumstances of its time."[19]

And again, [we] "do not simply confess with the immediate situation in mind, but with an eye on the future." [20]

Yet again: "We cannot yet foresee the consequences of the formulation and acceptance of this confession for the Dutch Reformed Mission Church, if it is indeed ready to accept those consequences for itself,"

> But in the end, for the church it cannot be about concerns about the sympathies it gains or loses, or concerns about the fortunate or less fortunate consequences the confession creates for its continued existence. These concerns are unnecessary, because according to Matthew 10 the confessing church *always* lives in the shadow of the Cross, and not without the assurance that the gates of hell shall not prevail against it. But no one can find comfort in this promise if he flees from the cross. [21]

In the second contribution, "The Confession of Belhar: A Crisis for the Dutch Reformed Churches?"[22] Durand drives the point home: "Is the Dutch Reformed Mission Church prepared to fully face the consequences of its confession, not only in its relationship with the (white) Dutch Reformed Church, but also *within itself*?"[23]

And on the crucial article which speaks of God as the One who promises justice to the poor and calls upon the church to stand where God stands, namely on the side of the poor and the wronged, Durand posits:

> The real question is *how* the DRMC will embody this confessional conviction in its continued critical confrontation with the political powers in South Africa.[24]

It is remarkable, from my point of view, how devastatingly relevant Durand's questions are for the church today and how they constitute the very challenge URCSA is facing in the debates on the inclusion of and justice for LGBTI persons. Out of the kairos of 1982 Durand foresaw the kairos of 2008.

I will argue that the three core issues in Belhar (unity, reconciliation, and justice) are the very ones which should guide the church in its continuing reflection on the integrity of its public testimony and prophetic faithfulness, and that they are particularly pertinent in the debate on sexual justice, which is one of the issues calling out for the prophetic witness of the church in South Africa and worldwide today. I will also argue that sexual justice is precisely one of those issues (as is gender justice) on which the confession rises above and beyond the immediate circumstances of its formulation and so prove Durand's point and our conviction that the confession can "outlive" those circumstances.

Some will perhaps argue that the "consequences" Durand was referring to were not those I am emphasizing, but instead more directly related to three burning issues at the time:

1. The relationship with the DRC, especially in regard to the remunerative power of that church and the DRMC's financial dependence on the white church.
2. The confrontation with the apartheid government ("the political powers in South Africa") as the Mission Church participated more actively and gave leadership in the struggle against apartheid.
3. The internal theological and political tensions and divisions with which the church had to grapple.

There were some in the DRMC that were distrustful of the theology that informed Belhar, because that theology, in my view, was directly rooted in liberation theology, rather than, as some would posit, some form of Barthian theology.[25] This was a generational, political as well as a theological problem, I think, compounded by the presence of those white "missionaries" serving in ministry in the DRMC and who had strong loyalties toward the DRC, the Afrikaner nationalist cause, apartheid and the conservative, distorted Calvinism that was the hallmark of white Dutch Reformed theology and the core of the moral and theological justification of apartheid.

For a whole generation of theologians in this mainly black church, a unique brand of black liberation theology, in important ways inspired as it was by the Reformed theology we discovered in the radical John Calvin, became the bedrock of our theological reflection and action.[26] There also were those black members and pastors who, despite the church's own strong, and growing, convictions on apartheid, found it increasingly harder to translate those convictions into practical political action. There were those who, for whatever reasons, voiced support for the apartheid government. Then there were those who were simply afraid—of the white church, of an aggressively oppressive regime, and of the price of costly discipleship, of the costs of prophetic engagement for the sake of justice.

All of these would play themselves out in the tumultuous decade that lay ahead and in events that at times threatened to pull the church asunder, and Durand was indeed acute in his understanding of the impact of the Confession of Belhar on these matters.[27] But this clearly could not have been his only concerns. If it were so, Durand himself would have remained captive of the paradigm created by apartheid and its attendant circumstances. As it is, the foundational argument which gives rise to his prophetic insight is his insistence that Belhar would "outlive" apartheid and its circumstances because it bases itself upon the church's fundamental confession that "Jesus is Lord." It grounded itself upon the "core issues at the heart of the gospel" namely justice, reconciliation, and unity, and that therefore it is a confession not only for the immediate present but indeed for the future.

In my view such an understanding explicitly leaves room for, no, more explicitly even, *calls for* an application and understanding of Belhar which rises above matters of race only. The fact alone that Belhar has anchored itself so firmly to the cause of justice testifies to this logic. So even though the confession was called forth by the historical moment of apartheid, and specifically by prevailing social, economic, and political injustices justified in the name of the gospel, the confession itself as prevailing truth goes beyond the contextual confines of its birth. Dirk J. Smit, another member of the drafting committee, makes the same point. A Reformed confession, he writes,

> is necessitated by a historical context, but its truth should extend further than the moment and the false teaching. The "yes" is much more important, critical and lasting than the "no"—*and should be a "yes" for others and elsewhere as well*, if it is indeed the "yes" and the truth of the gospel.[28]

Born in a "moment of truth," its truth transcends that moment, both in time and in circumstance. Precisely because it is truthful in its contextual moment, it can reveal the truth in and for other moments as well. A closer reading of the confession reveals the continued relevance of Belhar for the situation of wealth, poverty, and the intense inequalities in South African society today as well as globally. A comparison of the Belhar Confession and the Accra Confession of the World Alliance of Reformed Churches (now World Communion of Reformed Churches) of 2004 would further reveal the impetus of the Belhar Confession in the ecumenical church's witness vis-à-vis the global challenges of imperial domination, socioeconomic and ecological justice.[29]

I contend that in the choice for justice and human flourishing in the twenty-first century, in the new struggles for ecological, socioeconomic, and cultural justice, and especially as it pertains to the matters that go beyond race and are confronting the church in the realities of gender justice and justice for sexually differently oriented persons, lies the true value and applicability of Belhar. In the issues beyond the challenges of apartheid-racism it is crucial that the church testifies to a confession that has indeed "outlived" apartheid, and show that it can face the consequences of its prophetic faithfulness in the world and within itself. It is my further contention that in missing that understanding the synod, in its rejection of the wider validity of Belhar, had dramatically, perhaps fatally undermined the legitimacy of the church's own claim on the Confession of Belhar as well as the integrity of its prophetic witness in South Africa and the world today.

In the matter of sexual justice and in the debate at synod in 2008, the church was, for the first time perhaps, directly confronted with the consequences of its embrace of the Belhar Confession beyond the issue of race, apartheid, and the relationship with the Dutch Reformed Church. Indeed, it is precisely because the confession functioned so crucially and inspirationally in the struggle against racism and apartheid, proclaimed God so clearly as a God who seeks justice and calls the church to justice, a God calling so persistently upon the church to stand where God stands, namely against "every form of injustice," that the Uniting Reformed Church has taken upon itself the burden of solidarity in justice and faithfulness as regards the matters of gender and sexual justice. Every question Durand has raised 30 years ago stands as a challenge to our understanding of the confession and its validity for the situation in which we live in South Africa today.

Belhar as Defining Presence

Unlike other churches which have grappled with the issue of human sexuality, the URCSA does not only have the understanding and interpretation of Scripture and the legacy of ecumenical wisdom to work with. We have, as fundamental to all our theological deliberations, also the Belhar Confession. It brings with it a burden of responsibility URCSA cannot deny nor avoid. The Confession of Belhar, together with the three well-known confessions we have inherited from our Reformed roots in the Netherlands, form the confessional basis of the Uniting Reformed Church in Southern Africa. Together these four confessions (and the ancient creeds), are required to be believed, accepted, embraced by all members of URCSA, and undersigned by those who wish to enter her ministry as pastors. For URCSA, Belhar is the continuation and affirmation of the ecumenical creeds and it stands firmly within the Reformed theological tradition. It is our understanding of how this tradition with its particular dynamic theology could be applied to a particular situation in the new contexts in which we live. Belhar symbolizes the reception of the Reformed tradition, in contrast with, and opposition to the white Dutch Reformed churches and their theology of apartheid, in black South Africa. In essential ways, Belhar is for URCSA not just the acceptance, but indeed the validation of the Reformed tradition in the South African context and increasingly it is becoming that for other situations worldwide as well, as Belhar continues to gain acceptance and continues to become a theological point of reference and challenge for churches in the worldwide Reformed community and the wider ecumenical church.[30]

But for URCSA Belhar is more. It has fundamentally changed the life, outlook, and public witness of the church. Together with Scripture, the ancient beliefs of the Christian church, and the Reformed theological tradition it has become the foundation of all our theological reflection and action in the public square. Through Belhar we have sought—and it has placed us in—the company of believers who have, in life-threatening situations in the history of the church, looked toward the Word of God and the traditions of resistance in the ecumenical movement to seek a way of witnessing in moments of crisis and kairos where to the judgment of the church, the integrity of the Gospel, and the witness of the church in the world were at stake. In the more recent past, the Theological Declaration of Barmen *vis-á vis* the Nazi heresies in Germany (1934) was such a situation. The idolatry of racism and the false gospel of apartheid in South Africa was ours.

In the debates with the white Dutch Reformed Church for example, the point was often made that Belhar confirms in a special way the identity of URCSA, that its formulation and acceptance was a defining moment for us. That is to say, it is not the exclusive identity or even founding identity of the church: that identity was, is and forever will be Jesus Christ. But Belhar, more than any other document perhaps, *confirms* that identity, because in Belhar the stand the church takes, takes us closest to the cause of Yahweh and Jesus of Nazareth than in any other.

I need to express it even stronger: Belhar was not just a defining moment; it is a *defining presence* for us. By "defining presence" I mean first that whatever the moment of history, Belhar, and hence the church, will always be defined by its rootedness in, and commitment to unity, reconciliation, and compassionate justice. Second, that Belhar cannot and will not be confined to a single moment in our history, as if itself defined by that moment. In other words, Belhar cannot and will not be seen only as a response to racism, and even more narrowly, to apartheid only. In a post-1994 South African society, Belhar continues to define still today who and what we are, our understanding of the demands of Scripture, our response to the realities of the world we live in, our obedience to Christ in terms of the great global challenges facing the church today.

Third, it will always be defined by the fact that its conception was a *kairos* moment. In this moment of truth, and true to its *kairos* nature, it is not as if *we* have found and claimed the truth. It is the other way around: the truth has found, recovered, challenged, and reclaimed us. And because that defining presence is not only parochial but also ecumenical, not just local but global, Belhar can play the role it does for the worldwide ecclesial community as can be seen in its influence on the Accra Confession of the World Communion of Reformed Churches which deals with globalization, economic and ecological justice, for instance. Belhar's *kairos* conception is an ever-present challenge to the church to discern the signs of every time, to understand, and choose for the cause of compassionate justice, unity, and reconciliation.

Fourth, this confession came from within the community of the oppressed; those who had no voice, the least of those whom God could have chosen to speak through so powerfully to the powerful. They were those with no name in the streets (James Baldwin), but they dared to name God in the sanctuary as well as in the public square; not just within their racially separated spaces in racialized timidity, but in bold testimony to the world church and in the public places of power. Neither was the confession born of isolated, esoteric academic debate. It emerged from the lives and faith of ordinary oppressed people, their racial categorization delineating their lowliness; their struggles with the presence of evil and the promises of God, and it speaks with the eloquence of faith, not the certitude of sight. It was not commissioned by the powerful for the legitimization of earthly power. Instead, it places earthly power under the critique of heaven and earth: of the outraged God and the suffering people. In its words pulsates a life lived not under the protection of the throne but in the shadow of the cross. It bears the name of an apartheid-created, racially designed, crime-ridden, much maligned "colored" township which itself is a symbol of dispossession, rejection, malignant social engineering, and exclusion. Like the people on whose behalf it speaks, it bears in its testimony the marks of Christ. In its birth, its continued life, and in its prophetic presence, as we have seen over and over again, Belhar is a *skandalon*. But it is precisely as *skandalon* that it bears witness to the glory of Christ.

I would go further yet: because the confession is a defining presence in the ways I have described, it is also a legitimizing presence. The confession has given theological legitimacy to the church's participation in the antiapartheid struggle in a way that say, the Canons of Dordt never had and never could. The black Reformed church's struggle was not just against a racist, oppressive system; it was also against the white church's embrace of it, its blasphemous justification of it, its sinful profiting from it. It was a struggle *against* heresy, *for* the sake of the gospel. Now that the church has embraced it, found in it a fountain of inspiration during the darkest days of that struggle for racial justice and freedom on behalf of a whole nation; fought for it so passionately in the struggle with the Dutch Reformed Church, made Belhar its foundation for its stand on justice and God's preferential option for the weak, the poor, and the destitute for a quarter of a century, it can no longer selectively withdraw from the fight for justice whenever it feels like it, or when it becomes too uncomfortable or too risky.

The church cannot fail to respond to the distressing situations of poverty, inequality, and injustice of millions of South Africans in the present situation, simply because it finds it harder to speak and act prophetically now that, after 1994, political power is in black hands. Neither can the church act as if the oppression of women, the ongoing discrimination embedded in male micro-aggression,[31] and gender minimization[32] manifesting itself in appallingly sexist behavior and communicating hostile, derogatory, and negative slights and insults based on gender in society, in the workplace, or in the ministry of the church, does not matter. Embracing Belhar does not allow such benign neglect or cowardly silence. To withdraw from these struggles would in effect delegitimize *any* prophetic stand the church would wish to take on public issues in South Africa and globally today.

To rule a call on Belhar in the struggle for the rights and human dignity of LGBTI persons illegitimate—like the URCSA General Synod did in 2008—would in turn delegitimize *any* call upon Belhar by URCSA in the continuing justice struggles of the global poor or the reemergence of racism in South African society today. Indeed, it would bring into question the very validity of the church's witness for justice and reconciliation during the apartheid struggle itself. Seen in this light, Belhar's defining presence becomes an intensely self-critical presence.

Belhar indeed rises above and lives beyond the situation which was the immediate cause of its coming into being. The affirmation of the unity of God's people as "gift and obligation," the message of reconciliation God has entrusted to the church, the call to compassionate justice and the truth that through Jesus Christ we are the light of the world and the salt of the earth, called to be peacemakers, cannot possibly be confined to apartheid South Africa. This is not a call for "black and white together" in those incidental "open" services we have come to excel in in the constant efforts to avoid authentic church unity and genuinely nonracial congregations.

In all situations of oppression, rejection, and exclusion we celebrate the good news that God is a God who brings true justice among all humankind and that the church as the "possession of God"—not of human beings or cultural and ethnic groups or earthly powers—must stand where God stands: against all injustice and with the wronged, and that we are empowered by God's Holy Spirit to stand with the powerless against the powerful. The church is not in the service of empire, nor does it bow down to the dominant culture, the demands of patriotism or the dictates of political ideology. It is "the possession of God." God's embrace of humankind and the human condition in the incarnation of

Jesus Christ have far-reaching and radical consequences for our own humanbeingness and the relationships we foster and nurture. This the church celebrates.

That compelling passage from Calvin's *Institutes* we stood upon in 1982, in our appeal to the World Alliance of Reformed Churches when we called for apartheid to be declared a heresy, namely that "none of the brethren can be injured, despised, rejected, abused, or in any way offended by us, without at the same time, injuring, despising, and abusing Christ by the wrong we do...",[33] now stands as a *j'accuse* against *us*. We believe that we are called to confess all these things not through our earthly power, arrogance, or recklessness, says Belhar, but "in obedience to Jesus Christ, even though it may provoke the wrath of earthly authorities and human laws," because above all we know: Jesus is Lord.

The joy of belonging to Christ and to the community of believers, of knowing one's rootedness in the love of Christ and the love of the brothers and sisters; the joy of sharing that community in its fullness and the sharing of the fullness of one's own humanbeingness within that community and in the world: that joy is not to be denied any member of the body of Christ, in whom we all find, in the impressive formulation of the Heidelberg Catechism, our "only comfort in life and in death." That sense of belonging in Christ, and as a consequence with each other, is unbreakable and untouchable by any human law or ideology, by cultural or personal prejudice.

It is within this context also that Belhar calls upon us to remember that "we are obligated to give ourselves willingly and joyfully to be of benefit and blessing to one another (since) we share the one faith..." We are not offered this as an option we might or might not take. We are not forced, cajoled, or tricked into this: we are, as followers of Jesus, *obligated* as an outcome of the love of Christ. As true as this is of our racial relations, it is true of our other human relationships as well, especially in the church. We dare not deny this joy to LGBTI Christians and limit this obligation to only those who happen to share our sexual orientation. And having testified to itself the church testifies to the world by setting an example to the world in these and all other matters.

Belhar as Contextual and Situational Presence

It is important to once more underline the point that the context of racism and apartheid may have been the original *casus confessionis*, but it certainly does not proscribe it, nor does it denote the limits, or exhaust the depth and scope of the confession. We have already made the point that Belhar is universal in its applicability and in its inherent ability to speak to different situations in the world. In this part of our argument we approach this from yet another point of view. The theological truth Belhar proclaims transcends borders, geographical and otherwise; cultural, political, and human situations. That is the point of a kairos document such as the Confession of Belhar. The fact that Belhar is so understood by Christian churches from Korea to Palestine, from Africa to Europe to the United States, testifies to this. In other words, while Belhar indeed speaks of racism from the viewpoint of faith, Belhar is not defined by racism, nor is the confession contained or exhausted by it.

Much of the misunderstanding that surrounds Belhar, from others certainly, but also often from within URCSA circles, stems from the fact that Belhar is understood solely as a testimony against apartheid, bound historically and theologically to a particular political situation that existed at a particular time, and hence proscribed by that situation, and only applicable to that situation. If that were true, the white DRC's continuing distortions of Belhar would in fact be correct and the Uniting Reformed Church would have no leg to stand on. However, the theological basis of Belhar, the structure and the intentions as well as the language of the confession argue strongly that this is an impermissible reduction. It is a matter that touches the heart of the confession, and is crucial in our understanding of the impact of the confession on the life and witness of the church. It is, in short, a matter of confessional integrity.

The historical context of racism and apartheid is not the only context Belhar addresses and to which it speaks so powerfully. The confession lives by the affirmation with which it begins, that concludes Article One, and which deals with the unity of the church, namely that "true faith in Jesus Christ is the *only* condition for membership of this church." "This church" is not in the first instance URCSA, but rather the church of Jesus Christ. This is the faith of all who calls upon the name of Jesus Christ, who find in him their "only comfort in life and in death," and who follow him as the Messiah, the revolutionary teacher, and prophet from Galilee. This affirmation has much more radical consequences than might hitherto have been admitted to, perhaps because the confession is too readily read as a document responding to a "racial" situation, and because of the church's tangential tendency to submit to social pressure and political conservatism. Ironically in our times, for many in the churches "apartheid" or "racism" remains the safer, more comfortable, less offensive categories, while calls for gender and sexual justice posit the greater risks of solidarity.

The confession, for good reason, never mentions the word "apartheid," for the issue never was apartheid, but rather justice, unity, reconciliation; the integrity of the Gospel, the faithful obedience of the church and the Lordship of Jesus Christ. Neither *could* the focus be apartheid. Focusing on apartheid would have fatally removed the focus from Christ and would, both spatially and historically, have parochialized the confession beyond redemption.[34] The issue never was whether we wanted to be known as an "apartheid" or "antiapartheid" church. The issue always was whether we could discern the difference between a confessing church and a church with a confession.

Notice that the "forced separation of people on the grounds of race or color" is mentioned for the first time and only in Article Three which speaks of the "enforced separation of people on a racial basis" and in the "rejection" which follows. The affirmation of the "true faith in Jesus Christ" is related first to the rejection of any "absolutization" of "either natural diversity or the sinful separation of people" that "hinders or breaks the visible and active unity of the church," and next to the kind of belief that professes that genuine spiritual unity is truly being maintained "in the bond of peace whilst believers of the same confession are in effect alienated from one another for the sake of diversity and in despair of reconciliation." In other words, in seeking true unity our alienated reality cannot be condoned, tolerated, or alleviated by our "spiritual unity." The latter means nothing if the former is not real.

This holds not just for racial matters, even as at this very moment racial tensions are undeniably returning to South African society in ways not seen since the days of apartheid, and the issues of race and racism seem to reinvent and remanifest themselves with such vengeance in the United States and all countries in Europe. It pertains also to any other reality or perceived reality that "breaks the visible and active unity of the church," and it certainly cannot be contested that the unity of the church is as seriously threatened by the refusal of the church to truly embrace and welcome its LGBTI members, as it is by the growing wealth gap between the impoverished masses and the wealthy elites who both sit in the pews of our churches.

Liberating Language: Diversity, Dignity, Inclusion, Humanity

We shall have to say more about the language of Belhar here and how it acts as liberating, humanizing agent. Belhar not only advocates "embrace" as an act of love and justice, it also disputes against an understanding of "diversity" that is abused for reasons of negativity and rejection, instead of a diversity that celebrates the Other and the richness of difference. The diversity that is "absolutized" is the diversity that seeks to find a negative "otherness" that comes with enmity, distance, aversion, discrimination, degradation, and domination. That is the "diversity" as defined by apartheid ideology, which becomes the cause for separation, inferiorization, and exclusion. In doing so it eliminates dignity and the bond of humanity. To absolutize *this* diversity is to make it the foundation of the existence of the Other and so to pervert the meaning of genuine diversity. It is the breeding ground of injustice. The diversity that Belhar celebrates is the diversity that comes from celebrating both the richness of the creation of God and the dignity of the difference we see in the Other.

The foundation of the Other's existence is not the difference of skin color, gender, culture, or sexual orientation. Rather it is their humanbeingness, their being created in the image of God, sharing humanity in all its fullness with us. We dignify both the difference and the togetherness with our respect and love and the embrace of our common creatureliness as image bearers of God. The dignity of difference[35] is the dignity of personhood and being part of the greater human community. This is what the church celebrates and embraces. And this embrace is not the glorification of our ability to be "tolerant" as long as *our* cultural domination remains intact and normative. It is the celebration of the inclusiveness of the embrace of God.

Absolutizing natural diversity for the justification of exclusion while we should actually embrace and celebrate it not only breaks the visible and active unity of the church, but accepts that the church is doomed to live "in despair of reconciliation." This is a sinful attitude Belhar utterly rejects, because it despairs of, and makes insufficient the work of Christ in our lives. This despair is a deliberate rejection of the renewal in Christ in which "there is no longer Greek and Jew, circumcised and uncircumcised, barbarian, Scythian, slave and free; but Christ is all and in all" (Col. 3:11). On the contrary, it is our calling, gift, and obligation to live together as reconciled community. There is nothing that falls outside of this call and gift; nothing that makes us "despair of reconciliation" because we cannot despair of the work of Christ.

This goes indeed far beyond the issue of race. This addresses quite profoundly the historical and actual contexts of oppression, rejection, and exploitation of LGBTI persons, but also people mentally and physically challenged ("disabled persons") and women. It begins with the recognition that Belhar's understanding of the diversity mentioned above is a holistic, positive, enriching one, as opposed to the apartheid-inspired understanding of "diversity" that is negative and therefore leads to "natural" separation that should first be enforced by law and then sacralized by the church, as was the case under apartheid. It is a diversity based on mutual respect and openness, not a diversity which is required to adopt the values and cultural bent of the dominant; or conversely, a diversity that is considered to be contrary to the will of God, but enforced on an unwilling church by a secular Constitution, as is now the case in South Africa with the recognition of sexual diversity.

Belhar rejects the sinful absolutization with a view to inferioritize, separate, and discriminate, but expressly celebrates the diversity that affirms humanity and welcomes it as a gift from God for the richer life of the church. Belhar embraces that diversity as enriching and building the visible and active unity of the church. In this regard rejection of persons other than heterosexual or the degrading of women as if their "true faith in Jesus Christ" is not enough, but is in reality subjected to some form of human approval, something extra, or subject to their ability to "change" and become "more acceptable" (to us), is part of the sinful, heretical "doctrine" that Belhar rejects. Then it is not love of, and belief in Jesus Christ but patriarchy or heteronormativity that becomes the condition for membership of the church. Not only is our rejection of an LGBTI brother or sister a sin, but a sin also is, according to the confession, the "refusal earnestly *to pursue* this visible unity [with them] *as a priceless gift.*"

The hallmark of this very strong language is its inclusiveness. Inclusivity is also its intention, and it is an inclusion that is to be "earnestly" and actively "pursued." That means the undoing of injustice and the bringing of justice so that the visible unity can be realized. This assumes an activist church on behalf of justice. All manifestations of the sinfulness that "breaks the visible unity," "despairs of reconciliation," causes "alienation from one another," blesses the "enforced separation of people" on whatever grounds, are as applicable to the situations of separation and oppression and discrimination of LGBTI persons and women as they are to the realities of racial oppression and separation.

We must consider further the implications of the Confession that all human beings are created in the image of God. The Confession of Belhar grew out of a liberation theological understanding of the church on these matters since the early 1970s. We came to understand, in contrast to earlier times, that with regard to racism, we could no longer speak of it simply in individual, personal, that is to say, attitudinal terms. We understood racism in its historical, structural, systemic dimensions and manifestations as well. Racism, we discovered, is all the more devastating when it is linked with realities of power and powerlessness. Dealing with racism means dealing with power relations; with domination, subjection, and exploitation.

This same maturity of insight is called for in the matter of sexual justice. The injustices and suffering inflicted upon LGBTI persons are not just personal, a matter of attitudes; it is severely systemic and structural. Here too, power relations are at play. Heteronormativity rests in heterosexual power reflected in every area of society and all walks of life. This insight is even more important since it is the once-powerless who are in positions of power over LGBTI persons in South Africa today. It might be the power of the state, the power of structures in the church, the power of societal institutions such as the media, or the sheer power of cultural prejudice and sanction. It is for this reason that the Constitution of South Africa regards discrimination against homosexual persons a criminal act, as is the recognition, honoring, and protection of their rights considered a civil, legal, and political responsibility. I would argue that in its call upon the concept of *Ubuntu* the Constitution makes it also a moral responsibility. The Constitution means to protect the powerless against the powerful, an obligation Belhar claims as God's demand for the church.

The church began to speak of racism as "sin" because it denies, as we have stated before, the creatureliness, and hence the humanbeingness of others. It denies the truth that all human beings are created in the image of God, people whose humanity is confirmed and made sacred by the incarnation of God through Jesus Christ. In doing this, Calvin insists, we are acting with "the greatest inhumanity."[36] We are human in the likeness of God, which means not a physical likeness, but our unique, dynamic relation to God and hence to one another. God sees in us the marks and features of God's own countenance, so "whenever God contemplates his own face, he both rightly loves it and holds it in honour..."[37] Our humanity is confirmed by and in the humanity of the other; our own humanness is affirmed by our recognition of the humanness of the other, and therefore our existence is incomplete without that human recognition and reflection and our God-given capacity for intimate, caring, and loving relationships. Cultural, racial, ethnic, language, sexual, or any other difference cannot invalidate that basic truth that constitutes human life together. In Jesus Christ, these truths become utterly compelling.

We called racism a form of idolatry in which the one dominant group assumes, on the basis of pigmentation and the mythical belief in a social construct called "race," for itself a status higher than the other, and through political, cultural, military, and economic power, as well as socioeconomic and psychological structuring, seeks to play God in the lives of others. They demand from them a "correction" of their "deviant" (black) humanity that is in fact God-given: to be celebrated, not denigrated; to be embraced, not discriminated against; to be dignified with love, not vilified by ignorance and abuse.

And so we called apartheid racism a pseudo-gospel and a heresy because it claimed to have salvific power, made demands in the name of the gospel the gospel itself does not make, instituted conditions for and a threshold to membership of and full acceptance in the church other than faith in Jesus Christ alone, claimed to know better than God the way of salvation. We rejected the apartheid pseudo-gospel because it claimed that the most important thing about a person is not that she or he is a human being created in the image of God the Liberator, with inalienable rights, but his or her racial identity and pigmentation. It meant that racial identity determines, with an overwhelming intensity, everything in a person's life. This pseudo-gospel was perhaps willing to admit that God created us all, but added a "but..." That "but" was the beginning of the heresy, the human hubris and arrogance that dared to question the completeness, rightness, and gloriousness of God's creation.[38]

That view, we further determined, has all sorts of bitter consequences. Because it dehumanizes the other, reduces them to the caricature we, not God, created, they are stripped of their human dignity, of the freedom of being, choice, and options. Dislodged from the image of God, they are not fit to be considered in terms of pain or humiliation, dreams or aspirations, human degradation or human fulfillment and human rights. They become, in our sinful minds, the completed and completely distorted "other," the product of the perverted, racially obsessed imagination of the dominant group, the object of scorn. All the above-mentioned arguments that were, and still are, unquestionably valid in the struggle against racism and the racialized mind-set, are applicable to the situation of LGBTI persons.

This same process of thinking and action can be detected in homophobic bigotry. When Belhar rejects "any ideology which would legitimate forms of injustice and any doctrine which is unwilling to resist such an ideology in the name of the Gospel," this is precisely the ideologized theology the church embraces in its rejection of LGBTI persons that the Confession points to also.

To Call Upon God: Justice and Inclusivity

Moreover, the whole of Article Four, which deals with God as "the One who wishes to bring about justice and true peace on earth," speaks to the situation of LGBTI persons and women. The situation of the LGBTI person is in its deepest reality a situation of injustice. Their search for the recognition and protection of their humanity is a search for justice. In their woundedness, their vulnerability to the denial of their rights, the enmity of many in society and the church, and the rejection of their true and full humanity, LGBTI persons have an inalienable right to call upon the God "who in a special way (is) the God of the destitute, the poor and the wronged." Their suffering is no less wrong than the suffering of the widows and the orphans and it is in regard to their right to justice that

God "wishes to teach the people of God to do what is good and to seek the right."

Before God, there is no hierarchy of oppression and injustice. The injustice done to LGBTI persons is no less an abomination than the injustice done to the black poor and powerless. With God, justice is indivisible, as love is indivisible, as God is indivisible. Therefore, with regards to gays, lesbians, bi-sexual, trans-sexual, and intersexual persons, as it is with the oppression and marginalization women, the challenge is the same: in their struggle for the recognition of their rights to full humanity, the church also must learn "to stand where God stands," to witness and strive against "any form of injustice," so that also for those members of the body of Christ "justice may roll down like waters, and righteousness like an ever-flowing stream."

As the church seeks to follow Christ in the struggle for justice for the poor and the discriminated-against, so the church must follow Christ in this matter. This not only means that the church ought to support, uphold, and implement those rights afforded LGBTI persons in the Constitution of South Africa, the church ought to seek to actively safeguard and promote those rights within its own structures, its preaching and living, its worship and witness. Rejecting, as Belhar enjoins us, "*any* ideology which legitimates any forms of injustice..." means by the same token, or better still, by the same conviction, rejection of any form of oppression of women, or any form of bigotry, blatant or subtle.

This is the way in which the inclusiveness of the Confession of Belhar reflects the inclusiveness of the embrace of God. Seen through the lens of Belhar, only this could be the meaning and interpretation of the 2005 URCSA General Synod decision on this matter when synod spoke of its "embrace" of homosexual persons into the body of Christ. "Embrace" is inclusive. It does not tolerate any notion of distance. Not in terms of membership, nor in service or in ministry in any sense of calling recognized by the church. The only yardstick here, as with all members of the church, is "true faith in Jesus Christ." That is the meaning of unity, reconciliation, and justice. Inasmuch as that is denied, or something added to, we are reinstituting the heresy the Barmen Declaration pointed to in the German church and we have accused the white Dutch Reformed Church of in South Africa.

The confession states, "We believe that, in obedience to Jesus Christ, its only Head, the church is called to confess and do all these things, even though the authorities and human laws might forbid them and punishment and suffering be the consequence. Jesus is Lord." I argue that it is wrong to restrict this sentence to "governmental powers and authorities" only, even though this statement remains only too painfully true as we indicated at the start. Most African states criminalize homosexuality, and most recently according to news reports, the Gambian president Yahya Jammeh warned that all homosexual persons should leave the country "within twenty-four hours" otherwise "their heads would be chopped off." Since Yahya Jammeh threatened that his country's laws would be made stricter "than those in Iran," many gay persons have been arrested and otherwise persecuted.[39] "All homosexuals, drug dealers, thieves and other criminals" have to leave the country, says the president. In Zimbabwe President Mugabe described homosexual persons as "dogs" and "pigs," "not worthy of human consideration."[40]

More sophisticated perhaps, but with the same deadly, dehumanizing, soul-destroying logic, is US Supreme Court Justice Antonin's Scalia's judgment in his dissent from the Supreme Court's overturning of a Texas sodomy law, his lips dripping with disdain and contempt:

> State laws against bigamy, same-sex marriage, adult incest, prostitution, masturbation, adultery, fornication, bestiality are...called into question by today's decision.[41]

One cannot escape the conclusion: nonheterosexuality *by itself* is devoid of all humanity—it is the inevitable slippery slope toward bestiality. Such are the powers God's LGBTI children are up against. The church in South Africa cannot act as if, because our Constitution respects the human rights of LBGTI persons, this deplorable situation elsewhere is not our concern and as if these values are not under serious attack in our own country. Inasmuch as Belhar has been presented to the ecumenical church in hopes of its acceptance, URCSA, because of Belhar, has both a prophetic obligation and a pastoral responsibility for the brothers and sisters in those countries. As we so eloquently argued during the anti-apartheid struggle, ecumenical solidarity demands the pursuit of justice everywhere. Truly, Belhar is not a stick we wield as a weapon, but a staff on which we lean as we walk together.

In Christian circles the added element is the denial of the image of God in those whose sexual orientation differs from the heterosexual norm. And it is this deadly trio which create the climate and provide a priori the justification for the inhuman treatment of LBGTI persons, from societal rejection and verbal abuse to micro-aggression, violent attacks, "corrective rape," and murder. In South Africa the horrific violence visited upon women because they are women, is just as regularly visited upon LGBTI persons *because* they are what they are. Often this violence is seen as "sports," or treated as a joke, entertainment for macho men. If possible, this trivialization of violence is even worse than the violent deed itself.

But there is also the tyranny of cultural chauvenism, homophobic prejudices, and societal perceptions, in many cases driven by the media and propagated by churches, which exert enormous pressure over against what we know to be the call of the Gospel. These are the powers and authorities Belhar calls us to resist. There are frightening reasons why so many LGBTI Christians suppress their identity and even allow themselves to be forced into heterosexual marriages in order to hide their sexual orientation, causing untold suffering to themselves, their spouses, their families and in the end, the church. This is not a church reflecting the love Christ demands, the respect and dignity LGBTI persons deserve or a testimony to the glory of God.

It is worthwhile to quote the whole of Article Three, reading it not as a statement of faith about racial injustice, but as it is intended, a testimony against *all* forms of injustice, prejudice and exclusivity, and affirmation of the fundamental truths of the gospel of Jesus Christ and the inclusivity of God's embrace for any human situation:

> We believe that God has entrusted the church with the message of reconciliation in and through Jesus Christ;
>
> That the church is called to be the salt of the earth and the light of the world, that the church is called blessed because it is a peacemaker, that the church is witness both by word and deed to the new heaven and the new earth in which righteousness dwells;
>
> That God's life-giving Word and Spirit has conquered the powers of sin and death, and therefore also of irreconcilability and hatred, bitterness and enmity;
>
> That God's life-giving Word and Spirit will enable the church to live in a new obedience which can open new possibilities of life for society and the world;
>
> That the credibility of this message is seriously affected and its beneficial work obstructed when it is proclaimed in a land which professes to be Christian, but in which the enforced separation of people... promotes and perpetuates alienation, hatred and enmity;
>
> That any teaching which attempts to legitimate such enforced separation by appeal to the Gospel, and is not prepared to venture on the road of obedience and reconciliation, but rather, out of prejudice, fear, selfishness and unbelief, denies in advance the reconciling power of the Gospel, must be considered ideology and false doctrine.

In my view, the above considerations in light of the Confession of Belhar cannot but bring URCSA to accept and embrace LGBTI persons in the fullest sense of the word. That means that the church accepts:

1. That LGBTI persons, on the basis of their faith in Jesus Christ as personal Savior and Lord of their life and of the church, are without any reservation full members of the church of Jesus Christ.

2. That LGBTI persons deserve justice in the same way the church claims justice for the destitute and the wronged, both before and under the law, in civil society and in the church, and the church commits itself to actively pursue that justice in all areas of life.
3. That our commitment and calling to unity and reconciliation require that LGBTI persons, as confessing members of the church, have access to all the offices of the church, including the office of minister of the Word.
4. This access should, both in the interests of justice and pastoral concern, not be prejudiced by demands for celibacy if the relationship is one of love, respect, and real commitment. Should the criteria for heterosexual married persons apply, the church must then take a decision on support for, and the blessing of same-sex marriages as allowed by the Constitution.

It is perhaps best to conclude with two paragraphs from the report of the Task Team to the synod.[42]

"We have also discovered, inasmuch as those who are themselves not gay or lesbian can, just how deep are the pain and estrangement felt by homosexual [LGBTI] persons; just how horrifying for some of them is the prospect of being 'discovered' and 'exposed'; just how debilitating the humiliation they experience in the ways they are being discriminated against and talked about; just how destructive is the helplessness felt by the daily injustices done to them; and just how devastating the feelings of rejection and alienation they experience from the church and Christians. Most of all we have felt their total disorientation in the myriad ways church and society have questioned, undermined and denied their childhood of God. We have also felt the painful disillusionment of parents and family members, and with all of them, the loneliness no child of God need ever feel while there is such a thing as 'church'."

> As a church who experienced the pain and dejection of legal and personal discrimination because of race and skin colour, and through the grace of God have found the courage to resist and destroy it, URCSA is in a unique position to understand the reality with which [LGBTI] persons, their parents and family have to live, and to respond to it. We have come to know the God of compassionate justice and personal and political liberation, so the cry for justice from others in similar situations resonates with us. We know just how uplifting and empowering it is to know where God stands. Above all, we have come to know the power of the confession that Jesus is Lord, and how that enables us to work for justice, liberation and the humanisation of society and the world.

As nothing since the birth of the Confession of Belhar in 1982, not even the status of women in church life and ministry, the issue of sexual justice has forced URCSA to face the consequences of confessing our faith in Jesus Christ in new situations, and concerns about the well-being of the church once again abound.[43] But it is as Jaap Durand has said, and his words will remain as prophetic challenge before us:

> These concerns are unnecessary since a confessing church *always* lives in the shadow of the Cross and not without the assurance that the gates of hell shall not prevail against it. But no one can find comfort in this promise if he flees from the Cross.[44]

5

The End of Words? Kairos, Challenge, and the Rhetoric of the Barricades

Kairos and the End of Words

It will not be surprising that in our reflections on the meaning of kairos, prophetic preaching, that particular, extraordinarily difficult and dangerous calling of speaking truth to power, would loom large. And rightly so. Once kairos discernment turns a crisis into a kairos moment of conversion and commitment, prophetic witness and intervention are called for. For the poor and vulnerable the social, political, and economic crises caused by the abuse of power, rampant greed, and political indifference are not mere momentary disturbances. They do not appear and torture and then leave of their own volition or are magically removed by some benevolent source. They are the life-long condition of the oppressed and the downtrodden.

In the daily, uneven battles against the powers, overwhelming in their pervasive insidiousness, ruthless in their attempts to crush the people completely, to drain from them any sense of hope in the justice of God as we have heard John Calvin describe so eloquently, the oppressed hardly ever have a moment of respite. Facing the relentless propaganda of the powerful, and against the merciless erosion of their will to sustain meaningful life, what Homiletics and Preaching scholar Richard Lischer, in a very apt description, calls the "rhetoric of the barricades," the poor are first made powerless, then hopeless, then voiceless. They have, in a sense, come to "the end of words."[1]

Richard Lischer uses this expression differently and applies it to the calling of preaching. In reference to the famous and ever-haunting words of Irish poet William Yeats, Lischer observes,

> When true convictions give way to bigger and bigger lies told with increasingly "passionate intensity," the poet knows that it is time to keep

> silence...When the message of Jesus Christ can be Nazified or made the tool of racism, anti-Semitism, apartheid, or capitalism, it is time for preachers to shut up and take stock of themselves.[2]

Lischer then suggests that the "rhetoric of the barricades" should not be understood as words only. "What does one *say*," Lischer goes on to ask, "after a televised beheading? The proclamation of God's justice or God's love meets a wall of resistance first in the throat of the proclaimer, then in the ears of the hearer."[3] In that situation, the preacher has come "to the end of words." In more than one way this is true, and Lischer's call for an aversion in preachers for the emptiness of words is absolutely legitimate. Mouthing empty platitudes in the face of life's terror is a travesty.

Yet for the victims of these very real and present human-made atrocities—for every single one of those "isms" Lischer mentions are very much part of our experience right now—silence from those called to speak prophetic truth would create an unbearable void. We should not imagine that that void will remain empty just because the prophetic voices, for whatever reason, are silent. Political necessity and expediency, greed and the hunger for power quickly fill that void with the insidious propaganda of the official narrative, sanctioned by the palatable prophets of civil religiosity working relentlessly towards unfettered uniformity and coerced consent.

If the prophet, who is called to be "the voice of the voiceless" even if it is an isolated, lonely, sometimes trembling voice, remains silent, who will then open their mouth for those who cannot speak, are not allowed to speak, whose cry for justice is deemed too unworthy to listen to? In the victims of these ongoing atrocities there remains a deep longing for a word that is fundamentally different, hope-affirming, life-restoring. For them, in the midst of all those words and deeds of coercive, corrosive power, there must be a word that proclaims a different possibility, an alternative reality. So Lischer is right when he states elsewhere that despite everything, in the face of the crises confronting our world, "We cannot afford a moratorium on prophecy in these days."[4]

For indeed, we could also frame Lischer's questions differently, from below, as it were, from the perspective of those whose lives have been turned into constant crises by permanent injustices. What does one say after the death of yet another starving child, simply because of impoverishment gone over the edge of human endurance? Or when the dead body of yet another tortured activist in the endless struggles for justice is thrown on the doorstep of his parents' house or hung from a lamp post as a warning to others, or yet another family gathering is mistaken for a "terrorist gathering" and hit by drones? What does one say when yet another mother dies during childbirth because the police or the military at the check point or a road block refused to let them through?

What *does* one say when yet another law that legalizes dispossession or land theft is passed or when that dreaded Wall of infamy in Palestine cuts through yet another Arab-owned house and a family's life? What does one say when yet another black young man disappears into prison and is branded and disenfranchised for life because the poor person, walking on the street, is worth nothing to corporations and contractors; but when they are in jails and prisons they each generate revenues of $30,000–40,000 a year for the corporations who control and run the prison industrial complex in the United States.[5] *And this happens every day.* For the vast majority of God's children in the world, there is no respite. And it is not televised or even talked about much because so many in the rich world of power and privilege benefit from their misery.

But when in such situations the poor and defenseless are victimized into silence, does it mean that the prophet called by God has a right to claim that she has come to the end of words? In the time of the Nazi tyranny the horrors were such that one could hardly look upon them, let alone think about them in order to give words to such staggering realities. Yet, as the courageous preachers of the confessing church discovered, in such situations the very words of the preacher, the very act of preaching, become a significant form of resistance.[6]

In his fascinating and deeply moving book, *Preaching in Hitler's Shadow,* Dean Stroud presents some of the sermons of those incredibly courageous pastors of the Confessing Church in Germany during Hitler's reign of terror.[7] But preaching "in Hitler's shadow" meant that they were preaching not just in risky and dangerous times, they were preaching in the shadow of death. Literally. Yet such were their faith, courage, and commitment that not even entirely legitimate concerns for personal safety or the horror of Nazi atrocities "excused timidity in the pulpit."[8] Those called to faithful prophetic witness in Hitler's shadow could not afford to be silent in the face of the overwhelming Nazi propaganda machine and the even more overwhelming Nazi reality. In a letter to his wife from his prison cell on November 14, 1937, Pastor Paul Schneider wrote about the calling to prophetic preaching in Nazi Germany, expressing a truth many of us similarly felt in the struggle against apartheid: "It is not that I and all the rest of us have said too much in our sermons, but rather that we have said far too little."[9] Then, as now, the need for a prophetic word remains. It is, Lischer says in his superb definition of prophetic preaching, preaching that consists in

> speech and symbolic actions that follow the implications of God's holiness and revealed acts to their most concrete, vivid, and public conclusions.

> What is whispered in closeted places of fear and suffering, the prophet proclaims from the rooftops. Prophecy begins with the present state of things—King's refrain was, "Let us be dissatisfied"—and ends in the imagination of an alternative future.[10]

Prophetic preaching, I understand Lischer to say, is not just speech. It is speech *and* symbolic action. Hence the deliberate choice of the word "following." I understand that to mean that prophetic preaching is an event not just in the pulpit amidst praise and worship and quiet meditation, but on the streets, amidst the havoc, pain, and confusion wrought by poverty and hopelessness, where the senseless violence of the poor on the poor reflects the equally senseless but calculated violence of systemic, policy-sanctioned destruction of the poor. In this context of unholy suffering, the prophetic preacher insists that the holiness of God should not just be acknowledged in the sanctuary but followed in every area of life, and that God's holiness is revealed not just in acts of sanctification in the sanctuary where God is worshipped but in acts of liberation and justice in the dreaded places of fear and trepidation where the powers believe they hold sway. The preacher believes that those acts of liberation and justice are not vague, spiritualized, and privatized, but in fact concrete, vivid, and public.

What is whispered in "closeted places of fear and suffering" the prophet shouts from the rooftops. That is true. The pain of those who suffer dare not be silenced. Their cries, we have learned from Calvin, are the cries from a wounded God's very own heart. To attempt to silence those cries because they might offend the powerful and comfortable is an assault upon the holiness of God. That pain and suffering have to be *heard*. But what the prophet also shouts from the rooftops is what is whispered in those other closeted places: places of power and wealth, behind the closed doors of corporate board rooms and sacralized chambers of political power. Those places where a few make decisions that control and destroy the lives of millions half a globe away; where endless war equates seamlessly with endless profits, and where in matters of life and death there is no such thing as humbled hesitation or holy ground.

The prophet shouts from the rooftops that the world as it is is *wrong*. That the powers of this world are not invincible, that their word is not unchallengeable, that the present state of things is not irreversible, nor God-ordained; that discontent with evil is not abnormal or extreme or laughable, but rather a response to God's love of justice; that an alternative future is not just imaginable, but possible and urgent even though in the eyes of the powers the possibility of such a different world is absurd.

Walking with God

The prophetic preacher's sober assessment of the situation of our world, her realization of the reality of evil, does not paralyze her urge to speak: rather it informs it, shapes it, molds it, because always opposite the reality of the way the world is, is the reality of the world the way God desires it. The humility we feel at not being able to speak for God, or to speak in the name of God, does not nullify the call of God. That is the power of the prophet's rootedness among the people; that is where, as Calvin insists, the voice of God is heard in the cries of suffering and for justice: *vox victimarum, vox Dei*. It is for that reason too, that a prophetic theology adrift from or independent of the hopeful *sizwe* is unthinkable.

The fear of the consequences of the prophetic word may drive us up the wall, but it also drives us to our knees. The unspoken suffering of the people is a voice we cannot silence. Not with our realistic appraisals of life, not with our shocked contemplation of evil or our stupefied admission of the existence of evil, and not with the stunned silence which we hope will gain us, if not eternal understanding, then at least the temporary solace of some morsel of wisdom. Above all, we cannot escape the truth that the cries of the victims of the evil we deplore emanate from the very heart of the God we adore.

So, do what we may, we cannot escape or ignore that gut-wrenching compulsion that Jeremiah felt so keenly, despite his reluctance to speak, and which is the daily, sometimes bitter, bread of every prophetic preacher:

> If I say, "I will not mention Him,
>   Or speak any more in His name,"
> Then within me there is something
>   like a burning fire
>   shut up in my bones;
> I am weary with holding it in,
>   and I cannot. (Jer. 20:9)

There is a holy desperation in that "and I cannot" that we must not try to pacify, domesticate, or reshape into some kind of inoffensive, postmodernist gentility. It is the unadorned, raw utterance of resistance against God that has given in at last to the love of God, though with extreme reluctance. Resisting God is the opposite of walking with God, which is the injunction of that other prophet of social justice, Micah.

> He has told you, O mortal, what
>   is good;

And what does Yahweh require
of you
but to do justice, and to love
kindness,
and to walk humbly with your God. (6:8)

And "walking humbly with God," I have written in another place, is not simply an attitude of adoration and humility as some have suggested though it is certainly that as well. Neither is it an admonition to "know our place," wretched sinners and worthless humans before an omnipotent, omniscient, omnivorous God.[11] It is rather, an act of learning to read the heart of God, to hear the voice of God in the cries of the victims of our own ferocious greed, and in so doing to understand what Yahweh requires. And *that* cannot be done but in utter humility before God and before the ones we have hurt and damaged through our arrogance, injustice, and love of violence. Even though politics seems not to be able to do that since it gives the impression of weakness and timidity and opens up even a remote possibility that we might be wrong—*that we might have done wrong*—it is much less mystical than we have pretended, though often much harder than we are ready to believe:

> It means just what it says. It is walking with God through Egypt, *seeing* both the oppressive, heartless might of the Pharaoh *and* the pain and suffering of God's people. (Ex.3:7) It is standing in the midst of the slaves, counting the blows, bending under the weight, feeling the pain. It is understanding the power of the Pharaoh and the mercilessness of his slave drivers, and it is "to come down" to rescue, to liberate, to end the violence and the suffering. Walking humbly with God is walking from the brick-making yards through the palace gates to the throne, telling the Pharaoh, "Let my people go!" It is breaking down the wall of resistance between the will of the Pharaoh and the longing of the people, between the power of the Pharaoh and the cry for freedom. It is acknowledging the difference between making bricks for the Pharaoh and building the walls of Jerusalem.[12]

Walking humbly with God means being humbled by what we see, by what we are doing to others, by our capacity for harm and destruction in what we are wreaking upon God's creation. If we walk humbly with God we will gain the wisdom to hear the voice of God as God cries to the city (Micah 6:9–12). It is not a wailing as one finds in Jeremiah: "My anguish! My anguish! I writhe in pain! Oh, the walls of my heart!" (4:19). That kind of anguished cry we find earlier, in Micah 1:8. There Yahweh is depicted as a wailing woman, one in pain and in mourning; mourning the suffering inflicted on the poor by the oppression and injustices of the powerful: "For *this* I will lament and wail…"

The cause of God's lament is not the punishment to be inflicted upon two beloved cities; hence the strange words of 1:10: "Tell it not in Gath, weep not at all..." It is as if Yahweh is saying, "Don't you dare weep for the judgment that is coming to you, if you had no time or could find no compassion in your heart to weep for the injustices you have done, for the wounds you have caused, for the suffering you have inflicted upon the poor and downtrodden." Yahweh's anguish is because of the injustices inflicted upon the downtrodden and the defenseless. Every injustice, as we have heard Calvin say, is a wound inflicted upon the heart of God. God feels wounded and outraged in the persons of those who are victims of cruelty and wickedness.[13] And as a consequence, every cry uttered by the suffering poor is a cry from the heart of God: it is as if God hears Godself, when the oppressed cry "How long?"

Elsewhere Calvin considers it enough to state that oppression "utters a significantly loud cry of itself; and if the judge, sitting on a high watch-tower seems to take no notice of it, he is here plainly warned that such connivance shall not escape with impunity."[14] Now Calvin takes it one step further, making sure that it is understood that the cry for justice is not just a cry of oppression itself, sufficient on its own to call for a response in the doing of justice. The cry is in fact God's own cry: "It is as if the Lord hears himself, when *they* cry..." The seriousness of the matter cannot be overemphasized.

Micah teaches us that prophetic judgment is not emotional ranting and raving. He is meticulous as he lists the evil that those who oppress the poor "love." They "devise wickedness and evil deeds in their beds," that is they think of nothing else all night long, and when morning dawns, "they perform it." This should give us pause. First, Micah offers sober insight into the human psyche: unlike animals reacting on instincts for self-preservation and survival, humans *contemplate* the evil they wreak upon others. They *plan* exploitation and oppression; they *calculate* the profits and benefits of war and destruction. They *design* the language of justification, obfuscation, and trivialization: "collateral damage," "enhanced interrogation techniques," "We tortured some folks."[15] There is nothing spontaneous about it. Then Micah adds, with amazing insight into the workings of power, ancient and modern, "*because it is in their power*" (2:1). This is what lies at the core of their evildoing: raw, abusive power. There is no fuzziness, no naiveté, no ambiguity about this: it is pure, naked, abusive power.

One should read these words as the conclusion of every accusation the prophet makes: "They covet fields, and seize them; houses, and take them; they desire the inheritance of the lowly, and take it—*because it is in their power.*" Micah's graphic language depicts the viciousness of oppression: the oppressors "hate the good and love evil;" they "tear the skin off my people and the flesh off their bones." The evil of the injustices done is horrific and Micah is not interested in euphemisms as he describes it. One tastes Yahweh's outrage: They "eat the flesh of my people, flay their skin off them; break their bones in pieces, and chop them up like meat in a kettle, like flesh in a caldron" (3:2–3). And they do this because it is in their power to do so. Then Micah turns to that ever willing handmaiden of abusive power: the religious legitimation of civil religiosity, to the prophets who preach only what those they seek to please want to hear. Micah accuses these preachers of crying "Peace" because they themselves, in contrast to the poor, live well off the profits of their faithless complicity while the rich declare "war against those who put nothing in their mouths" (3:5). This is not the shalom that Yahweh desires and which Micah describes in the unforgettable, poetic dream of chapter 4. This is the murderous peace of violent pacification. It is the "peace" of the empire Israel's rulers are so eager to imitate. It is for *this* that Yahweh laments and wails.

There might be at least two other reasons for Yahweh's anguish, I think. Twice the prophet mentions one of them. In 3:1: "Listen, you heads of Jacob and rulers of the house Israel! Should you not know justice?" There is a sense of amazement in the question. And in 6:8: they cannot claim innocence or plead ignorance: they *know* what Yahweh requires. The prophet is referring to the Mosaic covenantal tradition, the foundation of Israel's existence and faith and the persistent theme of prophetic protest and resistance in Israel.[16] Doing injustice is denying the covenant. This they have imbibed with their mother's milk. It is what made ancient Israel unique among nations. This is why Yahweh makes "lamentation like the jackals, and mourning like the ostriches" (1:8).

The other reason is found in the well-known passage about what Yahweh requires (6:6–8). Reading the passage more attentively two things jump out, as it were. First is the sheer, overwhelming abundance of what they are offering Yahweh: burnt offerings of calves "a year old"; "thousands of rams" and "ten thousands of rivers of oil." These are not the offerings of the poor—two turtle doves (or two young pigeons) such as Joseph and Mary bring as they present Jesus to the Temple (Lk 2:24)—or perhaps a lamb, if they are lucky. These are the offerings of the extremely wealthy, offered out of the abundance and luxury of their ill-gotten riches and boundless prosperity. These they offer out of the arrogance of abundance and hubris. However, these are the very riches Yahweh condemns, because they are the fruits of oppression, dispossession, and exploitation. So they are offering Yahweh what Yahweh is bound to reject.

Second, though: running thinly disguised through the passage is a tone of irritated exasperation. One can almost see the pretended perplexity on the faces: "With what shall I come before the LORD?"; "Shall I come before him...?"; "Will the LORD be pleased with..."? This is not the tone of the contrite, worshipful heart. The barbed hyperbole turns into a crescendo of sarcasm as they come to the final offer to Yahweh: "Shall I give my firstborn...?" But this is exactly what Yahweh does *not* want; it is what Yahweh expressly forbids. From the viewpoint of the prophet this is absolutely outrageous, but simultaneously absolutely consistent with people who are drunk with their own power and who "walk in haughtiness" (2:3). It is with this haughtiness that the prophet, in responding, will contrast the humble walk with God.

In 6:9–12 however, Yahweh's cry is not an anguished lament. It is an amazing passage of verses that arrest the imagination. Here, Yahweh traverses the city streets, not aimlessly, but pointedly, naming the places of iniquity from whence emanates the misery of the poor. Yahweh utters a steady litany of deliberate judgment. But it is a *cry*: underneath the measured tones is the drumbeat of divine distress. Micah is specific: it is a cry to the *city*, but not the city as the urban, careless, heartless opposite of idyllic, communal, rural existence. The prophet does not offer sociological analysis. This is acute, clear-eyed political judgment. It is the city as the citadel of domination, the seat of all sorts of power, the dwelling place of the rich and privileged, where the poor and destitute live lives of cringing, desperate resignation in the shadow of shameless ostentation. Furthermore, it is not a cry against random and incidental injustices: the city represents entrenched, legalized, and legitimized systems of injustice that pervade every area of life. That is why Yahweh cries judgment and condemnation against the "tribe and the assembly," that is, the gatherings of the powerful elites who make decisions for the city, who devise the laws and policies that shape the political economy of the nation and control the lives of the people. The assembly, where the powerful make decisions for the poor but treat the poor as if they exist solely for the exploitative interests of the rich.

The city, where the exercise of power is most undeniable; where the great plans for perpetual enrichment and perpetual impoverishment are contrived in the palaces and the Temple; where the yawning gap between the rich and the poor is most stark, most disturbing, and most scandalous. The city: the center of commerce where the deals negotiated among the powerful crush the poor and favor the rich; where the business of making money continues undisturbed while the lives of the poor suffer devastating disruption. This is the place where the spoils from the exploitation of the disinherited rural poor are brought to swell the already overflowing coffers of the rich. The city: where the violence of the wealthy is sanctified by the soothing presence of the Temple, where the paid court prophets cry "Peace! Peace!", as the religious elites connive with the politically and economically powerful to oppress and exploit the poor.

It is here where the judgment of Yahweh resounds, echoing from those walls within which the powerful deem themselves safe and secure. This cry is not uncontrolled emotion, but clear-headed analysis of systemic oppression. This is not a whisper in the ear of one or two, but a loud cry of outrage and deliberate *j'accuse* to the ruling elites of the city where are stashed "the treasures of wickedness," where they keep "wicked scales and a bag of dishonest weights," measuring with the "scant measure that is accursed." "Shall I tolerate all this?" Yahweh asks. Again, with startling perspicacity Micah does not fail to understand and name greed and the perversion of justice in the courts for what they are: systematized violence. God cries to the city where "your wealthy are full of violence" and where the powerful speak with "tongues of deceit." God cries out against every instrument of oppression and exploitation used to crush the poor and the weak. It is in this sober deconstruction of the realities of his society that the prophet sets a model for the socioeconomic and political analysis so characteristic of kairos documents. Modern analysts of power and politics may do well to learn from this eighth-century prophet. Notice that the powerful elites are inflicting all this pain on the downtrodden and defenseless, but it is *Yahweh* who cries, "O my people, what have *I* done to you?" (6:3). Again Calvin's point is underscored. Micah foreshadows Jesus: "What you have done to the least of these, you have done to me" (Matt. 25:31–45). When Micah calls us to "walk humbly with God," this is what he wants us to understand. The cries of God overcome our end of words and give us new words to speak. It also means that the end of our words does not mean the end of our following God in humble determination to act out God's demands for justice.

For this reason the prophet interrupts himself in 2:6 to turn to that ever present demand from the powerful and those who profit from systemic oppression: "Do not preach—thus *they* preach—one should not preach of such things." Again and again, as we shall see with Amos as well, those who benefit from lies and deception cannot stand the word of prophetic truth. They want preachers who soothe and mollify, who seamlessly blend inoffensiveness with cowardice, who will say, "I will preach to you of wine and strong drink." How shall we understand this curious phrase? As biting sarcasm, I think. Shall we, the prophet seems to ask, make God the topic of a light-hearted happy-hour chat? After all, who speaks of judgment and condemnation over a glass of choice cabernet? Or shall excessive drinking and reveling and womanizing be the immorality I will address, never breathing a word about the immorality of socioeconomic injustice, of your violence against the defenseless, of your war against the poor, and of the systemic oppression which makes you rich? "Such a one would be a preacher for this people!"

The true prophet of God, however, is the preacher who will not satisfy the people with empty platitudes, soothing words, and the superficial telling of comforting stories; speaking of a God whose patience is never exhausted, who rewards the people for their self-styled "uprightness" while ignoring the injustices they do. They seek to disable the judgment of God with the love of God, proclaiming that a loving God cannot, and will not judge their wickedness: "Are these his doings?" they ask with the perplexity of the pampered. They seek a preacher who will speak of a God who, like them, does not see the misery of the oppressed and therefore is not disturbed by it; who, like them, do evil and forget about it as if it does not matter, because the poor do not matter; who tolerate wickedness because the profits it generates are just too great to resist; a God who has no option but to side with them because they are, in the jargon of globalized neoliberal capitalism, "too big to fail." Micah's God of justice, however, cannot forget: "Can I forget...?" Yahweh cries; and again, "Can I tolerate...?" Instead of seeking to be in their good graces by praising them, Yahweh announces judgment: "You shall bear the scorn of my people..." (6:16).

They seek to disempower the prophet with *their* power. But Micah is clear: over against their power the prophet speaks with a different kind of power: "As for me, I am filled with power, with the Spirit of the LORD, and with justice and might" (3:8). Theirs is the power of boundless arrogance, of ruthless intimidation and threat as we have seen in 2:1; his is the power of justice, of compassion, and servanthood. It is not the power *over others*; it is the power *shared with others* that makes such a fundamental difference in the practice of politics. It is not intimidation, coercion, and the threat of destruction that give him power; it is justice that gives him might. It is a reminder of true power rooted in the understanding of true authority, a power not divorced from the fear of the Lord as Calvin says elsewhere. It is, as well, a powerful reminder of the source of the strength of true prophetic witness, what Steve Biko called "the righteousness of our strength." This is the power that derives from the humble walk with God.

Walking humbly with God is walking with Jesus, *seeing*, not just looking at, the oppressed and the captives, working for their liberation, understanding not only that they are in prison but knowing also that someone is holding the key to that prison. Setting the captives free means taking possession of the key and unlocking the prison doors. It is walking among the poor and the destitute, sharing their struggles for life and dignity and bringing them the good news of God's justice. It is seeing the wounds of the broken-hearted and binding them, humbled into deeds of restitution and restoration and justice because we know that these are wounds we have inflicted. It is living among them the new reality of the reign of God that will challenge and break the deadly grip of the systems of domination and powers of enslavement on their lives.

It is walking with Jesus, restoring life to the bodies of children and thereby restoring life to the hearts of their parents. It is walking with Jesus, making the wounded whole, healing the sick, touching the untouchables and overturning the thrones of the Untouchables. Stepping aside to give women their rightful place, empowering them with dignity and the right to determine their destiny. It is weeping with those who mourn, releasing the life-giving power of the word of the kingdom; challenging the powerful on the matters of justice and mercy, in their temples and their palaces, giving notice that the reign of God is here.

Walking humbly with God is walking with Jesus, step by step through Gethsemane, perhaps not unflinchingly and fearlessly but nonetheless faithfully, running the gauntlet through the scoffers and the mocking laughter and the pointing fingers. It is walking with Jesus up that hill, bowed under the weight of the cross but not bowing before the powerful; hanging on that cross with him, not knowing with certainty but believing with all our heart that the grave has no power to hold us, just as it had no power to hold Jesus; that we will rise up with him in God's *apanastasia*, his resurrection which is God's rebellion against evil, against the bigger and bigger lies, against the death-dealing rhetoric of the barricades, against the powers of death and destruction. That is the walk with God that breaks down our resistance to prophetic faithfulness. It is also the walk that leads us inexorably right up to the barricades.

Kairos and the Rhetoric of the Barricades

Lisher's list of atrocities justified in the name of Jesus Christ is short but all the same horrifically accurate. All of these speak of systems of domination and violence, and central to all those is one salient feature: the power of coerced uniformity, of what Noam Chomsky and Edward S. Herman called "manufactured consent."[17] Lisher's list speaks of powers of domination that brook no dissent or critique; uniformity of opinion and behavior is essential. This is not so much to grant "permission" for atrocities to take place; the logic of the ideology necessitates the atrocity, makes it inescapable. It is much more that the atrocities should take place *in everybody's name*. If all are guilty everyone is innocent. Dissent destroys that logic, exposes that lie, annihilates that innocence, and hence cannot be tolerated.

In everybody's name, and in God's name: Nazi soldiers wore the slogan *Gott mitt Uns* (God with Us) on their belt buckles. South African theologian Johan Cilliers calls his analysis and assessment of white Dutch Reformed Church preaching during the apartheid era *God for Us?*[18] The question mark in the title does not signify doubt about the historic truth. Rather it questions the underlying assumptions of the theology of apartheid concerning God's approval of the ideology of apartheid and its attendant consequences. We recall Beyers Naudé's lament about loyalty within the ranks of Afrikanerdom, where loyalty to the ideology of apartheid converged with loyalty to God and God's purposes for the nation. "Anybody who is seen to be disloyal to his nation...is not only deemed a traitor, but in the deeper sense of the word, he is seen as betraying God."[19]

The politics of religious coercion is a powerful tool and Hitler, like all abusive powers, knew it well. The independence of the German regional churches (*Landeskirchen*) that is, not being subjected to a centralized authority, which gave space for the formation of the Confessing Church was, Dean Stroud writes, "an irritant to Nazi's."[20] As with all systems of domination and oppression, a hallmark of Nazism was the idea that every institution in Germany had to conform to Nazi ideology in a manner that made it structurally clear that "all paths led ultimately to Hitler."[21] This conformity was called *Gleichschaltung,* a synchronization of opinion which means everyone and every institution had to express a Nazi orientation and perspective. In this way, everyone and everything in the Third Reich had to conform to Nazi principles or be destroyed. "Whether internal or voluntary or external and coerced, the idea was that every man, woman, and child along with all institutions in Nazi Germany would live according to Nazi expectations." It was the "necessary step," was the quite shamelessly honest admission of Propaganda Minister Goebbels, "toward only one party, one conviction, one *Volk*. And all the other powers and forces have to subject themselves to this state or be pushed aside without mercy."[22]

I am still following the fascinating analysis of Dean Stroud. In April 1933, the Nazi parliament passed a law that would become known as the "Aryan Paragraph," which made it illegal for "Non-Aryans" to work in any bureaucratic capacity. All public servants who were not "racially pure" could no longer work in the public sector. The false prophets of Nazism, wrapping the message of the gospel of Jesus Christ in the flag of Nazi supremacism and racism rushed to bow down before the altar of uniformity. In September 1933, at the "Brown Synod," (brown being the color of Nazism) the German Christians demanded that all the churches of the Old Prussian Union incorporate the Aryan Paragraph. "Thus Nazi laws, not the Christian gospel, would dictate who could or could not preach the gospel in Germany...No longer was it true that Christian baptism incorporated a believer into the body of Christ, where there was no longer Jew or Gentile."[23]

Just a bit later that same September, the theology faculty at the University of Marburg put forth a detailed and closely reasoned report arguing for the exclusion of Jewish Christians from the office of clergy. Engaging *inter alia* the New Testament's proclamation in Galatians 3:27, 28 that in Christ there was no longer Jew or Greek, the report maintained that this was a spiritual statement that had nothing to do with biological differences.[24] It therefore had no moral or political consequences. The wild, Christian nationalist fervor of the Brown Synod was now legitimated by reasoned, scholarly, theological respectability.

It was a fateful year for Germany, but it was also a year of prophetic courage which would continue to inspire the church in Germany and the ecumenical movement throughout this disastrous period. That same September the Pastors' Emergency League was founded and in a strong statement written by Martin Niemöller and Dietrich Bonhoeffer, protested the Aryan paragraph. The seed for the Confessing Church was sown. Amazingly, considering the times, no less than 7,000 pastors joined the league, locked in opposition to Hitler and the German Christians. True to all kairos moments, the battle against Hitler was also the battle *within* the church, for the soul of the Christian Church.

But what would that battle entail? Did those pastors know what they were signing up for? Did they, in 1933, even remotely understand the nature of the evil they were facing? How many would remain steadfast, and how many would falter and fall under the weight of the combined power of state evil and church connivance? How many could even imagine what lay ahead, that the prophets of the Confessing Church would not all remain rock fast in that fierce storm that was brewing, but would be more like reeds shaking in the wind? Dietrich Bonhoeffer seemed to have understood this better than most. On January 20, 1934, he preached in London about the prophet Jeremiah. It was a sermon "full of feeling," revealing "the burning passion behind [Bonhoeffer's] reserve."[25] Jeremiah was called to be a prophet, Bonhoeffer preached, but he was "hunted game," struck down by "the arrow of the Almighty." He is a prisoner, Bonhoeffer said, his path is prescribed. "It is the path of the man whom God will not let go" despite his raw and insistent protestations. He will "never be rid of God" and it is the God who called him who will also lead him "down into the deepest situation of human powerlessness." God will make him a fool, but a fool who is "extremely dangerous to people's peace and comfort, so that he or she must be beaten, locked up, tortured, if not put to death right away." His congregation might not have fully understood what he was trying to say, but Bonhoeffer knew exactly where he was going:

> [Jeremiah] was upbraided as a disturber of the peace, an enemy of the people, just like those, throughout the ages until the present day, who have been possessed by God, for whom God had become too strong...how gladly would he have shouted peace and *Heil* with the rest...[26]

Like Jeremiah, Bonhoeffer felt "enticed," deceived by God. In that same sermon, identifying completely with the plight of the prophet Jeremiah, Bonhoeffer cries out: "How could we know that your love hurts so much, that your grace is so stern?...God, why are you so terrifyingly near us?" Love that "hurts"? Grace that is "so stern"? A nearness that "terrifies"? One feels hesitant to subject such words to analysis: it is holy ground, and every true prophet since Jeremiah has known it. Indeed, it would have been so much easier, so much safer, not to speak, not to challenge, not to prophesy, but just to shout *Sieg Heil!* and reap the benefits, be close to the throne, live a more restful, more immediately rewarding life.

The modern prophets who speak truth to power, secular as well as those who perceive their calling to come from God, will not escape the pressures of the barricades, the wrath of the powers, and the contestation with the modern prophets of the court. In the United States prophetic witness has come under renewed and severe pressure since the folly of the Iraq war. Almost as nowhere else in the world in the last 20 years or so, this has become clear and the frightening intimacy of political ideology and religious patriotism has taken on the biblical proportions the prophets railed against. "Freedom and fear, justice and cruelty have always been at war," said President George W. Bush just after 9/11/2001, "and we know that God is not neutral between them."[27] What Bush meant was that God is not neutral because God is "with us," and if God is with us God cannot stand in judgment of us. The waves of applause resounded not only in the chambers of Congress but across the nation. Whoever would dare to speak would speak condemnation over themselves. In summoning support for the war, English literature scholar and theologian Walter Herbert observes,

> The White House skillfully wove together themes of Christian piety and democratic principle, speaking about freedom and God's purposes in ways that sounded authoritative and familiar. Because the case for war drew on a shared vocabulary of public devotion, both secular and devout Americans supported the venture, or found it hard to frame the reasons for their opposition.[28]

But systems of domination leave nothing to chance, and almost always religious coercion is not the only weapon in their arsenal. In sometimes subtle, sometimes not so subtle ways, forceful shows of governmental power, threats, and draconian legislation reinforce the pressure on the populace to submit to the coercion and conform to the expectations set by the national agenda.

Apartheid had its formidable, and infamous, array of legislation for "national security" that made dissent and resistance not just unpopular but a matter of life and death. But it is remarkable, and for a South African who lived under and fought against apartheid, deeply disturbing, how far the United States, in its "National Defense Authorization Act," for instance, renewed for 2014, has gone down the road to adopt the worst characteristics of the Apartheid state in service of global apartheid.[29] The most controversial provisions, under the title "Counter-terrorism," allow for the indefinite detention without trial, one of the most detested means at the use of the apartheid regime. The use of torture on suspects is now well known and President Obama cannot seem to find a word of condemnation. Some forms of dealing with suspects, such as so-called rendition, and assassination by drones, remain unique to the United States.

The most recent revelations by former National Security Agency (NSA) employee Edward Snowden, himself an extraordinarily brave secular prophet, of the scope of surveillance, nationally and globally, by the NSA reveal, in large part, the unceasing attempts by governmental powers to reinforce the culture of consent through fear and threat. Not surprising at all is the intimidation of journalists like Glenn Greenwald, Naomi Klein, Naomi Wolf, and Chris Hedges, among others, who, in this matter, have taken up the role as secular prophets, calling attention to crises, seeing kairos moments in what governments want to keep closeted behind doors of utmost secrecy.[30]

Just as disturbing, as a specific example, is the attempt at stifling all dissent in the matter of Israel's occupation policies and oppression of Palestinians on university campuses in California. California legislators have passed a bi-partisan resolution (HR35) which constitutes a serious attack on academic freedom and the rights of students and faculty to raise awareness about human rights abuses by US-backed governments. In the resolution, the term "anti-Semitic" is so widely defined that any criticism of Israel's policies is "illegitimate." In this case, it is the young, secular prophets on the campuses who are being put under pressure to embrace the manufactured consent of the rhetoric of the barricades. California's universities, writes political scientist Stephen Zunes, "have long been a center of agitation for human rights and in opposition to US policies which support violations of human rights, whether it be the war in Vietnam, investment in apartheid South Africa, intervention in Central America or support for Israel's wars and occupation."[31]

But I must make one more observation that might help us understand the multiplicity of levels at which the power of manufactured consent works. Structures of domination have hegemonic power that is not always as obvious as draconian laws or abrasive propaganda through the mass media, but is as essential for the rhetoric of the barricades that silences and oppresses. In this I follow Jean and John Comaroff who have made us aware of hegemony not as raw power but rather as those insidious realities taken for granted as the natural shape of the world and everything that inhabits it; a form of power that is not always overtly felt and therefore not consciously resisted because its effects are rarely wrought by overt compulsion:

> They are internalized, in their negative guise, as constraints; in their neutral guise, as conventions; and in their positive guise, as values. Yet the silent power of the sign, the unspoken authority of habit, may be as effective as the most violent coercion in shaping, directing, even dominating social thought and action. [32]

In this view then, and I agree with the Comaroffs, the "rhetoric of the barricades" prophets have to contend with is not just the show of brutal force, the intimidation of oppressive laws, the subtle and not so subtle threats; the barrage of propaganda from the mass media, or the corrosive omnipresence of official narratives. It is also the insidiousness of hegemony as the Comaroffs describe it; the pressures of totalitarian loyalties ingrained in a culture of unquestioning belonging. So once again, as in the past, "throughout the ages until this day" we heard Bonhoeffer say, those who see a different world, who refuse to bow before the gods of uniformity but are searching for a new world and an alternative reality away from deception and destruction are marked for persecution because, as with Amos of Tekoa, "the land cannot bear their words" (Amos 7:10). But the "land" Amos is speaking of are those who control the land, who hold the power which feeds on the misery of the poor and oppressed, who know that the words of the prophets are words of judgment for them, but words of hope for the suffering people who place their faith in God. They cannot bear them.

The Voice Crying in the Wilderness

Speaking of the traditional sociocultural oppression of women in Africa and the destructive reinforcement of these harmful traditions by oppressive strands of the Bible, infusing oppressive patriarchal tendencies and practices with biblical authority, respected African theologian Mercy Oduyoye observes that even though the Christian heritage of the biblical, prophetic denunciation of oppression has served Africa well, much was left untouched and unchallenged:

> Biblical interpretation and Christian theology have had the effect of sacralizing the marginalization of women's experience, even in the traditional African religions. This distorts the essence of African womanhood... At this point, prophecy resumes its original character as a voice crying in the wilderness, ignored by the powerful and the respectable.[33]

On the oppressive strands of the Bible regarding the position and status of women and destructive patriarchal readings of those texts, unchallenged by a hermeneutic of suspicion, liberation, and inclusion, Oduyoye is right of course, and her pointed critique of the dismal failure of African theologians in this regard and our complicity in this ongoing evil is completely justified. Her argument emphasizes the need for strong, faithful prophetic witness against patriarchy, for such a liberative and inclusive biblical interpretation that would serve the liberation of women.[34]

However, the point I want to make here is a different one, in reference to "the voice in the wilderness." We have become used to reading the reference to "a voice crying in the wilderness" in Isaiah 40 as the prophetic voice of desperation, crying out in isolation and rejection, not heard nor heeded. But I suggest that rightly speaking, it is not so much the prophet who is in the wilderness, isolated and rejected, crying out a message nobody hears. It is, rather, the people who are in the wilderness, mired in hopelessness, confusion, and self-destruction, cast there by the powers who dominate their lives, who fear the dreams and hopes of the people for freedom, dignity and joy and therefore do whatever is necessary to crush those hopes. The prophet *joins* the people in the wilderness, standing with them in their loneliness and desolation, in solidarity and hope, seeking with them renewal of their hope in God and faith in the promises of God, knowing that the God of the wilderness is the God of the exodus and of freedom. Just because the people have been banished to the wilderness and their dreams of freedom and justice outlawed, does not mean that their faith and hopes have been destroyed: it is in the wilderness where Yahweh meets them, as Yahweh met Hagar, restored her hopes and her life as well as that of her child. So the point is not so much that the powerful ignore the voice—it is more that the *people*, in their destitution, can now hear that voice and be "comforted."

That is why Isaiah 40 does not begin with judgment directed to the mighty and the powerful, but with words of comfort spoken "tenderly" to the people, lost, bewildered, and afraid as they are. It marks a new beginning: the prophet announces the ways in which Yahweh will return justice to Yahweh's people. They have been roaming in the wilderness too long. "Enough!" Yahweh says. It is now time to speak comfort to the heart of Jerusalem. In sublime inversion, "Jerusalem" is here not the seat of the mighty and powerful where the subjugation of the people is plotted and where the powerful elites strove so mightily to imitate the ways of empire. Jerusalem is the city of the dream of God: city of justice and shalom, where the glory of God's justice shall be revealed, in this moment feared and rejected by the powerful, but alive and cherished in the hearts of the people. The people who believed that their banishment and suffering were God's punishment for their sins, that they suffered because they have somehow done something wrong; they shall no longer be punished for the crimes of the powerful. They have received "double," more than they deserve, now they will receive a double portion of God's compassionate justice. Now the Lord is about to turn that disjointed situation around. It is "beyond fathoming," the powerful do not understand it, but the powerless and the wearied do, and they "are strengthened" (vv. 28, 29).

Then the voice of the prophet cries out: "In the wilderness"—in this place of desolation and hopelessness, of despair and loneliness, where you have come to believe that Yahweh has forgotten and forsaken you, where the powers hold sway—"prepare the way of the Lord!" Then follow the ever captivating, hope-giving words in vv. 4–5, now in our minds forever linked not only to Isaiah but to Georg Handel whose ebullient, majestic music, and Martin Luther King Jr., whose soaring, hope-filled voice that last night of his life, captured the heart of Isaiah's prophetic intent:

> Every valley shall be lifted up,
> And every mountain and hill be made low;
> the uneven ground shall become level,
> and the rough places a plain.
> Then the glory of the LORD shall be revealed,
> And all people shall see it together.

For the first time we hear of the One who will not grow faint or weary (40:28), and in 42:4 we hear that that is so because the chosen Servant will not rest until justice is established in all the earth. The wilderness shall be tamed and overcome; where there is no way God will make a way—a *highway*. But not a highway for kings and emperors and their armies to travel on, on their way to conquer more lands, destroy more lives, subject more peoples to their brutal rule, but *the way of the Lord.* That is, the way of justice, of peace and freedom, the way Yahweh had intended for all God's children, the way of shalom. The prophet does not bemoan her loneliness and isolation, the prophet sees what is at present unimaginable: in the wilderness, a place of utter desolation and oppression, to where the people, their hopes and dreams and faith have been banished, meant to wither and die; there, in *that* place, the glory of Yahweh's compassionate justice shall be revealed, and *all flesh*, even those who now sit on thrones of power, oppression, and domination, shall see it. *Together,* at the same time as it is seen by the little ones of God. For one it shall be a judgment; for the other it shall be a vindication and a revelation of God's glory.

So that cry in the wilderness is not a cry of resignation, desperation, and self-pity because no one hears. It is a cry of defiant joy, of hopeful resistance. This time the shouts of "Make way!" are not to prepare the way for the lords of this earth with their chariots and garrisons; it is for the way of the LORD who comes to set the captives free. *Freedom is coming*, we sang during the struggle, *Oh yes, I know!* It shall come to pass, "for the mouth of the LORD has spoken." The One "who comes with might" will not oppress, humiliate, or destroy, but "will feed his flock like a shepherd; gather the lambs in his arms and carry them in his bosom, and gently lead the mother sheep" (40:11).

And not only shall the chosen One not grow weary or faint until justice is established, but all those "who wait upon the LORD shall renew their strength, they shall mount up with wings like eagles, they shall run and not be weary, they shall walk and not faint" (40:31). Strengthened by their faith and the vision of God's glory, they themselves shall run toward the fulfillment of justice. The image of the soaring eagle is not one of heavenly escapism, lifting up God's people above all reality. Nor is it an image of power and might intended to threaten, intimidate, and instill fear in the way empires of all times have employed this image and appropriated it for themselves. It is an image of renewed, emboldened agency. It is the weak and powerless who shall be empowered and "strengthened" (Is. 40:29).

"All flesh is grass," the voice cries. Again that "*all flesh*." Even those who think themselves immortal, who revel in their might and power, who trample upon the heads of the poor, who burn the dreams of the powerless to ashes and scatter them on the altars of self-gratification. *All flesh,* even those who claim greatness and "beauty," that is, unsurpassed glory and majesty, who act as if the lives of the downtrodden do not matter and can be snuffed out by one word. They are all like grass and shall wither like grass; like the flowers of the field they shall fade and die, and their greatness shall be no more. What remains is the Word of the Lord.

For ever. And that Word shall reveal the truth about the mighty, the great, and the powerful. God's promises will stand for the generations to come. No, the voice in the wilderness is not one that depicts despair, isolation, and rejection. It is the voice of hope undaunted, dreams rejuvenated, and faith renewed. That voice may be ignored, ridiculed, and detested by the powerful, but it is heard by the people and the people rejoice; it is heard by Yahweh, and Yahweh hears, sees, and acts.

That Sunday in January 1934, Dietrich Bonhoeffer saw the darkness that lay ahead for Germany, the church, and for himself, but he found a way to point the people to what really matters. He was the voice in the wilderness, speaking to the heart of God's people:

> The triumphal procession of truth and justice, the triumphal procession of God and his Scriptures through the world, drags in the wake of the chariot of victory a train of prisoners in chains. May he at the last bind us to his triumphal carriage so that, although in bonds oppressed, we may participate in his victory.[35]

But still a nagging question persists: what do we do with this? Is this not mere triumphalism pure and simple, the spiritual escapism of someone who rejoices in a delusionary victory of his own making because the struggle seems so long, so hard, and so hopeless? We should note, however, that Bonhoeffer is not speaking of the triumph of the struggle as if Hitler did not exist. Neither is he speaking of the triumph of the church. The triumphant church of Bonhoeffer's times is the "violet church" of the German Christians, "stamping their feet like mad" when Nazi loyalist Bishop Otto Dibelius speaks;[36] the church on the march with the Nazis, the church that shouts *Sieg, Heil!* and "*Gott mit uns!*" The church Bonhoeffer represents is the church under persecution. This is not a declaration of victory; it is not even a triumph of the vindication of prophetic witness: the prophet who speaks here would soon go back to Germany, to a life unimagined till now. He would, within ten years, die on the gallows even as the guns of the Allied forces could be heard just outside Berlin. It is, rather, an expression of the audacious hope of faith, the conviction of things not seen. He speaks of the "triumphal procession of truth and justice," a dream he would never see realized, but speaks of as though he could see it, like the prophet in the wilderness.

As Dietrich Bonhoeffer hears God's voice in London, hunting him down as God did with Jeremiah, Bonhoeffer pins his hopes on the "triumphal procession of truth and justice." That procession "drags in its wake" the prisoners in chains, those prophets who tried in vain to escape God's calling, who knew that for them there is no option but to follow God. We are not the triumphant troops—we follow "bound" to God's triumphal carriage. In that humble walk with God there are no certainties, no assurances, no guarantees—except the fragile faith that in the end God's truth and justice will triumph. And for that reason, we build, in the desert, a high way for our God, even though we ourselves may not live long enough to walk on it. Meanwhile, we walk in the way of the Lord. For the true prophet that must be enough.

6

Speaking Truth to the Tower: Kairos, Dissent, and Prophetic Speech

Kairos and Crisis

The gift of a kairos consciousness, I have argued above, is that it gives us the possibility to discern the signs of the times, to recognize a situation as a crisis that could be, or is in fact, devastating for the community. In many ways, the crisis is precipitated, created by the greed and indifference of the powerful. The crisis is to their benefit: they profit from it, hence they refuse to recognize it as a crisis. The prophet of God, on the other hand, recognizes the situation as a crisis because of her kairos consciousness, which allows her to see the situation through the eyes of the suffering, the weak, and the defenseless and as a result of her walking humbly with God. In this chapter the tower from the story of the Tower of Babel serves as a metaphor for the powers and principalities with which prophetic witness has to contend. The crisis presents itself in contradictory terms, such as T. Walter Herbert calls the Iraq war: a "catastrophic success," a devastating crisis for the citizens of Iraq but hugely profitable for those who instigated and waged this war, yet with long-term moral consequences equally as devastating for them.[1]

The Bible offers a premier example of such a crisis engulfing the world, swallowing up even the mighty Egyptian empire and the way it was made to benefit the rich and powerful: the famine described intermittently in Genesis 41–47, and specifically its effects on Egypt in Genesis 47:13–26. It is a crisis that devastates the poor and vulnerable, but it is a crisis from which the powerful in Egypt profit mightily. In all this Joseph, by this time a powerful prince of the Egyptian Empire without whose consent "no one shall lift up hand or foot in all the land of Egypt," (Gen. 42:44) plays a central, and ultimately shameful role as he turns this crisis for the poor into a seemingly endless profit-making venture for the empire, and the economic emergency measures meant to deal with the crisis into a lifetime punishment of dispossession and enslavement.[2] Joseph, in his role as representative of the empire, sees only the opportunities for exploitation and control. The true prophet, however, understands this moment as a kairos, a call to discernment, conversion, commitment, and action.

But those who have this discernment go against the grain, find themselves in opposition to the official interpretation of events, having to challenge the official narrative, in contention with the powers that rule from the Tower. This turns the kairos moment into a moment of confrontation; a crisis, to be sure, but a crisis of a different kind. Faithful prophetic witness cannot avoid this. The martyred Archbishop of El Salvador, Oscar Romero, understood this perfectly:

> A church that does not provoke any crisis, a gospel that does not unsettle, a word of God that doesn't get under anyone's skin, a word of God that doesn't touch the real sin of society in which it is being proclaimed, what gospel is that?[3]

Indeed: that is both the question and the challenge: a gospel that does not provoke a crisis within the crisis that is being denied, *because* the crisis is being denied to the detriment of those who suffer; a gospel that does not unsettle and disturb the comfortable in its call for justice and shalom, that does not get under power's skin, however thick that might be; what gospel is that? A crisis denied cannot be addressed, because it "does not exist." The crisis the prophet provokes is a crisis of conscience. I speak of a conscience that we do not of ourselves possess, but that is awakened in us by the promises of God; the conscience that calls upon those promises for God's sake and for the sake of the people. It is the conscience vulnerable to those who suffer and who are most easily wounded. It is not just knowing about right and wrong, it is being touched and moved by things we are normally inured to; not just the suffering of others, but their hunger for justice, their cries for freedom, their longings for dignity and human fulfillment.[4]

I have previously made the point that a constant—and crucial—feature of these situations is the desire on the part of those in power for the consensus of uniformity. Everyone is required to see things the way the powerful do; no dissent is allowed. The crisis is either presented as normal—this is the way things just are—or as unchallengeable and therefore unchangeable and irreversible. Often it is presented as something of a nature only properly understood by the experts, the elite interpreters of the dreams of the powerful against which the dreams of the powerless, the dreams of justice and freedom, stand no chance. They will tell the masses what to feel, think, and do. That is when prophetic witness, in its turn, provokes a crisis, albeit a different kind of crisis, because it turns the crisis into a kairos moment by identifying, exposing, and challenging the fables emanating from the Tower. In such situations two powers face each other: the power of manufactured consent and the power of prophetic dissent.

To focus our discussions on these issues, I propose, before we examine the story of the Tower of Babel, that we do a closer reading of two biblical examples of prophetic witness where crises were recognized as kairos moments of dissent and intervention. We will first pay attention to Micaiah, son of Imlah, then the prophet Amos, and finally turn to the story of the Tower of Babel. We will explore the crisis Micaiah is confronted with as a test of prophetic faithfulness and truth-speaking; we will read Amos in light of what I see as the similarities between his times and our present situation of global apartheid, and we will examine the story of the Tower of Babel with the issue of prophetic dissent in mind.

The obvious and superb example of prophetic dissent in the Bible is of course the prophet Elijah and his stand against Ahab, king of Israel and his wife Jezebel, plus the 450 priests of Baal in the service of the royal court. In the end though, the victory on Mount Carmel is drowned in bloodshed and a cloud of ambiguity remains hanging over that strange and disturbing day. Elijah's Carmel victory ends in a heart-rending scene under that solitary bush in the wilderness where he virtually gives up on life as he seems to give up on his prophetic calling, which in turn causes a dramatic confrontation with Yahweh who seems equally adamant not to allow the prophet to renounce his calling.[5] So for the prophet the risk lies by no means only in confrontations with earthly powers. The prophet, as we have seen with Elijah and Jeremiah and Bonhoeffer, has Yahweh to reckon with.

If the confrontation with Ahab and Jezebel presented Elijah with a difficult situation, however, the situation of another prophet, Micaiah ben Imlah, was even more complex and challenging (1 Kings 22:1–28).[6] Elijah was set against a wicked king supported by priests of Baal—not representing the God of Israel. Micaiah was confronted, to begin with, with that same wicked king, Ahab, this time bent on war, in the story simply referred to as "the king of Israel." But the situation is more complex. Also in the picture is a well-intentioned and cautious king, Jehoshaphat, seemingly more concerned about and open to "the word from the Lord" than his counterpart, yet also very open to the persuasions of Ahab: "I am as you are; my people are your people, my horses are your horses" (1 Kings 22:4). On top of that, Micaiah was facing the joint religious power of no less than 400 court prophets, who claimed and were convinced that *they*, not Micaiah, had heard, understood, and correctly interpreted the word of Yahweh. Theirs are the voices the king is eager to hear. Micaiah's voice, on the other hand, is offensive and too disturbing; an irritant.

So Micaiah faces several formidable obstacles in the forces allied against him. First, there is the power of a king eager for war, not in self-defense, but out of wounded personal and national pride and the desire for political hegemony and military primacy in the region.[7] The question Ahab puts to his advisers is rhetorical: he does not expect to be gainsaid; he has his mind already made up. Second, Micaiah has against him the nationalistic, patriotic fervor of the nation whipped up by the king in the double-edged phrasing of the question: "Do you know that Ramoth-gilead belongs to us, yet we are doing nothing to take it out of the hand of the king of Aram?" (v. 3). He means to shame his people, portraying them as weak, lacking in pride and courage, allowing the enemy to "take" what is theirs, they themselves being too cowardly to "take it [back]." It is the perfect patriotic pitch, even if, following Leo Honor, it is a lie, very much like the lies told by the Bush administration and the government of Tony Blair in the United Kingdom as justification for the invasion and occupation of Iraq. Third, there are the prophets of the court who offer religious legitimacy and the blessing of God upon the war effort. They represent, in contrast with Micaiah, the "moral majority." Our storyteller makes sure we get the point: "About four hundred of them." It is as if the 450 Baal prophets killed by Elijah have returned in full force, and with a vengeance. They offer an overwhelming force of religious sanctification of war and their certitude lies heavily in the scale; leaves no room for doubt or hesitation or debate: "Go up; for the Lord will give it into the hand of the king" (v. 6). The rapid pace of the narrative underscores Ahab's haste to go to war. The political issues are not in question. What is now introduced is the question of the validity of the prophetic word.[8]

In the discussion of the possibility of war, Ahab urges Jehoshaphat, king of Judah, to join him in the campaign. Jehoshaphat, not unwilling, but not convinced either despite the unison of voices claiming divine authority, insists: "Is there no other prophet of the LORD here...?" (v. 7). Jehoshaphat does not mean one other prophet of Yahweh besides the 400 prophets of Yahweh present. Hebrew Bible scholar Jerome Walsh points out that the prophets do not name the "Lord" in whose name they prophesy until v. 11 when they pointedly prophesy in the name of Yahweh. In Ahab's court, Walsh says, there was a continued tendency to blur the worship of Yahweh with worship to Baal and Asherah, "even to merge them into a polytheistic system." The point is superbly captured when Walsh raises the question, "Are Ahab's prophets equally at the service of Yahweh and of Baal or Ashera, depending on which deity the king wishes to consult at any given moment?"[9] Jehoshaphat already seems to discern this in the diplomatic emphasis he inserts into his first question in verse 5: "Inquire, pray, for the word of the LORD *today*."[10] The NRSV, along with most modern translations read, "Inquire first [before we go any further] for the word of the LORD." But that translation misses the subtlety in Jehoshaphat's emphasis "*today*," implying, "Even if you are not generally accustomed to inquire the word of the Lord, kindly do it on *this* occasion."[11] Within the context of this conversation that emphasis is not unimportant.

The king makes no secret of his feelings toward this "other" prophet. Apparently this Micaiah son of Imlah has a reputation: the king "hates" him. He never has "anything good" to say about the king. He prophesies only "disaster" (v. 8). Notice that Ahab does not mention Micaiah by name, even though he knows very well who the prophet is. But, more pointedly, he does not call him a prophet. He disdainfully refers to him as "one other." This could be mere pettiness on Ahab's part, but more likely it is a verbal preemptive strike, that particular way the powerful have of speaking of someone who displeases them, whose word is a priori to be considered worthless. The sneering tone of voice is not hard to imagine; one can virtually see the flaring of the nostrils, the turning down of the corners of the mouth, the dismissive wave of the hand. While the word "hate" may be too strong a translation as some maintain, the narrator nonetheless uses a word that clearly spells out Ahab's utter disdain for Micaiah; the animosity runs thick through the sentence.[12] Ahab uses the emphatic personal pronoun: "*I* hate him," perhaps expecting his personal disgust of Micaiah to be strong enough argument to persuade Jehoshaphat.

While Micaiah is being summoned with all haste, Zedekiah, apparently the leader of the four hundred, dramatizes his prophecy of victory by parading around with two horns of iron: "Thus says the LORD: with these you shall gore the Arameans until they are destroyed" (v. 11). Here, for the first time, Yahweh is mentioned, perhaps to add to the strength of the argument made to Jehoshaphat? But knowing what we do about the Ahab court religion, and understanding the uneven relationship between Ahab and Jehoshaphat evident in the text, is there an element of condescension here? "If that is what it takes to convince you, we can provide that also." So another layer is stacked up against Micaiah: the dramatic, frenetic presentation is a graphic prophetic activity not as such in need of words, although in this case Zedekiah strengthens the action by an oracle guaranteeing in Yahweh's name Ahab's victory over Aram.[13] It is a powerful tool, meant not just to impress the kings but to sway those in the public present there who might be wavering or are not yet entirely convinced. It shows his confidence, it reinforces the "word of the LORD," and it further inflames the listeners. No doubt, as a symbol of invincible aggressiveness it is also meant to simultaneously undermine Jehoshaphat's doubts and boost his low levels of confidence.

All along, the narrator not only builds up the tension, he makes us see the multiple difficulties Micaiah will face when he appears before the royal thrones. He reveals that the kings are not having this discussion in private chambers in the palace, but in public, in full view of the people, "at the threshing floor at the entrance of the gate of Samaria," a large, easily accessible, heavily trafficked area, no doubt deliberately chosen. And not only that. They are both "sitting on their thrones, arrayed in their robes," in full royal splendor and in full display of their royal power. Should Micaiah resist and dissent, it will be a thoroughly public rebuke, and hence not easily ignorable and forgivable. Zedekiah may have taken the dramatic lead, but, we are assured, all the prophets were prophesying "with one accord" (v. 13). Added to the power of the royal display and the public nature of the event then, is the power of the unanimity of religious opinion. "The words of the prophets with one accord are favorable to the king..." (22:13). It is pressure of formidable proportions.

And that is what the king's messenger is telling Micaiah as he fetches him. He does not threaten Micaiah. Rather, he urges him to conform, not to break the unity, not to challenge the other prophets, his colleagues; not to displease the king, not to shame the king in front of his royal visitor and his people, not to undermine the war effort, not to discourage the nation. "Let your word be like the word of them..." (v. 13). The messenger understands the pressure and the consequences of dissent and offers a word of wisdom. His is a reasonable request, made out of concern for the national good while simultaneously it is also good for Micaiah personally. Micaiah must now not think of himself only. Don't be proud, he seems to say, give in, you might even redeem your reputation. It cannot hurt to be a bit more popular among your colleagues. Now is not the time for prophetic bravado. Ahab may have been lenient in the past, but today such recklessness would be foolish. If Micaiah would only listen, it could be what our modern negotiators call a "win-win situation." If everyone is in agreement, the prophet should be too. Such holy consensus confirming so much earthly power must surely be of God. But that too, is a fable from the Tower: the prophet is always haunted by the question: *which* God, *whose* God, are they speaking of here?

It is then that Micaiah makes his intentions clear. A word from the LORD that seeks to please the king, persuade his visitor that what he suspects to be wrong is in fact right; a word that legitimizes the false prophecies of prophets on the king's payroll, that misleads the people into believing that this planned disaster in Ahab's mind is God's holy war—that might sound like good news for all concerned, but what kind of gospel is that? So Micaiah intends to provoke a crisis: "Only what the LORD says to me, *that* shall I speak" (v. 14). He displays the firm resolve one expects from the true prophet of God. "With a few bold strokes," writes Hebrew Bible scholar Leo Honor, "the author has depicted a great character, true and steadfast in his conviction, who was prepared to be different and who dared to stand alone."[14]

But the story comes up with two surprising moments. In front of the king, facing the array of powers stacked up against him, the pressures seem to overcome Micaiah and he appears to knuckle under: "Go up and triumph," Micaiah tells Ahab echoing the exact words of the majority, "the LORD will give it into the hand of the king" (v. 15). Ahab, however, promptly rejects this compliant response from Micaiah, and that is the second surprise: "How many times must I make you swear to tell me nothing but the truth in the name of the LORD?"

Does the king detect a sarcastic undertone that irritates him because Micaiah has done this before?[15] Does he simply want Micaiah to vindicate him in front of his guest? Ahab seems almost pleased that he was proved right regarding Micaiah's attitude. "Did I not tell you . . . ?"[16] Does Ahab want Micaiah to tell him only the truth when he speaks in the name of Yahweh?[17] All of this may be true; perhaps none of it matters. It's not just that Ahab is no fool: he senses when he is being lied to. More to the point is the question: does Ahab really care? It is not mere petulance directed at Micaiah we are seeing here; it is a dead serious confrontation with the God who seems to cross him every time. In the end he *does* go to war, no matter what Micaiah says—or God wants—he has no interest in the word of Yahweh if that word stands in the way of his own intentions. He does not *want* to hear the truth he adjures Micaiah to speak.

Pearls Before the Swine?

The truth of the matter is that the word of the LORD is wasted on him. This is an important issue for prophetic witness and one that seems to arise time and again. It calls for both critical discernment and extraordinary courage. It is what Dietrich Bonhoeffer understood so well in his objections to the proposal of talks between Karl Barth and Adolf Hitler as we have seen: "At the present time, I believe that any discussion between Hitler and Barth would be quite hopeless and, indeed, no longer to be sanctioned. Hitler has shown himself quite clearly for what he is, and the church ought to know with whom it has to reckon . . . " "Hitler ought not to and cannot hear; he is *obdurate,* and as such he ought to compel *us* to listen—the question is thus turned completely around." Bonhoeffer strengthens his point: "Isaiah didn't go to Sennacherib either."[18]

Hitler "is not in a position to listen," Bonhoeffer argues, not because the church has put him in that position, but because that is the position which secures his power—a position that he cannot give up, has no intention of giving up. He will talk to the church, not because he is desirous to hear the Word of God, but to compel the church to listen to *him*; not so that the Word could challenge and change him, but so that he could bend the Word of God to his will. So from the start it should be clear, Bonhoeffer argues, exposing and debunking the fable from the Tower that Hitler could be persuaded: the church does not go to testify, the church goes to listen. Bonhoeffer then stresses the point in two significant ways; first pointing out that the church, in trying to speak to Hitler, is naïve. The effort to "speak" to Hitler is "a laughable failure to understand what is really happening." Second, that at this point in history, it is not only that Hitler cannot hear; no, Hitler *"ought not to hear."* The exercise as a whole is pointless. Then comes the real point: "It is we who ought to be converted, not Hitler."[19]

I have seen this personally, and far too often, in the rounds of discussions between the church and the apartheid state or its religious agents, and more recently with the African National Congress government in South Africa and *its* religious agents: when do talks with the powers that be become senseless? When does what the church insists on calling "reconciliation" become just another form of political pietism? When is Christian witness pure legitimation of evil, or strengthening and abetting the evil doer in his evil? When does the church, in its endless willingness to be seen to talk to those in power in order not to lose their ear and the church's access to that power or to government largess, or to ingratiate itself with the public, simply end up standing in the way of justice? When do the words of the Gospel become pearls before the swine?

I suggest that this is what Micaiah knows. He has gone through this before; why should he throw pearls before swine? He does not stop prophesying God's truth. But he does stop the conversation with Ahab because it is a conversation merely meant to legitimize Ahab's power and bless Ahab's obduracy. He might please Ahab, or find approval with his court approved colleagues or applause with the court adoring public. But the question is: what about God? Ahab *knows* what Yahweh requires; hence his irritated response to Micaiah: "How many times must I tell you...?" A kairos consciousness is a consciousness that discerns this moment as well: the moment when the church no longer indulges in fruitless conversations with the powerful on whom the Word of the Yahweh is wasted. It is a moment to realize that at that point the Word is not engaged in order to challenge, confront, and transform, but in order to legitimize the obduracy that seeks to disempower the Word. The aim of that conversation is not conversion but justification; not the inducement of repentance before God but the blessing of rebellion against God. Do not throw pearls before the swine, Jesus warns.

When Archbishop Desmond Tutu was invited to a corporate lunch in Johannesburg to honor former British prime minister Tony Blair on September 2, 2012, he declined, stating that he could not in good conscience share a platform with someone who, like former president George W. Bush, ought to be charged with crimes against humanity before the International Criminal Court as the international community, applying different, and double, standards, charged African leaders such as Presidents Uhuru Kenyatta of Kenya and Charles Taylor of Liberia. Blair and Bush, Tutu maintained, "fabricated the grounds to behave like playground bullies and drive us further apart. They have driven us to the edge of a precipice where we now stand..." Pointing to the utter devastation of the war for the people of Iraq, the consequences for the world and the damage done to human relationships, Tutu argues that "leadership and morality are indivisible."[20]

The reactions to Tutu's decision were swift and damning. Journalist Giles Fraser, writing in the *Guardian* one day later, severely criticized Tutu, not for the Archbishop's argument, but for "the empty chair."[21] After all, Fraser argues, "Justice is about truth and reconciliation and not about the intoxicating serotonin of retribution." And not only did Tony Blair sit down with the Irish Republican Army and Mandela with apartheid's F. W. De Klerk, but "Jesus was often attacked for sitting down with those that morally respectable people had decided were beyond the pale." In the end, Tutu, unlike Jesus, was not interested in reconciliation, but was "about protecting his own innocence."

But that is the fable trumpeted from the Tower. Leaving Fraser's notion of "truth" completely aside, I should begin by pointing out, even though it is totally redundant in my view, that to accuse Desmond Tutu of reveling in the "intoxicating serotonin of retribution" is as far-fetched as it is preposterous. It is also utterly deceitful, deliberately turning the truth on its head. It is one more way of perpetuating the lie that sought to justify the 2003 Iraq war in the first place. The powerful rulers of two Western nations who not only made war against the people of Iraq in relentless retribution for a terrible crime the people of Iraq did not commit, in the process lying to their own public representatives, their people and the international community, shamelessly flouting international law, themselves committed a despicable act. But then, on top of it all, they also allowed the deliberate, shameful public spectacle of the death of Saddam Hussein, designed to shock and awe and terrify. In doing this, with astonishing glee before the whole world (who can forget George W. Bush's "Mission Accomplished!" triumphalism?) they are exactly the ones who were reveling in the "intoxicating serotonin" of retribution.

The Iraq war, as well as that in Afghanistan, and Yemen, and Pakistan, screams retribution. But such are the fables that emanate from the towers of power, as we shall see. When Tutu refuses to share a platform with Tony Blair and gives public testimony as to the reasons why, he *is*, in the most profound way, speaking truth to the Tower. And reminding Blair of his war crimes along with George Bush is not calling for retribution, it is prophetic judgment. It is calling for accountability, reminding the powerful that decisions have consequences. It is confronting Blair with wrongs the (Western) world continues to close its eyes to, because this world too, like Fraser, believes that Tony Blair, for some reason, "is no Charles Taylor."

Fraser's logic also believes that the people of Iraq are not worth the justice, nor the truth, nor the reconciliation Fraser claims he believes in and so glibly invokes. Tutu is not defending Taylor; far from it. He is simply asking why Blair's status (white, Western, former leader of a powerful Western nation) should excuse him from taking responsibility for crimes others (not white, not Western, not as powerful) are being called to account for. Tutu is protesting against "the powerful who can throw about their weight so callously and with so much impunity."[22] He is lifting his voice against the Western world that has not only remained largely silent about these war crimes and taken no actions against the high-placed perpetrators, but has in the process made the active instigators of the war, like former vice President Dick Cheney, first a much wealthier man and now is turning him into a media celebrity pontificating on the advantages of torture and the virtues of yet another war in Iraq. Tutu is publicly raising questions about the honesty and integrity of the processes of international law and in acting in the way he did, he is confronting not just Tony Blair (as in a private, one on one conversation) but the international community as well, with the call for justice, integrity, and equality. This is precisely what reconciliation and justice are all about. Fraser's idea of reconciliation knows no accountability or justice, let alone remorse and repentance. It is too cheap to be called reconciliation.

Tutu understands much better than Fraser that costly reconciliation does not lie in piling the costs on the bent shoulders of the powerless who already labor and are heavy-laden, whose burdens refuse them rest for their souls, but in the radical risks we take on behalf of others. He also knows, much better than Fraser that those in positions of power and privilege cannot define reconciliation nor affect it on behalf of others over whom they have power. Reconciliation, like forgiveness, cannot be defined and pronounced from the thrones of the powerful. It flows from the wounds of the crucified, and for forgiveness to be meaningful it has to be seen to flow from woundedness. Like Rizpah in that matchless story in 2 Samuel 21, Tutu, in his protest, shifts the focus away from the powerful, their duplicity and manipulation of faith and of God, to the victims of that power, and holds up their plight and their suffering as holy before God.[23]

Tutu does another thing. He speaks, not so much on behalf of the institutions of international criminal justice, but rather on behalf of the ravaged, devastated, silenced Iraqi people whose lives are precious in God's sight if not in the sight of those who call mass murder for the sake of profits and oil "making the world safe for democracy." That is the truth Tony Blair refuses to hear, but it is the truth without which genuine reconciliation is not possible. Like God in Micah, Tutu cries out on their behalf, in lamentation and outrage, and on behalf of the powerless, voiceless masses of the world whose fate, on a daily basis, lies in the hands of powerful men like Tony Blair and George Bush for whom nothing is impossible, because it is "in the power of their hand to do so," as we have heard Micah say. To lie about the reason for the war, Tutu is saying, is to seek the cause of the war with the people of Iraq whose suffering, first under Saddam Hussein (with whom the West made common cause for so long because it suited them) and now in the aftermath of the war, has still not ended.

In truth therefore, it is not his own, but *their* innocence Desmond Tutu is protecting even while he is relentlessly unmasking the pseudo-innocence of Western leaders and nations and their minions in the Western mainstream media. Tutu discerns the truth that the suffering of the people now profits the Western powers, same as their suffering under Saddam Hussein earlier profited the West. Fraser, like all servants of the empire, seeks to turn the truth on its head, blaming the victims of Western aggression for their own suffering. But it is not Tony Blair who is here made the victim of Tutu's supposed "intoxication" with retribution. It is the people of Iraq who are the real victims of Blair's and Bush's lust for power, war, and profits.[24] Tutu is making sure the world does not forget.

As I write this, Iraq is embroiled in an increasingly vicious internecine war. T. Walter Herbert's description of the Iraq war as "catastrophic success" continues to be vindicated.[25] Mr. Blair, seeing his ongoing role in the politics of the Middle East, has complained quite sharply that he is "unfairly blamed" for causing the current crisis in Iraq and that if Saddam had still been in power Iraq would be just as unstable. Tony Blair, writes journalist Juan Cole, is perhaps deliberately missing the point:

> His invasion of Iraq was illegal and based on deception and propaganda. That was what was wrong with it. A Quagmire that is the fruit of illegality and fraud is the worst…Blair's Attorney General, Lord Goldsmith,

> warned him in spring 2003 that there were no grounds in international law for a British invasion of Iraq, and that he and his government could face trial at the Hague if he went through with it. Blair hid the memo, quite dishonestly, from his cabinet.[26]

Tutu is "unlike Jesus" Fraser goes on to state, because Jesus sat down with those that "morally respectable people" thought were "beyond the pale." It is the problem with much of Western, liberal Christianity: it sounds biblical, and pious, but it isn't. It is not the message from the Gospel; it is a fable from the Tower. It is merely, I have written elsewhere, "the political pietism that protects the interests of the powerful," that presents us with an unbiblical, a de-politicized, de-justicized, spiritualized, disempowered, domesticated Jesus, meek in the face of the powerful, rendered speechless by the "honor" of merely being in their presence.[27] It is simply not true that Jesus "sat down" with everybody. Jesus did not sit down with the High Priest, or the Jerusalem elites; he simply spoke prophetic truth to their power as he did in Matthew 23. Before Pontius Pilate, Jesus refused even to say a single word (Jn 19:9). When he finally did speak to Pilate it was not to engage him in discussion but simply to remind him that, whatever Pilate might have thought, he had no power over him.

Rather than rushing to the palace to ingratiate himself with Herod when he heard that Herod had threatened his life and would snuff it out just as he had John the Baptist's, Jesus sent the king a curt, straightforward message: "Go and tell that fox for me: Listen, I am casting out demons and performing cures today and tomorrow, and on the third day I finish my work" (Lk 13:31, 32). In essentially the same message to John the Baptist in prison, the words were a prophetic consolation, an assurance that the liberating work of the Kingdom of God will continue despite John's predicament. Here, however, the words are words of defiance and resistance, a declaration that despite the threats to his life, Jesus will not sit down and negotiate with the powers of evil, or compromise his mission. It is enough to let them know that God's work will continue and God's will for God's people will be fulfilled. *Despite* Herod's power the power of the reign of God shall be seen: the lame *shall* walk, the blind *shall* see, the lepers *shall* be cleansed, the deaf *shall* hear, the dead *shall* be raised up, and the poor *shall* hear the good news that God has joined them in their struggle for justice (Matt. 11:4–5). Herod and his Roman masters, like the demons, will be cast out. That is all they need to know. For Jesus cozy chats with Pilate and lunch with Herod was not how he filled his days.

However, Jesus *did* sit down with tax collectors and prostitutes and lepers; with the despised and stigmatized of society; he did break bread with those not deemed worthy by the privileged elites. In opting for the poor, suffering, and marginal people of his time, write the authors of *The Zimbabwean Kairos Document*, as they seek to offer hope to their people in their struggles for justice against the increasingly oppressive Mugabe regime, Jesus sided with the struggling majority rather than the powerful political, economic, and religious leaders. He was so moved with compassion for the suffering outcasts that he made a deliberate choice to join them in their marginalization and in their struggles against it. In so doing Jesus "became an outcast himself, someone considered by the 'respectable' people of his time as cursed."[28] But these are hardly the Blairs and the Bushes of this world, the hard-nosed power mongers who know nothing of repentance or remorse or forgiveness, but who nonetheless claim innocence as if it were their right. It is a twisted, unholy logic to reel in the despised and rejected of the world who sought refuge and salvation in the love of Jesus in order to justify the arrogant intransigence of the powerful whose crimes were committed against the powerless and defenseless *in the name of Jesus*.[29] The Jesus Fraser likens Tutu to, is the Jesus who speaks only of forgiveness and love, never of justice and judgment; the Jesus who pampers the powerful and privileged, and pacifies the poor and powerless. But we have learned that following Jesus in his forgiveness of injustice means following Jesus in his outrage *at* injustice—*that* is following Jesus in his love.[30]

Jesus occupies the space in the Temple not because he is seeking conversation with the temple elite, but because he is reclaiming it as his *Father's* house, *not* blessing it as the den of thieves the powerful have turned it into. Jesus did not go into the Temple to give legitimacy to the oppression and exploitation the elites were engaged in; he entered the Temple in opposition to their power. Jesus did not at all desire to provide justification for their profitable collaboration with the Roman Empire in the oppression of his people. Tutu was not invited to speak truth to Tony Blair—in that power lunch with the investors of Johannesburg he would not have been given an inch of an opening—he was invited in hopes that he might give legitimacy to Tony Blair, and by extension to those who invited Blair because they profited from his politics. That he refused to do. He instead spoke truth to Blair and the world of power by refusing to sit down and break bread with him, as if the dead and dying children of Iraq whom Blair and Bush had robbed of life and hope and future do not matter. Those who were dead could not break bread with anybody, and those who were living did not have bread to share with anyone. A confined, scripted, polite chat with a glass of champagne in the hand might be a wonderful photo opportunity cherished by a certain type of journalist, but it is not a prophetic moment. Desmond Tutu discerned a kairos moment and turned it into a prophetic crisis.

"Go up and triumph"

At another level though, returning to Micaiah and Ahab, it is also the classic dilemma of the weary prophet: weary of fighting the life-threatening hatred and corrosive indifference of the powerful; weary of the complicity of colleagues who sell out the Word of Yahweh for the mess of pottage offered by royal approval and profitable patronage; weary of running up against the "rhetoric of the barricades"; weary of fighting with God. Micaiah, like Elijah, was "no better than his ancestors," no "great character, true and steadfast" whatever comes. He might have been thinking, "Ahab is going to do what he wants anyway. Let's just get it over with."

Micaiah shows what every true prophet knows: there are moments when one is just too tired of fighting against the odds, too tired of swimming against the stream; too tired of pretending that those moments of feeling like a reed in the wind do not exist. "Go up and triumph," he tells Ahab. He needs to be almost shamed into prophetic truth telling, not by Jehoshaphat, but by Ahab. Even Ahab instinctively knows that carrying fables to the Tower is not a prophet's calling. It is Micaiah's kairos moment.

But it is not really Ahab who makes him tell the truth. It is Yahweh who is quietly insisting. When in verse 15 he utters his compliant oracle, Micaiah simply begins, "Go up and triumph." In response to Ahab's derisive unbelief, he discloses a vision he did not share at first: he sees "Israel scattered..." Now, however, after Ahab's sarcastic jibe in his aside to Jehoshaphat—"Did I not tell you...?"—Micaiah utters the authoritative word: "Therefore, hear the word of Yahweh..." In response to Micaiah's first truthful oracle, Ahab, in verse 18, dismisses his words as simply a sign of personal animosity: this "prophet" is not to be taken seriously. He can have no objective appraisal of the situation; he is blinded by personal animosities and knows only doom and gloom. We should read the first word of verse 19 with emphasis, "*Then*"—after Ahab's dismissive "I told you so"—"Micaiah said, therefore..." Micaiah has given in, not to Ahab's contempt, but to Yahweh's insistence: "Hear the word of Yahweh..." He is indeed the true prophet: he does not indulge in carnivalesque future-foretelling; he sees what God sees, what is hidden from the eyes of those blinded by power, arrogance, and hubris. So first, he discloses, he sees Israel, "like sheep without a shepherd..." Ahab, in contrast, does not see, does not hear, and does not listen. He dismisses.

Now however, what Micaiah sees is not Israel in their scattered state. His gaze is transfixed on the Holy One. What he calls attention to first now, is not Ahab's army who should "go home in peace" before disaster strikes, but the awesomeness of the God Ahab dares to ignore and resist: "I saw the LORD sitting on his throne, with all the hosts of heaven beside him . . . " What is conspicuously displayed before him are Ahab and Jehoshaphat, sitting on their royal thrones decked out in splendor, surrounded by their advisors and counselors and hundreds of false prophets. What he *sees,* however, is Yahweh on the throne, "with all the hosts of heaven." Next to that magnificent and awe-inspiring sight, all else fades into insignificance. All earthly splendor and power are reduced to hollow pretentiousness. But this too, Ahab does not see. He does not see that it is this God, not Micaiah, "who has decreed disaster for you" (v. 23). He fights with Micaiah, but actually his battle is with Yahweh, and it is a battle he cannot win. Micaiah knows that he himself is still like a reed in the wind; like Jeremiah he must admit that "all my bones are shaking," (Jer. 23:9). but he dares to speak truth to power because he speaks in the name of a higher power.

So Micaiah speaks truth to power, and as always, it is a word earthly powers cannot stand, nor can it be endured by their paid prophets. Zedekiah hurls insults at Micaiah and strikes him in the face. It is not just about protecting his job or that he is personally peeved. The deeper issue here is the validity and authenticity of prophecy. Who speaks for God? And it is about the religious sanctification of the established order from which he profits. But it is about even more. With prophetic insight and courage Micaiah turns that question around: not only *who* speaks for God, but: for *which* God do you speak? Micaiah declares that the god for whom the 400 claim to speak is not the God of Israel, the God of justice and peace and compassion. And Zedekiah knows it. He reacts even before the king can—so much does he want to impress his master. But his eagerness to please the king proves Micaiah's point: there is a difference between prophetic truth and sycophancy.

The wrath of the king is not far behind, however. Micaiah is imprisoned and on specific royal instructions is kept in that agonizing state of always being on the edge of complete physical hunger: he is to be given the barest minimum to stay alive, "bread of affliction" and "water of affliction." It is more than just the physical torture of withholding nourishment which can drive one mad. It is also a daily reminder that in the eyes of the king his life is not worth much; it is hanging by a thread (v. 27). It is truly an affliction: a torturous uncertainty that plays havoc with the mind.

He will stay there until Ahab "returns in peace." In other words, even though Micaiah explains in as many ways as he can that Ahab's real battle is with Yahweh who has "enticed" him; in effect laid a trap for him: "So you see, [it is] the LORD [who] has decreed disaster for you"—and it is a trap from which Ahab will not escape—still Ahab defiantly insists that he will be victorious in battle and "will return in peace." At this point Ahab does not have to prove that he has power over the prophet—he is done with him. He thinks he has the power that can defy what Yahweh has decreed. The insult that Zedekiah has just screamed at Micaiah, Ahab now hurls in the face of Yahweh. If he could have slapped God he would have.

Still, the reader is given yet another telling glimpse of the man who thinks he can defy the God of Israel: we are allowed to suspect that deep down Ahab knows that the word of truth is ultimately in Micaiah's mouth and it terrifies him. Yet it does not deter him or even make him hesitate. Forever the wily schemer, Ahab comes up with a plan. Ahab decides to go into battle "in disguise," but, he tells Jehoshaphat, "you wear your robes." The narrator stresses the point: "So the king of Israel disguised himself and went into battle" (v. 30). Behind these words the reader discerns the amused question: Disguise himself for whom? To hide from whom? Certainly not from Yahweh who has already decreed disaster for him. The narrator does not amplify, but leaves us to ponder this in utter amazement: is Ahab merely a coward? Is this just monumental stupidity, or does his hubris simply know no end? Even from the man who acted "as if it had been a light thing for him to walk in the sins of Jeroboam, son of Nebat," (1 Kings 16:31) this is breathtaking.

In the end it is Yahweh who wins. The power of Ahab is broken and he dies an ignominious death, "propped up in his chariot," shot by an unknown soldier "who pulled his bow at random." But again, propped up to fool who? The Arameans could not have known it was Ahab, he was in disguise; but they spared Jehoshaphat, dressed in his kingly robes, because he was not Ahab. What the story wants to underscore is that the decree of Yahweh cannot be escaped and Ahab's play at power and cleverness becomes pure, and tragic, absurdity.

Micaiah, however, will see nothing of this. At the end of the prophetic confrontation he disappears from the story and we know nothing more of him. He knows only two things as he goes to jail: Ahab will not listen, and the small flame of resistance that flickered in Jehoshaphat has gone out. For the rest, he has no idea what will happen: what will become of him or whether he will even survive his days of "affliction." He does not know whether his prophecy will come true; he simply has to trust Yahweh: God will be true to God's word. The prophet speaks truth to power, but he knows he is not the rock upon whom everything depends. Through it all it is God who is his rock and his salvation. He himself is like a reed in the wind. Sometimes, that is all the prophet has to work with.

Kairos and the Rivers of Justice

"Nothing we know is sweeter than justice," John Calvin writes in his commentary on Amos, "when everyone gains his own right; for this serves much to preserve peace. Hence nothing can be more gratifying to us, than when uprightness and equity prevail."[31] When justice is not done however, when "they sell the righteous for silver and the needy for a pair of sandals"; when they "trample the head of the poor into the dust of the earth," (Amos 2:6,7) when as a result of perpetual injustice and perpetual impoverishment life becomes bitter as wormwood for the poor and afflicted, then God's judgment, as God's justice in defense of the weak and the wronged, shall be "a violent stream," writes Calvin:

> The LORD will certainly show to you how precious righteousness is. *It shall* therefore *run down* as violent *waters*, as an impetuous *stream*. "Judgement", he says, "shall rush upon you and overwhelm you".[32]

There are good reasons why I find Amos so intriguing a prophet and what he says so resonant with our times of global apartheid, and why it is important and instructive for us to reflect on the message of this prophet. First, Amos presents a relentless contestation of two powers: the power of oppression and the power of justice, the power exercised by the elites of Israel and the power of Yahweh intervening for the powerless, for Amos above all the God of justice. Second, like our world, his world is filled with the incessant rhetoric of domination: the voices of power and privilege, of supremacy and control, of cynical carelessness, dominate this world, drowning out the whispers of fear and cries of suffering which are seemingly only heard by Yahweh. It is the rhetoric of the barricades. The noise of power is backed up by the noise of official religiosity, a civil religion on the one hand providing legitimation for oppression and exploitation, and on the other acting as opiate for the people whose deep need for God's presence was not considered holy but exploited as useful tool for control. Religion flourished in the nation. "The populace thronged the shrines at festival time to practice an elaborate sacrificial ritual. Yahweh was trusted and patronized with presumptuous arrogance."[33] Third, Amos depicts two drastically different worlds: one of abject poverty and unrelenting misery, and another of wealth, comfort, bottomless prosperity, and the endless pursuit of personal happiness at the cost of the life of the poor. In their prosperity they "were immersed, as it were, in their pleasures," writes Calvin, "and satiety, as it ever happens, made them ferocious."[34]

Fourth, Amos' time was celebrated as a time of peace and prosperity. Jeroboam was one of a long line of rulers who in the judgment of the Deuteronomist "did evil in the sight of the LORD" (2 Kings 14:24). Yet under Jeroboam II, Israel knew her best years of prosperity and peace. The same is true for the kingdom of Judah. We are dealing with a period of both kingdoms' triumphant expansion and a series of military successes.[35] The international situation was auspicious; Assyria's imperial power had waned, the kingdom of Damascus had not yet fully recovered from earlier defeats by Assyria, and Jeroboam had made excellent use of the favorable international situation.[36] Yet the biblical judgment is not complimentary. The peace dividend does not benefit the whole population; it did not bring justice and equality and dignity to all, and precisely therein lies the "evil in the sight of the LORD." The elites prospered while the impoverishment of the masses worsened. Like in our day, the gap between the rich and the poor was unprecedented, unsustainable, and in terms of covenantal politics, intolerable. "The result was the stark contrast between the luxury of the rich and misery of the poor which Amos repeatedly indicts."[37] The peace and prosperity of the privileged came at the cost of the devastation and ruin of the weak and defenseless. As in our times, the politics of opportunism missed the opportunity for politics to allow peace and justice to embrace. However, the prophet does not make the mistake of equating the prosperity of the few with the justice Yahweh requires nor with the shalom Yahweh promises.

Fifth, Amos describes an obscene obsessiveness with making money. "The markets of Jeroboam's kingdom traded in human misery."[38] James Luther Mays writes as if describing our twenty-first-century global capitalist systems. The new moon and the Sabbath, when they could not carry on business, became an intolerable intrusion in the flow of business, and this while they have been instructed in the Sabbath economics Yahweh requires and that brings justice.[39] Their greed makes the one day lost to doing business seem like a year, is Calvin's interpretation. "If an hour is lost, they think that a whole year has passed away…'How is it', they say, 'there is no merchant coming? I have now rested one day, and I have not gained a farthing!'"[40] Calvin pushes beyond this and points at the core of the sin of profits over people and what today would be called "manipulation of the markets":

> [T]hey expected corn to be every month dearer; as those robbers in our day gape for gain, who from every quarter heap together corn, and thus reduce us to want; frost or rain may come, some disaster may take place; when spring passes away, there may come some hail or mildew; in short, they are, as it were, laying in wait for some evil…and the corn was then dearer, when there was no crop. Thus then there was a prey, as it were, provided for the avaricious and the extortioners.[41]

Calvin's choice of words here is unadorned and startlingly deliberate, provoking powerful images in the minds of his audience: *robbers* who *gape for gain,* who *reduce us to want; disaster;* (robbers) *laying in wait; prey* that is *provided for the avaricious and extortioners.* The evil purposefulness is undeniable and inescapable. Calvin not only knows how the capitalist economic system (even in its rudimentary form) works; he recognizes its greed, its inherently violent nature and despises it.

Sixth, all this prosperity, economic growth and peace, while the normal way of life for the elites, constituted a crisis of enormous proportions for the poor and vulnerable. In the eyes of Israel's God it was a scandalous situation and this is what Amos comes to condemn. For the elites, however, in Amos' time as it is in ours, the scandal is not in the gap between the rich and the poor, the oppression of the innocent, or in the hypocrisy of the national religion which Amos, in almost shocking terms, denounces as an affront to God. For them, the scandal lay in the words of the prophet from the south who was not intimidated by might and power, not beguiled by wealth and status, not impressed by false religiosity.

As with the prophet Micah (Micah 2:6) they did not hear him gladly, the rulers in Jerusalem, the pay-rolled priests under the leadership of Amaziah, and those "cows of Bashan" who ate and drank and made merry while they "oppressed the poor and crushed the needy." He was not polite, Calvin observes, "but proved that he had to do with those who were not to be treated as men, but as brute beasts; yea, worse in obstinacy than brute beasts…" They were "all stubbornness and wholly untameable…" The situation called for someone not ruled by diplomatic ambiguity, but who would "exercise towards them his native rusticity."[42] Their response was to get rid of him. "O seer, go! Flee away to the land of Judah, earn your bread there…" (7:12).

They did not want to hear a prophetic word from the LORD. They wanted to hear fables fabricated to please the Tower. They wanted a prosperity gospel that suited their contented lives and their prosperous lifestyle, uplifted their contented hearts and soothed their stunted consciences; a gospel that praised the "peace" their politics has wrought, even though that peace was a slow death for the powerless and the excluded. They did not want to hear that their wealth was not a blessing from God but rather the result of shameless exploitation and greed. They wanted a gospel that blessed their conspicuous consumerism and their reveling in luxury while they have not a thought for the poor whose lives they have ruined: the "ruin of Joseph," Amos calls them (6:4–7). They wanted a gospel that assured them that their "ebullient confidence"[43] in their prosperous economy and their political success was a sign of their trust in Yahweh and that their religious fervor was pleasing to God. It is not even that they did not want prophets; like in our imperial reality, they only wanted them to be patriotic, unquestioning, and uncritical.

In the face of the overpowering bombast of the powerful, the oppressed, and the downtrodden are made voiceless and powerless, their heads "trampled into the dust of the earth." It is not that the poor cannot speak for themselves or that they have nothing to say. They are *rendered* voiceless by incessant oppression. They are drained *of* life even as they are drained *by* life. They are crushed by taxes and levies from which the rich built "houses of hewn stone," and they are brought to ruin by the insatiable greed of those who govern them. They do not count, are deemed the price of "a pair of sandals." The law offers them no protection for the judges take bribes, which means they profit from the systems of oppression and exploitation they help create and in which they operate, and under which the poor suffer. There is no justice in their courts; their judgments are meant to uphold the system from which they benefit. As a result the needy are "pushed aside at the gate." It is not mere benign neglect we are seeing here; it is impassioned, aggressive malevolence. One must *feel* the violence in that "pushed aside," a phrase Amos uses more than once. Amos is talking about the law being turned into systemic lawlessness in the eyes of God, *before the very eyes of God.*

In their defense against the outrage of the poor and the judgment of God the powerful are throwing up the barricades. The poor, whose heads are "trampled into the dust" are speechless in the face of this rhetoric of power and carelessness, and hearing their wordless cries is the beginning of justice. But those who dare to step into the breach, who speak up for truth and righteousness in the gates are "hated" and "abhorred." The religious festivals in which they revel are not worship; they are a raucous assault upon the holiness and worthiness of God. These are evil times, and "the prudent" are counseled to "keep silent," an unknown voice, perhaps reflecting on the nature of such times seems to warn. It is as if this intrusion—deliberately creating an intrusive pause in the text—wants to hold the prophet, of Amos' time and for all such times, back for her own good (5:13). This cautionary note out of nowhere is not for nothing: all that clamor of cacophonous consent has but one purpose: to "command" the prophets, "You shall not prophesy" (2:12).

Into this din of oppressive falsity and arrogance Yahweh speaks. And it is for this reason that Amos does not begin his prophetic ministry with the customary formula, "This the LORD has whispered into my ear." In Amos the LORD does not "whisper"; Yahweh "roars." The word invokes the sound of rolling, growling thunder that reverberates throughout the book. It is a sound that rends the heavens and scorches the earth. As in every kairos moment, the stakes are high. Yahweh speaks for the silenced and the voiceless, determined that they *shall* be heard. Yahweh speaks *for* justice and *against* injustice. Therefore Amos' language is strong, passionate, vibrating with holy indignation. Yahweh's voice conjures up searing droughts, withering pastures, all-consuming fires. The poetic, rhythmic repetition of the "woes" and the condemnations is compelling and relentless: "For three transgressions…and for four…" It is a prophetic word that pulsates with divine power, divine anger, and divine lamentation. Again, as with Micah, this is an outraged, wounded, mourning God who speaks. God is outraged at injustice; God is wounded in the wounds of God's wounded people; God laments the unrelieved pain, the ruined lives, and the hardened hearts. This divine voice pulverizes all excuses, all justifications, all resistance. By the time Amos takes a breath with his rhetorical question, "Is it not indeed so, O people of Israel?" (2:11) the reader is already left almost breathless.

In arguably the most well-known oracle from this book, Amos speaks of justice (*sedaqa*) that should, and will, rush down "like waters," and righteousness (*mishpat*) like an ever-flowing stream" (5:24). What is striking here in his dream of another, different world is the bold juxtaposition with the omnivorous greed of the elites, their wealth, and insatiable hunger for power; the omnipresent but false religious fervor which Amos describes as in all ways extravagant and in screaming contrast to the people's silenced misery, their paucity of life, and their trivialized dignity. Over against this is the justice Yahweh demands which must "roll down like waters" and a "mighty stream." It is an exuberant abundance that will sweep away the injustices, set things right in the courts, in the community, and in all relationships. The prophet has no patience with theories of "trickle-down" economics and "rising tides" that are supposed to "lift all boats" as if the leaky boats of small-village fishermen are the same as the luxury yachts of the rich who benefit from the exploitation of the poor. "Justice and righteousness must roll down like the floods after the winter rains, *and* persist like those few wadis whose streams do not fail in the summer drought."[44]

This is the life in all its fullness Jesus speaks of as he fulfills the promise made to the prophet Isaiah not to rest or grow weary until justice is established in the earth (Is. 42:1–5; Matt. 12:15–21). Amos effectively neutralizes the propaganda from the Tower. Here there is no talk of small "windows of opportunity" the privileged grudgingly hold open for those from the "middle class" if they will only work hard, pull themselves up by their boot straps, "play by the rules," and as long as they do not challenge the systemic oppression that excludes the poor, and do not believe, as Micah exhorts us, that greed is violence against the poor.[45] No, here is the image of the doors flung open wide by a God "who opens and no one will shut" (Rev. 3:7,8).

So in the celebration of the coming of justice Amos is unrestrained: "The one who plows shall overtake the one who reaps, and the treader of grapes the one who sows the seed" (9:13). The delighted hyperbole of the prophet's language—"the mountains shall drip sweet wine and the hills shall flow with it"—says Calvin, means that "there will be no common or ordinary abundance" of God's blessings. They will "exceed belief."[46] This is the vision of a different world that the prophet sees despite the present, and God's people should not be allowed to forget this. In their present state of oppression the people may find that hard to believe, and the powerful may think it absurd even to imagine, but the prophet, in holding up an alternative reality, insists, "The time is surely coming, says the LORD..."

Babel and the Origin of Dissent

The last piece of interpretative biblical reflection I would want to call attention to is the story of the Tower of Babel, from Genesis 11. It is a well- known, for some perhaps well-worn, piece of scripture, subject of myriad interpretations. The passage has many imaginative misreadings, but one of the most damaging has been the use of the story of the Tower of Babel for the theological justification of apartheid.

Apartheid theology interpreted it as a deliberate attempt to defy God's command given at creation (Gen. 1:28) and repeated to Noah (Gen. 9:1,7) that humankind should divide into separate peoples with different cultures and different languages. Because this divine division is the indispensable basis for the peoples of the world to *be apart,* the very idea of "one city, one people, one language" is abhorrent and a defiance of God. In this theological logic God's command to "fill the earth" serves God's apartheid purposes: to separate the people and keep them apart.

During the 1930s and 1940s a Rev. C. R. Kotze from the Dutch Reformed Church preached such a sermon.[47] Making the point that God's will is the total and permanent separation of peoples he points to the Tower of Babel as a futile human effort to create one people and one language, the epitome of resistance against God. "For that reason God brings the confusion of languages, because God wants separate peoples and separate languages." The logic of God's acts regarding Babel becomes the logic of Pentecost where each "in their own language" proclaims the great deeds of God. Racial separation receives the sanctification of the Holy Spirit. Jesus might have prayed "that they all may be one," Kotze says, but that prayer does not avail much, for it "does not alter God's divine Counsel." The unbroken line of God's purposes is clear: "The tower of Babel, Deuteronomy and Pentecost proclaim to us: God has willed separate nations, languages and histories." And in an ironic twist after the condemnation of Babel, Kotze adds, "God builds a wall around his people." The sermon is not on Genesis 11, although Genesis 11 is its total focus, but on Isaiah 60:18, "You shall call your walls Salvation," and here the "salvation" the walls bring is the separation, distance, and isolation it secures from those other than the Afrikaner. So in a complete distortion of the text "salvation" lies not in faithfulness, in trust in God, in obedience to God or in faith in Jesus Christ—as one would expect a Christian to profess—but in walls of separation from others: in other words, in apartheid. This theology may be discredited by most of Christian theology today, but in South Africa, and elsewhere I suspect, it is by no means extinct.[48]

Most serious exegetes see in this story about a walled city and its heaven-high tower a warning against human arrogance and hubris. The narrator tells it with wry amusement: a city that is the envy of all, the epitome of human achievement, with formidable walls and a heaven-high tower, the self-centered pride in the repeated "let us," and especially in that "let us make a name for ourselves." Nonetheless Yahweh has to "come down" to see what they are so proud of. Every faithful Jew can smell the preposterousness of such a notion a mile off.

The city symbolizes empire, some scholars say,[49] and that is a valuable insight. The power, the arrogance, the hubris, the over-reaching, the "limitless self-congratulatory braggadocio"[50]: it all screams a warning to ancient Israel, living in the shadow of successive empires and learning hard and bitter lessons from the efforts within Israel by its own elites to imitate the ways of empire: this is precisely how things ought *not* to be.

While Claus Westermann is more interested in sociological theories of revolutionary upheavals that brought ancient, isolated groups of people in contact with different languages for the first time,[51] Dutch scholar A. van Selms emphasizes Babel's search for immortality as the sin that invites God's judgment. The "making of a name for themselves" is an effort to "overcome the boundaries set by death." Hence for van Selms, the "scattering" over the earth (v. 8) is God's punishment for this reach for immortality.[52] Not so for Walter Brueggemann though. Spreading abroad is willed by Yahweh. The fear of scattering is resistance to God's purpose for creation. The desire to stay "in their own safe mode of homogeneity, of self-serving unity" is to resist God's scattering activity.[53]

I have dealt with this text elsewhere and will here emphasize the main points of my exegesis and expand on my own reading of the text.[54] Indeed the question of human pride and overreach, resistance to God's purposes—these are key elements in the story. Their resistance to being "scattered" is defiance of God's desire at creation to fill the earth, to work it, to shape it until all the earth, like the garden, becomes space for life, a dwelling place for God and all God's creation. All of these activities take place under the canopy of the blessing Yahweh gives to humankind. It is a call for all humankind to do this *together*. Babel turns that blessing into curse they should avoid at all costs, hence their resistance to being "scattered." In this rebellion against God their unity, their sameness of mind and thought have become so precious that they dared not risk it in exposure to the world outside the walls: the pain, the daily struggles of people, their suffering, their needs or the challenges they pose to what it means to be human together in the world. Babel has developed, Brueggemann observes correctly, "a fortress mentality, a world free of the danger of the holy and immune from the terrors of God in history."[55]

They need divine sanction to make this work. But what they need even more is the voice of a god against the voice of God. If Yahweh wills them to scatter, they need a counter-god who will tell them to build a city so that they can *avoid* being scattered. They need a god who will bless what they do, no matter how senseless or sinful. They need a god who understands the "real world" of politics, who grasps the intricate demands and the supremacy of national security; who comprehends the need for unity in times of crisis and challenge. They do not need a God of dissent, resistance and judgment, who calls for obedience and openness and justice. They need a god of compliant compatriotism. They have no need for the God Isaiah speaks of: "Let the wicked forsake their ways, and the unrighteous their thoughts... for your thoughts are not my thoughts, nor are your ways my ways, says the LORD... For as the heavens are higher than the earth, so are my ways higher than your ways, and my thoughts higher than your thoughts" (Is. 55:7–9). They need a god whose thoughts *are* their thoughts, and whose ways *are* their ways. Hence the Tower, with steps, whose top "reaches into the heavens" where they will go and replace the God of heaven and earth with a god of their own making and likeness, who will be called by the name they will make for themselves.

"Let us make a name for ourselves," Babel says; let us become the envy of those foolish enough to respond to God's will, even if they know that what God wills is against their own interests. Let them envy the greatness a people united in one voice and one purpose can attain. So this is the epitome of Babel's civilization: life without God but with gods who serve at their pleasure, with a heaven-high tower for direct communication with the divine; greatness without justice and compassion, security without humanity, reveling in their isolation, celebrating their stunning achievement: one people, one language, one goal; one, enclosed city where all think alike and speak alike. "Oh blessed uniformity!" is the battle hymn of the Republic of Babel.[56]

So in our reading of the story verse 4 is crucial. But we must take verse 1, with which the narrator frames the story, far more seriously than do the apartheid theologians of yesterday and today. "Now the whole earth had one language and the same words." These are the words picked up by Yahweh in verse 6: "And the LORD said, 'Look, they are one people, and they have all one language; and this is only the beginning of what they will do; nothing that they propose to do will now be impossible for them.'" These are strange, ominous-sounding words, and so are they meant to be read.

What was intended as a blessing for humankind has now been turned into a threat to humankind. The unity of our common humanity has been turned into a dangerous sameness. The fantasy of our creativity which blossoms in our obedience to God has been harnessed, compressed into a slave mentality that has lost all sense of freedom. No one dares to break the pattern of speech or challenge the pattern of thinking. Raising doubts about the ways of the people is a threat to the unity of the people. Raising questions about the walls around the city is an onslaught on the security of the city. Questioning the Tower is a sin against the gods.

But the strangeness of Yahweh's words does not end there. "This is only the beginning," God says, "nothing that they propose now will be impossible for them." God sounds frightened, and rightly so. God is not afraid for Godself, however, God is afraid for *us*. What will become of God's world and God's people when what is unthinkable in God's mind becomes possible for us? When there is just sameness, when we are required to all speak the same language, when dissident voices are not listened to, but ridiculed, persecuted, and silenced, and when those who turn against the Tower are ruthlessly crushed by the Tower, then nothing they propose to do will be impossible, for there is no one to warn, and no one to stop them. And this is only the beginning! Who knows to what terrible depths of inhumanity humanity will be plunged by those drunk with the power of the Tower?

History has multiplied Richard Lisher's list a hundredfold. Centuries-long crusades with blood rising to the bridles of horses, was only the beginning of a history of genocide, dispossession, and enslavement in the name of the One who is the Prince of peace. We have made the unthinkable the possible and thus the utterly banal: from the burning of "witches"—women who frightened us with their strength and wisdom, to "faggots"—those whom God created sexually other. From Hitler's gas ovens to Pot Pol's killing fields. From Bosnia's ethnic cleansing to ethnic cleansing in modern-day Israel to Rwanda's holocaust. There the mass murders had a grim double edge: they not only emanated from a terrifying uniformity of thinking, speaking, and acting; they worked in reverse as well: they actually "brought Hutus together," like nothing else could, binding them ever closer in the horror of a shared, unspeakable transgression. A stunned Philip Gourevitch, in conversation with a Hutu justifying the killings ("*All* Tutsis were enemies!") asks: "Even senile grandmothers and infants? Even the fetuses ripped from the wombs of Tutsis after radio announcers had reminded listeners to take special care to disembowel pregnant victims?"[57]

From the Sharpeville massacre and the killing of Soweto's children under apartheid—the people's oppressor—to the Marikana massacre under the African National Congress—the people's liberation movement. Because four little girls in a Birmingham church were no price at all, 500,000 dying Iraqi children were "a price worth paying." The cluster bombs killing innocent children at birthday parties but sparing buildings for later use, and young girls' faces drowned in acid because they dare claim the right to education. Whole communities destroyed because of merciless ecological aggression, multitudes of species wiped out forever as we display our mindless, deadly mastery of creation. Meanwhile we desperately cling to the fables from the Tower that all this violence has salvific power, that Jesus, or Allah, or Yahweh, is with us, and that our clones can replace what our drones destroy.

If God had only known how right God would be, Genesis 6 where we are told that human beings had become so shockingly violent and destructive that God "regretted" having created them might have followed Genesis 11.

But Genesis 11 is not the story of the Tower and its politics of fear and compulsion, and it is not a story of the glorification of violence as "solution" to problems. God is determined not to let the flood return. God seeks a better way and the story of the Tower of Babel becomes above all the story of the origin of prophetic dissent. The language of verse 8 does not echo, but is in stark contrast, no, in *rebellion* to the repeated "come, let us" of verses 3 and 4. Yahweh's "come let us" in verse 8 is the voice of dissent, and it comes to disturb and counter the deadly sameness of language and thinking that makes the unthinkable possible, and normal. If "the whole world" has only one language and the same words, and there is no voice left in Babel that speaks in the different, challenging, and liberating tongue of truth; if there is no one that will take the critical step away from the Tower to witness to the Tower, then Yahweh self will take the risk of prophetic dissent. In reading the story therefore, the accent should not fall on the multiplicity of languages, but rather on the single voice of dissent: Yahweh's. Yahweh comes down to do what all prophets must: to speak truth to the Tower; to destroy the fables that emanate from the Tower, to rescue those who languish in the shadow of the Tower. It is Yahweh who is the origin and source of prophetic dissent. Yahweh's "come let us" is not resigned despair, but an invitation to revolutionary dissent. Not a declaration to destroy the world but Yahweh's intention to save the world.

The confusion that follows, then, is not so much a result of the multiplicity of languages; it is the confusion in the ranks of the powerful, totally confounded when prophetic truth is spoken. It is the shock of seeing that those living in the shadow of the Tower have been given the power to speak truth to the Tower; that the paralyzing spell of uniformity and manufactured consent can be broken. For in the shadow of the Tower, within the walls of Babel, truth *is* a different language, a life-giving and redemptive language. And when it speaks of "God's great deeds of power," it speaks of an entirely different kind of power, and it can be heard in every tongue of every nation as indeed it is at Pentecost. So there is, after all, a connection between Babel and Pentecost, though completely different than the connection imagined by apartheid theology, then and now.

The "bewilderment," "amazement," "perplexity," and the "astonishment" of the Pentecost crowd with which the text of Acts 2 fairly bristles, is the turned-around and redeemed confusion of Babel. In Genesis 11 the emphasis falls on the malevolent confusion of the powerful. In Acts 2 it falls on the joyful amazement of the powerless. In Genesis 11 it signals the end of oppressive, coercive power of the powerful. In Acts 2 it celebrates the outpouring of life-giving, world-transforming power given to the powerless. The peoples of the world, so meticulously noted by Luke (2:5–12) are hearing this, and they will indeed "be scattered" across the earth to spread the good news of God's liberating power.

Luke's "every nation under the heavens" was also every nation under the brutal heel of the Roman empire; every single one of them required to call Caesar "Lord" and "Savior" and to bow down before the imperial image in worship of the Emperor. All of them knew that the power of Rome had nailed Jesus to the cross. Now they hear Peter call not Caesar, but Jesus, "Lord," in defiance of every sacred imperial decree. Now, every one of them, *each in their own tongue,* hears the gospel: "But God raised him up, having freed him from death, because it was impossible for him to be held in its power" (Acts 2:24). The power of the empire that spread "shock and awe" everywhere as "the sole super power of the ancient world"[58] and at a time when Rome's authority, after years of bloody internal strife, was once again ruthlessly established over all the world, is now again challenged, engaged, and defied.[59] Pentecost is the feast of the power of prophetic dissent and prophetic truth-telling.

7

Combative Love and Revolutionary Neighborliness: Kairos, Solidarity, and the Jericho Road

Kairos Consciousness and Prophetic Ministry

If the parables Jesus told should be read as "subversive speech" and the Jesus telling them as "pedagogue of the oppressed" as William R. Herzog holds[1]—and I think he is right—then the inner-city ministry of Dr. J. Alfred Smith Sr., pastor emeritus of Allen Temple Baptist Church in Oakland, California, ecumenical leader and public theologian, is itself a parable of prophetic ministry. It is a ministry imbued with what above I have called a kairos consciousness. However, a kairos consciousness is a subversive consciousness which in turn is rooted in a subversive piety. I see in him, as I do in Archbishop Desmond Tutu, such a subversive piety,

> springing from a spirituality of combative love that took him from the pulpit and the quiet of his prayer room to the struggle and from the crucifix on the wall to the streets where his people suffered on the crosses of racist oppression.[2]

It is a piety of liberation, rooted in God's compassionate justice for the poor, the oppressed, and the suffering, and a deep and abiding love for all God's children. But because it is a piety characterized by combative love, it is always subversive. It subverts the unjust status quo upheld by the powers of oppression and destruction. This piety is subversive because it is neither sentimentalized nor privatized. It is not captive to ideology or obeisant to earthly powers. Rather it is captive to God's inclusive love and compassionate justice, and the sacrificial solidarity and resistance of Jesus of Nazareth.[3]

As reflected in the title of his fascinating autobiography, J. Alfred Smith characterizes his ministry as "The Jericho Road" ministry.[4] It is a book that describes his life from growing up as the child of a single mother, through his struggles with life to find and take hold of his destiny; his calling and his work; his discovery of what it means to be black in America and his participation in the civil rights movement, to finding and understanding his calling as pastor, preacher and prophet. It is a testimony to prophetic faithfulness.

Through it all his life was guided not by certitude but by faith, not by comfort but by hope, not by a resigned piousness but by a spirituality of struggle. We learn how he has come to understand that if one says "Jesus," one must perforce also say "justice," and through his preaching, counseling, and prophetic witness he has shared that understanding with the multitudes who over the years heard him so gladly.

When he finally understood that his was a life called to the ministry, he knew that it was not going to be a ministry that cries "Peace! Peace!" where there was no peace; a ministry that longed for comfort in the adoration of the comfortable; that sought refuge in the protection of the reputable. To the contrary, he saw his ministry as among those with no reputation at all: the poor and the downtrodden, the marginalized and the afflicted; those, as James Baldwin called them, "with no name in the streets."[5] If they were exposed to the vicissitudes of life and the vagaries of power, he was going to be exposed. Because they were vulnerable, he made himself vulnerable. He would seek to uplift his people with the dream of the Promised Land, but he would not placate them with otherworldly piousness. He would encourage them with the truth of God's promises, but he would not deceive them with the lie that they were not still wandering in the wilderness. He would comfort them with the love of Jesus: "Come to me, all you who are weary and are heavy-laden, and I will give you rest" (Matt. 11:28). But he would also strengthen them with the truth-laden power of the prophet,

> Thus says the Lord: Act with justice and righteousness
> and deliver from the hand of the oppressor anyone
> who has been robbed.
> And do no violence or wrong to the alien,
> the orphan, and the widow, or
> shed innocent blood in this place. (Jer. 22:3)

His would not be a ministry of the highway, smoothly and effortlessly bypassing the ugly blemishes of the city, an eight-lane elevated platform from where the city offers only vistas of grandeur, and exiting only into the leafy suburbs of stately homes, safe lanes, and oblivious living. His would be a ministry of the road running *into* and *through* the city, the road lined with hovels and shacks, foreclosed small shops and ramshackle houses with boarded-up windows. That city where dangers lurked in the shadow of every high-rise cowering under the assault of angry graffiti; where children played, not in parks where it is safe, but in the streets where gangs battle for territory; where people walked, not in carefree nonchalance, but in fear and trepidation; where the air is scarred by the smell of uncollected garbage, thick with the stench of hope that has died. His would be a Jericho Road ministry.

The Jericho Road Ministry

But what does it mean: this Jericho Road ministry? Note, first of all, that J. Alfred Smith speaks of a "Jericho Road *ministry*." In our contemporary context, where "ministry" has assumed the banality of the platitudinous, that is a significant emphasis. For him the word "ministry" indicates that this is more than just a temporal or a temporary occupation. More importantly, it is more than a transient insight, a fad to be replaced by another catchy slogan tomorrow, as so much of what is called "ministry" in so many churches has become. Their idea of ministry is to sloganize Jesus, using catchy phrases that would suit "the market" they are targeting, fashioning a gospel fit for sleek consumerist psychologizing. They look at God's people with a keenly exploitative eye: they do not see people whose needs are to be kept holy before the Lord; they see people with needs to be manipulated, often in ways that reduce people to their needs only, for the sake of control and material gain. They separate people from their needs and when the needs can no longer be exploited for profit, the people are discarded as needless, unneeded, and unheeded. Then new needs are found and targeted.

For J. Alfred Smith, and for those called to prophetic ministry, this is decidedly not so. People, whoever and wherever they might be are God's people, created in God's image, for whom Christ died; whose needs—spiritual, economic, social, political, communal, and personal, *are* to be held holy before God. As a result his ministry is immersed in the lives of the people, as it is immersed in the love of God in Jesus Christ. And between the two there is no dichotomy. It is a holistic, prophetic ministry that understands and seeks to respond to the pain and suffering, the struggles and hopes of God's people.

That is why it is a Jericho Road ministry: it is a concretized prophetic calling. It means walking the road the people have to walk, facing the dangers the people face, taking the risks the people have to take in order to survive. It means resisting the seduction of religious propriety that deems it unseemly for the pastor's feet to gather dust; foregoing the privilege of accepting the ride offered by the comfortable and better situated parishioner concerned with the well-being of the pastor, to finish the rest of the way in air-conditioned comfort; understanding that no church business *at* the end of the road is as pressing as the business of this journey *to* the end of the road.

In J. Alfred Smith's reading, the Jericho Road ministry is a ministry of compassionate justice, of prophetic clarity and prophetic faithfulness; of pastoral tenderness and worldly holiness. By that I mean a holiness that stands in absolute opposition to what shames God in the world because it stands in absolute awe before God. It understands that the evil humanity is capable of should be made impossible, because it is unthinkable before God. If we understand what is unthinkable before God we will understand better why nothing is impossible for God, and hence not only for God Jesus assures us, but for all those who believe (Mk 9:23).

A Man Went Down from Jerusalem...

The characterization, "The Jericho Road ministry" is taken from the well-known parable of Jesus in the gospel of Luke, chapter 10:25–37. The drop from Jerusalem, 2700 feet above sea level, to Jericho 17 miles away, 800 feet below sea level—a 200-feet drop per mile—is barren, almost denuded of any vegetation, hilly, with numerous hiding places for bandits. It is a "notoriously treacherous road."[6]

In connection with the reading of this parable, scholars have pointed to the fact that the enmity between Jews and Samaritans was visceral, volatile, and sustained, and theologically, culturally, socially, and politically this was not unimportant.[7] Jews looked down upon Samaritans as a people with an inadequate theology (Samaritans accepted only the first five books of the Hebrew Bible—the "Books of Moses"); they were considered by some to be the descendants of the people brought to Palestine by the Assyrians and other conquering nations in the process of imperial colonization, and hence associated with that imperialism Jews experienced as so harsh and oppressive; and last but not least they were seen as people of "doubtful descent," in other words, people of mixed race, even though the Judeans—and Jesus himself, as scholars such as Cain Hope Felder and Curtiss Paul DeYoung have convincingly argued—were racially mixed, people of Afro-Asian descent.[8]

By themselves and within the contemporary context these facts do have significance. However, it seems that first of all we should understand that the parable is not in the first instance about Jews and gentiles, or even Jews and Samaritans. Neither is it told in order to highlight ethnic prejudices of long ago, even though these certainly play a role.[9] It is also not about an argument between Jesus and a lawyer trained in the Torah, nor about the fact that at that stage of Jesus' ministry the lawyers, scribes, and priests, the elite rulers of Israel had, in their collusion with the Roman imperialists and exploitation of the people, developed such a hatred for Jesus because of his radical understanding and application of the Law, his deep connection with the common people, and his prophetic, critical, political stance. How all these elements find their place shall hopefully become clearer as we progress.

It is telling that in the parable the ethnic identity of the victim on the road is not a point explicitly raised. In my view, identity is only important in as far as the word "Samaritan" comes with such negative connotations that the role ascribed to the Samaritan in the parable had to be significant for Jesus' audience.[10] As far as this is concerned, Jesus seems to be making two points. First, the ethnic identity of the victim should make no difference to our expression of love and neighborliness. It is irrelevant. The neighbor is anyone in need of our solidarity, whose situation in and of itself is an appeal to our sense of compassion and justice. The Other, whoever they may be, is a neighbor, because their appeal to us is based on our being human together, sharing our childhood of God, both being endowed with the image of God, in whose humanity my humanity is authenticated. This is what Africans would call *ubuntu*. Second, the one who understands this is the one from whom, in view of the prejudices of that society, this is the least expected. The neighbor is our kin, our flesh and blood, but it has nothing to do with a shared ethnic or national or racial identity. It is a splendid example of how Jesus presents and represents the inverted order of God's reign, God's tendency to turn reality around, to choose for the least, the despised and the unimpressive, thereby challenging and exposing prejudice, pride, bigotry, and hypocrisy—in other words, lovelessness. The parable of the Pharisee and the tax collector in the gospel of Luke is an impressive example of this (Lk 18:9–14).

The parable begins with a question from a lawyer to Jesus concerning the way "to inherit eternal life" (v. 25). Jesus directs the lawyer to the Torah: "What do you read there?" Of course the answer is that one should love the Lord God with all one's heart and soul and strength, "and your neighbor as yourself" (vv. 26–28). "Do this," Jesus says, "and you shall live." Then the lawyer, "in trying to justify himself," asks the crucial question which forms the heart of the matter: "And who is my neighbor?" It is then that Jesus responds by telling the parable. The story unfolds and the characters pass by: the traveler who becomes the one attacked, the bandits, the priest and the Levite, and finally the Samaritan, who sees the wounded man, stops, attends to the victim, and takes him to the inn in Jerusalem.

There seems to be a fair amount of consensus that the twin issues of neighborliness and love seem to be at the heart of the parable.

At the outset it is important to know that Jesus is saying that our understanding of love and neighborliness reveals our understanding of God. This is how crucial it is. How we shall live, *whether* we shall live, in other words, how we shall find meaningful life with and in God, depends on how we find meaningful life with the neighbor. The love for the neighbor becomes the litmus test, the touch stone for our love for God. God cannot be loved without loving the neighbor. Our faithfulness to the law of God is authenticated by the love of the neighbor. The writer of the First Letter of John understood this well when he, without hesitation, labeled as "liars" those who refused to accept this basic scriptural truth: "For those who do not love a brother or sister who they have seen, cannot love God whom they have not seen" (1 Jn 4:20). The issues of love and neighborliness, however, are framed within that other, crucially important question: what *kind* of love; and what *kind* of neighborliness might Jesus have in mind? The parable is told to illustrate and illuminate exactly this issue.

The parable shows who understands this, and who does not. But the right understanding opens the door to life—the life Jesus spoke of and came to realize, the life permeated by the active longing for and the embrace of the reign of God, the life infused and driven by justice, truth, mercy, and compassion; the life in which human life flourishes; the life in the fullness of shalom, which the Scriptures tell us is God's intention for all God's children. "Do this," Jesus says, "and you shall live."

Across the ages, as is still the case today, the parable has been interpreted in different ways.[11] I shall name three of these interpretations that have a bearing on our discussion here. There is first, the Jericho Road as allegory; second there is the Jericho Road as metaphor; and third there is the Jericho Road as fantasy.

In the Jericho Road allegorized, interpreters have, following the early Church Fathers, understood the parable to be an allegory, a literary device in which characters in stories symbolize ideas and concepts. Then the story becomes a moral lesson for life. In this interpretation, every point and character in the parable is given a moral application. Usually four themes were emphasized: the ruin of the human race (the attack on the defenseless traveler); the devil's persecution (the robbers); the inadequacy of the Law (the Priest and the Levite); and lastly Christ's mercy (the Samaritan).[12]

When the Jericho Road story is metaphorized, it becomes a metaphor for the kingdom of God. In our life we will encounter such Jericho Road episodes and the test is then whether we, in the face of the misfortune of another, will behave like the Priest and the Levite, or like the Samaritan. This will determine our "Christian character," our closeness to the kingdom of God. Sometimes the story is told as a metaphor of life. The parable becomes what is called an "example story." It is turned into "life's highway" and we are called upon to follow the example set by the "good" character and avoid the example set by the "bad" characters.

Then there is what I would call the Jericho Road as fantasy. The Jericho Road is again turned into "the road of life" on which we all (have to) travel. It is presented as a road on which all persons, regardless of their station in life, travel equally, with equal choices and equal outcomes. We all meet life's mishaps, are all overcome by life's challenges and disappointments, all confronted by adversaries we are all called to face. Like the victim on the Jericho Road, we are all disappointed when the help we expect is not given. So the parable becomes a story about life in general, about the human condition in general. How we face this and get through this determines our being Christian in the world.

But the Jericho Road as fantasy has another aspect, totally oblivious of the paradox inherent in the interpretation that is given. In wealthy, privileged churches and poor churches alike this parable will become the example story we have mentioned before: exhorting the listener to be sensitive to the victims on "life's highway," and to follow the example of the Samaritan, that is Christ. Both rich and poor will understand themselves to be both victim and Samaritan in the general human sense, as well as in the particular sense. Both will be exhorted to follow the example of the Good Samaritan, to help the victim along the road. This generalization is the first problem we encounter with all of these interpretations.

Kairos and the Jericho Road

On my reading, however, this interpretation does not reflect Jesus' intent with this parable and neither is it the understanding that drives J. Alfred Smith's naming of his ministry. And here is why:

In all these interpretations, the parable is entirely spiritualized. The Jericho Road becomes the "road of life," a spiritual pilgrimage. The characters, and as a result their actions as well, all become spiritualized. There is no engagement with the reality of life.

In contrast, Jesus was not telling the story to demonstrate a spiritual journey of life. Jesus was telling the parable to illustrate the realities of life as faced by real people who had to travel that route every day. Jesus knew that when people traveled from Jericho to Jerusalem, they were likely to be attacked, robbed, hurt, and sometimes killed. Talking of life's dangers and realities as if they were mere spiritual illustrations of a spiritual journey cannot be Jesus' intent. Jesus' intent was not metaphoric.

For Jesus, the blood on the ground was not symbolic of something—it was real. Likewise, the demands of the reign of God for that situation may not be spiritualized—they are real.

The fantasized Jericho Road, where all of us travel along "life's highway," encountering difficulties common to all of human existence, is equally unreal and inadequate. Even if one works with the "highway of life" metaphor, one cannot speak of it as if those traveling on it are all equal, facing the same challenges on equal footing. There are some travelers who are far better equipped to deal with the dangers of this treacherous road. The rich and powerful do not travel like the poor: they can afford to buy protection which the poor cannot do. They can find ways of defense against robbers and bandits which the poor cannot do. In truth, the rich and powerful who travel this road in protected comfort are as much to be called bandits who threaten the lives of the poor, who exploit and rob them of all they have. The poor, especially poor women and children, the weak and the marginalized are always vulnerable.

When they travel they are exposed to dangers in a way the powerful and privileged never are. Traveling on "life's highway" in our world today the poor, and the marginalized do not have the same preparation, the same opportunities, the same protection, the same confidence and defense mechanisms that decent education, stable jobs, patriarchal privilege, heterosexual normativity, and generational wealth provide. It is fantasy to think that traveling on "life's highway" we are all equal. In a word, it is simply dishonest: the leafy streets of protected suburbs are clearly not the Jericho Road of the ghetto, the African township, or the sprawling squatter camps of the cities of the global South.

The fantasized Jericho Road of our pious sermonizing is one where it is possible to believe we can create a system where enormous wealth can be created for the few at the cost of the impoverishment of the masses and that that wealth will eventually trickle down to the poor, because we are all "on life's road together": the vacuous belief that "all boats are lifted by the rising tide." That belief is a fantasy. The magnificent yachts of the rich are not the leaky boats of the poor. A Jericho Road ministry *knows* that it is a fantasy and hence will struggle with the poor to create a more just system, fight for more equality, and struggle for a more equitable distribution of wealth, power, and social goods. There are some scholars who call the parable "banal" precisely because, in their view, the parable encourages superficial charity, merely binding the wounds, taking some victim to a soup kitchen, instead of addressing the root causes of the problem. I agree with New Testament scholar Luise Schotroff that this is a superficial reading of the text.[13] The parable has far more radical implications than such a reading allows.

Martin Luther King Jr., in his famous address on the Vietnam War, also fell back on the parable of the Good Samaritan, and even though he cannot resist the temptation of the highway metaphor, and thus cannot step away from the "example story" interpretation, he rightly sees the parable as more than just a call for charity after the fact: "On the one hand," he says, "we are called to play the Good Samaritan on life's roadside; but that will only be an initial act. One day we must come to see that the whole Jericho Road must be transformed so that men and women will not be constantly beaten and robbed as they make their journey on life's highway. True compassion is more than flinging a coin to a beggar; it is not haphazard and superficial. It comes to see that an edifice which produces beggars needs restructuring."[14]

Martin Luther King Jr. does indeed help us to see the call for systemic change in the parable, and John Dominic Crossan is not wrong when he says that our parable under discussion, rather than being an example story, is to be understood as "a challenge parable; a story that challenges listeners to think long and hard about their social prejudices, their cultural assumptions, and, yes, even their religious traditions."[15] But the point Jesus wants to make I think, is even more radical than this. What these interpretations all fail to see is that it is crucial, in the first telling of the story, to remember *who* Jesus' listeners were: namely the poor peasants of Galilee, the oppressed and viciously exploited masses who lived under the iron fist of the Roman Empire and the Temple Elites.[16] They were also a people embroiled in ongoing struggles of resistance against Roman imperial rule, keenly aware of the ruthlessness of these powers.[17] But equally then, in the retelling of the story, the addressees of the story today, the people who not just occasionally travel on the Jericho Road, but who have to spend their whole lives *on* the Jericho Road, not only have to know that it is Jesus telling the story. They also have to ask "which Jesus is telling the story?"

It certainly cannot be the depoliticized,[18] dejusticized[19] Jesus of Western Christianity, or the blond, blue-eyed Christ who became the standard bearer and principal justifier of imperial lust for power, war, and domination; the one who sanctified the colonization of our lands and our minds, who blessed oppression, slavery, despoliation, and dispossession, and left us orphans, discarded on earth and homeless in heaven.

For those of us who are the descendants of slaves it cannot be the Jesus Vincent Harding speaks of so vividly; the Jesus we first met on the slave ships:

> We heard his name sung in praise while we died in our thousands, chained in stinking holds beneath the decks, locked in with terror and disease and sad memories of our families and homes. When we leaped from the decks

> to be seized by sharks we saw his name carved in the ship's solid sides. When our women were raped in the cabins, they must have noted the great and holy books on the shelves. Our introduction to this Christ was not propitious and the horrors continued on America's soil.[20]

Neither can it be the Jesus of the European colonizer, whose Gospel came to us in the form of a "fabulous ghost," as South African catechist and hymn writer John Ntsikana describes it in a poem from 1884:[21]

> Some thoughts till now never spoken
> Make shreds of my innermost being;
> And the cares and fortunes of my kin
> Still journey with me to the grave.
>
> I turn my back on the many shams
> That I see from day to day;
> It seems we march to our very grave
> Encircled by a smiling Gospel.
>
> For what is this Gospel?
> And what salvation?
> The shade of a fabulous ghost
> That we try to embrace in vain.

Already then Ntsikana, on behalf of his own as well as of coming generations, struggled with the inexpressible paradox of Africans having given their lives to Christ, yet now being "encircled" by a "smiling Gospel." One feels the contradictions: a gospel that is "good news" and "liberation from captivity" *encircles*? The black Christian is not liberated, Ntsikana says, she is *suffocated*. And moreover, suffocated by a "smiling Gospel": Is the mocking done by those who made the Gospel into a sham, an instrument of oppression and exclusion, or—unthinkable though it might be—is this Christ himself laughing at us, mocking us for being so credulous, so laughably naïve? Have we, in embracing this Gospel, become no more than a laughing stock for others? We are, he writes, "marched to our graves," to all kinds of death, because this Gospel, brought to us by those who enslaved and dispossessed us, brings us no understanding, no sharing of the pain, no comfort for our tormented souls.

Ntsikana expresses not just the discovery of pain and "sham," but also a sense of betrayal and outrage. But deep down he knows: this smiling, mocking Gospel is not real, and neither is the "salvation" it purports to bring: it is but the "shade of a fabulous ghost" we try, but cannot really, embrace. It is in the struggle with this paradox that black Christians would come to understand the difference between the Christianity that came with the colonizer and the power of the gospel of Jesus the Messiah. We would learn that this colonized and colonizing Gospel is one we *should not* embrace. It is in this struggle that Ntsikana's "fabulous ghost" would take on flesh and blood and bones in the reality of the black Messiah.[22]

No, the Jesus who told the Jericho Road story is the Jesus who introduced himself as the anointed One of God, the one upon whom the Spirit of the Lord rests, who proclaimed good news to the poor, came to set at liberty the oppressed, to set the captives free, to heal the brokenhearted, and to announce the acceptable year of the Lord, and not just for Israel, but for the nations (Lk 4:16–18).

That is a revolutionary program and the Jesus of that program is a revolutionary Jesus. That is the reason for his resistance to the Roman Empire and its works of destruction, oppression, dehumanization, and dispossession.[23] That's also the reason for the constant tensions and confrontations with the ruling elites of Israel in Jerusalem: the priests, the scribes, and the lawyers in the Temple; and with Herod, the vassal king of the Romans in Judea, that vile imitation of Roman imperial arrogance. That is also the ultimate reason for his death on a cross; an utterly shameful death preserved especially for intransigent and rebellious slaves, violent criminals and rebels against Roman imperial authority. That is why the parables of Jesus are "subversive teachings," and why Jesus is the "pedagogue of the oppressed" as William R. Herzog II correctly calls him. "Jesus' proclamation of the reign of God, including its attendant theology and ethics, grew out of his social analysis. He did not proclaim the reign of God in a vacuum or teach theology and ethics devoid of social context."[24]

This Jesus, argues New Testament scholar Obery M. Hendricks Jr., was not just an itinerant wisdom teacher. He was a political, social, and religious revolutionary. To say that Jesus was a political revolutionary, writes Hendricks,

> Is to say that the message he proclaimed not only called for a change in individual hearts but also demanded sweeping and comprehensive change in the political, social, and economic structures in his setting in life: colonized Israel. It means that if Jesus had his way, the Roman Empire and the ruling elites among his own people either would no longer have held their positions of power, or if they did, would have to conduct themselves very, very differently. It means that an important goal of his ministry was to radically change the distribution of authority and power, goods and resources, so all people—particularly the little people, or "the least of these", as Jesus

> called them—might have lives free of political repression, enforced hunger and poverty, and undue insecurity.[25]

This is the Jesus who told the parables, including the parable of the Good Samaritan. And that is why Jesus' last question: "Which one of these three, do you think, was a neighbor to the one who fell into the hands of the robbers?" (10:38) opens up such radical possibilities. This is a crucial insight missing from the interpretations we have discussed.

Combative Love and Revolutionary Neighborliness

But what would a revolutionary Jesus mean by telling this story? Jesus means, I believe, to tell us the true meaning of radical, combative love; of true, radical, revolutionary neighborliness. Way back in 1974, in a then startlingly fresh approach, French theologian Jean Cardonnel raised a question, as disturbing and challenging now as it was then, the question I believe Jesus was trying to get the lawyer to ask. It is a question that at once reveals the real-life situation Jesus was recalling and the revolutionary nature of what is called for in such a situation. What would have happened, Cardonnel asks, if the Samaritan had come upon the scene *while the robbers were still attacking their victim*? What would then be the act of true love toward the neighbor? Should he have waited, hung back, until they have finished and departed for him to then perform his act of mercy? Or would the true act of love have been to intervene and stop the bandits from causing harm to their victim?[26] That, I submit, is the question. It is a question that immediately exposes the total inadequacy of all spiritualizing, all generalized allegorizing, and all fantasized sermonizing, because it raises another, even deeper question: if love intervenes, what form would this intervention take? In any case, *that* is the question both *driven by* love and *expressive of* love.

Cardonnel argues that true love of neighbor is not just a healing love, a love that tends the wounds but fails to ask where the wounds come from, and who made them. It certainly is not a sentimentalized love that speaks vaguely of "setting a good example"; it is a "combatant love, which needs to be transformed into an inventive, prophetic, pioneering, creative love." That is the love of the Jericho Road. It is a love not lured into safe, distant deeds of charity, a love not afraid to engage the situation as one finds it, a love that seeks to understand the causes of suffering and seeks to engage these causes, not just their consequences. It is a love that not only seeks to understand *who* caused the wounds, but also *why*? A love that asks not only how to stop the bleeding, but how to stop the *wounding*.

Cardonnel speaks of the difference genuine love makes in this situation:

> The essential difference between, on the one hand, the Samaritan, the common man, the man of the people, the man who disappears in the crowd, and, on the other hand, the priests, the economists, the psychologists, and the experts in power and authority lies in this: the first-named needed no religion, no doctrine or precise definition of his field of labour, in order to love, in order to exercise empathy, in order to act in a loving fashion and to experience solidarity with the other.[27]

We turn once again to Dietrich Bonhoeffer, theologian of the resistance against Hitler, the Nazi's and the complicity of the Christian church. The sharpened kairos consciousness of Dietrich Bonhoeffer saw with prophetic clarity what was at stake as the church grappled with what the Nazis called "the Jewish question." Bonhoeffer knew, as all true prophets would discover in other times, that at heart this had nothing to do with "the Jewish question," as for us today it has nothing to do with the "race problem," the "gender problem," or the "queer problem." Fundamentally and principally the question then was as it would always be: "How radical is your love? How revolutionary is your neighborliness?" It goes without saying that here, as I do with reconciliation elsewhere, I speak of love not as a sentimental concept, but as a political force for change and the common good.

At the time when he decided to join the resistance, Bonhoeffer reflected on the realities of the German situation. He did not philosophize about the general ruinous condition of humankind; he did not spiritualize the kingdom of God. He did not flee into academic theological vagueness or eschatological escapism, even though that would have been safer. With our parable in mind, we return to Bonhoeffer as he pondered "three possibilities" open to the church in life and death situations where fundamental choices must be taken on behalf of the victims of oppression. Having established that the church challenges the state as to its actions toward the people; and that the church has an obligation toward the victims of any societal order (whether they are Christian or not), Bonhoeffer comes to the only possibility proper for the church in such a situation:

> The *third* possibility is not just to bind up the wounds of the victims beneath the wheel, but to seize the wheel itself.[28]

We have reflected on the richness of these words before, but we can now turn to them with different emphasis. In light of our parable, what Bonhoeffer was asking, in effect, of the church and of himself was this:

what is the calling of love and neighborliness in this situation in which we come upon the Jericho Road scene while the robbers were still attacking? Hitler was still very much present, in control of the machine that was crushing his victims. The third option was really the only option left, if one were not, like the priest and the Levite, to turn away and walk away. For Bonhoeffer the call of love in his situation was to join the resistance and, as a consequence the plot to take Hitler's life.

Not merely incidentally, facing the same historic decision with consequences of the same significance, this is also the question that confronted Albert Luthuli and Nelson Mandela in South Africa's struggle for freedom after that crucial moment in our history, the Sharpeville massacre. And even though the two men came to radically different conclusions, I will argue that the fundamental question that drove them was the same.

Perhaps we should briefly remind ourselves again of the context. In December 1961, after the Sharpeville massacre in March of the year before, the African National Congress made the decision to embark on a military strategy and formed its armed wing, Umkhonto we Sizwe, meaning "the spear of the nation" (MK). On June 12, 1964, Mandela, Walter Sisulu, and six others were sentenced to life imprisonment. At that time, according to University of KwaZulu-Natal historian Scott Couper, Luthuli proceeded to issue a statement, much quoted since, fiercely debated and "frequently used to support the claim that he supported the initiation and the formation of MK."[29]

Luthuli's statement began by stating that the ANC had "never abandoned" its method of what he called a "militant, non-violent struggle, and of creating a spirit of militancy in the people." That raised at least two issues. First, that even though a decision was taken to form a military wing, for Luthuli militant, nonviolent action was still an option, in fact remained foundational for the liberation movement. Second, and crucially, Luthuli states that the claim on "militancy" with all the richness of its attendant symbolism for any revolutionary movement should not be restricted to the choices for violent struggle only. There is such a thing as "a spirit of nonviolent militancy" that could be instilled in people, and for him it should always remain a real, live option.[30] Despite his own convictions, however, he did not openly criticize the move toward armed tactics. Indeed he insisted that no one could blame those "brave, just men" who resorted to a military option given the circumstances. They were, in Luthuli's eyes, still "seeking justice" albeit by the use of violent methods, and still represented "the highest in morality and ethics in the South African political struggle." By sending them to prison, he added in a remarkably perceptive sentence, the South African courts have in fact "sentenced this morality and ethics to an imprisonment it may never survive."[31]

These words have caused a great and continuing debate on the question of violence, the ANC's decision and Luthuli's attitude toward it. Even though, Scott Couper remarks, "nationalistic commentaries rarely state categorically" that Luthuli supported the initiation of violence, they "frequently *imply* it," because, they argue, Luthuli's own words—"no one can blame brave just men [for choosing violence]"—pave the way for that understanding. This interpretation and its rationalization are not always honest,[32] but I think that from an ANC viewpoint it is nonetheless understandable. Because of this decision the ANC had invested almost all of its years and energy in exile in the armed struggle, the defense and the justification thereof. It was vitally important for the credibility of the liberation movement in their view, to claim that the struggle for freedom had therefore been won by military means. The almost ritualistic glorification of violence and the constant characterization of the violent struggle as the heart of the "National Democratic Revolution"—which in turn is at the heart of the ANC's vision—made that stance not only unavoidable but an absolute necessity.

The fact that it did not happen that way, and that the ANC guerrilla forces, without in any way belittling their fervor, commitment, and sacrifices they believed were for a good cause, nevertheless never stood a realistic chance against the best equipped and trained military force on the continent, did not really matter. What also did not seem to matter is that the struggle was ultimately and finally won by the internal forces and their persistent, sacrificial nonviolent resistance rather than by the sporadic acts of violence done by MK or APLA (the military wing of the Pan Africanist Congress), or for that matter, by the so-called Self-Defence Committees the ANC had set up in the Vaal Triangle townships during the states of emergency in South Africa half-way through the eighties. For them, what matters are the romanticized revolution and the sacrifices of MK soldiers. It is almost as if the sacrifices of those who stayed home and fought the daily battles on apartheid's killing fields in a nonviolent revolution for almost two decades did not count.[33]

The statement as a whole is remarkable in that it reveals a generosity of spirit that is more than just "leaving space for democratic decisions." One should not underestimate the serious tensions the pro-military decision created between Luthuli and members of the ANC, including, and perhaps especially Mandela who had to defend the decision publicly. Yet Luthuli's love for Christ and for the justice Yahweh requires led him, according to his own testimony, to participation in the struggle. This is the love that led him to love all his people, black and white, including those in his organization who, like Mandela, differed seriously from him on this crucial matter and derided him for his dissent.[34]

But let us further examine Couper's discussion of this matter. Couper makes the point that Luthuli "could not and did not support the formation and launch of MK because his domestic and international constituency bound him to never countenance the loss of moral high ground."[35] That is strongly plausible, but if that were the only "smoking gun evidence" for Luthuli's nonviolent stance, one would perhaps be right in describing him as more opportunistic than principled. In this same vein follows the argument that Luthuli, in essence, deferred to Martin Luther King Jr. Luthuli took seriously King's reading of Reinhold Niebuhr that helped King to be cautious about humanity's "potential for evil" which many pacifists, wrote King, "fail to see." "All too many had an unwarranted optimism concerning man and leaned unconsciously toward self-righteousness."[36] Scott Couper concludes, "Luthuli was, in King's words, wary of perceiving himself as 'self-righteous' and 'not free of the moral dilemmas' faced by Mandela and the others who also had lost patience."[37] So, by Couper's reckoning, at least part of Luthuli's ambiguity should be understood in light of the ambiguity of Martin Luther King Jr. on this point. Luthuli, like King, was a "strategic pacifist" rather than an "ideological" one.

In response, we should first turn to what seems to be the core of the debate. The debate centers almost exclusively on the question whether Luthuli would have called himself a pacifist. Luthuli, like King, counted many pacifists among his circle of friends and supporters, but never joined a pacifist organization. Defenders of the 1961 MK decision insist he was not pacifist and therefore must have supported the decision and the violent struggle. More than once, Couper points to Luthuli's declaration, "I am not a pacifist, I am a realist."[38] Still, he comes to the conclusion that Luthuli, both as a struggle activist, a leader of the movement, and as a Christian, could never have chosen for violence. His nonviolent stance throughout was too consistent. "He did not, as an individual, nor as the ANC president general, ever advocate or justify violence prior to or after the 1961 decision to form MK, to which he had been party."[39]

But perhaps the issue here is not so much whether Luthuli would describe himself as a pacifist, strategic or not, trying to grasp "the moral high ground" over against Mandela and Tambo. Perhaps the question is not whether he, with an eye on his international support base, felt compelled to follow Martin Luther King Jr.'s reticence as to perceptions of "self-righteousness." Is, all these other considerations aside, the simple truth not that Luthuli's understanding of the call of Christian discipleship on this issue was fundamental in his beliefs and actions? Couper suggests that Luthuli's "strong Christian leanings...combined with his belief that a violent solution would be suicidal for oppressed and oppressors alike and the advent of new strategic opportunities afforded by his reception of the Nobel Peace Prize persuaded him against supporting the initiation of violence by MK."[40] Fundamentally it was these convictions, rather than politics, that caused the tensions between Luthuli and his movement and Luthuli and Mandela on this sensitive issue.[41]

This brings Couper closer to Luthuli's truth, in my understanding. One cannot deny the fundamental convictions based on Luthuli's understanding of the way of Jesus of Nazareth. That much is certainly true, and to me that sounds more in line with Luthuli's consistent thinking and actions than to explain his nonviolence as more or less a political response to the demands of his domestic and international supporters, or in terms of his relationship with Martin King Jr. Moreover, if one considers the fact that Martin Luther King Jr. and Albert Luthuli had never met, with King working in the United States under a completely different set of circumstances, why would Luthuli be so much more concerned with King's opinion of him than the opinion of his peers in South Africa and the movement he had led for so long despite his admiration for the American leader? And considering his banning that had made his leadership far more complicated and more difficult to exert, why would he hope for "more opportunities" for nonviolent action, which he could no longer lead and personally inspire with his presence, especially if he had to concede Mandela's point about white intransigence over a protracted period of time? It was a point Luthuli himself had made repeatedly and in his statement in court Mandela quotes him in this regard.

Neither could it simply have been the utilitarian consideration whether nonviolence as a strategy "works." It often does not work, and purely on political analysis, South Africa at the time, as well as later in the final phases of the struggle in the seventies and eighties, did not offer much in the way of evidence that it would work. At the same time there was not much evidence that violence as strategy for resistance in the South African situation "worked." What fundamentally drove Luthuli was that nonviolence as a way of resistance and therefore as a strategy of struggle was indeed the way of Jesus of Nazareth; that politically and strategically it could indeed be very effective, and that it did offer the greater future for oppressed and oppressor alike, creating space for the reconciliation without which no revolution is really complete.

Luthuli himself had long had the sense to take into consideration that arguments for nonviolent struggle would become increasingly difficult to make in the face of the viciousness of apartheid oppression. And even though this did not make him choose violence it does explain his insistence that he was not a "pacifist." I understand this to mean that Luthuli was wary of making pacifism an ideological platform as it so often is understood, bringing with it the moral entrapments he eschewed and knew were not helpful in the South African situation. Moreover, despite his holding on to his own convictions on this matter, and while he was tireless in trying to persuade others to hold onto this view, which the ANC, he believed, had "never abandoned," he was, under the circumstances, not prepared to force others to hold the beliefs he did. Is it then not more probable that Luthuli hesitated to take a stance which resolutely, as a matter of doctrine and unbending principle, and under all circumstances would condemn the use of violence, not so much for himself, but to create freedom of choice for others? Nonviolence, after all, is a philosophy no one can be coerced into; one has to freely, willingly, soberly, and courageously embrace it, consciously opening oneself to the consequences it brings.

For himself, that he has said again and again, violence would never be acceptable, but he was willing to accept that for others, situations may arise in which they found themselves without options left. In that case, Luthuli would not be a partner, but he would remain a steadfast witness to an alternative possibility. He could not follow them, but he would not condemn them—both as a realist about the South African situation and as a Christian driven by hope for the South African situation. Luthuli understood the reasons why some in South Africa *would* turn to violence. He knew very well, as he stated in his Nobel Peace Prize acceptance speech, that "in my country, South Africa, the spirit of peace is subject to some of the severest tensions known to men."[42] Unforgettable is his pain-filled cry from the heart:

> How long before the Union's African people are seeking a new embodiment of new wishes? How long before, out of the depths they cry, "If the man of peace does not prevail, give us the men of blood?"[43]

That is not a rallying call for the justification of violence. It is a cry of mourning for the hardness of heart in white South Africa, and the temptation for the people, in response to that hardness, to risk their soul in embracing what is closest to their oppressors' hearts. In South Africa at the time, and at every stage of the struggle, one would be utterly irresponsible if one did not take that into consideration. If one wanted to lead credibly one had to keep in mind that; without consideration of our own historical context and the hugely hypocritical stance on this matter of the supporters and beneficiaries of apartheid at home and abroad a doctrinaire attitude would not be helpful or add to one's integrity in discussing the question of violence and the arguments for or against it. One could not simply call people under such extreme duress to nonviolence as if it were the most natural of responses. That was already, and constantly, done by too many from within the comfort of their far-removed places of safety, protected privilege, and unthreatened wisdom. One had to persuade the masses who were risking their lives in a struggle that was nonviolent only from their side that even though violence was an option, nonviolence was the better, life-giving option.

Nelson Mandela's famous statement before the court in his trial was a reasoned, scientific appeal, devoid of emotion, to understand the choice for violence. That is one reason why one should take this issue so seriously and respond to it with the same seriousness with which it was posed. But that was years after, in a rationale in his trial. In situations of extreme violent oppression such as South Africa was, and in the actual moment of confrontation, it was the appeal to violence that was the emotional appeal, far easier to make, calling upon those natural desires for revenge and retribution, those longings for "heroism" that always live just beneath the surface in all of us. In contrast, it was the appeal to nonviolence that had to be reasonable, well-considered, politically and philosophically responsible and persuasive. In such situations it is always the harder choice.

Violence appeals to the feelings and responses in the heated moment of confrontation, in which the consequences are almost always confined to, and justified by the immediate gratification of the need for retribution and the urge of a response to oppression and the call of freedom. Nonviolence calls for the consideration of the possibility that one might be seen as weak, meekly crumbling before the violent onslaught, not willing to make the sacrifices necessary for freedom. Nonviolence has to persuade people of a more distant, but infinitely more real victory than the immediate satisfaction of a victory written in blood. It has to persuade people to make the same sacrifices unrelieved by retribution; to believe in and hope for things not yet seen, but nonetheless essential for a peaceful, humane future. In my experience that is always the harder choice.

Mandela's famous words, "an ideal for which I am prepared to die," were meant as an expression of his willingness to give his life in the struggle for freedom and dignity, even if it has to be a violent struggle. And in the minds of many, that makes him the struggle hero he has rightly become. But the choice for nonviolent struggle reveals one's willingness to die for the same ideals, in the process of which, however, one is willing to lay down one's life, but not willing to take the life of the other, hoping that on the other side of the revolution the room created by this sacrifice would be a possibility for reconciliation and shared freedom. This was not only Albert Luthuli's choice, but the choice of the generation after 1976, that, especially during the eighties, turned the struggle into a wave of nonviolent, militant deliberateness that the apartheid edifice could not withstand. And that, I contend, was what Mandela knew when he stepped out of prison in 1990.

Couper makes the valuable point that Luthuli's statement makes the subtle but important distinction between "sympathy" and "support." Sympathy or solidarity with Mandela and the others, he argues, "does not assume support or agreement with their methods." He then continues, "Luthuli also made the same distinction between the ANC as an organization he led as president general and the 'brave just men' who could not be blamed if their patience became exhausted."[44] That much, I think, is clear. The ANC that Luthuli led has indeed never, throughout its existence, abandoned the method of "a militant, nonviolent struggle." The historical record, which Mandela would recall during his statement at trial, verified this. "However," Luthuli continues, "in the face of the uncompromising white refusal to abandon a policy which denies the African and other oppressed South Africans their rightful heritage—freedom—no one can blame brave and just men from seeking justice by the use of violent methods..." That historical record would now be changed, but not nullified.

But we need to dig even deeper. Luthuli, in insisting that Mandela and the others remained "brave, just men," even in their decision for the use of violence, compels us, in following his logic, to ask a different question, all the more important because, besides being a *political* question, is also a *moral* question, namely: who *created* this dilemma? Who is really to blame for the decision to turn to violence? Certainly not the leaders of the ANC, whose patience, after years of nonviolent struggle, had finally worn out? And Luthuli knows where the blame lies: with the white government who refuses to abandon a policy of racist oppression, especially in the light of decades of extraordinary patience and endurance: "How easy it would have been," Luthuli makes plain in his Nobel Lecture, "for the natural feelings of resentment at white domination to have been turned into feelings of hatred and a desire for revenge against the white community..."[45] But that did not happen.

And the reason why it did not happen was not accidental. Nor was it simply because of the pressures of white power. It was because, "deliberately and advisedly, African leadership for the past fifty years...had set itself steadfastly against racial vaingloriousness."[46] This is a strong choice of words, and as we have noted before, it once again underlines Luthuli's generosity of spirit. The African leadership, in Luthuli's view, resisted the temptation to see in violence a proof of their dedication to freedom, a vindication of the validity and quality of their leadership, a measurement of the integrity of their struggle. They refused to have their response to oppression dictated to by the immorality of the apartheid mindset. Neither was turning the violence of the white oppressors against them evidence of some kind of muscular African "manhood."

That, Luthuli argues, is all vainglory: it is no achievement, he is saying, to ape the mindless destructiveness of one's oppressor.

So Luthuli's words here are not uttered to justify violence. They are meant to put into perspective the historical circumstances, to expose the hubris and hardheartedness that forced South Africa's oppressed people into decisions they, given a choice, would rather not have taken. They are meant to raise the issue of ultimate moral responsibility. Indeed, keeping the brutality of apartheid rule in mind, Luthuli argues, those who take such decisions against such odds, laying their lives on the line for the sake of justice, are indeed "brave" and "just." It is the South African government and its immoral legal system that had brought new, and greater, risks to the South African situation: "They [the apartheid regime and its beneficiaries] have put the highest morality and ethics in the liberation struggle in a prison where it might not survive."

Luthuli was not referring to the decision by Mandela and the ANC to ultimately turn to violence I think. He was referring to those high and impeccable moral standards, embodied by Mandela and the others, in fact by the oppressed people of South Africa as a whole, that have kept the struggle nonviolent for so long, that have honored the noblest goals of the struggle for decades in the face of the immorality of unspeakable oppression. It was those high moral standards which were now punished with imprisonment, where "it might not survive." If Mandela and the others would now turn as bitter, as filled with racist hate as their oppressors, convinced of the justness of revenge and retribution, and if that would be the message sent to their people, who would have to take ultimate responsibility?

If understood thus, what Couper calls even "more difficult to explain," might not be so difficult to explain after all. He refers to the words in the statement that describe Mandela and the others as possessing "the highest morals and ethics within the liberation struggle." This is how I understand Luthuli: If black leadership had done all they could, if they had led their people with all deliberateness on a path of nonviolent resistance despite the odds, the unbearable provocation, the harshness and the brutality of the regime; nonetheless all the time working toward a vision "of a non-racial, democratic South Africa which upholds the rights of all who live in our country to remain there as full citizens, with equal rights and responsibilities with all others..."[47]—who would now point the finger of blame?

Who would call them immoral? Certainly it cannot be the representatives of one of the most brutally racist regimes of the twentieth century, perpetrators of a system declared a crime against humanity? It cannot be the supporters and beneficiaries of apartheid who grew fat and comfortable feeding on the violence of apartheid and the exploitation and oppression of South Africa's black masses. Their immorality in creating, maintaining, and supporting the immorality of an evil system precludes them from ethical judgment. And certainly not Albert Luthuli, who understood that not everyone in the struggle who did not share his views had therefore become "immoral"? He would rather honor them than belittle them as "immoral" in the eyes of an evil regime who had no claim on honor, and of a world who through its complicity and complacency with apartheid had together *caused* the fateful decision to be taken.

But there is a still deeper reason for Luthuli's words, I think, and this brings us back to our question whether this whole argument is merely about (some form of) pacifism, and it returns us to our parable. I think Luthuli understood that at the very heart of the issue lies not the question of pacifism, or who exhibits the higher morality. Rather, Luthuli understood that it was about the question Cardonnel called our attention to: What happens if this (revolutionary, combative) love is expressed *during* the struggle, not *after*?[48] It is the question Jesus raises in the parable: how combative is your love, and how revolutionary is your neighborliness? At its essence it was love for the oppressed people of South Africa, and the love for justice that made them join the struggle despite the dangers, the risks, and the sacrifices. It was for love of a country where at that moment, Luthuli lamented,

> The brotherhood of man is an illegal doctrine, outlawed, banned, censured, proscribed and prohibited; where to work, talk, or campaign for the realization in fact and deed of the brotherhood of man is hazardous, punished with banishment, or confinement without trial, or imprisonment; where effective democratic channels to peaceful settlement of the race problem have never existed these three hundred years; and where white minority power rests on the most heavily armed and equipped military machine in Africa.[49]

In his now famous address to the Court from the dock, Mandela was at pains to point out the long road of what he called "anxious assessment" that preceded the decision to turn to violence.[50] He and his comrades spoke of the need for "responsible leadership to canalize and control the feelings of the people;" how, if left unaddressed, those feelings would explode into "outbreaks of terrorism" that would produce "an intensity of bitterness and hostility between the races." He recounted the long litany of state violence as response to nonviolent resistance, how "all lawful modes of expressing opposition" had been closed by legislation. He told the Court that the "volunteers," mendaciously described by the apartheid prosecutors as "soldiers of a black army pledged to fight a civil war against the whites" were in fact called volunteers "because they volunteer to face the penalties of imprisonment and whipping which are now prescribed by legislature for such acts." They volunteered not to kill and rape and pillage, but to sacrifice and serve.

He repeatedly made the case against the dangerous and ultimately fatal intransigence of the apartheid regime, and again and again stated how difficult it was for them to make this decision. "This conclusion was not easily arrived at. It was only when all else had failed, when all channels of peaceful protest had been barred to us, that the decision was made to embark on violent forms of political struggle... We did so, not because we desired such a cause, but solely because the Government had left us with no other choice." Then Mandela added words of inescapable portent and historical responsibility: "There comes a time in the life of any nation when there remain only two choices—submit or fight." Their love for the people and their love for freedom, their dignity, and their concern for South Africa's future left them no choice: they decided to fight. For the moment, Luthuli's hope that the fight against apartheid would remain nonviolent was set aside. It would take a new generation to rekindle that hope.

Like Bonhoeffer, both Mandela and Luthuli were driven not by hatred or vengeance or the desire for retribution or murder, or what Luthuli called "vainglory," but by the fundamental question: what is the quality of my love for the neighbor? What does love for the people, oppressed and oppressor alike, mean in this situation? What does it mean "to grab the spokes of a wheel?" What is the dictate of love while the robbers are still doing harm to the victim on the road? For Jesus in occupied Judea, for Bonhoeffer in Nazi Germany, and for Albert Luthuli and Nelson Mandela in apartheid South Africa, *this* was the ultimate question. For Mandela, it meant a turn to violence in response to the violence of the oppressor. Luthuli could not make that choice.

But if the crucial issue here is the issue of combative, revolutionary love rather than a debate about pacifism, there is no contradiction between the Mandela of 1961 and the Mandela of 1990. It was his love for all the people of South Africa, white and black, that made Mandela make the choice for forgiveness and reconciliation. And who knows what role the extraordinary magnanimity of Luthuli might have played in his decision?

I remain convinced that Luthuli made the wiser choice. I do not think Nelson Mandela was correct when he launched MK in the belief that military means would advance the struggle. But for far too many across the world, Mandela is the hero he was because of his choice for violent struggle. That is far too simplistic, I think. For me, Mandela is a hero because he took that step only after much debate, intense, and intensely honest internal struggle, and critical, agonizing hesitation. It was not ideological recklessness, the gratification of retribution, or superficial desires for heroism that drove him. That would be what Luthuli called "vaingloriousness." Nor was he afraid to embrace it once again when the time came in 1990. The "cherished ideal" for which he was prepared to die, was not "military struggle." The ideal was the continuing fight against white domination and black domination, the dream of "a democratic and free society in which all persons live together in harmony and with equal opportunities."[51]

The argument has been put to me that the fact that Mandela refused to renounce violence when it was set as condition for his release by the National Party government in the 1980s, is proof of his life-long commitment to violence. It is another reason for his iconic status. But they have it wrong. If that were true Mandela's embrace of the politics of reconciliation as "at the heart of the struggle all along," would have been hypocritical and cynical in the extreme. If Mandela had accepted that condition, he would have denied the historical circumstances that drove the ANC to that decision. Such denial would have removed the blame from the apartheid government, cleansed the historical record of the truth that the deepest reason for it all was not a desire for violence on the side of the oppressed, but the ruthless use of violence as means of domination and the worship of violence as salvific power by white South Africa.

Acceptance of such a condition would have meant sanctifying the hypocrisy of a regime which was still, at that very moment, unleashing unrelenting violence against nonviolent protesters in the streets of South Africa while daring to speak of nonviolence to Mandela. Acceptance would have been vainglorious: putting one's own freedom above the freedom of one's people, blessing the apartheid regime with legitimacy when one's spiritual children, their struggles and their courage have called into question the regime's very right to even dictate terms of freedom to their leader and to themselves, and were paying the highest price for that refusal.

And now, looking back at 1990, with Mandela emerging from prison, recognizing the impact and nonviolent militancy of the internal struggle since 1976 and especially 1983 that finally and ultimately broke the back of apartheid oppression, reminding the ANC and the world that the militant, nonviolent tradition of the struggle was indeed never abandoned but embodied in and embraced by a new, nonracial generation; Mandela calling for all violence to cease and for his people to respond not with hatred or retribution but with forgiveness and reconciliation, proclaiming that reconciliation has "always been" at the heart of our struggle for justice and freedom, is it not the wisdom of Luthuli and the deepest traditions of the struggle that have ultimately triumphed? I think it is.

"Who is Neighbor to the One...?"

On the Jericho Road where the victims lie bleeding, sentimental love and distanced neighborliness look the other way for fear of being compromised, of being drawn into fights they have no stomach for. They look on, wringing their hands in spasms of agony at what is happening to the victims crushed by the wheel, or wait until the robbers have taken their fill of blood, momentarily departed, and then they offer darting, in-between deeds of charity before the robbers return.

Combatant love and revolutionary neighborliness however, cannot look away, cannot stand aside, cannot wait for intermittent, safe charity. It is not afraid of the contamination of solidarity. Instead it intervenes, steps into the breach, takes the risk of attack and retribution, taking upon itself the violence intended for the victim. It wrests control of the wheel out of the hands of the violent perpetrator and stops the cycle of destruction. That is the combative love that leads to the revolutionary neighborliness that Jesus talks about and J. Alfred Smith understood for his ministry.

At this point the parable reveals at least three things to us. First, the combatant love flows from understanding the revolutionary Jesus when he, in response to the lawyer's question, "And who is my neighbor?" turns the question around and asks, "Who is the neighbor to the one who fell into the hands of the robbers?" Now, in Jesus' question, the emphasis is no longer on the choices of the passers-by. The focus is on the one who suffers, who is bleeding, the one in need of solidarity, healing, and liberation. The terms of engagement are not set by the powerful by the side of the road or by the robbers lurking in wait; they are being set by the victim of the violence from which the powerful benefit. The lawyer question, "Who is my neighbor?" affirms the power of decision in the hands of the unharmed, unthreatened, and uncommitted passers-by, who by their silence and unconcern aid and abet the evildoers. The Jesus question, however, "Who is the neighbor of the one...?" displaces the power to the one who bleeds. And this power is not the coercive, needful power of victimhood—it is the compelling and liberating power of suffering. Now the neighbor is not an innocuous, de-contextualized entity about whom we can speak in vague, generalized, or spiritualized terms. Jesus is clear who he is speaking about and he is emphatic: "The one who fell into the hands of the robbers." The neighbor is not the one who happens to walk by, nor the one we feel free to choose. It is the one under attack, to whom harm is being done in our very presence, and perhaps in our very name.

Now we are told not to get deflected by concentrating on the sins of the passers-by. Jesus is not one to encourage our tendencies of finger-pointing. We are told not to see the world through the eyes of the rich and powerful, the settled and comfortable, who can afford to look away, to not become involved because it would compromise their political position with those in power. Not through the eyes of those more concerned about religion—"the tithing of mint, dill and cumin," Jesus would say elsewhere—than about faith, love, compassion, and justice. We should see the world through the eyes of the suffering, the victims of the violence not just of the bandits, but also of the carelessness and neglect of the respectable elites who see the victim, and then cross the road to pass by on the other side. That is revolutionary.

Second, the question unmasks the callousness of the powerful, here portrayed in the priest and the Levite, who look at the victim without really seeing her; the hypocrisy of the professionally religious for whom religion is a tool of power and exclusion, not an invitation to inclusion, compassionate solidarity and servanthood. It unmasks them as participants in, and beneficiaries of the violence that is inflicted upon the vulnerable. From them no love or solidarity should be expected. No, this comes from the totally unexpected: the Samaritan, the one looked down upon, the one without the proper status and qualifications, and without adequate, acceptable religion, the one with no standing who had no right to be on that road. After all, what would a Samaritan want in the city of Zion? That is revolutionary.

Third, the symbols and proprietors of official religion see and look away, turn away and walk away, not so much for fear of the attackers that might still lurk nearby. It might very well have been the case, but of that the text does not give clear indication. What the text does indicate clearly is their religious position, their rank in the hierarchy of the Temple elite, their self-perceived closeness to the Temple and hence to the holiness of God, which is all threatened by the possibility of contamination by the victim lying in the ditch.

But the Jesus who tells the parable is the Holy One who, in the words of the incomparable Christ hymn preserved in Philippians 2, "though he was in the form of God…emptied himself, taking the form of a slave, being born in human likeness…humbled himself," and in so doing he became the contaminated one, even to the point of subjecting himself to "death on a cross" (2:6–8). And *therefore,* Paul says, *for that very reason,* "God also highly exalted him and gave him a name that is above every name…" It is the slave that is proclaimed Lord, and it is the contaminated one before whom "every knee in heaven and on earth and under the earth" shall bend. It is the name of the contaminated One that every tongue shall confess, "to the glory of God the Father" (2:9–11). The one willing to contaminate himself with the stigmatized and despised form of the slave, is the one who is called Lord, because he was driven by a revolutionary, combatant love.

But there is more: Jesus was revolutionary because his revolutionary neighborliness and combatant love were far more radical than the revolutionary fervor of the attackers. The "bandits" in the parable might have been plain, criminal robbers, like the criminals we know. But even then, Jesus would have understood that the people who are now called robbers and bandits have once been landowners and providers, secure in the covenantal justice Yahweh had provided. But they had been robbed and dispossessed themselves, driven into debt-slavery through exorbitant, unbearable taxes by the Romans and the Temple both; that they lost their land, their livelihood, and their dignity through the exploitation and legalized robbery South African New Testament scholar Ernest van Eck describes so well:

> This then, was the situation of the peasantry in Palestine in the time of Jesus. Taxation was exploitative: Rome assessed its tribute and then left Antipas and the Temple elites free to exploit the land to whatever degree they saw fit. The elites thus lived at the expense of the non-elite—shaping the social experience of the peasantry, determining their quality of life, exercising power, controlling wealth and enjoying high status in the process. Social control was built on fear and the relationship between the ruling elite and the ruled peasantry was one of power and exploitation.[52]

But most likely the bandits were those resisters to Rome's oppressive rule, rampant in first-century Palestine, who rose up violently against the oppressors of the people of Judea, the Romans, and the elites in Jerusalem who were their internal collaborators.[53] They were freedom fighters, fighting for the freedom of the people of Judea and Galilee who suffered so much under the brutal Roman yoke. They turned the violence of their oppressors against them in what they believed was a noble struggle for liberation. And in that struggle, inevitably, the innocent get hurt. That was not allowed to distract them, because for all revolutionaries *the cause* always justifies the means and no life, no matter how innocent, is more sacred than the cause. Those who fall victim to the cause are what the imperialists call "collateral damage," or the even more cynical "eggs" that must be broken to make an omelet. Revolutionaries, on the other hand, speak of "the blood of the martyrs that waters the tree of freedom." But they are really saying the same thing. The bottom line is the justification of violence and the trivialization of the pain of the innocent. To question that violence is to question not only the efficacy of it; it is to question its salvific power, which, in situations where violence is glorified, always becomes an article of faith. It is to question the belief that violence is the god we need, to whom, in the first and the last resort, we turn for liberation, to whom we bow in submission and worship.

Jesus says "no" to this fatal imitation of the imperial way of life. A revolution without humanity is no revolution; a struggle without spirituality is doomed to make as many victims as the systems of oppression they are fighting. That is why the Samaritan stops. He stops not just to bind the wounds. He stops to challenge and break the cycle of violence; the violence of the bandits who kill in the name of the struggle, and the violence of the passers-by who benefit from oppression and the very violence they pretend not to see; who turn the other way, claiming the neutrality of religious noninvolvement. Jesus does not reject the struggle against oppression; he turns the revolution in a fundamentally different direction. He reminds the revolution of the power of love; a love that is revolutionary because it is humanizing; and combative because it challenges the combatants for freedom in that it dares to offer a correction to an understanding of the cause of freedom that embraces the inhumanity of the empire. It is not the turn to violence, it is in fact the embrace of compassionate, combative love that is revolutionary, Jesus says, turning our concepts of revolution on their head. Jesus makes the Samaritan stop because the struggle, in order to be genuinely revolutionary, has to be ubuntufied.

That is why J. Alfred Smith is still on the barricades today, making sense of suffering, "preaching until justice wakes."[54] That is why for him the struggle is not yet over, beginning with the struggle for prophetic faithfulness in a Christian church that has lulled justice to sleep. A prophet who walks the Jericho Road, he knows: electing a black president all by itself does not make America a nonracial or even a "post-racial" society; let alone a just or a safe society. He knows: every child that goes to bed hungry at night; every child that is robbed of a decent education; every woman that is the victim of violence at home or in the streets or the targeted victim of baptized bigotry from the pulpit; every poverty-stricken community that is the victim of systemic violence, every victim of HIV/AIDS or mental illness that is also the victim of ostracism and stigmatism; every young man who dies before his time in the inner cities of America because his life span is the same as that of a peasant in Bangladesh; every black person in prison who is the victim of mass incarceration as a measure of social control and political disenfranchisement, "the new Jim Crow" in America;[55] every innocent civilian killed by a drone; every endangered child for whom the dreams of a meaningful life have turned into a nightmare of hopelessness and despair; every LGBTI person, despised, targeted, and excluded because of heterosexual hegemony and bigotry; every soldier who sacrifices their life in every senseless war waged for profit or national vanity—he knows: in America or in the global community, they all still walk the Jericho Road.

The kairos-conscious prophetic preacher/theologian/Christian knows the Jericho Road will not be transformed by the shallowness of charity, the pious talk of post-racialism, the fantasies of sentimental sermonizing, or the mindless, blood-filled anger of despair. It will be transformed only by the clear-eyed vision of prophetic faithfulness, the hard work of genuine social transformation and the dedication to economic justice; by struggle infused by a spirituality of struggle, by the power of combatant love and of revolutionary neighborliness; by the continued presence of a Spirit-filled Jericho Road ministry, which by looking to Jesus and through the eyes of Jesus will see the victims along the road.

It is because of his faithful walk on the Jericho Road that J. Alfred Smith can dream of a new generation of preachers who will find their sense of purpose in servanthood and prophetic ministry, achieving the goals he has set for his ministry:[56].

- Mentoring for prophetic ministry;
- Working for interfaith unity;
- Intercession for the entire nation;
- Advocating for women in ministry and for gender and social justice; for solidarity with victims of racism, sexism, ageism, classism, and homophobia;
- Responsible stewardship and economic justice;
- Eradicating what he calls "modern towers of Babel" and working for a "multilingual, multiethnic, Pentecost";
- and finally to deepen American spirituality through prayer, discovering joy in sorrow, strength in weakness, hope in despair, and triumph in tragedy.

In this way, J. Alfred Smith says, we can regain Christian credibility and create hope not just for America but for the world:

> The Christian credibility and the bright horizons of newness of life in Christ will dawn on the world. The contrast between the hell of the inner city and the peace of the suburbs will be diminished, and the extremes of inordinate wealth and grinding poverty will be overcome. The chasm between rich and poor will be bridged, and the great obscenity within America will be stifled by the Word of truth.[57]

8

That Which Avails Much: Kairos, Public Prayer, and Political Piety

An Open Letter to Minister Kader Asmal[1]

This chapter contains the text of the open letter I wrote in 2001 to Prof. Kader Asmal, then Minister of Education in the Cabinet of President Thabo Mbeki. So a word about context might be in order. I have found the open letter a very efficacious form of getting a point across, especially for an audience outside the church or one's own congregation where a sermon might have served the same purpose and the issue is one that concerns society as a whole. I have used it before, when in 1979 I wrote such an open letter to the then Minister of Justice in the cabinet of President P. W. Botha, Alwyn Schlebusch, responding to his threats to the churches of the South African Council of Churches who, having passed a number of resolutions regarding civil disobedience had put themselves on a direct collision course with the apartheid regime. The minister was also responding to my call, at the same conference, on the churches not only to support individual acts of civil disobedience, but also public acts of mass protest; to challenge not just individual draconian laws, but the whole system of apartheid as inherently unjust, inherently violent, and inherently evil.[2]

Those decisions, coming in the aftermath of the Soweto youth revolt of June 16, 1976, and as it was still sweeping the country, characterized the radicalization of (black) Christianity in South Africa, the changing role of those churches in the antiapartheid struggle in South Africa; by the same token significantly heightening the tensions between those churches and the apartheid regime.[3] The churches' role as militant, nonviolent vanguard of the struggle was to become more clearly delineated. In similar fashion, Archbishop Desmond Tutu (then Bishop of Johannesburg), had written his open letter to Prime Minister John Vorster in early 1976, foreseeing with remarkable clarity the Soweto uprisings as inevitable consequence of the apartheid government's oppressive policies, and uttering the solemn warnings of the prophet to those in power. Clearly those two letters are in response to what we discerned as kairos moments for South Africa and the church.

This letter from 2001 addresses the Minister's reaction to an ecumenical public prayer service held on March 21, Human Rights Day in South Africa's calendar. For those who were in the struggle March 21 also marks the Sharpeville massacre of 1960 and the massacre of township protesters at Uitenhage in the Eastern Cape in 1985. It was in the context of an ANC-organized human rights rally that the Minister launched his attack on the Christian gathering a few miles away for being "sectarian" and "exclusive," presumably because it was a Christian meeting. He alleged that in contrast to the ANC rally, the prayer meeting was organized for whites and "coloreds" only, excluding (black) Africans, a strange allegation to make, seeing the clearly nonracial character of the prayer meeting at Newlands Stadium. Professor Asmal seemed particularly peeved that some politicians from the Democratic Alliance, the official opposition in South Africa's parliament, were seen at the prayer gathering, not playing any public role, but associating themselves with the gathering and call to prayer. It was as much the angry, scathing tone of the Minister's speech and its contents that drew public attention.

As it happens, this particular prayer service was initiated by the more conservative Christian groups in South Africa with whose theological stance on issues such as gender and sexual justice for example I am in total disagreement, as the reader will have discovered in the pages of this book. For this reason there was some hesitation before I decided to write and publish the letter. In the end, though, and for that particular historical moment, I considered the principle involved and the need for prophetic, public testimony more important than my fundamental theological and political differences with those groups.

The letter was not meant to defend such conservative, and for me, highly objectionable beliefs, and many of us who supported the call for public prayer for "transformation" were deeply offended when some of the speakers did utter them at the prayer service during the course of the day. I do not believe that theirs is the correct understanding and interpretation of the biblical message regarding these matters, neither are they reflective of the inclusive love of God come to life in Jesus of Nazareth. I was not unaware of the fact that many in those groups would rather not be associated with me or my theological and political convictions as expressed in this letter, and they would not see this letter as in line with, and hence not reflective of their own views and beliefs at all.

So in a sense, while addressing the Minister, the letter was also a witness to those groups, an attempt to offer an understanding of prayer that is more than the pietistic, private affair so many have made of it, as well as much more than, and entirely different from, the uncritical public patriotic piety that makes of prayer a handmaiden of governmental power, bowing before and blessing that power whatever the uses of it, rather than speaking truth to that power, whatever the consequences of that prophetic stance may be. "By default, coercion, or intention," writes theologian John De Gruchy, such patriotic piety remains "captive to the interests of the nation or the state,"[4] incapable of uttering the prophetic or liberating word. It was to emphasize precisely this point that I made explicit reference in this letter to the Call for a Day of Prayer in 1985, when we asked the churches to pray publicly for the downfall of the apartheid government.[5]

On that day in South Africa, commemorating the killing of the children in Soweto on June 16, 1976, we turned our silent agonies into a public cry for justice and deliverance. On that day too, we publicly confessed our belief in the spirituality of struggle, in the inextricability of prophetic protest and subversive piety. We were not praying to the ANC, nor to the revolutionary forces in their underground struggle against apartheid. We were—as Nicholas Wolterstorff correctly observes in his insightful reflections on this call to prayer—praying to God, putting in God's hands all our work, our struggles, our sacrifices, our bewilderments, our hopes. We found ourselves compelled not only to name the injustice that we petitioned God to remove but compelled also to name the righting of injustice that we, in the expectation of faith, thanked God for bringing about. "To do that," Wolterstorff says, "is to identify the signs of Christ's redemptive action (in history)," even if, he adds, that makes many people "extremely nervous."[6] We prayed in faith, and we prayed in the hope that Christ would indeed bring about his reign of justice, that God will deliver us from the chains of apartheid; that God will confound the ruthless and that the power of God's kingdom would be seen on earth. That hope is not the hope that God may perhaps hear our prayers and respond. We believed passionately that God *did* hear. It was with us as with Dietrich Bonhoeffer, as Eric Metaxas writes of him, incidentally reiterating Woltertorff's point about that "nervousness": "What made him stand out, to some as an inspiration, to others as an oddity, and to others as an offense, was that he did not *hope* that God heard his prayers, but *knew* it."[7]

Following Karl Barth, we believed that the obligation laid upon us by the Scriptures to pray for those in authority brought grave responsibilities. In praying for government the church must not become part of "the perversion of the state," or Christians become "traitors of their own cause."[8] For Barth, like for us, political responsibility and the ever-present possibility of confrontation with the state are inherent in one's obligation to pray for the government. "For the church to take its prayers *for* the state seriously is to take the office of government more seriously than the government itself does" writes Charles Villa-Vicencio, one of the drafters of the *Theological Rationale* published in support of the call to prayer.[9]

We wanted to make one other point. In this public prayer we were testifying to the truth that the god of apartheid who sanctioned our oppression and the massacre of our children, however much the apartheid Christians, their churches, and their government wanted to claim God, was not, could not ever be, the God of Jesus Christ; that the apartheid God was indeed a false god, an idol, as the prophet Jeremiah taught us, a "scarecrow in a cucumber field" who cannot hear, speak, or walk; and one that "had to be carried" by the brutal might of apartheid. We wanted to publicly testify to our faith in the God of the Magnificat: the One who "brings down the mighty from their thrones." So even though those who came to pray put so much, including their lives at risk—praying for justice is costly, we have found—we had heard Jeremiah: "Do not be afraid of them..." (Jer. 10:5) And so in 1985, across South Africa, we prayed:

> This day, oh God of mercy
> we bring before you all those
> who suffer in prison,
> who are oppressed,
> who mourn those who died in freedom struggles
> in places like Soweto, Cross Roads, Uitenhage,
> Sharpeville, and many places not known to us.
> Deliver us from the chains of apartheid, bring us all
> to the true liberty of the sons and daughters of God.
> Confound the ruthless, and grant us the power of your kingdom.

The God we prayed to was the God who had heard the cry of Ishmael (Gen. 21:17) and seen the plight of Hagar, the slave woman (Gen. 16:13) as God heard the cry of the slave people of Israel, seen their misery and came down to deliver them (Ex. 3:7, 8). Our prayers were political, of course, but the Psalms teach us, argues Hebrew Bible scholar Gerald D. Sheppard, that all prayers, even when spoken in private, are a political activity: "Prayer seeks to articulate reality, attribute aspects of reality to God, summon God to act, and nurture courage to persevere or provoke changes in the conduct of the one who prays. The question is, strictly speaking, not whether prayer is political, but what politics pertain to this or that particular prayer."[10] And so it was with us. We prayed not just for the downfall of the apartheid regime and the coming of justice, we prayed for courage and integrity, for truthfulness in witness and for faithfulness in endurance in the struggle, and for the joy of the hope for things not yet seen but believed and fought for.

The South African *Kairos Document*, in speaking of the actions the church must take toward justice and transformation, states that "it is not enough for Christians to pray for a change of government."[11] The *Kairos Document* is right of course. But I think it would be wrong to think that this is some oblique critique of the call to pray for the downfall of the SA regime. The *Kairos Document* is warning against prayers as a form of escapism, merely, perhaps in some desperation, expressing the longing for a different, more just, more humane rule before God in the hope that there might be some supernatural intervention without the human agency that requires actions, commitment, and sacrifice. The call to prayer was decidedly different. It was a call in the midst of the struggle, to those already committed to and in the struggle. It was a call to publicly confess our acknowledgment that in this struggle we are dependent on the love and mercy of the God of justice. It underlines our belief in the spirituality of struggle and expresses our conviction that God, who hears the prayers and cries of the oppressed as John Calvin taught us, indeed, who hears *Godself* in the prayers of the oppressed will respond to the longing of God's own heart and bring God's promises of justice and peace to life in our lives.

At issue here, as the reader will discern, is the matter of public piety, the meaning of prayer, and the Minister's strong reaction to a gathering of Christians publicly at prayer. At issue is also the call to public, prophetic witness regarding the boundaries of governmental power and when, in the judgment of the church, the state oversteps those boundaries. I consider this a kairos moment, coming as it did at a time when the churches in South Africa were not nearly as strong and as public in our prophetic witness towards the ANC government as we were vis-à-vis the apartheid regime.[12] Already there were signs that the ANC government would not brook prophetic critique from the churches who it once regarded as allies in the struggle. The infamous and disastrous $6 billion arms deal made by the government in the 1990s, riddled by corruption as it was, and representing a tragic distortion of priorities, caused serious clashes between government and Christian activists, even though churches as institutional bodies remained curiously silent on this highly important issue for quite some time.[13]

Of course, we should have known better. The ANC was quite clear, from Oliver Tambo in exile to Nelson Mandela in a democratic South Africa, that in their view it is the political leadership who leads. The people are merely called to follow since the leadership is the undisputed "revolutionary vanguard." "The primacy of the political leadership is *unchallenged and supreme,* and all revolutionary formations and levels (whether armed or not) are subordinate to this leadership" said ANC leader Oliver Tambo in an important policy statement.[14] At the time Oliver Tambo was of course speaking in exile, and the formations he was speaking of were the formations within the ANC organization. But African scholar Krista Johnson's point, in her careful discussion on this matter, is precisely to show how easily the ANC took that rule with them into a democratic South Africa and the "contradictions" it creates for South Africa's ruling party and as a result, for the government and the nation as well.

Politically this would prove increasingly difficult. Theologically, it flew in the face of what I regarded very much as my inheritance, that radical Calvinism that believes that the Lordship of Jesus Christ is over every single inch of life, and its conviction that Christian witness against ought to enter the real world and challenge it, shape it, subvert it, revolutionize it until it conforms to the norms of the kingdom of God—justice, mercy, equity, compassion, peace, inclusion, and humanness. Prayer is naturally very much at the heart of all this. The tensions between governmental powers and those prophetic voices in the churches on the arms deal issue for instance, as well as later on—from the stance of the Thabo Mbeki administration vis-à-vis the challenge of the HIV/Aids pandemic to corruption to the persistent questions of power, privilege, poverty, and justice in post-1994 South Africa should not have surprised us as much as it did.[15]

Therefore, it was important for the church at that particular historic moment to bear public witness to the newly elected ANC government, and to have the courage of our convictions in the same way as we witnessed to the apartheid regime. Understanding the import of that moment, I thought, would in large measure determine the course of prophetic Christianity in democratic South Africa for the immediate future. Because of the silence of the prophetic church since 1994, moreover, we saw how the void created was filled by other voices, voices that sought closeness to and acceptance of imperial political power, voices that spoke for religious exclusivism, homophobia, and patriarchal domination; voices that would so dramatically change the Christian landscape in South Africa. In truth, it was these voices that spoke louder that day in Newlands Stadium.

This letter sought to reclaim the prophetic voice and its right, and obligation, to speak into the political realities of South Africa. So the matter is both spiritual and political, as all prophetic witness always is. The title reflects the important role of prayer in the struggle for freedom in South Africa, and the prophetic task of the church in discerning and acting upon a kairos moment in the new era of South Africa's search for enduring democratic authenticity. Political piety of which I am speaking here can either be the genuine subversive piety rooted in the belief that

God is a God of justice and of history, a belief publicly acted upon in obedience to Christ for the sake of the common good; or the political pietism politics most often indulges in and almost always requires from us, as I believe the Minister did on this occasion as the attentive reader will discover.

Then subversive political piety becomes a prophetic critique of political pietism.[16] The public prayer for justice, as are the acts of undoing injustice and doing justice are all deeply rooted in this subversive piety and it follows our acts of private prayer and submission before the God of heaven and earth. It is in the awe-filled silence before the glory of God that our souls tremble, and where we find the courage to speak boldly before the world. Our souls tremble before God so that our knees won't have to tremble before the world. We are awed by the presence of the Living One so that we need not be overawed in the presence of earthly power.[17] It is this subversive piety that our public prayers for justice should seek to express.

Goodwood Prison
Private Bag X04
Edgemead,
23 March 2001

Prof. Kader Asmal
Minister of Education
Parliament Buildings
Cape Town

My dear Kader,

It was with great sadness that I read of your attack on the Christian prayer gathering held on Wednesday 21 March. I must confess to some, though not total surprise. I have sometimes wondered how long it will take for our ANC government to launch such an open attack on Christians for being Christians. The ANC, it is known, has a culture of tolerance, not only for the wide divergence of viewpoints and beliefs in society as a whole, but also for within the movement itself. You yourself are a cultured man with a high level of understanding for the views of others; an erudite man, for whom I have much respect. What is it, then, that made you lash out so harshly against Christians gathering to pray in public for issues that must, surely, trouble the government as deeply as they do us?

I was not present at Newlands on Wednesday (what would I have given to be there!) because I am, as you know, still incarcerated, my hopes of an early release having been dashed again and again. But we prayed here too, the prisoners at Goodwood prison, for peace and genuine reconciliation, for true justice and an end to violence, mayhem and crime; for good government and for the fulfillment of the dreams of the poor; for the kind of transformation of our society and our country that is more than mere change. So in spirit we were at Newlands and we felt ourselves one with those persons, lifted up together by the songs of praise and worship while we lay in our cells, and joined together before the throne of God. I praise God that such an event was possible and actually happening, where Christians from all persuasions, black and white, Protestants and Catholics, "main-line", Pentecostal and Charismatic, could be united by the call for prayer, in the firm belief that God answers prayer. So when your attack came you were also attacking me, as well as all those Christians who are members of the ANC, and I feel obliged to respond.

I tried to seek some understanding of what it is that vexed you so much and caused such an ugly, ill-advised outburst of intolerance. I know that some are already saying that it was out of pure frustration because the ANC rally itself could, according to the media, draw no more than 300 persons, and that on such an important day in our political calendar, in contrast with the Christian prayer service which attracted over 45,000. Surely it cannot be that. If there is unhappiness about the numbers the ANC is able to draw at public meetings on such auspicious occasions as Human Rights Day, then surely the ANC must search for the answers within itself. And we must take note of the fact that a Christian gathering *is* able to draw the masses in such huge numbers and politics in general, and the government in particular would be wise to learn from it.

One should hardly have to mention that Christians, like any other group, have the right, constitutionally, to gather and give public expression to their beliefs. No apologies, no excuses, no explanations. More important, over and above the Constitution, we believe that Christians have a calling, a *duty* to pray. I will not bother you with references to biblical texts, but I can assure you, they are all there. We pray for all persons in authority, for the government, for the church, for all people in need. We pray that the world in which we live may be changed, that *people* may be changed because we hold the conviction that all real and lasting change somehow comes from within and find expression in our life together as a society and a people. And prayer is not doctrinal formulations or the mumbling of magical formulas. Neither is it an escape from our daily responsibilities. Rather it is a call to take up those responsibilities, not on our own, but in total dependence on the grace of God and in the power of the Holy Spirit of God.

Yes, for this very reason our prayers are sometimes political. They must be, because all the world is the Lord's, and there is no area of life, not a single inch, that is not subject to the lordship of Jesus Christ. So politics and politicians cannot consider themselves outside the demands of the gospel or outside the circle of prayer. We pray for politics, not because we feel so much at home there, in that world of intrigue and compromise, of betrayal and power, of immense temptation and awesome responsibility, but because even there we assume our positions as believers. Even there we must dare to name God, to confess God from within the womb of politics, and so to challenge every idolatry that seeks to displace God in the lives of God's people. And so we come together to pray for transformation, political and societal and economic; and we prayed for personal transformation, for conversion, so that people might be driven by inner conviction rather than by political expediency.

We pray also because we believe passionately in the power of prayer. Prayer changes things, Christians say, and that is true. It is that conviction, you may perhaps remember, that inspired us in 1985 to call for a day of prayer for the downfall of the apartheid regime. We prayed then in the midst of a storm too, and we were viciously condemned by all who felt themselves threatened by a God who listens to the prayers of the oppressed. We were vilified by those whose interests could not abide the changes we were praying for. But the thing is, God heard our prayers, things changed, and apartheid is no more. Mandela could come out of prison, and you could come home from exile.

You call the Newlands gathering "sectarian", "exclusive" of those who were not white, "colored" or Christian. But that is manifestly untrue. Are you saying that Christians in this country are only "white" and "colored"? That black people are not Christian, or not interested in prayer? Or even worse, were not invited? But they were there, in their thousands, calling upon God to do what God has done before: give deliverance, respond with love and compassion, work liberation for God's people. It may well be that the [ANC] rally at Langa township was so sparsely attended because so many of the people expected there were at Newlands!

In fact, the utterly undesirable distinction between "whites", "coloreds" and "Africans" was not made by the Christian gathering, but by you. I hope it is not intentional, for it is so much against what the ANC professes. It certainly is very much the antithesis of the Christian faith and what was the reality on Wednesday. God's liberation for which we prayed is not just for "Christians", but for all our people, all in need, for all those oppressed by poverty, injustice, fear and violence.

And it is not as if this is something new. We have always believed this. God is a God of justice and liberation and those deeds of liberation can be seen throughout history, beginning with the liberation of the people of ancient Israel from slavery. And Christians have shared this faith with others in this country as long as anyone can remember. My own participation in the struggle for liberation in this country was based on, and inspired by, my faith in Jesus Christ, but that fact never gave rise to the desire to be exclusive of others. The very first time I was arrested by the apartheid regime was in 1979 on the bridge to Gugulethu, and as we marched to be arrested I was flanked by two Muslims: Hassan Solomon and Faried Esack. We did not then think in terms of exclusivity because I happened to march with my Bible in my hands. Nor did we think it exclusive when Muslims met on Friday and prayed in their mosques while I was not allowed to enter even when in interfaith services Sheik Gabier spoke in my church from my pulpit. Throughout those years we never thought that Muslims or others were "wrong". We just knew that we could not live without Jesus. And that we could not live without publicly acknowledging that.

What you saw on Wednesday, Minister, was not an exhibition of Christian exclusivity, but the continuation of a long tradition within the Christian church, who believes the words of Jesus, "Ask, and it shall be given you; search, and you will find; knock, and the door will be opened for you." Without this passionate belief in the power of prayer, without our faith in Jesus the Messiah, Christians would never have been able to join the struggle and to make the tremendous contribution they did make. Through all those years of struggle we were not so much inspired by slogans and speeches and vague dreams of "freedom" and "democracy" which, for millions, even today remain largely unfulfilled. Nor were we driven by philosophical concepts many did not even understand. We were, simply, and wonderfully, inspired by our faith. So we did what we did, in the name of Jesus. It did not then offend our comrades of other faiths. Why should it now? We were not ashamed of our faith then. Why should we be now?

When we marched and demonstrated for the exiles to come home, for Nelson Mandela and the others to be released, for the detainees to be set free, for the banned to be unbanned, we prayed and we believed. When we were tear gassed and beaten, set upon by dogs, detained and tortured, publicly humiliated and scorned; when we lay bleeding, dying and afraid, we were inspired, not by Marx or Lenin, but by our faith in Jesus of Nazareth. We faced the viciousness of the regime and we took the pain, *not* because we strove for ideological perfection or were lured by the false dream of some worker's paradise, but because Jesus said, "Do not be afraid, I have overcome the world." We did not ask if Mandela was a Christian, whether the exiles were communists, atheists or agnostics, or whether those detained shared our faith. We prayed and God's love sustained us and drove us to act.

Now today, there are millions who feel that what we have fought for has not been realized. They are deeply disturbed that our new democracy is threatened by crime and violence, by corruption in high places, public and private, by injustice in the courts, and by relationships poisoned by hatred, racism and class consciousness. They are deeply concerned by the abuse of women and children, by an ever-growing gap between the rich and the poor, and by a casual indifference, a frightening carelessness by those who have the power to make a difference. They come together to pray because they are deeply convinced that transformation that is only social, economic and political, however indispensable, is not enough. They believe that we need the power of God in our lives so that transformation can be fundamental. Let me be bold, Minister: South Africa would not be free today if there were not such people, and South Africa needs them today more than ever before. As you reflect on the history of South Africa, as you did last Wednesday, please do not forget this. More than anything our struggle was sustained by prayer and faith. I know. I was there. Denying this historical truth will only exacerbate our already grave situation.

According to the newspaper, you said that "The ANC is different from the Christian gathering. We do not care what race or of what faith you are. We do not celebrate Human Rights Day like those people. We celebrate it with joy and love. We do not exclude anybody." With all respect, Minister, that is a statement of stunning ignorance. First of all, at the heart of the Christian faith is the belief that "there is no Jew or Greek, bond or free, male and female, but all are one in Christ." The universality of the work of Jesus of Nazareth was one of the most revolutionary characteristics which marked the movement that took his name. That Western Christianity and racist churches in this country have denied this for so long does not make it any less true. And in Goodwood prison, certainly, on Wednesday prayers were offered in English and Afrikaans, in Xhosa and Sotho, and even in Arabic.

Second of all, I would venture to say that one would have to go far to match, never mind beat, the unbridled joy that reverberated around Newlands Stadium on Wednesday. It is a joy that is not affected whether a speaker turns up or not, or speaks well or not, or says the right things or not. It is a joy that stems from the truth that Jesus has the power to save and change lives. It is a joy that surpasses all human understanding, so that even in prison on Wednesday we sang and danced and worshipped, not because we were going home that night, but because we knew the truth about Jesus and about ourselves, and that truth has set us free. It is the same joy that sustained us even when the apartheid regime breathed fire and destruction. And I remember the songs that filled the air when we confronted riot squads in the streets of our townships and when they surrounded our churches. It was the joy of knowing that the man with the gun in the hand cannot at the same time hold onto our freedom too, and that if he wants to hold onto his own freedom he will have to lay down the gun.

We are told that you are upset because the day of prayer "looked like a Democratic Alliance[18] rally." Please do not give the DA more credit than they deserve. Whether or not the DA leadership in the Western Cape were present because of political opportunism might be true, but that is not the issue now. The point is rather; Where were the ANC leadership? Those who are Christians and members of the ANC must wonder about that. Why were we not represented? Why are we afraid to be associated with prayer in public? Wednesday's celebration was a celebration of prayer, a heartfelt cry on behalf of all South Africa's people to the God who promised us, "If my people who are called by my name humble themselves, pray, seek my face, and turn from their wicked ways, then I will hear from heaven, and will forgive their sins *and heal their land*." We should have been there, not to speechify or pontificate, but to pray.

Like you, I am distressed that some used the prayer gathering as an occasion to launch an attack on non-heterosexual persons. You are right: that *is* against the spirit of Human Rights Day. It is also, I strongly believe, against the spirit of Jesus of Nazareth. Many, many Christians, of whom I am one, do not agree with them. We differ fundamentally on our understanding of the Bible on this and other matters. I find the condemnation of Lesbian, Gay, Bi-sexual and Trans-sexual persons, many of whom are committed Christians, wrong, lacking in compassion and distasteful. On this point, conservative Christians share the same views as conservatives in other religions. I want to sincerely ask the forgiveness of all those who attended, or listened or watched, who wanted to share in the spirit of the day and were profoundly hurt by those remarks. But let us not try to score political points off the ignorance or pain of others. Instead of making this a point of condemnation [of the gathering] we should use this as an invitation to open discussion and honest conversation, also within the Christian church. On the whole, the issues that unite us [as a people] are more, and of greater import, than those that divide us. Our differences can be overcome.

So far from attacking the Christian gathering, the government should applaud it, support it, embrace it. True transformation shall not come to South Africa through new laws only, or more money for the police services, or more new prisons. It is clear to me also that politics alone is not the answer. For all the lofty political language our politicians from all sides now habitually employ, for all the constitutional guarantees we believe to have in place, for all the talk of a "rainbow nation", we know something fundamental is wrong. The vision of our politics has become the victim of our politics, our communal life has become confused, cheap and endangered; our public conversation through our politics and our media has long been, and still is superficial, mean spirited, and uninspiring. Our nation is in danger of losing its soul. Nothing less than the restoration of our covenant with God and with one another will save us. For Christians, that God is the God of Jesus whom we call Christ. What we need is a change of heart, a revolution of the spirit, an understanding of ourselves more than mere propaganda to make us feel good, and certainly more than the sectarian, hapless despair that so often poisons our public debate.

We need a conversion of the soul. That cannot be done by parliament although what happens in parliament can reflect it. It cannot be done by politics although our political discourse and actions may be fundamentally changed by it. It can only be done by a spiritual force greater than ourselves, more powerful than our speech, more lasting than our dreams. That is what Christians are trying to do when we pray: submit ourselves to that greater power which is God, so that we may be used by God for the good of our nation.

The vision that our politicians so often speak of seeking cannot come from those on high, from the privileged and the powerful. The father of my own Reformed tradition, John Calvin, has warned us that those in power rarely have the vision to use power for the sake of goodness. That vision has to be born amongst the people, carried within their hearts, warmed by the fire in their souls, nurtured by their acts of selfless love. That is what this call to prayer is all about. I cannot imagine that anyone in government could be against that. Let me assure you: what has happened last Wednesday, and what will continue to happen in South Africa is much bigger than petty party politics, and cannot be exploited, manipulated or stopped by it.

I hope you will think again about your words. Let us not fight. Not on this issue. No good will come of it. History is littered with the debris of once powerful regimes who thought they could take on God and the church. The National Party government in South Africa is only the most recent example of such utter foolishness. That is a fatal mistake born of the arrogance of power. The ANC must not make that mistake. Let us not fight. Let us rather take hands and together fight against the forces that seek to destroy our nation and the future of our children. Christians will continue to pray. We invite you to join us. If you cannot pray with us, please do not stand in our way.

I hope fervently that you are not scandalized by my writing to you. Things have changed and many at this moment are embarrassed to know me now and I apologize if I do cause such embarrassment to you now. The stain of leprosy which prison brings has added deeply to the pain of the last seven years. Now is not the time to discuss the reasons why I am here. Like so many others, I am sure you know why. But I am a Christian, one who knows God's forgiveness and mercy, and although I am, in the eyes of the world, "fallen from grace", I have found that God's grace is sufficient for me and that God's mercies are new every morning. That is the promise upon which I dare to stand and in which I continue to rejoice. Although as Paul says, I am truly the very least of all saints, this grace was also given to me to bring to all God's children the boundless riches of Christ.

I am also well aware that I have, in the normal sense of things, no "mandate" [from the leadership], that precious stamp of legitimacy the ANC prizes so highly, so that you may be tempted to put this letter aside. I hope you do not, for my mandate comes from Christ, whose servant I still am. I am in chains, but the Word of God is not bound. And it is to that Word I seek to be obedient. I am in prison, but Christ, in his mercy, is not ashamed of me, and therefore I am called not to be ashamed of the gospel of Jesus Christ and it is to that gospel and that name I now witness. I come to you with nothing more than this. And with nothing less than this.

Please allow me to end with another word from Paul, who had failings and fears like all of us, but who through the grace of God has left a marvelous legacy of Christian faith and witness for us all to follow: "Now to Him who by the power at work within us is able to accomplish abundantly more than we all we can ask or imagine; to Him be the glory in the church and in Christ Jesus to all generations, forever and ever."

May grace and peace be with you,
Nkosi sikilel' I Afrika!

Yours faithfully,
Allan Boesak.

PS: Because of the public import of the issue at hand I shall treat this as an open letter.

Notes

Introduction

1. It is not my intention to reintroduce the discussion around the word *kairos* as it is found in the New Testament and the meaning it has gained since it was first used as a theological concept to indicate uniquely urgent moments in history that call believers to discernment, decision, and action. That has already been superbly done by Paul Tillich, see his chapter on "Kairos" in *The Protestant Era* (Chicago: University of Chicago Press, 1938). See also Robert McAfee Brown (ed.), *Kairos: Three Prophetic Challenges to the Church* (Grand Rapids, MI: Wm. B. Eerdmans, 1990), 2–7.
2. See *Kairos Palestine, 2009, a Moment of Truth, a Word of Faith, Hope, and Love from the Heart of Palestinian Suffering*, www.kariospalestine.ps; see the responses, from South Africa: http://kairossouthernafrica.wordpress.com/about; from Kairos USA: www.kairosusaorg; from the United Kingdom: *Time for Action, a British Response to a Moment of Truth, the Kairos Palestine Document*, www.kairosbritain.org.uk; *Kairos Palestine, The Iona Call*, http://amosaicof peace.wordpress.com/2012/07/25/kairos-palestine-the-iona-call-20. See also the Master's degree program on Kairos Studies at Colgate Rochester Crozier Divinity School, Rochester, NY, USA, www.crcds.edu
3. Recently, French Prime Minister Manuel Valls admitted to the existence of a "geographic, social, ethnic apartheid" in his country through the relegation of some people to the suburbs, ghettos; the ethnic divisions, the more and more emphatic role skin color plays in French society, discrimination because of skin color "or because she is a woman." "The word 'apartheid' is specifically surprising," writes news agency teleSUR, "as it suggests that the segregation logic has been at least partly built up through public policies, or failed policies of housing, education, employment, and is not merely the result of a social crisis." http://readersupportednews.org/news-section2/318-66/28177-french-prime-minister-there-is-ethnic-apartheid-in-france, accessed January 22, 2015. Such admissions make clear to what extent "apartheid" is no longer to be regarded as a historic

South African phenomenon, but has come to describe deeply systematized situations of discrimination, racism, domination, and violence in the world in general.

4. According to South African economics scholar Patrick Bond, the term "global apartheid" was first used by former South African president Thabo Mbeki at the welcoming ceremony of the World Summit for Sustainable Development in Johannesburg, 2002: "We have all converged to confront the social behaviour that has pity neither for beautiful nature nor for living human beings. This social behaviour has produced and entrenches a global system of apartheid. The suffering of the billions who are the victims of this system calls for the same response that drew the peoples of the world into the struggle for the defeat of apartheid in this country." See Patrick Bond, "Is the Reform Really Working?", *The South Atlantic Quarterly*, 103, 4, (2004), 817–839. See on global apartheid as a challenge for the church and people of faith, my analysis within the framework of the *Accra Confession*; Allan Aubrey Boesak, *Dare We Speak of Hope, Searching for a Language of Life in Faith and Politics* (Grand Rapids, MI: Wm. B. Eerdmans, 2014), Chapter 2, 43–66 and further references there. On global violence, war, and peace, see *Dare We Speak of Hope*, Chapter 4, 90–122. For further analysis see Patrick Bond, *Against Global Apartheid. South Africa Meets the World Bank, IMF, and International Finance* (London and Cape Town: Zed Books, 2004).
5. See, for example, Robert Reich, "The Bankruptcy of Detroit and the Division of America," http://readersupportednews.org/opinion2/279-82/257525-focus-the-bankruptcy-of-detroit- 6 September 2014, accessed September 8, 2014.
6. John De Gruchy has raised the question of John Calvin's theology and its relationship with modern liberation theology, and here I endeavor to take that conversation further. See John W. De Gruchy, "Toward a Reformed Theology of Liberation: A Retrieval of Reformed Symbols in the Struggle for Justice," in David Willis and Michael Welker (eds.), *Toward the Future of Reformed Theology, Tasks, Topics, Traditions* (Grand Rapids, MI, and Cambridge, UK: Wm. B. Eerdmans, 1999), 103–119
7. See Richard Lischer, "Anointed with Fire: The Structure of Prophecy in the Sermons of Martin Luther King Jr.," in Timothy George, James Earl Massey, and Robert Smith (eds.), *Our Sufficiency Is of God, Essays on Preaching in Honor of Gardner C. Taylor* (Macon, GA: Mercer University Press, 2010), 231.
8. See Richard Horsley (ed.), *In the Shadow of Empire: Reclaiming the Bible as History of Faithful Resistance* (Louisville, KY: Westminster John Knox Press, 2008). See Gunther Wittenberg, *Resistance Theology in the Old Testament, Collected Essays* (Pietermaritzburg: Cluster Publications, 2007). Both Wittenberg and West read the Bible as "primarily a potential source for liberation rather than a source of oppression," see vii.
9. See Charles Villa-Vicencio, "Quo Vadis? The Dangerous Memory of the Gospel," *The Link*, 47, 2, (April–May, 2014), 3–10.

1 Hearing the Cry and Reading the Signs of the Times: A Humanity with a Kairos Consciousness

1. See Clint Le Bruyns, "The Rebirth of a Kairos Theology? A Public Theological Perspective," paper presented at the Brazil-South African Consultation on Citizenship and Interculturality, Unisa, Pretoria, March 23, 2012, available at http://www.academia.edu/148082/The_Rebirth_of_Kairos_Theology_A_Public_Theological_Perspective, accessed November 3, 2013. Le Bruyns writes, "I recall how much this process of reading the *Palestinian Kairos Document* and attempting a South African response forced us to ask questions about our own life-situation and the public role of theology and church. It pushed us to revisit our own kairos document and the quality of public theology for liberation, justice and dignity it envisaged and called for. I remember how much the Palestinian Kairos Document seemed to be helping us reconnect with our South African context..." op. cit., 5. The authors of *Call to Action, a U.S. Response to the Kairos Palestine Document* write, "We begin with a confession of sin to Palestinians in the State of Israel, the West Bank, Gaza, East Jerusalem, the diaspora and in refugee camps in Gaza, the West Bank, Lebanon, Jordan, and Syria. As U.S. Christians we bear responsibility for failing to say 'enough!'...We have failed to speak the truth as we see it and in so doing follow Jesus' path of love and forgiveness as the way to justice and peace. But now we are called to speak the truth..." Kairos USA 2012, 1, 2. Gerald O. West speaks of the "complicity of the churches" who since 1994 "have withdrawn into what the Kairos Document referred to as 'Church Theology.'" See Gerald O. West, "People's Theology, Prophetic Theology, and Public Theology in Post-liberation South Africa," Ujamaa Centre, School of Religion, Philosophy and Classics, University of KwaZulu-Natal, http://academia.edu/7263452
2. The *Kairos Document* can be accessed at http://www.sahistory.org.za/archive/challenge-church-comment-political-crisis-south-africa-kairos-document-1985.
3. See Clint Le Bruyns, "The Rebirth of Kairos Theology?", 5. As of this writing, at least one theological seminary in the United States, Colgate Rochester Crozier Divinity School in Rochester, New York, has launched a Master's in Theology degree program called "Kairos Studies."
4. Cf. Allan Boesak, "Kairos Consciousness," http://kairossouthernafrica.wordpress.com/kairos-consciousness, accessed November 3, 2013.
5. See Clint Le Bruyns, op. cit. Cf. "Latest Draft: Constitution of Kairos Southern Africa," http://kairossouthernafrica.wordpress.com/about, accessed November 3, 2013.
6. For a compilation of kairos documents since 1985 see *Kairos, the Moment of Truth, the Kairos Documents*, compiled and edited by Gary S. D. Leonard, Ujamaa Centre for Biblical and Theological Community Development and Research, (2010), http://ujamaa.ukzn.ac.za/Libraries/manuals/The Kairos Documents.sflb.ashx. For a discussion of the contents and intent of kairos documents see Dirk J. Smit, "Kairos Documents," in Dirk J. Smit, *Essays in*

Public Theology, Collected Essays 1, Study Guides in Religion and Theology 12, Publications of the University of the Western Cape, ed. Ernst Conradie (Stellenbosch: Sun Media, 2007), 251–254.

7. For the concept of "pseudo innocence" see Allan Aubrey Boesak, *Farewell to Innocence, a Socio-Ethical Study on Black Theology and Black Power* (Maryknoll, NY: Orbis Books, 1977).
8. John Calvin, *Commentary on the Twelve Minor Prophets*, Habakkuk 1:2.
9. See e.g. Allan Boesak, *The Tenderness of Conscience, African Renaissance and the Spirituality of Politics*, (Stellenbosch: Sun Media, 2005), 223–224.
10. See Paul Lehmann, *The Transfiguration of Politics, Jesus Christ and the Question of Revolution* (London: SCM Press, 1975), 235; see also Allan Boesak, *The Tenderness of Conscience*, 224.
11. For a brilliant reflection on injustice as wounding God, see Nicholas Wolterstorff, "The Wounds of God: Calvin's Theology of Social Justice," in Nicholas Wolterstorff, *Hearing the Call, Liturgy, Justice, Church and World*, ed. Mark R. Gornik and Gregory Thompson (Grand Rapids: Wm. B. Eerdmans, 2011), 114–132. I return to this crucial matter in chapter 2, below.
12. See "Latest Draft: Constitution of Kairos Southern Africa." http://kairossouthernafrica.wordpress.com/about, accessed November 3, 2013.
13. I return to this important discussion in chapter 2 below.
14. See West, "People's Theology," 11, quoting Ramaphosa from *City press* and other newspaper reports.
15. Allan Boesak, *The Tenderness of Conscience*, 224.
16. See Allan Boesak "Kairos Consciousness." I reflect more fully on this particular point in Allan Aubrey Boesak, *Dare We Speak of Hope? Searching for a Language of Life in Faith and Politics* (Grand Rapids, MI, and Cambridge, UK: Wm. B. Eerdmans, 2013), 62, 63.
17. See Naim Stifan Ateek, *A Palestinian Christian Cry for Reconciliation* (Maryknoll, NY: Orbis Books, 2008), 11.
18. See the introduction to "Kairos India 2000," Leonard (ed.), op. cit., citing habil James Massey, "Kairos India 2000: A Process of Reflection for Social Activists, http://www.cca.org.hk/clusters/fmu/resources/urm/up9p/99build1.htm/.
19. This is an extremely important point emphasized in every kairos document. In the 1989 *Kairos Document* on behalf of kairos Christians from the Philippines, South Korea, Namibia, South Africa, El Salvador, Nicaragua, and Guatemala titled "The Road to Damascus," the kairos theologians write, "The particular crisis or *kairos* that has led us to the writing and signing of this proclamation of faith is the conflict between Christians in the world today. We have wished to make it quite clear that we believe that those Christians who side with the imperialists, the oppressors and the exploiters of people are siding with the idolaters who worship money, power, privilege and pleasure. To misuse Christianity to defend oppression is heretical. And to persecute Christians who are oppressed or who side with the oppressed is apostasy—the abandonment of the gospel of Jesus Christ." See Gary S. D. Leonard, (ed.), op. cit., 189.

20. See *Challenge to the Church: A Theological Comment on the Political Crisis in South Africa. The Kairos Document 1985*, http://www.sahistory.org.za/archive/challenge-church-theological-comment-crisis "Whereas the characterization in the 1980s was in terms of political engagement," writes Gerald West, "'church theology,' in our current context would have to be framed in economic terms. From the side of the state, 'church theology' forms of Christianity are attractive alliance partners, given their reluctance to engage with the state on structural matters, such as economic systems. The state is content to cede the moral terrain to this religious sector, which would include the condition of the nation's soul, provided of course this was understood as the collective personal morality of the nation," West, op. cit., 12.
21. Walter Brueggemann, *The Prophetic Imagination* (Philadelphia: Fortress Press, 1978), 13.
22. Ibid.
23. Cornel West, *Democracy Matters: Winning the Fight Against Imperialism* (New York: Penguin Press, 2007), 114–115.
24. See Charles Villa-Vicencio and John De Gruchy (eds.), *Apartheid Is a Heresy* (Grand Rapids: Wm. B. Eerdmans, 1982).
25. See G. D. Cloete and D. J. Smit (eds.), *A Moment of Truth, the Confession of the Dutch Reformed Mission Church* (Grand Rapids: Wm. B. Eerdmans, 1984).
26. Brian D. McClaren, *Why Did Jesus, Moses, the Buddha, and Mohammed Cross the Road? Christian Identity in a Multi-faith World* (Nashville, NY: Jericho Books, 2012), 82, cited in Mark Braverman, *A Wall in Jerusalem, Hope, Healing, and the Struggle for Justice in Israel and Palestine* (New York: Jericho Books, 2013), 74.
27. M. M. Thomas, "Issues Concerning the Life and Work of the Church in a Revolutionary World," in A. H. van den Heuvel (ed.), *Unity of Mankind* (Geneva: W.C.C., 1969), 89–98. For discussion of the controversy at the time see Allan Aubrey Boesak, *Farewell to Innocence, A Socio-Ethical Study of Black Theology and Black Power* (Maryknoll, NY: Orbis Books, [1977], 1984), 80–90.
28. See Le Bruyns, op. cit., 5.
29. The interrelatedness of these movements and struggles is illustrated by a description of the Occupy Movement of 2011: "The Occupy movement was part of a much larger global protest and revolt in 2011. It began when Tunisian fruit vendor, Mohamed Bouazizi, drenched himself in paint thinner and then lit a match to protest against police harassment and government callousness. His death ignited large-scale rallies and demonstrations for democracy and economic justice across Arab cities in Tunisia, Egypt, Libya, Syria, Bahrain, Yemen, Algeria, and other countries... Encouraged by political populism in the Arab world, *Adbusters* [magazine in Canada] issued a challenge for Americans: 'Are you ready for a Tahrir moment?'", see Joerg Rieger and Kwok Pui-lan, *Occupy Religion, Theology of the Multitudes* (Lanham, MD: Rowman and Littlefield, 2012), 2. Rieger and Pui-lan quote *Time* magazine: "In 2011, protesters did not just voice their complaints; they changed the world." The point here of course, is not to claim that all these

struggles are similar, but rather that there is an interconnectedness to all struggles for justice, all the more pertinent because of the globalized reality of our world.

30. Elizabeth Schüssler Fiorenza, "An Invitation to 'Dance' in the Open House of Wisdom: Feminist Study of the Bible," in Cho Hee Ann and Katherine Pfisterer Darr (eds.), *Engaging the Bible: Critical Readings from Contemporary Women* (Minneapolis: Fortress Press, 2006), 83, cited in Cheryl B. Anderson, *Ancient Laws & Contemporary Controversies, The Need for Inclusive Biblical Interpretation* (New York: Oxford University Press, 2009), 17.
31. See Joerg Rieger, *Christ and Empire, from Paul to Postcolonial Times* (Minneapolis: Fortress Press, 2007), Chapter 1; see also John Dominic Crossan, "Roman Imperial Theology," in Richard A. Horsley, (ed.), *In the Shadow of Empire, Reclaiming the Bible as a History of Faithful Resistance* (Louisville and London: Westminster John Knox Press, 2008), 59–73. Crossan writes, "Before Jesus existed, and even if he had never existed, these were the titles of Caesar the Augustus: Divine, Son of God, God, and God from God; Lord, Redeemer, Liberator, and Savior of the World. When those titles were taken from him, the Roman emperor, and given to a Jewish peasant, it was a case of either low lampoon or high treason. Since the Roman authorities did not roll over in their togas laughing, we may presume that Pilate, acting for them, got it precisely correct. He publicly, officially, and legally executed Jesus for nonviolent revolution against their imperial power," 73; John Dominic Crossan, *God and Empire: Jesus Against Rome, Then and Now* (San Francisco and New York: HarperOne, HarperCollins, 2007); see also Allan Aubrey Boesak, *Dare We Speak of Hope?*, 151–152.
32. Tom Engelhardt, "American Jihad 2014," http://readersuportnews.org/opinion2/277-75/21359-american-jihad-2014?tmpl=compon..., accessed September 1, 2014.
33. James Cone, *Black Theology and Black Power* (Minneapolis: Seabury Press, 1969), 38, 39.
34. James Cone, "Black Theology and the Black Church: Where Do We Go from Here?", in James Cone and Gayraud Wilmore (eds.), *Black Theology and Black Liberation* (Maryknoll, NY: Orbis Books, 1993), 106.
35. See e.g. Boesak *Farewell*, 72–98. See also James Cone, *God of the Oppressed*: "Unless we black theologians can make an adequate distinction between divine revelation and human aspirations, there is nothing to keep Black Theology from identifying God's will with anything black people should decide to do at any given historical moment," (New York: Seabury Press, 1972), 84–85.
36. Dietrich Bonhoeffer Works, 8, 515–516; see also Allan Aubrey Boesak, *Dare We Speak of Hope?* 80–81.
37. See Mary Elizabeth King, *A Quiet Revolution: The First Palestinian Intifada and Nonviolent Resistance* (New York: Nation Books, 2007); see also Stephen Zunes, *Supporting Non-Violence in Syria*, truth-out.org/news/item/13774-supporting-non-violence-in-syria?tmpl, accessed January 8, 2013.

38. Paul Lehmann, *Ethics in a Christian Context* (New York: Harper & Row, 1963), 117.
39. Cf. Allan Boesak, *Black and Reformed, Apartheid, Liberation and the Calvinist Tradition* (Maryknoll, NY: Orbis Books, 1984), 110.
40. Bonhoeffer in his letter to Henriod, see Frederich Schlingensiepen, *Dietrich Bonhoeffer, Martyr, Thinker, Man of Resistance*, trans. Isabel Best (London and New York: T&T Clark, 2010), 159.
41. See John De Gruchy, "South African Theology," in William Dyrness and Veli-Matti Kärkkainen (eds.), *Global Dictionary of Theology* (Downers Grove: IVP, 2008), 841–845, Le Bruyns, op. cit., 1.
42. See John W. De Gruchy, "Toward a Reformed Theology of Liberation: A Retrieval of Reformed Symbols in the Struggle for Justice," in David Willis and Michael Welker (eds.), *Toward the Future of Reformed Theology* (Grand Rapids: Wm. B. Eerdmans, 1999), 103–119. There De Gruchy (p. 106) writes, "Our contention, then, is that just as it is legitimate and possible to be a Roman Catholic theologian of liberation, so it is legitimate and possible to be a Reformed theologian of liberation." For De Gruchy's take on the 1985 *Kairos Document* and its relationship with liberation theology, see e.g. his *Liberating Reformed Theology* (Grand Rapids: Wm. B. Eerdmans; Cape Town: David Philip, 1991).
43. Op. cit., 1, 2.
44. I refer here also to the theology of the first missionaries of the London Missionary Society perhaps especially Johannes Theodorus van der Kemp and and his early colleagues who came to South Africa and on the basis of their faith and their understanding of the call of the Gospel, threw in their lot with the indigenous peoples of South Africa, took up the fight for justice and human rights against the colonial regime and the settlers and their churches, a point I make in *The Tenderness of Conscience*, 103–131. But see especially Richard Elphick's comprehensive and convincing study *The Equality of Believers, Protestant Missionaries and the Racial Politics of South Africa* (Charlottesville: University of Virginia Press, 2012); also John W. De Gruchy, *The Church Struggle in South Africa* (Minneapolis: Fortress Press, 2005), Chapter 1.
45. See Allan Aubrey Boesak, *Dare We Speak of Hope?* 67–70.
46. See Albert John Luthuli, *Let My People Go! The Autobiography of Albert Luthuli* (Cape Town: Tafelberg and Mafube, 2006), 232–236.
47. See John W. De Gruchy and Charles Villa-Vicencio (eds.), *Apartheid Is a Heresy*.
48. Vuyani S. Vellem, *The Symbol of Liberation in South African Public Life: A Black Theological Perspective,* unpublished PhD thesis, University of Pretoria, 2007, 83.
49. See Charles Villa-Vicencio, "Quo Vadis? The Dangerous Memory of the Gospel: South Africa, Palestine and the Papal Visit to the Holy Land," *The Link*, 47, 2, April–May 2014, 3–10. The quotation is on p. 5.
50. See Letty M. Russell, *Human Liberation in a Feminist Perspective: A Theology* (Philadelphia: Westminster Press, 1974), 58.

51. A more detailed and very helpful discussion on liberation theology is found in Justo L. González and Catherine Gunsalus González, *Liberation Preaching, the Pulpit and the Oppressed* (Nashville: Abingdon, 1980), Chapter 1.
52. Hugo Assmann, *Theology for a Nomad Church* (Maryknoll, NY: Orbis Books, 1976), 129–145.
53. See Obery M. Hendricks Jr., *The Politics of Jesus, Rediscovering the True Revolutionary Nature of Jesus' Teachings and How They Have Been Corrupted* (New York: Doubleday, 2006), 70–71; Richard A. Horsley, *Galilee* (Minneapolis: Fortress Press, 1995).
54. Seen from this perspective Cheryl Anderson's important work offers not just new insights into liberation theology but is a necessary corrective of a "blind spot" in liberation theology.
55. Dirk J. Smit, "Kairos Documents," op. cit., 254. See Leonard (ed.), op. cit., 209–239. Why it is included as a "kairos document." The one notable exception seems to be "A Kairos for Kenya" which is markedly different in style and character than other kairos documents. Lacking the stringent sociopolitical and economic analysis, the "challenge to the church," the sense of urgency and prophetic confrontation with those who perpetrate injustice so characteristic of kairos documents, it reads more like a supplication to the Kenyan government. Its motto at the start of the document, "Come now, let us reason together," from Isaiah 1:18, becomes more political appeasement than prophetic exhortation and the text quoted at the end of the document, "Let justice flow like a stream and righteousness like a river that never runs dry" (Amos 5:24) becomes an expression of wishful thinking rather than an authoritative proclamation to the powers that be.
56. See Allan Boesak, *The Tenderness of Conscience*, Chapter 5.
57. See Le Bruyns, op. cit., 4, 5; see also Allan Boesak, *The Tenderness of Conscience*, Chapter 5.
58. See e.g. Allan Boesak, *The Tenderness of Conscience*; Tinyiko Sam Moluleke, "May the Black God Stand Up, Please!: Biko's Challenge to Religion," in Andile Mngxitama, Amanda Alexander, and Nigel C. Gibson (eds.), *Biko Lives! Contesting the Legacies of Steve Biko* (New York: Palgrave Macmillan, 2008), 115–126; *The Evil of Patriarchy in Church, Society and Politics*, papers from a consultation hosted by Inclusive and Affirming Ministries (IAM) in partnership with the Department of Religion and Theology of the University of the Western Cape and the Centre for Christian Spirituality, published by IAM (Stellenbosch, 2009); Allan Boesak, *Running with Horses, Reflections of an Accidental Politician* (Cape Town: JoHo! Publishers, 2009), especially Chapters 11, 13, and 18; and Allan Aubrey Boesak and Curtiss Paul DeYoung, *Radical Reconciliation: Beyond Political Pietism and Christian Quietism* (Maryknoll, NY: Orbis Books, 2012).
59. Op. cit., 5.
60. Op. cit., 5.
61. Le Bruyns seeks, in my view not very successfully, to locate the discussion of kairos theology as prophetic theology within the framework of "public theology" widely regarded in theological circles in the global South as being promoted from within Euro-American theological circles as a theology that sought to replace liberation theology.

62. Ateek, op. cit., 12, 13.
63. Idem.
64. See Naim Stifan Ateek, *Justice, and Only Justice: A Palestinian Theology of Liberation* (Maryknoll, NY: Orbis Books, 1989); also Naim S. Ateek, Marc H. Ellis, and Rosemary Radford Ruether (eds.), *Faith and the Intifada: Palestinian Christian Voices* (Maryknoll, NY: Orbis Books, 1992).
65. Le Bruyns, op. cit., 5, 6.
66. See Douglas A. Hare, *Matthew, Interpretation, a Bible Commentary, for Teaching and Preaching*, James Luther Mays, Patrick D. Miller, and Paul J. Achtemeier (eds.) (Louisville, KY: Westminster John Knox Press, 1993), 122; *The New Interpreter's Bible*, Vol. VIII (Nashville: Abingdon Press, 1995), 267; Warren Carter, *Matthew and the Margins, a Socio-Political and Religious Reading*, Journal for the Study of the New Testament Supplement Series, Stanley E. Porter (exec. ed.), (Sheffield: Sheffield Academic Press, 2000). "John challenged and conflicted with religious and political elites including Herod Antipas. So: did they go out to see Herod 'blown about', attacked by John's critique of urban power, wealth, and alliance with Rome, and /or punished by God?" Carter, *Matthew*, 251. There is also the suggestion that since the reed as symbol appeared on some of Herod's coins, Jesus means to say that John is not to be bribed or bought to speak in Herod's favor.
67. See *Letters and Papers from Prison*, enlarged edition (ed.), Eberhard Bethge, trans. R. H. Fuller et al., (New York: Macmillan, 1972), 347–348.
68. See Allan Boesak, *The Fire Within, Sermons from the Edge of Exile* (Cape Town: New World Foundation, 2004; and Glasgow: Wild Goose Publications, 2007), Introduction.
69. Kelly and Nelson, op. cit., 509.

2 At the Heart of It All: Kairos, Apartheid, and the Calvinist Tradition

1. John Calvin, commentary on Isaiah 58:6–7 See also Nicholas Wolterstorff, "The Wounds of God: Calvin's Theology of Social Justice," in Mark R. Gornik and George Thompson (eds.), *Hearing the Call, Liturgy, Justice, Church, and World* (Grand Rapids, MI/Cambridge, UK: Wm. B. Eerdmans, 2010), 114–132. The quotation is on pp. 126–127.
2. It should be noted that although I speak mostly of the white Dutch Reformed Church (NGK) within whose orbit the three black Dutch Reformed churches, the Dutch Reformed Mission Church, the DR Church in Africa and the Reformed Church in Africa (formerly Indian Reformed Church) most immediately lived and functioned, the particular interpretation of Reformed theology I am referring to was practiced by all three white Reformed churches in South Africa; the DRC, or NGK, the Hervormde Kerk (NHK), and the Gereformeerde Kerk (GK). Support for apartheid and the embrace of the theology of apartheid as moral and theological justification of the ideology and policies of apartheid were mainstays of all three. As a result the Hervormde

Kerk, who like the DRC, was a member of the World Alliance of Reformed Churches, was suspended together with the DRC for its theological support for apartheid and its racist practices in the church. The Gereformeerde Kerk never was a member of WARC. All three churches made "Christian Nationalism" foundational for their interpretation of Reformed theology.

3. Christiaan Frederick Beyers Naudé was a white Afrikaner, a Dutch Reformed minister with incontestable Afrikaner credentials and destined for great things within the Afrikaner community and perhaps the country as a whole. He was one of the selected few (and in his time the youngest) who gained membership of the Afrikaner Broederbond, a highly exclusive and influential secret society of Afrikaner males who basically functioned as a parallel government. The Sharpeville massacre on March 21, 1960 and its aftermath had a powerful impact on Naudé. He became an impeccable foe of apartheid and a despised and ostracized figure in his own community while simultaneously turning into a hero for black people in general and my generation within the black Dutch Reformed churches in particular. His influence in my life was huge and his courage and integrity remain an inspiration for many still today. He was one of very few private citizens offered a state funeral by the ruling ANC government.
4. In the aftermath of the Sharpeville massacre the member churches of the World Council of Churches, and under its auspices met in Cottesloe, a suburb of Johannesburg, to discuss the massacre and its consequences for South African society and South African churches. The statement issued from the gathering became known as the Cottesloe Declaration. I return to, and discuss in more depth, both the Sharpeville massacre and the Cottesloe Declaration in chapter 3 below.
5. The Group Areas Act of 1950 was the title of three acts of the Parliament of South Africa enacted under the apartheid government. The acts assigned racial groups to different, racially designated residential and business sections in urban and rural areas. One effect of the law was to exclude all persons classified as "non-white" from living in the most developed areas which were exclusively restricted to whites. This led to arbitrary dispossession and forced removals on a huge scale, though not on the same levels as the 1913 and 1936 Land Acts. The Group Areas Act was repealed on June 30, 1991 by the Abolition of Racially Based Land measures Act, No. 108 of 1991.
6. Cf. Danie Langner, *Teen die Héle Wêreld Vry—Knegte van die Allerhoogste: Koot Vorster—Segsman of Profeet?* (Pretoria: Griffel Publishers, 2007), 103.
7. Langner, *Teen die Héle Wêreld Vry*, 104, 105. For the peculiar term "Boere-Calvinisme" ("Boer Calvinism," perhaps better understood as "Afrikaner Calvinism"), see Langner, 103, 153, 154. In Afrikaans though, the term "Boer," and Langner's use of it at this particular historic moment would have added significance, reflecting the reemergence of Afrikaner ethnic nationalism in South Africa after 1994. For a very useful discussion of the roots of Afrikaner Calvinism see T. Dunbar Moodie's classic, *The Rise of Afrikanerdom, Power, Apartheid, and the Afrikaner Civil Religion* (Berkeley: University of California Press, 1975), 22ff.

8. For a discussion on this issue see Allan Boesak, *Running with Horses, Reflections of an Accidental Politician* (Cape Town: JoHo! Publications, 2009), Chapter 1.
9. See the testimony of Prince Dibeela, younger generation theologian from Botswana, until 2014 Secretary-General of the United Congregational Church in Southern Africa, cf. Prince Dibeela, "In Pursuit of a Liberating Humanism, Reflections in Honour of Allan Aubrey Boesak," in Prince Dibeela, Puleng Lenkabula, and Vuyani Vellem (eds.), *Prophet from the South, Essays in Honour of Allan Aubrey Boesak* (Stellenbosch: Sun Media, 2014), 226: "I am part of the generation that came into theological consciousness in the eighties, at a time when Southern Africa was groaning and experiencing the birth pains of liberation. It was a difficult time to be a Christian, let alone a Reformed Christian because of the farcical and supposedly Calvinistic hermeneutics of the Dutch Reformed Church in South Africa at the time. The scandalous, systemic justification of apartheid did a great blow to the church as a credible community of transformation and liberation."
10. See Allan Aubrey Boesak, *Black and Reformed, Apartheid, Liberation and the Reformed Tradition* (New York: Orbis Books, 1984).
11. See David P. Botha, "Church and Kingdom," in Margaret Nash, (ed.), *Thy Kingdom Come* (Johannesburg: SACC, 1988) who makes a virtually unassailable argument for not only this fact, but for the irreplaceable role of the DRC in the preparation for apartheid rule. De Gruchy, *The Church Struggle* (Grand Rapids: Wm. B. Eerdmans, 1985), 9, 10 also refers to this fateful decision and calls it a theological position "somewhat removed from the theology propounded by the reformer from Geneva." Botha is much more direct.
12. Still one of the most comprehensive and thorough critiques of the theology of apartheid as it was formulated in the DRC's 1974 apologia, *Ras, Volk en Nasie en Volkereverhoudinge in die Lig van die Heilige Skrif* (Cape Town: N.G. Kerkuitgewers, 1974), is Douglas Bax's quite superb study *A Different Gospel: A Critique of the Theology of Apartheid*, (Parkview, Johannesburg: The Presbyterian Church of South Africa, 1979).
13. Boesak, *Black and Reformed*, 86.
14. Cf. Steve Biko, *I Write What I Like, a Selection of His Writings* (Johannesburg: Ravan Press, 1996), 58–59.
15. Helmut Gollwitzer, *Die Kapitalistische Revolution* (Munich: Kaiser, 1974), 45.
16. In the *Sunday Times*, November 8, 1970, cited in Charles Villa-Vicencio, "An All-pervading Heresy: Racism and the English-speaking Churches," in Charles Villa-Vicencio and John De Gruchy (eds.), *Apartheid Is a Heresy* (Cape Town: David Philip, 1982), 59.
17. See John De Gruchy, "Toward a Reformed Theology of Liberation," in David Willis and Michael Welker (eds.), *Toward the Future of Reformed Theology, Tasks, Topics, Traditions* (Grand Rapids: Wm. B. Eerdmans; Cambridge, UK, 1999), 106.
18. Idem.
19. Boesak, *Black and Reformed*, 84.

20. Raymond Beddy, *Inleiding tot die Geskiedenis van die Khoikhoi en San as Afrikane, vanaf die Evolusionêre Ontstaan in Noord Afrika tot die Hede in Suid Afrika* (Bloemfontein: Handisa Media, 2007), 48.
21. At that point, the DRC in the Cape colony was under the authority of the classis of Amsterdam of the Reformed Church in the Netherlands who had decreed that all slaves and persons from the indigenous communities who became Christians and joined the church would become members of the DRC. The process of racial segregation in the church would not take firm hold till the middle of the nineteenth century after the DRC in South Africa received autonomy from the mother church in Holland in 1824.
22. Richard Elphick, "Evangelical Missions and Racial 'Equalization' in South Africa, 1890–1914," in Dana L. Robert (ed.), *Converting Colonialism, Visions and Realities in Mission History, 1706–1914* (Grand Rapids, MI: Wm. B. Eerdmans; Cambridge, UK, 2008), 112–133. The quotation is on p. 112.
23. Elphick, op. cit., 112–113.
24. This is my direct translation of the Afrikaans rhymed version of the Genevan Psalms, from *Psalms en Gesange*, Nederduits Gereformeerde Kerk and Nederduitsch Hervormde Kerk (Cape Town: N.G. Kerkuitgewers 1976), Psalm 74.
25. See Elphick, "Evangelical Missions," in Dana L. Robert (ed.), op. cit., 113: "Their (the Khoi's) grievance was not only political but ecclesiastical and theological as well."
26. See Walter Brueggemann, *The Prophetic Imagination* (Philadelphia: Fortress Press, 1978), 13.
27. The fierceness of this battle is perhaps best illustrated by the history of controversy surrounding the formation and acceptance of Confession of Belhar as well as the search for theological identity and self-understanding independent of the white Afrikaner version and understanding of Calvin's theology in the black Reformed churches in South Africa.
28. Boesak, *Black and Reformed*, 86.
29. Boesak, *Black and Reformed*, 87–90. In this struggle we drew inspiration from the whole of the Reformed tradition including the Reformed confessions from the Dutch tradition and the Heidelberg Catechism, see *Black and Reformed*, 93, 96–99.
30. See, Allan Boesak, *Running with Horses, Reflections of an Accidental Politician* (Cape Town: JoHo! Publishers, 2009), 9. This Calvinist bent has sometimes been misunderstood as with e.g. Michael Walzer, who calls Calvin an "ideologist" rather than a theologian because of Calvinist theology's capacity "to activate its adherents and to change the world," cf. Walzer, *The Revolution of the Saints, a Study in the Origins of Radical Politics* (London: Weidenfeld & Nicolson, 1966), 27. In my view this misunderstanding arises because of a lack of insight in the meaning of Calvin's view of the world "as the theatre of God's glory," his understanding of God as a God of justice, as well as his understanding of the Lordship of Jesus Christ over all of life, and the supremacy of the Word of God as these must find practical expression in the life of the believer. For a brilliant explication of this see

Nicholas Wolterstorff, "The Wounds of God: Calvin's Theology of Social Justice," in Nicholas Wolterstorff, *Hearing the Call:* "What characterized the Calvinist movement as a whole," writes Wolterstorff, "was its dynamic restlessness; much of that can be traced to Calvin himself—to his actions in Geneva, but also to his words," op. cit., 128.

31. See Nicholas Wolterstorff, "The Wounds of God: Calvin's Theology of Social Justice," in Mark R. Gornik and Gregory Thompson, op. cit., 118–128.
32. Wolterstorff, op. cit., 119.
33. John Calvin, *Opera*, 45, 613. See also Boesak, *Black and Reformed*, 90.
34. *Institutes*, Book IV, 17, 38. I use here the translation by John Allen (Philadelphia: Presbyterian Board of Education, 1936). It was the administering of the sacraments that first gave cause to the accommodation of racism in the life of the DRC in the nineteenth century and that led to the infamous decision of the Synod of 1857, see De Gruchy, op. cit., 7–9. This text also played a key role in our argument before the World Alliance of Reformed Churches' 1982 General Council to declare the theological and biblical justification of apartheid a heresy.
35. See Allan Boesak, "God Made Us All, But...," *Black and Reformed*, 100–110.
36. *Opera*, 53, 639. *Sermon LIII* on I Timothy 6:17–19.
37. *Opera*, 21, 432.
38. Cf. Allan Aubrey Boesak, *The Tenderness of Conscience, African Renaissance and the Spirituality of Politics* (Stellenbosch: Sun Media, 2005), 203–204. See also Nicholas Wolterstorff, *Until Justice and Peace Embrace* (Grand Rapids: Wm. B. Eerdmans, 1983), and Wolterstorff, *Justice, Rights and Wrongs* (Princeton: Princeton University Press, 2008).
39. Calvin, Sermon CXL on Deuteronomy 24:14–18.
40. Abraham Kuyper, in his address before the Christian Social Congress in 1891, cited by Nicholas Wolterstorff, *Until Justice and Peace Embrace*, 73. See also Boesak, *Tenderness*, 207. It is these insights derived from true radical Calvinism in my view that make Kuyper universal and outlive his sometimes unbearable racism and European chauvinism.
41. This is how Calvin ends that famous passage in the *Institutes*, IV, xx, 32.
42. See Boesak, *Black and Reformed*, 32–41; see also Allan Boesak, *Running with Horses*, 21–71.
43. See Boesak, *Black and Reformed*, 94.
44. The continued, deliberate misrepresentation of our theological points of view, even today among the "new" generation of DRC theologians, shows precisely how disturbing this question has remained for white Reformed Christians in South Africa; see Langner, op. cit., 147, 152, 153. Also the continued resistance to the acceptance of the Confession of Belhar to the exclusion of all logic and reason is evidence of this seemingly inextinguishable trend.
45. Calvin, *Institutes*, IV, XX, 4. Even though some call the Romans 13:1–7 passage "rhetorical hyperbole" from Paul (see William Bouwsma, *John Calvin, a Sixteenth-Century Portrait* (New York and Oxford: Oxford University Press, 1988), note 9, 286, there is no question of the universal impact of

this view since the sixteenth century, and not just within churches of the Reformed tradition. Besides, we read this not as "rhetorical hyperbole" but rather as a vital critical notion built into the expectation of government displaying in its actions the image of God. A government that does not respond to this expectation as "servant of God for your good" loses its legitimacy, opens itself to fundamental critique and should be resisted, see Allan Boesak, "What Belongs to Caesar? Once Again Romans 13," in Allan Boesak and Charles Villa-Vicencio (eds.), *When Prayer Makes News* (Philadelphia: Westminster Press, 1986), 138–156.

46. Even though many read this as an expression of Calvin's conservative yearning to accommodate the empire, I think that Calvin may have intended this as a double-edged sword: it is a prophetic, critical reminder that the king is king *under* God who is after all "King of kings, to whose will the desires of all kings ought to be subject, to whose decrees all their commands ought to yield." Besides, the "minister of God" is a direct reference to the "servant of God" *(leitourgos)* the term Paul uses in Romans 13 where the emphasis is on government as servant of God... "*for your good*." The earthly ruler, as minister of God, ought to reflect the rule of God, namely justice, mercy, compassion, inclusion. Calvin writes as an exile from France, to a king whose heart "is presently turned away and estranged from us—even inflamed against us—still I hope that we may recover its grace..." So the respectful tone is not only because those in authority deserve such respect, it is also sensible politics. Yet even in his diplomatic caution the prophetic edge is not at all blunted. So he ends with the salutation, "Most powerful and shining king," which sounds, on the face of it, almost sycophantic. Still, Calvin balances that as the reminder comes back even here as Calvin tells the king who really has the last word: The faithful, who are suffering now (under this king), "await the strong hand of the Lord which will doubtless be shown forth in its season and will appear armed to deliver the poor from their affliction and to punish the scornful." Then follows the last sentence, "May the Lord, King of kings, *establish your throne in justice, and your seat in equity.*" Emphasis added. Even Francis could hardly have misunderstood that.
47. *Institutes*, IV, xx.
48. *Institutes*, IV, xx. Calvin constantly employs words such as "esteem" and "reverence" with regard to earthly rulers. Still, it is important to note that Calvin speaks of the "sacred majesty" with which God has invested *legitimate authority*. The understanding is clear: not all who *claim* authority has God's blessing.
49. *Institutes*, IV, xx, 25.
50. Nicholas Wolterstorff deals in detail with Calvin and Romans 13 in his *The Mighty and the Almighty* (New York and Oxford, UK: Oxford University Press, 2011).
51. See Allan Boesak, "What Belongs to Caesar?"
52. See Versahni Pillay, "Cursed If We Criticize Zuma? Think Again," Mail & Guardian (Online), October 8, 2013, available from http://mg.co.za/article/2013-10-08, cursed-if-we-criticise-zuma-think-again/ accessed July 14, 2014.

53. See Boesak, "What Belongs to Caesar?"; see also especially the whole body of recent New Testament studies dealing with this subject, e.g. Richard A. Horsley (ed.), *Paul and Empire, Religion and Power in Roman Imperial Society* (Harrisburg, PA: Trinity International Press, 1997); Richard A Horsley (ed.), *Paul and Politics, Ekklesia, Israel, Imperium, Interpretation* (Harrisburg, PA: Trinity International Press, 2000), and the bibliography cited there.
54. See Allan Boesak, "What Belongs to Caesar?"; Nicholas Wolterstorff, *The Mighty and the Almighty*, 83–104.
55. *Institutes*, IV, xx, 24. I agree with Calvin: "He would justly be deemed insane who disapproved of such a government."
56. See Calvin's *Institutes*, IV, xx, 32.
57. *Institutes*, IV, xx, 32.
58. See Don Compier, *What Is Rhetorical Theology? Textual Practice and Public Discourse* (Harrisburg: Trinity International Press, 1999); see also Dirkie Smit, "Resisting 'Lordless Powers'?", in Prince Dibeela, Puleng Lenkabula, and Vuyani Vellem (eds.), *Prophet from the South, Essays in Honour of Allan Aubrey Boesak*, 33–68; also Serene Jones, *Calvin and the Rhetoric of Piety*, Columbia Series in Reformed Theology, Columbia Theological Seminary (Louisville, KY: Westminster John Knox Press, 1995). In the introduction to her work, Jones describes Calvin's *Institutes* as follows: "Here, the reader finds Calvin, a master of both French and Latin eloquence, skillfully practicing his talent for sharp and enlivening prose. Here, one also discovers Calvin's theology unfolding as more than a straightforward summary of doctrine; it unfolds as carefully detailed and rich language, wrought by the pen of one of early modern Europe's most powerful rhetoricians" (p. 2).
59. *Institutes*, IV, xx, 32, italics added.
60. Cf. Walzer, *Revolution of the Saints*, 67ff. I first raised this issue in a paper read at a symposium on the 150th anniversary of the Great Trek at the University of the Western Cape, Bellville, during the second state of emergency in 1988, see Allan Boesak, *Trektragiek: 'n Histories-Teologiese Perspektief op Diaz, die Huguenote en die Groot Trek*, unpublished paper, 1988.
61. Theodore Beza, *Concerning the Rights of Rulers Over Their Subjects and the Duty of Subjects towards Their Rulers*, see Walzer, *Revolution*, 75ff. In the case of the first an ordinary citizen has the right to resist; in the case of the second, Beza argues, the matter is more complicated. Even today, Beza is open to both a conservative and a progressive reading. But in my view the key here remains the test of "legitimacy" Beza introduces, and Beza's insistence on the "ordinary right…to defend the lawful constitution of their country." Such ordinary rights were the routine provisions of divine providence, "miracles were unnecessary"; see Walzer, *Revolution*, 80.
62. Francis Hotman, *Franco-Gallia or, an Account of the Ancient Free State of France*, published in 1573, see Walzer, *Revolution*, 76ff.
63. Commentary on The Acts of the Apostles, 3:17.
64. See *The Anchor Bible Dictionary*, Vol. 5, David Noel Friedman (ed.) (Doubleday: New York, 1992), 975.
65. *Commentary* on Acts 5:29.

66. *Commentary* on Matthew 2:9. Italics added.
67. *Commentary* on Isaiah 14:7–8.
68. *Commentary* on Matthew 2:9.
69. *Commentary* on Isaiah 3:12.
70. *Commentary* on Exodus 5:9.
71. *Commentary* on Exodus 5:12. Calvin understands the boundaries: "[The Pharaoh] is deaf to every excuse of his officers...there is no more feeling in him than in a stone." Bonhoeffer, in his rejection of the decision to (still) seek discussions with Hitler by sending Barth to him, understood these boundaries as well as Calvin, and it would lead to another kairos moment and a different kind of decision: "From now on, I believe, any discussion between Hitler and Barth would be quite pointless—indeed, no longer to be sanctioned. Hitler has shown himself quite plainly for what he is, and the church ought to know with whom it has to reckon...," Bonhoeffer in his letter to Erwin Sutz, see Eric Mataxas, *Bonhoeffer: Pastor, Martyr, Prophet, Spy*, (Nashville: Nelson Thomas, 2010), 249. Return to this important insight in chapter 3 below.
72. See Nicholas Wolterstorff, *The Mighty and the Almighty, an Essay in Political Theology* (Cambridge, UK, and New York: Cambridge University Press, 2012), 67–82.
73. See John Witte, *The Reformation of Rights: Law, Religion, and Human Rights in Early Modern Calvinism* (Cambridge and New York: Cambridge University Press, 2007), Chapter 1.
74. See Wolterstorff, The Mighty and the Almighty, 75–77.
75. Op. cit., 74.
76. See Richard A. Horsley, *Jesus and the Powers, Conflict, Covenant, and the Hope of the Poor* (Minneapolis: Fortress Press, 2011), 51–54.
77. Horsley, op. cit., 51.
78. Idem, 51.
79. Commentary on Exodus 1:17. "Although tyrants do not easily allow their commands to be despised, and death was before their eyes, (the midwives) still keep their hands pure from evil. Thus, sustained and supported by their reverential fear of God, they boldly despised the command and the threatenings of Pharaoh..." Then Calvin turns to the application of these insights to the questions of justice and injustice in his day: "...[F]or many would be preposterously wise, whilst, under pretext of due submission, they obey the wicked will of kings in opposition to justice and right, being in some cases the ministers of avarice and rapacity, in other of cruelty; yea, to gratify the transitory kings of earth, they take no account of God; and thus, which is worst of all, they designedly oppose pure religion with fire and sword. It only makes their effrontery more detestable, that whilst they knowingly and willingly crucify Christ in his members, they plead the frivolous excuse, that they obey their princes according to the word of God; *as if (God) in ordaining princes, had resigned his rights to them; and as if every earthly power, which exalts itself against heaven, ought not rather most justly to be made to give way...* [T]he example of these midwives is abundantly sufficient for the condemnation; especially when the Holy Spirit himself commends them, as not having obeyed the king, because they feared God." Emphasis added.

80. Commentary on Acts 5:29.
81. *Institutes,* III, viii, 7. Emphasis added.
82. Wolterstorff, *Hearing the Call*, 129.
83. Cf. Wolterstorff, idem, 130.
84. *Institutes*, IV, xx, 20, 25, and 29.
85. *Commentary on the Twelve Minor Prophets*, Habakkuk 2:6, Vol. 4, 93–94.
86. *Institutes*, IV, xx, 31.
87. See Dietrich Bonhoeffer, *Letters and Papers from Prison, Dietrich Bonhoeffer Works*, Vol. 8, quoted in John De Gruchy, "In Praise of Courage," in Ernst Conradie and Christoffel Lombard, *Discerning God's Justice in Church, Society and Academy, Festschrift for Jaap Durand* (Stellenbosch: Sun Press, 2009), 62.
88. David Held and Anthony McGrew (eds.), *The Global Transformations Reader* (Cambridge, UK: Cambridge University Press, 2000), cited by Jonathan Sacks, *The Dignity of Difference, How to Avoid the Clash of Civilizations* (New York: Continuum, 2006), 29.
89. For the full text of the Accra Confession see *Proceedings of the General Council of the World Alliance of Reformed Churches*, Accra, Ghana, 2004 (Geneva: WARC, 2004), 153ff. The World Alliance of Reformed Churches is since 2010 the World Communion of Reformed Churches.
90. *Institutes*, IV, xx, VI.
91. Paul Lehmann, *The Transfiguration of Politics* (New York: Harper & Row, 1975), 39.
92. "Calvinism understood that the world was not to be saved by ethical philosophizing, but only by the restoration of the tenderness of conscience," see Abraham Kuyper, *Six Stone Lectures* (Grand Rapids: Wm. B. Eerdmans, 1931), 123. For the way in which I understood and worked this out see my *The Tenderness of Conscience*, Chapter 7.
93. Kuyper, *Six Stone Lectures*, 88.
94. I speak of public theology not as a separate discipline or expression of a new theology, but as the prophetic theology expressed and practiced in the public square.
95. Kuyper, op. cit., 126.
96. Kuyper, op. cit., 88; see also Boesak, *Tenderness*, 214.
97. See Wolterstorff, *Hearing the Call*, 132.
98. See William Stacy Johnson, *John Calvin: Reformer for the 21st Century* (Louisville, KY: Westminster John Knox Press, 2009), 109.

3 The Time for Pious Words Is Over: Kairos, Decision, and Righteous Choices

1. Bonhoeffer's letter to Karl-Friedrich Bonhoeffer, January 14, 1935, see Geffrey B. Kelly and F. Burton Nelson (eds.), *A Testament to Freedom, the Essential Writings of Dietrich Bonhoeffer* (San Francisco: HarperSanFrancisco, 1990), 447. Bonhoeffer speaks tellingly of "peace and justice or Christ himself." He

writes this as his testimony of faith, to a brother who apparently found, he says, "all these thoughts completely insane."

2. See "Letter to a Woman to Whom Bonhoeffer Was Engaged," Kelly and Nelson, op. cit., 447–448.
3. Kelly and Nelson, op. cit., 445.
4. See Dean G. Stroud, *Preaching in Hitler's Shadow, Sermons of Resistance in the Third Reich* (Grand Rapids: Wm. B. Eerdmans, 2013).
5. Bonhoeffer in a letter to Rüdiger Schleicher, April 8, 1936, see Kelly and Nelson, op. cit., 449.
6. "Letter to a Woman to Whom Bonhoeffer Was Engaged," Kelly and Nelson, op. cit., 448.
7. I have spoken about this aspect of Bonhoeffer's theology in a different context, ever more aware of the complexity and astounding relevance of Bonhoeffer's thinking as it emerges even in a single phrase as is also evident throughout this work, see Allan Aubrey Boesak, *Dare We Speak of Hope? Searching for a Language of Life in Faith and Politics* (Grand Rapids, MI and Cambridge, UK: Wm. B. Eerdmans, 2013).
8. DBWE, 10, 342.
9. See Ferdinand Schlingensiepen, *Dietrich Bonhoeffer, 1906–1945, Martyr, Thinker, Man of Resistance* (London and New York: T&T Clark, 2010), 49.
10. See Schlingensiepen, op. cit., 49.
11. Schlingensiepen, op. cit., 111.
12. Bonhoeffer wrote in his diary, "[God] certainly sees how much personal feeling, how much anxiety there is in today's decision, however brave it may seem... So one can only ask God to judge us and to forgive us... At the end of the day I can only ask God to give a merciful judgment on today and all its decisions. It is now in his hand," see Eric Metaxas, *Bonhoeffer, Pastor, Martyr, Prophet, Spy* (Nashville: Thomas Nelson, 2010), Chapter 6, "The Great Decision." The citation is on p. 336.
13. Cf. C. F. B. Naudé, "Obedience to God," in *My Decision* (Johannesburg: The Christian Institute, 1963), 11. The Christian Institute was the nonracial organization founded by Beyers Naudé at the time of the tensions with the Dutch Reformed Church and in the aftermath of Sharpeville. Its goal was to foster a sense of justice and reconciliation through ecumenical conversations and Bible study, to encourage Christians to come together across the racial divide and join with each other in the struggle against apartheid. The Christian Institute, the Johannesburg newspaper *The World* and its editor Percy Qoboza, as well as a number of activists and organizations were banned by the apartheid regime on October 19, 1977. Naudé and the Cape Director of the Christian Institute, Rev. Theo Kotze received banning orders on the same day. As was usual, the bannings lasted for seven years, subject to renewal by order of the Minister of Justice.
14. *Pro Veritate*, October 6, 1970, 9. Even in the choice of these words Naudé echoes Bonhoeffer: "The time when people could be told everything by means of words, whether theological or pious, is over"; see Dietrich Bonhoeffer,

Letters and Papers from Prison, ed. Eberhard Bethge, trans. Reginald Fuller, Frank Clark et al. (New York: Simon and Schuster, 1997, [1953]), 279.

15. See Charles Villa-Vicencio, *Trapped in Apartheid, a Socio-Theological History of the English-Speaking Churches* (Maryknoll, NY: Orbis Books, and Cape Town: David Philip, 1988), 107–117.
16. See Scott Couper, *Albert Luthuli: Bound by Faith* (Scottsville: University of KwaZulu-Natal Press, 2010), 86.
17. Nelson Mandela, "An Ideal for Which I Am Prepared to Die," in Tom Clarke (ed.), *Great Speeches of the Twentieth Century* (London: Preface Books, 2008), 232–233
18. For the complete text of the Cottesloe Declaration see Piet J Naudé, *Neither Calendar nor Clock, Perspectives on the Belhar Confession* (Grand Rapids: Wm B. Eerdmans, 2010), 226–232.
19. Cf. Beyers Naudé, *My Land van Hoop* (Cape Town: Human & Rousseau, 1995), 159. This biblical text was fundamental to both Dietrich Bonhoeffer, the Confessing Church in Germany and Albert Luthuli on their resistance to tyrannical and illegitimate regimes, as well as to a new generation of Christian activists in the struggle in South Africa since. The text reads, "We must obey God rather than human beings."
20. See Piet J. Naudé, op. cit., 233–236.
21. Cf. Albert Luthuli, *Let My People Go!*, passim; see also Scott Couper, op. cit., and the numerous documents, articles, and pamphlets produced by the liberation movements and their leaders throughout these times referenced in his work.
22. See Allan Boesak, *Running with Horses, Reflections of an Accidental Politician* (Cape Town: JoHo! Publications, 2009), Chapters 5, 6, and 7 which reflect on my reasoning behind the call for the United Democratic Front and the introduction of "the politics of refusal" as the driving force behind the resistance to the 1983 constitution and the "reforms" of the P. W. Botha era.
23. Italics mine.
24. "I see no clever strategy in leaving [whites] to attribute fictitious attitudes to us when in fact we have *real* attitudes of our own... [our aim is] to ensure that if the whites are ignorant of the realities, the fault does not lie with us." Cf. Albert Luthuli, op. cit., 176–177, emphasis original.
25. Albert Luthuli wrote at the time, "And now, as never before, the government is responsible for the civil violence that takes place...," cf. Luthuli, *Let My People Go!*, 228.
26. Below, I return to this issue within another context.
27. Beyers Naudé, "Christian Involvement in the Struggle for Human Rights and Justice," in L. C. Hansen (ed.), *The Legacy of Beyers Naudé, Beyers Naudé Centre Series on Public Theology Volume 1*, 114.
28. Beyers Naudé, "Christian Involvement," Hansen (ed.), *Legacy*, 114.
29. See DBWE, 12, II/13. For an excellent contextual discussion on this matter see also Ferdinand Schlingensiepen, *Dietrich Bonhoeffer*, 126, 313. Bonhoeffer is not here speaking of the steering wheel of a car. Schlingensiepen makes the

point that early writers in English on Bonhoeffer were not familiar with the German expression *dem Rad in die Speichen fallen,* which means to bring a wheel to a standstill by seizing its spokes. See Schlingensiepen, op. cit., n 15, 389, and his reference to Renate Wind's introduction of the expression to English readers, cf. Renate Wind, *Dietrich Bonhoeffer: A Spoke in the Wheel*, trans. John Bowden (Grand Rapids, MI: Wm B. Eerdmans, 1991), 66.

30. Denise Ackermann, "Beyers Naudé: The Public Theologian," L. C. Hansen (ed.), *Legacy*, 73.
31. See Charles Villa-Vicencio, *Trapped in Apartheid*, 111, 112: "Most of those churches found themselves forced by (white) public opinion fuelled as it was by frantic anti-WCC propaganda unleashed by the South African media, government threats and their considered responses to the WCC decision, into an alliance against that organisation... [They were] not prepared to face the fundamental issues involved in the PCR challenge."
32. Villa-Vicencio, *Trapped in Apartheid.*
33. Beyers Naudé, "The Flame of Fire and Sledgehammer," sermon preached on November 3, 1963, *My Decision*, 12–20: "It is [God] who brings matters to a head, it is he who brings his Church, his servants, his children to total obedience to his Word. It is he who comes to us with a Word that flames like fire, which shatters like a hammer blow to bring us back to the fundamentals of our faith...," 17. See also Len Hansen (ed.), *Legacy*, 41–45. The quotation is on p. 44.
34. "Obedience to God," sermon preached on September 22, 1963, *My Decision*, see also Hansen (ed.), *Legacy*, 28.
35. DBWE 13, 397ff., cf. Schlingensiepen, op, cit., 171.
36. It should perhaps not be necessary any longer to point out that this conversation between the woman and the serpent had nothing to with sex, or with "proving" that "from the beginning" women were "weaker," physically and morally; or with establishing the "satanic" origin of women's "skills in and powers of seduction." In reality the woman's inquiry has to do with the gaining of wisdom and knowledge.
37. DBWE 13, 307ff., Schlingensiepen, op. cit., 171.
38. See Paula M. Cooey, "Finding Jesus in Today's Horror, the Powerful Resistance of Le Chambon," in Michael G. Long, *Resist! Christian Dissent for the 21st Century* (Maryknoll, NY: Orbis Books, 2008), 19, 20.
39. Beyers Naudé, "Confessing the Faith in South Africa Today," Hansen (ed.), *Legacy*, 129.
40. Ackermann, "Public Theologian," Hansen (ed.), *Legacy*, 70.
41. In speaking of forced removals as a "slow process of death," Naudé says, "And you know, I must feel the agony of this because I know that the people who are in control and in power doing this, these are my people. I cannot deny that I am an Afrikaner. I am nothing else but an Afrikaner... yet in that sense I don't see myself to be there—then the *agony of that separation...*" (my emphasis). Then Naudé poses the issue that "separates" him from the Afrikaner: "What are the basic roots, what are the deepest roots of such an injustice, of such inhumanity? How do we continue to justify it, and that in

the face of the fact that the whole world outside is turning like South Africa? This is wrong, this is inhuman, and this is evil..." See Beyers Naudé and Dorothee Sölle, *Hope for Faith. A Conversation* (Grand Rapids and Geneva: Wm. B Eerdmans and WCC Publications, 1986), 9–10.

42. Earlier in his ministry before the turning point of 1960, Naudé's sermons uncritically reflected the Afrikaner's religious mind, political convictions, and cultural inclinations and show no meaningful challenge to the theology of apartheid. After Sharpeville he would turn resolutely, and permanently, away from all that. See Murray Coetzee, Len Hansen, and Robert Vosloo (eds.), *Vreesloos Gehoorsaam, 'n Keur Uit Beyers Naudé se Preke, 1939–1997, Beyers Naudé Centre Series for Public Theology* (Stellenbosch: Sun Media, 2013).
43. Beyers Naudé and Dorothee Sölle, op. cit., 27.
44. DBWE, 14, 678–689.
45. See Schlingensiepen, ibid., 277. Bonhoeffer deliberately capitalizes the last few words—even the adjectives, which are not usually capitalized in German—to emphasize an extremely important matter in the context of Nazi Germany: that they referred to Jesus' brothers and sisters in the flesh, namely the Jews, as well as the outcasts, the despised, and marginalized in Germany's Nazi-controlled society, and those "who do the will of my Father" who Jesus claims as family in Mark 3:33.
46. Beyers Naudé, "Reconciliation," *My Decision*, 20–27; see also Hansen, *Legacy*, 141.
47. Naudé and Sölle, *Hope for Faith*, 11.
48. "Steve Biko: The Man and His Message," Hansen, *Legacy*, 79.
49. Charles Villa-Vicencio calls both recent documents from Kairos Southern Africa "cautious and restrained," see Charles Villa-Vicencio, "The Dangerous Memory of the Gospel: South Africa, Palestine and a Papal Visit to the Holy Land," essay, p. 15, published in somewhat shortened form as "Quo Vadis?", in *The Link*, 47, 2, April–May 2014, 3–10, see www.ameu.org. For references to serious critique of the December 2012 letter to the ANC by Kairos Southern Africa, the South African Council of Churches and other groups, see Ignatius Swart, "Revival of a Kairos Consciousness: Prolegomena to a Research Focus on Religious and Social Change in Post-Apartheid South Africa," Inaugural Lecture, University of South Africa, November 19, 2013, 4, n 12, 13, 14: "In effect this letter could be criticized for its fear of the state's authority, for not daring to speak out sufficiently against the erstwhile 'liberator's' corruption." Swart, though himself not as critical as this, and approaching the documents from a different perspective for his research purposes, does remark that "if viewed through the lens of Boesak's description, a closer look into the contents of this first letter of 17 pages may well lead one to discover a text that appears too benign in the way it approached the ANC and that, as such, had given way to the kind of sentimentalism and romanticism that Boesak refers to...," p. 4. I have elsewhere pointed to one, perhaps unintended, not further explicated but nonetheless pertinent critique in the December 2012 letter in the use of the phrase "post-Marikana South Africa"; see Allan Aubrey Boesak, *Dare We Speak of Hope? Searching for*

a Language of Life in Faith and Politics (Grand Rapids: Wm. B. Eerdmans, 2014), 6, 8.

50. See Piet Naudé, *Neither Calendar nor Clock*, 222. The text of the Belhar Confession is on 219–223.
51. See Beyers Naudé, "The Need for Political Reform," Hansen, *Legacy*, 95: Their task will be difficult, Naudé says, in light of the "tragic ignorance" of the Afrikaans electorate "deliberately maintained by the Afrikaans press, the radio and the Afrikaans churches." They will, Naudé warns, discover "widespread apathy," will be subjected to vilification, be called "*Kafferboeties,*" (the American equivalent is "n...lover"; the Nazi German equivalent was "Judenknecht"—"Jew servant"), liberalists or communists. Here too Naudé is consistent: "A crucial test for their concern for and commitment to change will be their willingness to take a determined stand in public in the face of similar accusations."
52. "Obedience to God," *My Decision*, 10; see also Hansen, *Legacy*, 29.
53. "Obedience to God," *My Decision*, 11; see as well Hansen, *Legacy*, 29.
54. See Allan Boesak, "The Black Church and the Future," *Black and Reformed, Apartheid, Liberation and the Calvinist Tradition* (Maryknoll, NY: Orbis Press, 1984), 22.
55. Beyers Naudé, "Steve Biko, The Man and His Message," Hansen, *Legacy*, 78. Apartheid racism had made of blackness a question of skin color by which one's (sub)humanity was measured, a color that denoted shame and inferiority. It was the genius of Black Consciousness to turn blackness into both a claim on full humanity and, under apartheid, a *condition*, of oppression yes, but then also of resistance to oppression and of yearning for freedom. For blacks and for the whites who joined the struggle it became a condition that denoted liberation and liberative action.
56. Beyers Naudé, "Steve Biko: The Man and His Message," Hansen, *Legacy*, 79, italics added.
57. It was from Adam Clayton Powell Sr., that great black preacher/politician, that Dietrich Bonhoeffer had learned the phrase "cheap grace" which he embraced and used with immortal effect in his work and life's testimony: "Reverend Adam Clayton Powell Sr., the renowned and dynamic pastor of Abyssinian Baptist Church of Harlem, coined the term 'cheap grace', to refer to white Christian America's tolerance of Jim Crow, lynching, and racism. Dietrich Bonhoeffer, who is usually associated with the term 'cheap grace', learned this ethical principle from Powell while attending his church during his student days at Union Theological Seminary...Bonhoeffer was able to transport the lessons learnt from the black church to deal with the rising anti-Semitism of his native Germany," see Miguel de la Torre, *Liberating Jonah, Forming an Ethics of Reconciliation* (Maryknoll, NY: Orbis Books, 2007), 95. De la Torre in turn learned this from Ralph Garlin Clingan, *Against Cheap Grace in a World Come of Age: A Study in the Hermeneutics of Adam Clayton Powell, 1865–1953, in His Intellectual Context* (New York: Peter Lang, 2002). Most scholarship on Bonhoeffer's time at Abyssinian Baptist concentrates only on the influence on Bonhoeffer of the church's passionate worship style, the music, and the emotional manifestations, De la

Torre remarks. "It is interesting to note that few Euroamerican scholars are willing to explore the intellectual contributions the black church, and Adam Clayton Powell in particular, made to Bonhoeffer's scholarly development. We are left asking why?" Indeed. See also Reggie L. Williams' excellently developed argument along these same lines, tracing Bonhoeffer's radicalized thinking on this point to the theology of the Harlem Renaissance writers with whom he became acquainted in his interactions with Harlem and Abyssinian Baptist Church during his stay in New York City. See Reggie L. Williams, *Bonhoeffer's Black Christ, Harlem Renaissance Theology and the Ethic of Resistance* (Waco, TX: Baylor University Press, 2014).
58. "Steve Biko: The Man and His Message," Hansen, *Legacy*, 79.
59. For the full text of the Accra Confession see *That All May Be One, World Alliance of Reformed Churches 24th General Council Proceedings* (Geneva: WARC, 2005), 153–160.
60. Beyers Naudé, "Reconciliation," *My Decision*, 24; see as well Hansen, *Legacy*, 140.
61. DBWE 13, 30ff.
62. See Beyers Naude, "Flame of Fire and Sledgehammer," *My Decision*, 14–16; see as well Hansen (ed.), *Legacy*, 42–43, bold in original.

4 The Inclusiveness of God's Embrace: Kairos, Justice, the Dignity of Human Sexuality, and the Confession of Belhar

* It is not my intention to enter into another review of the arguments regarding biblical texts on this particular issue. The literature on the biblical arguments is vast, increasing and easily accessible. For my own views on the biblical interpretation regarding these texts see Allan Aubrey Boesak, "'Founded on the Holy Bible...', A Bible-believing Judge and the 'Sin' of Same-Sex Relationships," *Journal of Gender and Religion in Africa, Vol. 17, No. 2, 2011, Special Issue: Same-Sex Sexuality in South Africa*, Center for Constructive Theology, University of KwaZulu Natal, 5–23. This chapter is concerned with the Belhar Confession, a particularly important text for the Uniting Reformed Church in Southern Africa (URCSA) as well as for other churches in the Reformed family who have accepted the Belhar Confession as standard of faith. For the URCSA the confession is vital, since it had played such a crucial role in the church's stand on and struggle against racist apartheid oppression, and historically sees itself in succession to such hallowed documents as the Barmen Declaration of the Confessing Church in Nazi Germany. In this, the Belhar Confession has the same goals as the South African *Kairos Document* which became such a ringing call for justice in so many different contexts in the world and is now, with the rising understanding of intensifying global struggles for justice, dignity, equality and peace, gaining new relevance and power worldwide. URCSA's oft-stated desire is for the Belhar Confession to be embraced by all churches in the worldwide

family of Reformed churches, since its relevance cannot and should not be limited to the apartheid situation in South Africa which would not be as relevant for other churches in other situations where the struggle for racial justice is not the main issue. This claim to transcendent relevance which URCSA itself makes is also at the core of the argument in this chapter.

1. The report, titled "Report on Homosexuality to the General Synod of the Uniting Reformed Church in Southern Africa" was prepared by a working group designated by the previous synod (2005) and had done its work over the four years spanning the two synod meetings. We will not speak of "homosexual" persons here because transgender, bisexual, and intersexual individuals resist the construction of mutually exclusive categories for gender identities, (male or female), and sexuality (heterosexual or homosexual). Therefore these groups are contesting the binary nature of these constructions themselves and not just the different values placed on them in a patriarchal, hetero-normative system of domination; cf. Cheryl B. Anderson, *Ancient Laws & Contemporary Controversies* (New York: Oxford University Press, 2009), 18. In this chapter we shall mostly refer to Lesbian, Gay, Bisexual, Transsexual, and Intersexual (LGBTI) persons.
2. At the 1982 synod, in the debate on the proposal that the time had come for the church to discern and confront the signs of our times, and that the only appropriate response in light of the gravity of the situation was a new confession of faith, the words "kairos moment" were expressly used. Subsequently, the volume edited by Gerhard D. Cloete and Dirk J. Smit, dealing with the Belhar Confession, its origin and meaning for the church was titled *A Moment of Truth: The Confession of the Dutch Reformed Mission Church* (Grand Rapids, MI: Wm. B. Eerdmans, 1984). Thus three years before the *Kairos Document*, the DRMC used the word kairos to describe a moment of crisis for the country and the church and to call for prophetic discernment, commitment, and action on the part of the church.
3. Among others, the report recommended that "homosexual persons express their intimate relations within the context of...Christian marriage blessed by the church"; and, "As confessing members of the church of Jesus Christ homosexual Christians shall, on the basis of their faith in Jesus Christ have access to all the offices of the church, and upon fulfillment of all the academic requirements for the ministry, to the office of minister of the Word." See "Report on Homosexuality," *Agenda for Synod: Fifth General Synod of the Uniting Reformed Church in Southern Africa, Unity in Diversity, 29 September-05 October 2008 Hammanskraal* (Wellington: Bible Media, 2008), 83–153. The recommendations are on 149–151.
4. The change was proposed by the former scribe of synod Rev. Colin Goeieman who wisely saw the folly of leaving those words standing in the Acts of synod.
5. Calvin, *Institutes*, III, vii, 6.
6. See Nicholas Wolterstorff, "The Wounds of God: Calvin's Theology of Social Justice," in Mark R. Gornick and Gregory Thompson (eds.), *Hearing the Call, Liturgy, Justice, Church, and World* (Grand Rapids, MI/Cambridge, UK: Wm. B. Eerdmans, 2010), 126.

7. As a result, and in light of what I considered to be a litmus test for the church in Africa and the integrity of its prophetic witness and the quality of its compassion and sense of justice even before the recent tragic events in Uganda, I decided to resign from all the positions I held in the Cape and General Synods. I could not in good conscience be an official representative of a church who in taking this position, betrayed so much of its own tradition, its confession, and what it had stood for in the past.
8. See Editorial, *The Cape Times*, June 2, 2011.
9. *Ancient Laws*, 18, quoting Rev. Kelvin Calloway, in Kelly Brown Douglas, "Heterosexism and the Black American Church Community: A Complicated Reality," Marvin M. Ellison and Judith Plaskow, (eds.), *Heterosexism in Contemporary World Religion: Problem and Prospect* (Cleveland: Pilgrim Press, 2007), 199.
10. Cf. Miguel De La Torre, *Doing Christian Ethics from the Margins* (Maryknoll, NY: Orbis Books, 2004), 14, cited in Cheryl B. Anderson, *Ancient Laws*, 44.
11. It has been pointed out that the word "homophobia" is perhaps not the most suitable to use. It implies a fear of LGBTI persons because they somehow threaten society. The "fear" society professes to have thus totally erases the very real fear LGBTI persons themselves have, living with suspicion, hatred, rejection, and exclusion, and the violent consequences these increasingly produce. It turns the reality of victimization around. Moreover, that this fear is irrational, unjustifiable, and totally misplaced does then not enter the discussion. It is better to call it by its name: a shameful form of bigotry with disastrous and deadly consequences. For an excellent, detailed discussion of the term, even though no alternative term for "homophobia" is proposed see Louis-Georges Tin, *The Dictionary of Homophobia, A Global History of Gay & Lesbian Experience*, trans. Marek Redburn, with Alice Michaud and Kyle Mathers (Vancouver: Arsenal Pulp Press, 2008), 11–17.
12. As I write this, President Museveni has just signed the most strident "anti-gay" legislation into law, to the great delight of Christian legislators and many churches. It is chilling, but unusually instructive to note how, now that in the United States the cultural climate is changing and making anti-LGBTI bigotry more and more difficult, fundamentalist US Christianity, with all its destructive economic and ideological imperial power, is exported to Africa, with murderous implications for LGBTI persons in Africa, wreaking devastation in African societies and African churches. A day after the bill was signed into law the public hunt was already under way. Another Ugandan newspaper, *The Red Pepper*, read "EXPOSED! Uganda's 200 Top Homos Named" with several photographs to the headline. See http://www.cnn.com/2014/02/25/world/africa/uganda-anti-gay-law/index.html, accessed March 6, 2014.
13. Risdel Kasasira, "World Condemns Killing of Gay Activist," *Daily Monitor*, January 28, 2011, retrieved March 6, 2014.
14. In 2011, the media reported on the deaths of three teenage boys who were allegedly tortured to death at a so-called conversion camp in South Africa. As a consequence of the belief that LGBTI persons have an "acquired

condition" and can be changed, or have been driven by sinful desires which can be corrected by prayer and other methods, Raymond Buys died two weeks after being put on life support two months into a three-month "training course" provided by Alex de Koker's Echo Wild Game Ranger's camp. He had severe brain damage, a broken arm, bruises, and emerged severely malnourished, dehydrated, and covered in cigarette burns. Two other young men, Erich Calitz (25) and Nicolas Van Der Walt (19) died after severe brain injuries obtained at this same Ranger's camp, see http://www.huffingtonpost.com/2013/04/30/gay-south-african-conversion-deaths_n_318620.htm, accessed June 3, 2013. See also University of Cape Town constitutional law expert Pierre de Vos, "South Africa: Black Lesbians, No Justice," *Africa Files*, http://www.africafiles.org/printableversion.asp?id=21543, accessed, June 4, 2013: "When people talk about the transformation of the judiciary and our legal system they will not mention the name of Zoliswa [the young lesbian who was killed in Khayelitsha township near Cape Town on February 4, 2006], or any victims of serious crime who seldom seem to have seen even a modest chance of receiving at least a semblance of justice..." See also Melissa Turley, "South Africa: The Fight for Acceptance in the Rainbow Nation," http://www.globalspost.com/dispacthes/globalpost-blogs/rightas/South-Africa-lesbian-violence, accessed June 4, 2013.

15. See Jeff Stuart, "Junkets for Jesus," *Mother Jones* magazine, November–December 2010, 61. The bill dramatically expands punishment for same-sex relationships or even behavior, already illegal in Uganda, and calls for the death penalty of "serial offenders" and imprisonment for failing to report gays and lesbians to authorities. See also Lerato Mogoatlhe, "Killing and Dying in God's Name—Being Gay in Uganda Is Like Being Sentenced to Death," *Sunday Independent*, December 15, 2010. See as well Jeff Sharlett, *The Family: The Secret Fundamentalism at the Heart of American Power* (New York: HarperCollins, 2008). The bill signed into law keeps the prison sentences but has dropped (under the severe international pressure) the death penalty clause. The consideration of the death penalty, however, does speak to the state of mind of lawmakers and their Christian backers in Uganda and the United States. The same kind of legislation is being pursued in Sudan, Rwanda, and the Democratic Republic of the Congo, countries where one would expect the most pressing concerns would be the ravages of continuing (civil) wars, poverty, Western capitalist exploitation, and the poor state of human rights, especially as regards women and children.
16. See J. J. F. Durand, "A Confession—Was It Really Necessary?" in G. D. Cloete and D. J. Smit (eds.), *A Moment of Truth: The Confession of the Dutch Reformed Mission Church* (Grand Rapids: Wm. B. Eerdmans, 1984), 33–41.
17. These are the Heidelberg Catechism, the Belgic Confession, and the Canons of Dordt.
18. *Moment of Truth*, 46.
19. Ibid., 46.
20. Ibid. 46.
21. Ibid., 48.

22. See Cloete and Smit, *Moment of Truth*, 116–126.
23. Ibid., 132.
24. Ibid., 133.
25. See for example Piet J. Naude, *Neither Calendar nor Clock, Perspectives on the Confession of Belhar* (Grand Rapids: Wm. B. Eerdmans, 2011), 77–79. In my view, much of this argument is sometimes inspired by a desire to secure greater acceptability of the confession by the main stream of the white Dutch Reformed Church. In the tortuous debates on the Confession with the DRC the issue of the "origin" of Belhar came up repeatedly. I argue that the "origin" of the Belhar Confession should not be sought in a specific proposal in a specific moment in a church gathering as if it was created *ex nihilo*, as it were, in one single, spontaneous moment. The birth of Belhar was a process borne by the development of theological thinking since 1976, perhaps even earlier with the idea of a "confessing church" in the thinking of the Christian Institute. It was a process of both unlearning the distorted Calvinism of the white DRC and learning a new understanding of Reformed theology within the ecumenical context of liberation theology. This is not to say that Karl Barth, especially the early Barth of Safenwil and the early struggle against Hitler, had no impact on us and our theological formation; to the contrary. The fact that there are clear comparisons in style with the Barmen Declaration of the German Confessing Church, of which Karl Barth was a major authorial contributor, and that justice as theological category plays an important role in the theology of Barth, however, does not make the theological content of the confession "Barthian." I contend that a close reading of the confession confirms that the influences on the formation of the theology that informed the prophetic stance of the Dutch Reformed Mission Church at the time both theologically and in its active participation in the struggle and hence also the contents of the Belhar Confession, came more from black liberation theology and an understanding informed by the radical Calvinist Reformed tradition, in which I include the early Barth. That was the theology that most infused our thinking at the time. One should also take into account contemporary theological documents that saw the light of day at the time and most clearly reflected contemporary black theological thinking such as the 1981 "Charter of the Alliance of Black Reformed Christians in Southern Africa," see John de Gruchy and Charles Villa-Vicencio (eds.), *Apartheid Is a Heresy* (Grand Rapids: Wm B. Eerdmans, 1983), 161–168; see also Allan Boesak, *Black and Reformed, Apartheid, Liberation and the Calvinist Tradition* (Maryknoll, NY: Orbis Books), 1984, which includes essays from as early as 1974, especially Chapter 9, "Black and Reformed: Contradiction or Challenge," especially 94–99, which stems from 1981; and the "Theological Declaration for the Call to Prayer for the End of Unjust Rule" in 1985, see Allan Boesak and Charles Villa-Vicencio (eds.), *When Prayer Makes News* (Philadelphia: Westminster Press, 1986). The context of the Belhar Confession is historically more naturally this expression of liberation theology than classical Barthian European theology. We must resist the constant temptation and postcolonial colonialist tendency to ascribe every significant theological development and action in the black church a postiori

to the influence of white European-centered theology, as if black people had no original theological thinking of their own, and as if black liberation in the church and outside of it always depended on white intervention and is legitimate and acceptable only when validated by white theological approval.

26. See e.g. Allan Boesak, 1984, *Black and Reformed*, and more recently, Allan Boesak, *The Tenderness of Conscience: African Renaissance and the Spirituality of Politics* (Stellenbosch: Sun Press, 2005). Compare also my argument in chapter 2 above.
27. For an example of a sermon addressing these tensions in the Dutch Reformed Mission Church caused by the church's stand on the questions of justice and the choice for participation in the struggle against apartheid during the 1980s see my "At the Risk of Unity," in Allan Boesak, *Walking on Thorns, Sermons on Christian Obedience* (Grand Rapids, MI: Wm. B. Eerdmans, 1984), 11–18.
28. Dirk J. Smit, 2007, "Reformed Faith, Justice and the Struggle Against Apartheid," in E. Conradie, (ed.), *Essays in Public Theology, Collected Essays 1, Study Guides in Religion and Theology 12, Publications of the University of the Western Cape* (Stellenbosch: Sun Press), 34 (italics added).
29. See Allan Boesak, Johann Weusmann and Charles Amjad-Ali (eds.), *Dreaming a Different World, Globalisation and Justice for Humanity and the Earth—The Challenge of the Accra Confession for the Churches* (Stellenbosch: The Globalisation Project, 2010).
30. The influence of Belhar on the Accra Confession, adopted by the World Alliance of Reformed Churches at Accra, Ghana in 2004, and dealing with matters of empire, global economic justice, and ecological responsibility, is an excellent example of this, both in the history of the debates and the formation of the Accra Confession and in the text of the confession itself. For further perspectives on Belhar as defining presence and especially on the meaning of standing with God in God's suffering in the world, see Allan Boesak, "Standing Where God Stands: The Confession of Belhar after Twenty-Five Years," *Studia Historiae Ecclesiasticae*, July 2008, XXXIV, 1, 143–172.
31. See Mary L. Jensen, Mary Sanders, and Steven J. Sandage, 2010, "Women's Well-Being in Seminary: A Qualitative Study," *Theological Education*, 45, 2, 2010, The Association of Theological Schools, The Commission on Accrediting, Pittsburg PA, 109.
32. The phenomenon of women, their worth and contribution being ignored or minimalized, the trivialization of gender issues, the resistance to validation of contributions and expertise of women. Cf. Jensen et al., "Women's Well-being," *Theological Education*, 111.
33. *Institutes*, IV, xvii, 38.
34. See Allan Boesak, "To Stand Where God Stands," op. cit., 156.
35. The phrase comes from Jonathan Sacks, *The Dignity of Difference: How to Avoid the Clash of Civilizations* (New York: Continuum, 2006).
36. See Calvin's commentary on Isaiah 58:6–7; see also Wolterstorff, *Hearing the Call*, 126.
37. *Institutes*, III, xviii, 5.

38. See Allan Boesak, "God Made Us All, But..." *Black and Reformed*, 100–110.
39. Most recently President Jammeh called LGBTI persons "vermin" and "a threat to humanity" and vowed his government would fight them "in the same way it fights malaria-causing mosquitoes." See http://www.ndtv.com?article/world/gambia-s-yahya-jammeh-calls-gays-vermin, accessed May 20, 2014. Even more recently Jammeh threatened to kill any person who flees Gambia and claims persecution of LGBTI persons in seeking asylum abroad. See Trudy Ring, "Gambian President on Gay Asylum-Seekers: 'I Will Kill Them'," Advocate.com, May 16, 2014, accessed May 20, 2014.
40. President Mugabe reiterated his views in his 2014 Independence Day speech "filled with anti-gay rhetoric," calling LGBTI persons "not human." See Gaystars News, April 18, 2014, http://gaystarsnews.com accessed May 20, 2014. See also "It's Not Just Uganda: Behind the Christian Right's Onslaught on Africa," *The Nation*, April 4, 2014, http:www.thenation.com/blog/179191/its-not-just-uganda-the-Christian-rights-onslaught-on-africa, accessed May 20, 2014.
41. Cf. David G. Myers and Letha Dawson Scanzoni, *What God Has Joined Together: The Christian Case for Gay Marriage* (San Francisco: HarperCollins, 2005), 125.
42. "Report of the Task Team on Homosexuality," *Agenda for Synod*, 86.
43. Women were accepted into the ministry of the DRMC in 1986 in a debate that took less than an hour. This is not to say that full gender justice has been attained—far from it. Women's struggle for justice and well-being is still very much a struggle in the URCSA. It does say much though about the theological climate created by the Belhar Confession in which that particular debate took place at the time.
44. Durand, "A Confession, Is It Really Necessary?", Cloete and Smit, *Moment of Truth*, 48.

5 The End of Words? Kairos, Challenge, and the Rhetoric of the Barricades

1. See Richard Lischer, *The End of Words, The Language of Reconciliation in a Culture of Violence* (Grand Rapids, MI, and Cambridge, UK: Wm. B. Eerdmans, 2005), ix. Lischer speaks of preachers coming to the "end of words," but this very apt phrase describes the situation of people pushed to the edge of hopelessness just as well.
2. Op. cit., 5.
3. Op. cit., 5.
4. Richard Lischer, "Anointed with Fire, The Structure of Prophecy in the Sermons of Martin Luther King, Jr.", in Timothy George, James Earl Massey, and Robert Smith Jr. (eds.), *Our Sufficiency Is of God, Essays on Preaching in Honor of Gardner C. Taylor* (Macon, GA: Mercer University Press, 2010), 231.

5. See Chris Hedges, *Truthdig*, "The Business of Mass Incarceration," www.truthdig.com/report/item/the_business_of_mass_incarceration_20130728/ accessed July 28, 2013. "In 2011," a report commissioned by the Samuel DeWitt Proctor Conference states, "the prison industry market totaled $34.4 billion in revenues and represents a growth of 9.1% from 2000 through 2011." See *A Nation in Chains, A Report of the Samuel DeWitt Proctor Conference* (Chicago: Samuel DeWitt Proctor Conference, 2014), 48. The report, presenting a three-year research project and the findings of nine statewide justice commission hearings on mass incarceration, offers a wealth of extremely valuable information on the matter of mass incarceration and is obtainable from the Samuel DeWitt Proctor Conference, admin@sdpconference.info
6. See Dean G, Stroud, *Preaching in Hitler's Shadow, Sermons of Resistance in the Third Reich* (Grand Rapids: Wm. B. Eerdmans; Cambridge: UK, 2013), 3, 4.
7. Dean G. Stroud (ed.), *Preaching in Hitler's Shadow*, 47.
8. Op. cit., 46.
9. Stroud, op. cit., 47.
10. "Anointed with Fire," in *Our Sufficiency*, 231.
11. See for example John Calvin, *Commentaries on the Twelve Minor Prophets*, Commentary on Micah 6:6–8: "The true way then of walking with God is, when we thoroughly humble ourselves, yea, when we bring ourselves down to nothing; for it is the very beginning of worshipping and glorifying God when men entertain humble and low opinion of themselves."
12. See Allan Boesak, *The Tenderness of Conscience, African Renaissance and the Spirituality of Politics* (Stellenbosch: Sun Media, 2005), 233–234.
13. See Nicholas Wolterstorff on "The Wounds of God: Calvin's Theology of Social Injustice," in Mark R. Gornik and Gregory Thompson (eds.), *Hearing the Call: Liturgy, Justice, Church and World* (Grand Rapids: Wm. B. Eerdmans, 2011), 127.
14. John Calvin, commentary on Psalm 83, *Commentary on the Book of Psalms, Vol. III* (Edinburgh: Edinburgh Printing Company, 1847), trans. James Anderson, 322.
15. President Obama's now infamous line in admission of the systemic torture programs the United States engaged in since 2003. See http://www.theguardian.com/world/2014/aug/01/obama-cia-torture-some-folks-brennan, accessed February 5, 2015.
16. See Richard Horsley, "Introduction," in Richard A. Horsley (ed.), *In the Shadow of Empire, Reclaiming the Bible as a History of Faithful Resistance* (Louisville, KY: Westminster John Knox Press, 2008), 6. See also Gunther Wittenberg, *Resistance Theology*.
17. Noam Chomsky and Edward S. Herman, *Manufactured Consent: The Political Economy of the Mass Media* (New York: Random House, 1988).
18. Cf. Johan Cilliers, *God for Us? An Analysis and Assessment of Dutch Reformed Preaching during the Apartheid Years* (Stellenbosch: Sun Media, 2006).

19. See Beyers Naudé and Dorothee Soelle, *Hope for Faith, A Conversation* (Grand Rapids: Wm. B. Eerdmans, and Geneva: WCC Publications, 1986), 9–10.
20. Dean G. Stroud, op. cit., 26.
21. Op. cit., 27.
22. Op. cit., 27.
23. Op. cit., 29.
24. Op. cit., 29. This same exegesis of Galatians 3:27 and the same argument was followed in the same detail by the apartheid theologians in their defense of racial supremacy and the Dutch Reformed Church's defense of racially divided churches within the Dutch Reformed family.
25. *Dietrich Bonhoeffer Works English (*DBWE), Geffrey B. Kelley (ed.) (Minneapolis: Fortress Press, 2001), 13, 347ff. See Ferdinand Schlingensiepen, *Dietrich Bonhoeffer, Martyr, Thinker, Man of Resistance*, trans. Isabel Best (London and New York: T&T Clark, 2010), 158.
26. DBWE, Vol. 13, 351–353; see also Eric Metaxas, op. cit., 208–210.
27. George W. Bush, "Address to a Joint Session of Congress and the American People," United States Capitol, September 20, 2001. www.whitehouse.gov/news/releases/2001/09/20010920-8.html, cited in T. Walter Herbert, *Faith-Based War, from 9/11 to Catastrophic Success in Iraq* (Oakville and London: Equinox, 2009), 1.
28. Herbert, op. cit., 2.
29. See "National Defense Authorization Act for Fiscal Year 2012": http://en.wikipedia.org.wiki/ National_Defense_Authorization_Act_for_Fiscal_Year 2012 (accessed November 20, 2012).
30. See Glenn Greenwald, "Detaining My Partner: A Failed Attempt at Intimidation," readersupportednews.org/news-section2/421-national-security/18975-detaining-my-partner-a-failed-attempt-at-intimidation?tmpl=1&page= accessed August 20, 2013. "This is obviously a rather profound escalation of their (US and UK governments) attacks on the news-gathering process and journalism. It's bad enough to prosecute and imprison sources. It's worse still to imprison journalists who report the truth. But to start detaining the family members and loved ones of journalists is simply despotic…If the UK and US governments believe that tactics like this are going to deter or intimidate us in any way from continuing to report aggressively on what these documents reveal, they are beyond deluded." Glenn Greenwald is the journalist at the UK-based Guardian newspaper who first began to report on the documents Edward Snowden was revealing on the spying activities of the US National Security Agency which had sent shock waves around the world. On August 19, Greenwald's partner, David Miranda, was detained by UK police as he entered London's Heathrow airport, "under Schedule 7 of the Terrorism Act of 2000." See also Chris Hedges, "Let My People Go," www.truthdig.com/report/item/let_my_people_go 20140810
31. See www.huffingtonpost.com/stephen-zunes/california-state-assembly_b_1842841.html accessed July 24, 2013.
32. See Jean Comaroff and John L. Comaroff, *Of Revelation and Revolution: Christianity, Colonialism and Consciousness in South Africa*, Vol. 1

(Chicago: University of Chicago Press, 1991), 22, cited in Gerald West, "Explicating Domination and Resistance: A Dialogue between James C. Scott and Biblical Scholars," in Richard A. Horsley (ed.), *Hidden Transcripts and the Arts of Resistance, Applying the Work of James C. Scott to Jesus and Paul* (Atlanta: Society of Biblical Literature, Semeia Studies, No. 48, 2004), 173–194. The quotation is on p. 177.

33. Mercy Amba Oduyoye, *Daughters of Anowa, African Women and Patriarchy* (Maryknoll, NY: Orbis Books, 1995), 175, 176.
34. See Oduyoye, op. cit.; also and especially Cheryl B. Anderson, *Ancient Laws & Contemporary Controversies, the Need for Inclusive Biblical Interpretation* (New York: Oxford University Press, 2009). See also the excellent contributions in *The Evil of Patriarchy in Church, Society and Politics*, proceedings of a consultation organized by Inclusive and Affirming Ministries in partnership with the Department of Religion and Theology, University of the Western Cape, and the Centre for Christian Spirituality, Stellenbosch, South Africa, September 5 and 6, 2009.
35. *Dietrich Bonhoeffer Works*, ed. Keith Clements, 353, Metaxas, op. cit., 210.
36. Bonhoeffer in a letter to Erwin Sutz, December 25, 1931. The "violet church" refers to the violet cross on the official church flag. See Kelly and Nelson, *A Testament to Freedom, The Essential Writings of Dietrich Bonhoeffer* (San Francisco: HarperSanFrancisco, 1990), 405. This church, Bonhoeffer writes in one of his lectures on "The Nature of the Church," "has been harmoniously absorbed into the culture as a whole!...It is not a question here of a proper place but of a *privileged* place...It is the place of Christ present in the world." See Kelly and Nelson, op. cit., 89.

6 Speaking Truth to the Tower: Kairos, Dissent, and Prophetic Speech

1. See T. Walter Herbert, *Faith-Based War: From 9/11 to Catastrophic Success in Iraq* (London and Oakville: Equinox, 2009).
2. For a fuller explication of my views on Joseph's role in the famine in Egypt and its effects on the people see Allan Aubrey Boesak, *Dare We Speak of Hope? Searching for a Language of Life in Faith and Politics* (Grand Rapids, MI, and Cambridge, UK: Wm. B. Eerdmans, 2014), Chapter 6.
3. Oscar Romero, *The Violence of Love: The Pastoral Wisdom of Archbishop Oscar Romero*, translated and compiled by James R. Brockmen (New York: Harper & Row, 1988), 64.
4. See G. H. ter Schegget, *Het Geheim van de Mensenzoon* (Baarn, Netherlands: Wereldvenster, 1972), 131–144; see also Allan Boesak, *The Tenderness of Conscience, African Renaissance and the Spirituality of Politics* (Stellenbosch: Sun Media, 2005), 222.
5. For a superb discussion of this see Jerome T. Walsh, *Berit Olam, 1 Kings, Studies in Hebrew Narrative and Poetry*, David S. Cotter OSB (ed.), (Collegeville, MN: Liturgical Press, 1996), 264–278.

6. I was fascinated and inspired by this story from an early age, and this text from 1 Kings 22:14 became the text of my entry sermon after my ordination in Immanuel Dutch Reformed Mission Church congregation in Paarl on February 24, 1968: "But Micaiah said, as the LORD lives, whatever the LORD says, that I will speak."
7. Some scholars argue that the form of Ahab's question is an indication that Ramoth-gilead had not been included among the cities to be returned when Ahab set the conditions for the truce. Accordingly he was the aggressor, asking for more than was called for by the conditions of the truce set after the battle of Aphek, see Leo L. Honor, *Book of Kings 1, A Commentary, The Jewish Commentary for Bible Readers* (New York: Union of American Hebrew Congregations, 1955), 309.
8. See Richard D. Nelson, *First and Second Kings, Interpretation, a Bible Commentary for Teaching and Preaching* Patrick D. Miller (ed.) (Atlanta: John Knox Press, 1987), 147.
9. Walsh, op. cit., 347, n 5: "Is it coincidence that Zedekiah (whose name is explicitly Yahwistic: 'Yahweh is Righteousness') is the son of 'Chenaanah'... whose name sounds suspiciously like 'Canaanite'?"
10. The New American Bible translates, "Seek the word of the Lord at once," but the KJV and the *Holy Bible from Ancient Manuscripts*, following the Peshitta, are closer to the Hebrew text; see also Leo Honor's translation, op. cit., 310.
11. See Honor, op. cit., 310.
12. See Walsh, op. cit., 346.
13. See Walsh, op. cit., 347.
14. Honor, op. cit., 312.
15. So argues Honor, op. cit., 317.
16. See Nelson, op. cit., 148.
17. See Walsh, op. cit., 349.
18. See Eric Metaxas, *Bonhoeffer, Pastor, Martyr, Prophet, Spy*, 249, emphasis original.
19. See Geffrey B. Kelly and F. Burton Nelson (eds.), *A Testament to Freedom, The Essential Writings of Dietrich Bonhoeffer* (San Francisco: HarperSanFrancisco, 1990), 435, 436.
20. See http://www.theguardian.com/politics/2012/sep/02/tony-blair-iraq-war-desmond-tutu, accessed October 8, 2013.
21. See Giles Fraser, "Desmond Tutu Should *Not* Have Shunned Tony Blair," theguardian.com, Monday, September 3, 2012, accessed October 8, 2013. It is not my intention to enter into Fraser's argument why he considers that "Blair is not Charles Taylor" and hence less deserving of criminal charges, or why he finds Blair's arguments for the war more understandable. It is perhaps important to note Frank Chikane's wry remark in his discussion of the Iraq war as seen from the South African perspective, "No one will be taken to international Criminal Court in The Hague. Those who were involved are beyond and above the jurisdiction of the ICC as an understanding of justice in this case depends on how weak or powerful one is." See Frank Chikane, *The Things That Could Not Be Said, from*

A{ids} to Z{imbabwe} (Johannesburg: Picador Africa, 2013), 64. My concern here is Fraser's understanding of reconciliation which he accused Tutu of undermining.

22. See http://frontapagemag.com/2012/mark-d-tooley/archbishop-tutu-shuns-tony-blair, accessed October 8, 2013. Quoting Tutu calling bin Laden "a child of God," Tooley asks, "But is Tony Blair excluded from Tutu's circle of divine love?" But this is a distorted question. Tutu's speaking truth to Blair does not exclude Blair from God's or Tutu's "circle of love." But in my view Tooley seeks a sentimentalized love that never confronts or challenges, nor calls to conversion. That love is not biblical.
23. See for my explication of the Rizpah story as related to reconciliation, Allan Aubrey Boesak and Curtiss Paul DeYoung, *Radical Reconciliation, Beyond Political Pietism and Christian Quietism* (Maryknoll, NY: Orbis Books, 2012), Chapter 2. The reference here is on pp. 36, 37.
24. Secret memoranda obtained through the freedom of information Act in Britain show secret meetings between ministers in the Blair Cabinet and senior oil executives discussing how British oil companies could benefit from the invasion of Iraq. See Paul Bignell, "Secret Memos Expose Link between Oil Firms and Invasion of Iraq," *The Independent*, April 19, 2011. See also Naomi Klein, *The Shock Doctrine, The Rise of Disaster Capitalism*, Part VI, "Iraq, Full Circle Overshock," (New York: Metropolitan Books, 2007), 325–382. Frank Chikane, writing from the vantage point of an insider in the Mbeki administration in South Africa during the war, makes the same point. See Frank Chikane, *The Things That Could Not Be Said*, 58–66. "The war appeared like an opportunity to test modern war machinery. It was like children playing with newly-acquired high-tech toys. But these high-tech machines were striking human beings," p. 62. On the same matter, Chikane quotes former Federal Reserve Chairman Alan Greenspan, "I am saddened that it is politically incorrect to acknowledge what everyone knows: the Iraq war is largely about oil." Greenspan in *The Guardian*, UK, September 16, 2007, see Chikane, op. cit., 64.
25. See T. Walter Hebert, *Faith-Based War.*
26. So Archbishop Tutu could have been even more scathing in his critique of Mr. Blair had he wanted to, but his reasons for not attending that luncheon with Tony Blair are certainly vindicated. See Juan Cole, "Blair-Bush & Iraq: It's Not Just the Quagmire, But the Law-breaking and Deception," http://readersupportnews.org/opinion2/277-75/24248-focus-blair-bush-iraq-its-not-just-the-quagmire, June 15, 2014, accessed June 16, 2014.
27. See Allan Aubrey Boesak and Curtiss Paul DeYoung, *Radical Reconciliation, Beyond Political Pietism and Christian Quietism* (Maryknoll, NY: Orbis Books, 2012), 106–108.
28. See "A Call to Prophetic Action! Towards the Jubilee Year 2000, for a Socially Just, Democratic, and Prosperous Zimbabwe, The Zimbabwean Kairos Document," in *Kairos*, Leonard, (ed.), 302.
29. See T. Walter Herbert, *Faith-Based War.*
30. See Allan Aubrey Boesak and Curtiss Paul DeYoung, *Radical Reconciliation*, 108.

31. John Calvin, commentary on Amos 5:8, *Commentaries on the Twelve Minor Prophets.*
32. Calvin, commentary on Amos 5:24, emphasis original.
33. See James Luther Mays, *Amos, A Commentary, The Old Testament Library* (Philadelphia: Westminster Press, 1969), 3.
34. Calvin, Commentary on Amos, 1:1.
35. See Francis I. Andersen and David Noel Freedman, *Amos*, The Anchor Bible (New York: Doubleday, 1989), 21ff.
36. See Mays, op. cit., 2. "Taking advantage of these favourable circumstances, Jeroboam had pursued a vigorous policy of expansion east of the Jordan with great success. Along with political success came a burgeoning prosperity for many in the nation. The older homogenous economic structure of Israel gave way to sharp distinctions of wealth and privilege." See also Andersen and Freedman, Amos, 22–23: "Israel and Judah has few if any worries about the great powers to the northeast and southwest, Assyria and Egypt."
37. Cf. Mays, op. cit., 2, 3.
38. See Mays, op. cit., 142. "Amos speaks of men who miss no trick of trade; they sell refuse for profit...[they] are blind to the reality of the man whom they exploit," 144–145.
39. "Sabbath economics requires faith: a firm confidence that the world will continue to operate benevolently for a day without human labor, that God is willing and able to provide enough for the good life. Sabbath promises seven days of prosperity for six days of work. It operates on the assumption that divine providence surpasses human productivity." See Shanta Premawardhana, "Greed as Violence, Methodological Challenges in Interreligious Dialogue on the Ethics of the Global Economic Crisis," *Journal of Religious Ethics*, 2011, 39.2:223–224, 231, quoting Walter Brueggemann, "The Liturgy of Abundance, the Myth of Scarcity," *Christian Century*, March 24–31, 1999, 342–347.
40. Commentary on Amos 8:5.
41. Commentary on Amos 8:5.
42. Commentary on Amos 1:2.
43. See Mays, op. cit., 2.
44. Mays, op. cit., 109.
45. See Shanta Premawardhana, op. cit., 224. Premawardhana cites from a report of the World Council of Churches' Churches' Commission on International Affairs (CCIA) reinforcing my earlier point that these crises are often manufactured: "The accumulation of wealth and the presence of poverty are not simply accidents, but are often part of a strategy for some people to accumulate power and wealth at the expense of others. As such, greed is a form of violence which on personal, community, national, regional, and international levels isolates and injures us."
46. Commentary on Amos 9:13.
47. Rev. C. R. Kotze, *Die Bybel en ons Volkstyd, Preke 1930–1946* (Bloemfontein: Sacum Bpk., 1955), 37–44. He speaks of "modern builders of Babel's tower," those who "want to break down the walls in every area of life; who despise

the language (Afrikaans), who want to erase the color line. Where God has willed two peoples they want to create one; every one equal, white and black, yellow and brown—all one! They are the ones who awaken the wrath of God…"

48. See a very recent sermon posted on *Wasklip's Blog*, an apparently right-wing South African blog on which many sermons preached along these lines can be found. A sermon on Genesis 11 begins this way: "Where did apartheid start? In our country? No. Apartheid began with the tower of Babel where God confused peoples' languages…because [what they were doing] was against the commands of God." The sermon follows the apartheid theology logic through to Pentecost, adds the scene in Revelation 7:9 of the multitudes appearing "before Jesus' throne still as separate peoples and nations." It ends with the question, "[in light of all this], therefore, is apartheid a sin?" See "Hoekom Apartheid?????????" http://wasklip.wordpress.com/category/hoekc, accessed September 2, 2013 (my translation). I am grateful to Johan Cilliers for directing me to this.
49. See *Genesis, The Interpreter's Bible*, Vol. I (New York and Nashville: Abingdon Press, 1952), 546: The arrogance and self-satisfaction in the five times-repeated "let us… " is a characteristic of imperial power. "If there was a throne of God, they would climb up and occupy it."
50. So Walter Brueggemann on Assyria in a discussion on Isaiah 10:5–19, "Faith in the Empire," in Richard Horsley, (ed.), *In the Shadow of Empire, Reclaiming the Bible as a History of Faithful Resistance* (Louisville, KY: Westminster John Knox Press, 2008), 31.
51. See Claus Westermann, *Genesis 1–11, A Commentary*, trans. John J. Scullion S. J. (Minneapolis: Augsburg Publishing, 1974), 543: "Was there a time when this was not the case, when everyone spoke the same language? It was not a theoretical question, but the result of social upheaval."
52. See A. van Selms, *Genesis I, Prediking van het Oude Testament* (Nijkerk (the Netherlands): G.F. Callenbach, 1967), 160–166.
53. See Walter Brueggemann, *Genesis, Interpretation, A Bible Commentary for Teaching and Preaching*, James Luther Mays (ed.), (Atlanta: John Knox Press, 1982), 98–99.
54. See Allan Boesak, *The Fire Within, Sermons from the Edge of Exile* (Cape Town: New World Foundation, 2004; Glasgow: Wild Goose Publications, 2007), 1–16.
55. Brueggemann, op. cit., 100.
56. See Allan Boesak, *The Fire Within*, 7. Much of the following passages rely on my exegesis there.
57. "The massacres of the early nineties can be seen as dress rehearsals for what proponents of Hutuness themselves called the 'final solution' in 1994," writes Philip Gourevitch, *We Wish to Inform You that Tomorrow We Will Die With Our Families* (New York: Picador, 1998), 94. "Few refused to participate and assertive resistance was extremely rare," Gourevitch, op. cit., 96.
58. See Richard A. Horsley, *Jesus and the Powers, Conflict, Covenant, and the Hope of the Poor* (Minneapolis: Fortress Press, 2011), 22.

59. "This was not a good time for a god other than Jupiter to reach out to the peoples of the *oikoumene*, (inhabited parts of the earth) in a world mission...It was a particularly bad time for proclaiming a crucified messiah as Lord and Savior...If there had been any doubt as to whom the world belonged, Rome in 70 had settled the case once for all...Rome's great victory over the Judeans and the destruction of the Jerusalem Temple marked the beginning of a new era. From now on Rome's domination would remain uncontested." See Bridgett Kahl, "Acts of the Apostles, Pro(to)-Imperial Script and Hidden Transcript," in Richard A. Horsley, (ed.), *In the Shadow of Empire*, 139–141.

7 Combative Love and Revolutionary Neighborliness: Kairos, Solidarity, and the Jericho Road

1. See William R. Herzog II, *Parables as Subversive Speech: Jesus as Pedagogue of the Oppressed* (Louisville: Westminster John Knox Press, 1994).
2. See Allan Aubrey Boesak and Curtiss Paul DeYoung, *Radical Reconciliation, Beyond Political Pietism and Christian Quietism* (Maryknoll, NY: Orbis Books, 2012), 135–136.
3. Op. cit., 136.
4. J. Alfred Smith Sr. (with Harry Louis Williams II), *On the Jericho Road: A Memoir of Racial Justice, Social Action and Prophetic Ministry* (Valley Forge, PA: Judson Press, 2004).
5. James Baldwin, *No Name in the Street* (New York: Dell Publishing, 1972).
6. Cf. Klyne Snodgrass, *Stories with Intent, A Comprehensive Guide to the Parables of Jesus* (Grand Rapids: Wm. B. Eerdmans, 2008), 345.
7. Cf. Luise Schotroff, *The Parables of Jesus* (Minneapolis: Fortress Press, 2006), trans. Linda M. Maloney, 134; *Anchor Bible Dictionary*, Vol. 5 (New York: Doubleday, 1992), 941–947.
8. See Cain Hope Felder, *Troubling Biblical Waters: Race, Class, and Family* (Maryknoll: NY: Orbis Books, 1989), 37; also Curtiss Paul DeYoung, *Coming Together in the 21st Century, The Bible's Message in an Age of Diversity* (Valley Forge, PA: Judson Press, 2009), 53–54.
9. See Luise Schotroff, op. cit., 134.
10. As far as the juxtaposition of Samaritan, priest and Levite is concerned, John Dominic Crossan writes, "Priest and Levite versus Samaritan represent the positive and negative cultural polarities of first-century Jewish tradition..." Crossan speaks of a "cultural paradox, a social contradiction in terms": "For centuries before the time of Jesus, there had been tension between Jews and Samaritans, and a 'good Samaritan' was more paradox than cliché." John Dominic Crossan, *The Power of Parable, How Fiction by Jesus Became Fiction About Jesus* (New York: HarperCollins, 2012), 60.
11. See Snodgrass, *Stories with Intent*, 350–352; Simon Kistemaker, *The Parables of Jesus* (Grand Rapids: Baker Book House, 1980), 174.

12. See the discussion in Snodgrass, *Stories with Intent,* 15–17.
13. See Schotroff, op. cit., 136. Schotroff disagrees with this judgment. She believes the parable is about how "a teaching about love can become deed," 134.
14. Martin Luther King Jr., "A Time to Break the Silence," in James M. Washington (ed.), *A Testament of Hope, The Essential Writings of Martin Luther King, Jr.* (San Francisco: Harper & Row, 1986), 241.
15. Crossan, op. cit., 62.
16. See William R. Herzog II, "Why Peasants Responded to Jesus," in Richard A. Horsley (ed.), *Christian Origins: A Peoples History of Christianity,* Vol. I (Minneapolis: Augsburg Press, 2005) 47–70.
17. See e.g. Richard Horsley, *Jesus and the Powers, Conflict, Covenant, and the Hope of the Poor* (Minneapolis: Fortress Press, 2011). "Jesus worked among people subject to the Roman Empire. His renewal of Israel, moreover, was a response to the longings of those people, who had lived under the domination of one empire after another for centuries, to be free of imperial rule. Israelite tradition from which Jesus worked in his mission bore the marks of a prolonged struggle of the people both to adjust to and resist the effects of the powers of empire." See p. 17.
18. See Richard A. Horsley, *Jesus and Empire: The Kingdom of God and the New Disorder* (Minneapolis: Fortress Press, 2003), 6–12.
19. See Nicholas Wolterstorff, *Justice: Rights and Wrongs* (Princeton: Princeton University Press, 2008), 96ff.
20. Vincent Harding, "Black Power and the American Christ," in Floyd B. Barbour (ed.), *The Black Power Revolt: A Collection of Essays* (Boston: P. Sargent, 1968), 86.
21. See Es'kia Mphahlele, *ES'KIA: Education, African Humanism & Culture, Social Consciousness, Literary Appreciation* (Johannesburg: Kwela Books, 2001), 298. See also Allan Boesak, *The Tenderness of Conscience: African Renaissance and the Spirituality of Politics* (Stellenbosch: Sun Media, 2005), 136–137.
22. See Allan Boesak, *Tenderness,* 137.
23. See e.g. Richard A. Horsley, *Jesus and Empire: The Kingdom of God and the New World Disorder;* Obery M. Hendricks Jr., *The Politics of Jesus—Rediscovering the True Revolutionary Nature of Jesus' Teachings and How They Have Been Corrupted* (New York: DoubleDay, 2006); see also Allan Aubrey Boesak and Curtiss Paul DeYoung, *Radical Reconciliation.*
24. Cf. Herzog, *Parables as Subversive Speech,* 264.
25. Obery M. Hendricks, *The Politics of Jesus,* 5.
26. See J. Cardonnel, "Van konservatieve erfenis naar revolutionaire traditie," *Tijdschrift voor Theologie,* special number, *Religie van de Toekomst, Toekomst der Religie,* University of Nijmegen, 1974, 116.
27. Cardonnel, op. cit., 116.
28. Dietrich Bonhoeffer Works, Geffrey B. Kelley (ed.) (Minneapolis: Fortress Press, 2001), 12, II/13.

29. Much of the following rests on the excellent work of Scott Couper, *Albert Luthuli, Bound by Faith*, (Scottsville: UKZN Press, 2010), 152–184. The full text of the statement can be found in Couper, op. cit., 235–236.
30. This distinction would prove to be crucially important when we, in the process of the formation of the United Democratic Front some 20 years later, would debate the question of violence and nonviolence, especially since those devoted to ANC politics would very much see violence as a live option, perhaps an inevitable one, seeing as this was still official ANC policy, unchanged since 1961. We chose for Luthuli's nonviolent militancy.
31. Couper, op, cit., 175.
32. See Couper, op. cit., 204–206.
33. It is remarkable that those who choose the way of violence never have to defend their decision as "unrealistic," even though violence rarely "works" and its consequences remain devastating for those who engage in it as well as for those who are its victims. Contrarily, the defenders of nonviolence are almost always automatically seen as "unrealistic." Hence the necessity for even Luthuli and Martin Luther King to point out that they were "realists," not "pacifists."
34. One must not underestimate the embarrassment Luthuli's views caused Mandela and the others in the ANC who advocated violence. In his autobiography, Luthuli is bold on the matter of violence and nonviolence: "We do not struggle with guns and violence, and the supremacists' array of weapons is powerless against the spirit." On his African tour Mandela meanwhile, no doubt referring to Luthuli, told the conference in Ethiopia that it was a "crime for the leadership to hesitate to change tactics when those tactics proved futile." In a subsequent report (July 24) to the ANC Working Committee Mandela went even further: "Some of [Luthuli's] statements have been extremely unfortunate and have created the impression of a man who is a stooge of the whites." Couper, op. cit., 156.
35. Couper, op. cit., 168.
36. Couper op. cit., 170, quoting Martin Luther King Jr., from *The Autobiography of Martin Luther King Junior*, found at http://www.stanford.edu/group/King/publications/autobiography/chp_3.htm
37. Op. cit., 177.
38. Op. cit., 170.
39. Op. cit., 178.
40. Op. cit., 177.
41. Op. cit., 160: "His publicized views directly contradicted Mandela's views found in MK's manifesto." These views "deeply disturbed many of his more militant colleagues."
42. Couper, op. cit., 219.
43. Couper, op. cit., 182.
44. Op. cit., 177.
45. Couper, op. cit., 230.
46. Idem.
47. Idem.

48. See Cardonnel, op. cit., 120.
49. Couper, op. cit., 225.
50. See Nelson Mandela, "I am Prepared to Die," http://www.historyplace.com/speeches/mandela.htm, accessed January 30, 2014.
51. "I am Prepared to Die," op. cit., 11.
52. See Van Eck E., 2011, "When Neighbours Are Not Neighbours: A Social-scientific Reading of the Parable of the Friend at Midnight, (Lk.11:5–8)," *HTS Teologiese Studies/Theological Studies* 67, (1), Art. #788, 14 pages. DOI 10.4102/hts.v6i1.788,222
53. See Richard A. Horsley with John S. Harrison, *Bandits, Prophets, and Messiahs: Popular Movements in the Time of Jesus* (Minneapolis: Winston, 1985); and Richard Horsley, *Jesus and the Spiral of Violence: Popular Jewish Resistance in Roman Palestine* (San Francisco: Harper & Row; Minneapolis: Fortress, 1995).
54. See J. Alfred Smith, *Making Sense of Suffering: A Message to Job's Children: A Guide to Teaching and Preaching the Book of Job* (Progressive National Baptist Convention, Board of Education, 1988); see also J. Alfred Smith Sr., *Speak Until Justice Wakes, Prophetic Reflections from J. Alfred Smith Sr.*, Jini M. Kilgore (ed.) (Valley Forge, PA: Judson Press, 2006).
55. The expression is from Michelle Alexander, *The New Jim Crow: Mass Incarceration in the Age of Colorblindness* (New York: New Press, 2010). The life expectancy comparison is found in Christopher J. L. Murray, Sandeep Kulkarni, and Majid Ezzati, "Eight Americas: New Perspectives on U.S. Health disparities," *American Journal of Preventive Medicine*, 29, no. 5, Suppl. 1 (2005): 6. See as well Allan Aubrey Boesak and Curtiss Paul, DeYoung, *Radical Reconciliation*, 151–158.
56. J. Alfred Smith, *On the Jericho Road*, 239.
57. J. Alfred Smith, ibid., 239.

8 That Which Avails Much: Kairos, Public Prayer, and Political Piety

1. This letter was first published in part by several South African newspapers, then as a chapter in Allan Boesak, *Running with Horses, Reflections of an Accidental Politician* (Cape Town: JoHo! Publishers, 2009), 246–257. The letter itself is unedited. The introduction was written for this publication.
2. See Allan Boesak, *Black and Reformed: Apartheid, Liberation and the Calvinist Tradition* (Maryknoll, NY: Orbis Books, 1984), 20–31, especially 27–31.
3. The text of the 1979 letter can be found in Allan Boesak, *Black and Reformed*, 32–41.
4. See John De Gruchy, "Prayer, Politics and False Piety," in Allan Aubrey Boesak and Charles Villa-Vicencio (eds.), *When Prayer Makes News* (Philadelphia: Westminster Press, 1986), 104.
5. The "Theological Declaration" accompanying the Call and made public at the time reads, in part, "We have prayed for our rulers, as is demanded of us

in the scriptures. We have entered into consultation with them, as required by our faith. We have taken the reluctant and drastic step of declaring apartheid to be contrary to the declared will of God, and some churches have declared its theological justification to be a heresy. We now pray that God will replace the present structures of oppression with ones that are just, and remove from power those who persist in defying God's laws, installing in their place leaders who will govern with justice and mercy." Cf. Allan Boesak and Charles Villa-Vicencio (eds.), *When Prayer Makes News* (Philadelphia: Westminster Press, 1986), 26.

6. See Nicholas Wolterstorff, "Seeking Justice in Hope," in Wolterstorff, *Hearing the Call: Liturgy, Justice, Church, and World*, ed. Mark R. Gornik and Gregory Thompson (Grand Rapids, MI/Cambridge, UK: Wm. B. Eerdmans), 185. See also Nicholas Wolterstorff, *Journey Toward Justice, Personal Encounters in the Global South* (Grand Rapids: Baker Academic, 2013), 237–243. It will be clear that there is a vast difference between such a call for prayer and the political rituals of civil religiosity as expressed in the "Prayer Breakfasts" habitual in America, such a powerful phenomenon of political pietism, and so needful to the political establishment that not since Dwight Eisenhower has any American president dared to miss it.
7. Eric Metaxas, *Bonhoeffer, Pastor, Martyr, Prophet, Spy* (Nashville: Thomas Nelson, 2010), 237, my emphasis.
8. See Karl Barth, *Community, State and Church: Three Essays*, ed. Will Herzberg (New York: Doubleday and Co. 1960), 136.
9. See Charles Villa-Vicencio, *Trapped in Apartheid, a Socio-Theological History of the English-Speaking Churches* (Maryknoll, NY: Orbis Books, 1988), 154–155.
10. Cf. Gerald T. Sheppard, "'Enemies' and the Politics of Prayer," in Norman K. Gottwald and Richard A. Horsley (eds.), *The Bible and Liberation, Political and Social Hermeneutics* (Maryknoll, NY: Orbis Books, 1993), 376–391. The citation is on p. 389.
11. See *The Kairos Document*, second edition, 74, 75. It is noteworthy that this remark is made in the section on "civil disobedience." The Christians who responded to this call in the face of extraordinary harsh opposition from many church hierarchies, condemnation in the secular and Christian media and threats from the apartheid regime, were those Christians who already in 1979 accepted the challenge of participation in mass campaigns of civil disobedience, not just participating but leading those campaigns in the actions of the United Democratic Front between 1983 and the end of 1989.
12. See Allan Aubrey Boesak, *The Tenderness of Conscience, African Renaissance and the Spirituality of Politics* (Stellenbosch: Sun Media, 2005), Chapter 5, especially 154ff.
13. On the arms deal and one Christian activist's persistent, costly struggle against it and the tensions with government caused by that persistence, see Terry Crawford-Browne, *Eye on the Money, One Man's Crusade Against Corruption* (Cape Town: Umuzi, 2007).
14. Oliver Tambo, cited in Krista Johnson's insightful article, "Liberal or Liberation Framework? The Contradictions of ANC Rule in South Africa,"

Journal of Contemporary African Studies, 21, 2, May 2003, 321–328. The emphasis is mine. That the ANC could not distinguish between what was necessary for its proper working *in exile,* and what would now be proper in a democratic society, would prove to be a huge problem, especially since the root of the matter was not just practical questions of internal discipline, but of principle, namely that of "democratic centralism." Under Nelson Mandela already, but certainly under Thabo Mbeki it would be made clear that for the ANC the churches are now regarded as just another nongovernmental organization; hence the expectations still guiding the ANC in its relations with the churches, that the churches should not debate or question the "national agenda," but merely accept and support it. Their role is not one of prophetic watchfulness and prophetic witness (this concept remains hard for the ANC to grasp and accept) but of unquestioning political support and nonpolitical volunteerism, see Allan Boesak, *The Tenderness of Conscience*, 160–164.

15. For an expanded argument on this matter see Allan Aubrey Boesak, *The Tenderness of Conscience*, 154–164.
16. For my use of the terms "political pietism," and "subversive piety," see Allan Aubrey Boesak and Curtiss Paul DeYoung, *Radical Reconciliation, Beyond Political Pietism and Christian Quietism* (Maryknol, NY: Orbis Books, 2012), Introduction, Chapter 1, and Chapter 8, "Subversive Piety: The Re-radicalization of Desmond Tutu," especially 134–141.
17. I follow the thinking of Abraham Kuyper in this, see Allan Boesak, *The Tenderness of Conscience*, 232.
18. The Democratic Alliance is the official opposition in South Africa's parliament.

Bibliography

Abedine, Saad and Elizabeth Landau. "Ugandan Tabloid Prints List of 'Homosexuals'." *CNN*, February 25, 2014: http://www.cnn.com/2014/02/25/world/africa/uganda-anti-gay-law/index.html

Ackermann, Denise. "Beyers Naudé: The Public Theologian." In *The Legacy of Beyers Naudé*, edited by L. C. Hansen. Beyers Naudé Centre Series on Public Theology Volume 1. Stellenbosch: Sun Press, 2005.

Adams, Richard. "Invasion of Iraq Was Driven by Oil, Says Greenspan." *The Guardian*, September 16, 2007: http://www.theguardian.com/world/2007/sep/17/iraq.oil

Alexander, Michelle. *The New Jim Crow: Mass Incarceration in the Age of Colorblindness*. New York, NY: New Press, 2010.

Anderson, Cheryl B. *Ancient Laws & Contemporary Controversies: The Need for Inclusive Biblical Interpretation*. New York, NY: Oxford University Press, 2009.

Assmann, Hugo. *Theology for a Nomad Church*. Maryknoll, NY: Orbis Books, 1976.

Ateek, Naim Stifan. *Justice, and Only Justice: A Palestinian Theology of Liberation*. Maryknoll, NY: Orbis Books, 1989.

———. *A Palestinian Christian Cry for Reconciliation*. Maryknoll, NY: Orbis Books, 2008.

Ateek, Naim Stifan, Marc H. Ellis, and Rosemary Radford Ruether, eds. *Faith and Intifada: Palestinian Christian Voices*. Maryknoll, NY: Orbis Books, 1992.

Baldwin, James. *No Name in the Street*. New York, NY: Dell Publishing, 1972.

Baptiste, Nathalie and Foreign Policy in Focus. "It's Not Just Uganda: Behind the Christian Right's Onslaught in Africa." *The Nation*, April 4, 2014: http://www.thenation.com/blog/179191/its-not-just-uganda-behind-christian-rights-onslaught-africa

Barth, Karl. *Community, State and Church: Three Essays*. Will Herzberg, editor. New York, NY: Doubleday, 1960.

Bearing Witness Report: A Nation in Chains, A Report of the Samuel DeWitt Proctor Conference. Chicago, IL: Samuel DeWitt Conference, 2014.

Beddy, Raymond. *Inleiding tot die Geskiedenis van die Khoikhoi en San as Afrikane, vanaf die Evolusionêre Ontstaan in Noord Afrika tot die Hede in Suid Afrika*. Bloemfontein: Handisa Media, 2007.

Bignell, Paul. "Secret Memos Expose Link between Oil Firms and Invasion of Iraq." *The Independent*, April 19, 2011: http://www.independent.co.uk/news/uk/politics/secret-memos-expose-link-between-oil-firms-and-invasion-of-iraq-2269610.html

Biko, Steve. *I Write What I Like: A Selection of His Writings*. Johannesburg: Raven Press, 1996.

Boesak, Allan Aubrey. *Black and Reformed: Apartheid, Liberation, and the Calvinist Tradition*. Maryknoll, NY: Orbis Books, 1984.

———. *Dare We Speak of Hope?: Searching for a Language of Life in Faith and Politics*. Grand Rapids, MI: Wm. B. Eerdmans, 2014.

———. *Farewell to Innocence: A Socio-Ethical Study on Black Theology and Black Power*. Maryknoll, NY: Orbis Books, 1977.

———. *The Fire Within: Sermons from the Edge of Exile*. Cape Town: New World Foundation, 2004; Glasgow: Wild Goose Publications, 2007.

———. "'Founded on the Holy Bible...': A Bible-Believing Judge and the 'Sin' of Same-Sex Relationships." *Journal of Gender and Religion in Africa* 17, no. 2 (2011). 5–23.

———. "Kairos Consciousness." Kairos Southern Africa: http://kairossouthernafrica.wordpress.com/kairos-consciousness/

———. *Running with Horses: Reflections of an Accidental Politician*. Cape Town: JoHo! Publishers, 2009.

———. "Standing Where God Stands: The Confession of Belhar after Twenty-Five Years." *Studia Historiae Ecclesiasticae* 34, no. 1 (July 2008). 143–172.

———. *The Tenderness of Conscience: African Renaissance and the Spirituality of Politics*. Stellenbosch: Sun Press, 2005.

———. "Trektragiek: 'n Histories-Teologiese Perspektief op Diaz, die Huguenote en die Groot Trek." Unpublished paper, University of the Western Cape, 1988

———. "What Belongs to Caesar?: Once Again Romans 13." In *When Prayer Makes News*, edited by Allan Aubrey Boesak and Charles Villa-Vicencio. Philadelphia, PA: Westminster Press, 1986.

Boesak, Allan Aubrey and Charles Villa-Vicencio. *When Prayer Makes the News*. Philadelphia, PA: Westminster Press, 1986.

Boesak, Allan Aubrey and Curtis Paul DeYoung. *Radical Reconciliation: Beyond Political Pietism and Christian Quietism*. Maryknoll, NY: Orbis Books, 2012.

Boesak, Allan Aubrey, Johann Weusmann, and Charles Amjad-Ali, eds. *Dreaming a Different World: Globalisation and Justice for Humanity and the Earth—The Challenge of the Accra Confession for the Churches*. Stellenbosch: The Globalisation Project, 2010.

Bond, Patrick. *Against Global Apartheid: South Africa Meets the World Bank, IMF, and International Finance*. London and Cape Town: Zed Books, 2004.

———. "Is the Reform Really Working?" *The South Atlantic Quarterly* 103, no. 4 (2004). 817–839.

Bonhoeffer, Dietrich. *Berlin: 1932–1933*. Larry L. Rasmussen, editor. Isabel Best, David Higgins, and Douglas W. Stott, translators. Best, editors. Dietrich Bonhoeffer Works, vol. 12. Minneapolis, MN: Fortress Press, 2009.

———. *Letters and Papers from Prison*. Eberhard Bethge, editor. Reginald Fuller, Frank Clark, et al., translators. New York, NY: Simon and Schuster, 1997 [1953].
———. *Letters and Papers from Prison*. John W. De Gruchy, editor. Isabel Best, Lisa E. Dahill, Richard Krauss, and Nancy Lukens, translators. Dietrich Bonhoeffer Works, vol. 8. Minneapolis, MN: Fortress Press, 2010.
———. *London, 1933–1935*. Keith W. Clements, editor. Isabel Best, translator. Dietrich Bonhoeffer Works, vol. 13. Minneapolis, MN: Fortress Press, 2007.
———. *Theological Education at Finkenwalde*. H. Gaylon Barker and Mark Brocker, editors. Douglas W. Stott, translator. Dietrich Bonhoeffer Works, vol. 14. Minneapolis, MN: Fortress Press, 2013.
Boring, M. Eugene. "The Gospel of Matthew." In *The New Interpreter's Bible: A Commentary in Twelve Volumes*, vol. VIII. Nashville, TN: Abingdon, 1995.
Botha, David P. "Church and Kingdom." In *Thy Kingdom Come*, edited by Margaret Nash. Johannesburg: SACC, 1988.
Bouwsma, William. *John Calvin: A Sixteenth-Century Portrait*. New York, NY: Oxford University Press, 1988.
Braverman, Mark. *A Wall in Jerusalem: Hope, Healing, and the Struggle for Justice in Israel and Palestine*. Nashville, NY: Jericho Books, 2013.
Brueggemann, Walter. "Faith in Empire." In *In the Shadow of Empire: Reclaiming the Bible as a History of Faithful Resistance*, edited by Richard A. Horsley. Louisville, KY: Westminster John Knox Press, 2008.
———. *Genesis*. Interpretation: A Bible Commentary for Teaching and Preaching. James Luther Mays, editor. Atlanta, GA: John Knox Press, 1982.
———. "The Liturgy of Abundance, the Myth of Scarcity." *Christian Century* (March 24–31, 1999).
———. *The Prophetic Imagination*. Philadelphia, PA: Fortress Press, 1978.
Bush, George W. "Address to a Joint Session of Congress and the American People." United States Capitol, September 20, 2001: http://georgewbush-whitehouse.archives.gov/news/releases/2001/09/20010920-8.html
Calvin, John. *Institutes of the Christian Religion*. John Allen, translator. Philadelphia: Presbyterian Board of Education, 1936.
Cardonnel, J. "Van konservatieve erfenis naar revolutionaire traditie." In *Tijdschrift voor Theologie*, special number, *Religie van de Toekomst, Toekomst der Religie*. Netherlands: University of Nijmegen, 1974.
Carter, Warren. *Matthew and the Margins: A Socio-Political and Religious Reading*. Journal for the Study of the New Testament Series. Stanley E. Porter, editor. Sheffield: Sheffield Academic Press, 2000.
Chikane, Frank. *The Things That Could Not Be Said: From A[ids] to Z[imbabwe]*. Johannesburg: Picador Africa, 2013.
Chomsky, Noam and Edward S. Herman. *Manufactured Consent: The Political Economy of the Mass Media*. New York, NY: Random House, 1988.
Cilliers, Johan. *God for Us?: An Analysis and Assessment of Dutch Reformed Preaching During the Apartheid Years*. Stellenbosch: Sun Press, 2006.
Clingan, Ralph Garlin. *Against Cheap Grace in a World Come of Age: A Study in the Hermeneutics of Adam Clayton Powell, 1865–1953*. New York, NY: Peter Lang, 2002.

Cloete, G. D. and D. J. Smit. *A Moment of Truth: The Confession of the Dutch Reformed Mission Church*. Grand Rapids, MI: Wm. B. Eerdmans, 1984.

Cole, Juan. "Blair-Bush & Iraq: It's Not Just the Quagmire But the Lawbreaking & Deception." Reader Supported News, June 15, 2014: http://readersupportednews.org/opinion2/277-75/24248-focus-blair-bush-and-iraq-its-not-just-the-quagmire-but-the-lawbreaking-and-deception

Comaroff, Jean and John L. Comaroff. *Of Revelation and Revolution: Christianity, Colonialism, and Consciousness in South Africa*, vol. 1. Chicago, IL: University of Chicago Press, 1991.

Compier, Don. *What Is Rhetorical Theology?: Textual Practice and Public Discourse*. Harrisburg: Trinity International Press, 1999.

Cone, James. "Black Theology and the Black Church: Where Do We Go from Here?" In *Black Theology and Black Liberation*, edited by James Cone and Gayraud Wilmore. Maryknoll, NY: Orbis Books, 1993.

———. *Black Theology and Black Power.* Minneapolis: Seabury Press, 1969.

———. *God of the Oppressed*. New York, NY: Seabury Press, 1972.

Cooey, Paula M. "Finding Jesus in Today's Horror: The Powerful Resistance of Le Chambon." In *Resist!: Christian Dissent for the 21st Century*, edited by Michael G. Long. Maryknoll, NY: Orbis Books, 2008.

Couper, Scott. *Albert Luthuli: Bound by Faith*. Scottsville: University of KwaZulu-Natal Press, 2010.

Crawford-Browne, Terry. *Eye on the Money: One Man's Crusade Against Corruption*. Cape Town: Umuzi, 2007.

Crossan, John Dominic. *God and Empire: Jesus Against Rome, Then and Now.* New York, NY: HarperCollins, 2007.

———. *The Power of Parable: How Fiction by Jesus Became Fiction About Jesus*. New York, NY: HarperCollins, 2012.

———. "Roman Imperial Theology." In *In the Shadow of Empire: Reclaiming the Bible as a History of Faithful Resistance*, edited by Richard A. Horsley. Louisville, KY: Westminster John Knox Press, 2008.

De Gruchy, John W. *The Church Struggle in South Africa*. Minneapolis, MN: Fortress Press, 2005.

———. "In Praise of Courage." In *Discerning God's Justice in Church, Society, and Academy: Festschrift for Jaap Durand*, edited by Ernst Conradie and Christoffel Lombard. Stellenbosch: Sun Press, 2009.

———. *Liberating Reformed Theology*. Grand Rapids, MI: Wm. B. Eerdmans, 1991.

———. "Prayer, Politics, and False Piety." In *When Prayer Makes News*, edited by Allan Aubrey Boesak and Charles Villa-Vicencio. Philadelphia, PA: Westminster Press, 1986.

———. "South African Theology." In *Global Dictionary of Theology*, edited by William Dyrness and Veli-Matti Kärkkainen. Downers Grove, IL: InterVarsity Press, 2008.

———. "Toward a Reformed Theology of Liberation: A Retrieval of Reformed Symbols in the Struggle for Justice." In *Toward the Future of Reformed Theology: Tasks, Topics, Traditions*, edited by David Willis and Michael Welker. Grand Rapids, MI: Wm. B. Eerdmans, 1999.

de la Torre, Miguel. *Doing Christian Ethics from the Margins*. Maryknoll, NY: Orbis Books, 2004.

———. *Liberating Jonah: Forming an Ethics of Reconciliation*. Maryknoll, NY: Orbis Books, 2007.

de Vos, Pierre. "South Africa: Black Lesbians, No Justice." Africa Files: http://www.africafiles.org/printableversion.asp?id=21543

DeYoung, Curtis Paul. *Coming Together in the 21st Century: The Bible's Message in an Age of Diversity*. Valley Forge, PA: Judson Press, 2009.

Dibeela, Prince. "In Pursuit of a Liberating Humanism: Reflections in Honour of Allan Aubrey Boesak." In *Prophet from the South: Essays in Honour of Allan Aubrey Boesak*, edited by Prince Dibeela, Puleng Lenkabula, and Vuyani Vellem. Stellenbosch: Sun Press, 2014.

Douglas, Kelly Brown. "Heterosexism and the Black American Church Community: A Complicated Reality." In *Heterosexism in Contemporary World Religion: Problem and Prospect*. Cleveland, OH: Pilgrim Press, 2007.

Durrand, J. J. F. "A Confession—Was It Really Necessary?" In *A Moment of Truth: The Confession of the Dutch Reformed Mission Church*, edited by G. D. Cloete and D. J. Smit. Grand Rapids, MI: Wm. B. Eerdmans, 1984.

Elphick, Richard. *The Equality of Believers: Protestant Missionaries and the Racial Politics of South Africa*. Charlottesville, VA: University of Virginia Press, 2012.

———. "Evangelical Missions and Radical 'Equalization' in South Africa, 1890–1914." In *Converting Colonialism: Visions and Realities in Mission History, 1706–1914*, edited by Dana L. Robert. Grand Rapids, MI: Wm. B. Eerdmans, 2008.

Engelhardt, Tom. "American Jihad 2014." Reader Supported News, January 6, 2014: http://readersupportednews.org/opinion2/277-75/21359-american-jihad-2014

The Evil of Patriarchy in Church, Society and Politics. A Consultation Held at Mont Fleur Conference Center. Stellenbosch, 2009: http://www.iam.org.za/gix/wp-content/uploads/2013/12/EvilOfPatriarchyReport.pdf

Felder, Cain Hope. *Troubling Biblical Waters: Race, Class, and Family*. Maryknoll, NY: Orbis Books, 1989.

Fiorenza, Elizabeth Schüssler. "An Invitation to 'Dance' in the Open House of Wisdom: Feminist Study of the Bible." In *Engaging the Bible: Critical Readings from Contemporary Women*, edited by Cho Hee Ann and Katherine Pfisterer Darr. Minneapolis, MN: Fortress Press, 2006.

Fraser, Giles. "Desmond Tutu Should Not Have Snubbed Tony Blair." *The Guardian*, September 3, 2012: http://www.theguardian.com/commentisfree/2012/sep/03/desmond-tutu-snubbed-tony-blair

Friedman, David Noel, ed. *The Anchor Bible Dictionary*. 5 vol. New York, NY: Doubleday, 1992.

"Gambia's Yahya Jammeh Calls Gays 'Vermin,' Says to Fight Like Mosquitoes." *New Delhi Television*, February 19, 2014: http://www.ndtv.com/article/world/gambia-s-yahya-jammeh-calls-gays-vermin-says-to-fight-like-mosquitoes-485233

Gollwitzer, Helmut. *Die Kapitalistische Revolution*. Munich: Kaiser, 1974.

González, Justo L. and Catherine Gunsalus González. *Liberation Preaching: The Pulpit and the Oppressed*. Nashville, TN: Abingdon, 1980.

Gourevitch, Philip. *We Wish to Inform You That Tomorrow We Will Die With Our Families*. New York: Picador, 1998.

Greenwald, Glenn. "Detaining My Partner: A Failed Attempt at Intimidation." Reader Supported News, August 10, 2013: http://readersupportednews.org/news-section2/421-national-security/18975-detaining-my-partner-a-failed-attempt-at-intimidation

Hansen, L. D., ed. *The Legacy of Beyers Naudé*. Beyers Naudé Centre Series on Public Theology Volume 1. Stellenbosch: Sun Press, 2005.

Harding, Vincent. "Black Power and the American Christ." In *The Black Power Revolt: A Collection of Essays*, edited by Floyd B. Barbour. Boston: P. Sargent, 1968.

Hare, Douglas A. *Matthew*. Interpretation: A Bible Commentary for Teaching and Preaching. James Luther Mays, Patrick D. Miller, and Paul J. Achtemeier, editors. Louisville, KY: Westminster John Knox Press, 1993.

Hedges, Chris. "The Business of Mass Incarceration": http://www.truthdig.com/report/item/the_business_of_mass_incarceration_20130728

———. "Let My People Go." *truthdig*, August 10, 2014: http://www.truthdig.com/report/item/let_my_people_go_20140810

Held, David and Anthony McGrew, eds. *The Global Transformations Reader*. Cambridge, UK: Cambridge University Press, 2000.

Helm, Toby. "Tony Blair Should Face Trial Over Iraq War, Says Desmond Tutu." *The Guardian*, September 1, 2012: http://www.theguardian.com/politics/2012/sep/02/tony-blair-iraq-war-desmond-tutu

Hendricks Jr., Obery M. *The Politics of Jesus: Rediscovering the True Revolutionary Nature of Jesus' Teachings and How They Have Been Corrupted*. New York, NY: Doubleday, 2006.

Herbert, T. Walter. *Faith-Based War: From 9/11 to Catastrophic Success in Iraq*. Oakville: Equinox, 2009.

Herzog II, William R. *Parables as Subversive Speech: Jesus as Pedagogue of the Oppressed*. Louisville, KY: Westminster John Knox Press, 1994.

———. "Why Peasants Responded to Jesus." In *Christian Origins*, edited by Richard A. Horsley. A People's History of Christianity, vol. 1. Minneapolis, MN: Augsburg Press, 2005.

Honor, Leo L. *Book of Kings 1: A Commentary*. The Jewish Commentary for Bible Readers. New York, NY: Union of American Hebrew Congregations, 1955.

Horsley, Richard A. *Galilee*. Minneapolis, MN: Fortress Press, 1995.

———, ed. *In the Shadow of Empire: Reclaiming the Bible as History of Faithful Resistance*. Louisville, KY: Westminster John Knox Press, 2008.

———. *Jesus and Empire: The Kingdom of God and the New Disorder*. Minneapolis, MN: Fortress Press, 2003.

———. *Jesus and the Powers: Conflict, Covenant, and the Hope of the Poor*. Minneapolis, MN: Fortress Press, 2011.

———. *Jesus and the Spiral of Violence: Popular Jewish Resistance in Roman Palestine*. Minneapolis, MN: Fortress Press, 1995.

Horsley, Richard A. with John D. Hanson. *Bandits, Prophets, and Messiahs: Popular Movements in the Time of Jesus.* Minneapolis, MN: Winston, 1985.

Jensen, Mary L., Mary Sanders, and Steven J. Sandage. "Women's Well-Being in Seminary: A Qualitative Study." *Theological Education* 45, no. 2 (2010). 99–116.

Johnson, Krista. "Liberal or Liberation Framework?: The Contradictions of ANC Rule in South Africa." *Journal of African Studies* 21, no. 2 (May 2003). 321–328.

Johnson, William Stacy. *John Calvin: Reformer for the 21st Century.* Louisville, KY: Westminster John Knox Press, 2009.

Jones, Serene. *Calvin and the Rhetoric of Piety.* Columbia Series in Reformed Theology, Columbia Theological Seminary. Louisville, KY: Westminster John Knox Press, 1995.

Kahl, Bridgett. "Acts of the Apostles: Pro(to)-Imperial Script and Hidden Transcript." In *In the Shadow of Empire: Reclaiming the Bible as History of Faithful Resistance.* Louisville, KY: Westminster John Knox Press, 2008.

Kairos 1985. "Challenge to the Church: A Theological Comment on the Political Crisis in South Africa. The Kairos Document, 1985." South Africa History Online: http://www.sahistory.org.za/archive/challenge-church-theological-comment-political-risis-south-africa-kairos-document-1985

Kairos Britain. "Time for Action: A British Christian Response to *A Moment of Truth*, the Kairos Palestine Document." Kairos Britain: http://www.kairos-britain.org.uk/resources/documents/Time-for-Action/Time-for-Action.pdf

Kairos Iona. "Kairos Palestine: The Iona Call 2012." A Mosaic for Peace, July 25, 2012: http://amosaicforpeace.wordpress.com/2012/07/25/kairos-palestine-the-iona-call-2012/

Kairos Palestine 2009. "A Moment of Truth: A Word of Faith, Hope, and Love from the Heart of Palestinian Suffering." Kairos Palestine: http://www.kairo-spalestine.ps/sites/default/Documents/English.pdf

Kairos Southern Africa. "Latest Draft: Constitution of Kairos Southern Africa." Kairos Southern Africa: http://kairossouthernafrica.wordpress.com/about/

Kairos USA 2012. "Call to Action: U.S. Response to the Kairos Palestine Document." Kairos USA: http://kairosusa.org/wp-content/uploads/2013/12/Kairos-USA-Call-to-Action.pdf

Kasasira, Risdel. "World Condemns Killing of Gay Activist." *Daily Monitor.* January 28, 2011.

Kelly, Geffrey B. and F. Burton Nelson, eds. *A Testament to Freedom: The Essential Writings of Dietrich Bonhoeffer.* New York, NY: HarperCollins, 1990.

King Jr. Martin Luther. *The Autobiography of Martin Luther King, Jr.* Clayborne Carson, editor. New York, NY: IPM/Warner Books, 2001.

———. "A Time to Break the Silence." In *A Testament of Hope: The Essential Writings of Martin Luther King, Jr.*, edited by James M. Washington. San Francisco, CA: Harper & Row, 1986.

King, Mary Elizabeth. *A Quiet Revolution: The First Palestinian Intifada and Nonviolent Resistance.* New York, NY: Nation Books, 2007.

Klein, Naomi. *The Shock Doctrine: The Rise of Disaster Capitalism*. New York, NY: Metropolitan Books, 2007.

Kotze, C. R. *Die Bybel en ons Volkstyd: Preke 1930–1946*. Bloemfontein: Sacum Bpk., 1955.

Kuyper, Abraham. *Six Stone Lectures*. Grand Rapids, MI: Wm. B. Eerdmans, 1931.

Langner, Danie. *Teen die Héle Wêreld Vry—Knegte van die Allerhoogste: Koot Vorster—Segsman of Profeet?* Pretoria: Griffel Publishers, 2007.

Le Bruyns, Clint. "The Rebirth of Kairos Theology? A Public Theology Perspective." academia.edu: http://www.academia.edu/1484082/The_Rebirth_of_Kairos_Theology_A_Public_Theological_Perspective

Lehmann, Paul. *Ethics in a Christian Context*. New York, NY: Harper & Row, 1963.

———. *The Transfiguration of Politics: Jesus Christ and the Question of Revolution*. London, UK: SCM Press, 1975.

Leonard, Gary S. D., ed. "Kairos, the Moment of Truth: The Kairos Documents." Umajaa Centre for Biblical and Theological Community Development and Research, 2010. http://ujamaa.ukzn.ac.za/Libraries/manuals/The_Kairos_Documents.sflb.ashx

Lischer, Richard. "Anointed With Fire: The Structure of Prophecy in the Sermons of Martin Luther King Jr." In *Our Sufficiency Is of God: Essays on Preaching in Honor of Gardner C. Taylor*, edited by Timothy George, James Earl Massey, and Robert Smith. Macon, GA: Mercer University Press, 2010.

———. *The End of Words: The Language of Reconciliation in a Culture of Violence*. Grand Rapids, MI: Wm. B. Eerdmans, 2005.

Luthuli, Albert John. *Let My People Go!: The Autobiography of Albert Luthuli*. Cape Town: Tafelberg and Mafube, 2006.

Mandela, Nelson. "An Ideal for Which I am Prepared to Die." In *Great Speeches of the Twentieth Century*, edited by Tom Clarke. London, UK: Preface Books, 2008.

Mays, James Luther. *Amos: A Commentary*. The Old Testament Library. Philadelphia, PA: Westminster Press, 1969.

Metaxas, Eric. *Bonhoeffer: Pastor, Martyr, Prophet, Spy*. Nashville, TN: Thomas Nelson, 2010.

McLaren, Brian D. *Why Did Jesus, Moses, the Buddha, and Muhammad Cross the Road?: Christian Identity in a Multi-Faith World*. Nashville, NY: Jericho Books, 2012.

Mogoatlhe, Lerato. "Killing and Dying in God's Name—Being Gay in Uganda is Like Being Sentenced to Death." *Sunday Independent*. December 15, 2010.

Moluleke, Tinyiko Sam. "May the Black God Stand Up, Please!: Biko's Challenge to Religion." In *Biko Lives!: Contesting the Legacies of Steve Biko*, edited by Andile Mngxitama, Amanda Alexander, and Nigel C. Gibson. New York, NY: Palgrave Macmillan, 2008.

Moodie, T. Dunbar. *Afrikaner Civil Religion*. Berkeley, CA: University of California Press, 1975.

Mphahlele, Es'kia. *ES'KIA: Education, African Humanism & Culture, Social Consciousness, Literary Appreciation*. Johannesburg: Kwela Books, 2001.

Murray, Christopher J. L., Sandeep Kulkarni, and Majid Ezzati. "Eight Americas: New Perspectives on U.S. Health Disparities." *American Journal of Preventive Medicine* 29, no. 5, suppl. 1 (2005).

Myers, David G. and Letha Dawson Scanzoni. *What God Has Joined Together: The Christian Case for Gay Marriage.* New York, NY: HarperCollins, 2005.

"National Defense Authorization Act for Fiscal Year 2012." Wikipedia: http://en.wikipedia.org/wiki/National_Defense_Authorization_Act_for_Fiscal_Year_2012 (accessed November 20, 2012).

Naudé, C. F. B. "Christian Involvement in the Struggle for Human Rights and Justice." In *The Legacy of Beyers Naudé*, edited by L. C. Hansen. Beyers Naudé Centre Series on Public Theology Volume 1. Stellenbosch: Sun Press, 2005.

———. *My Decision.* Johannesburg: The Christian Institute, 1963.

———. *My Land van Hoop.* Cape Town: Human & Rousseau, 1995.

———. "The Parting of the Ways." *Pro Veritate* 6 (October 1970).

———. "Steve Biko: The Man and His Message." In *The Legacy of Beyers Naudé*, edited by L. C. Hansen. Beyers Naudé Centre Series on Public Theology Volume I. Stellenbosch: Sun Press, 2005.

Naudé, C. F. B. and Dorothee Sölle. *Hope for Faith: A Conversation.* Grand Rapids, MI: Wm. B. Eerdmans, 1986.

Naudé, Piet J. *Neither Calendar nor Clock: Perspectives on the Belhar Confession.* Grand Rapids, MI: Wm. B. Eerdmans, 2010.

Nelson, Richard D. *First and Second Kings.* Interpretation: A Bible Commentary for Teaching and Preaching. Patrick D. Miller, editor. Atlanta, GA: John Knox Press, 1987.

Oduyoye, Mercy Amba. *Daughters of Anowa: African Women and Patriarchy.* Maryknoll, NY: Orbis Books, 1995.

Pillay, Versahni. "Cursed if We Criticize Zuma? Think Again." *Mail & Guardian*, October 8, 2013: http://mg.co.za/article/2013-10-08-cursed-if-we-criticise-zuma-think-again/

Premawardhana, Shanta. "Greed as Violence: Methodological Challenges in Interreligious Dialogue on the Ethics of the Global Economic Crisis." *Journal of Religious Ethics* 39, no. 2 (2011).

Proceedings of the General Council of the World Alliance of Reformed Churches. Geneva: WARC, 2004.

Psalms en Gesange: Nederduits Gereformeerde Kerk and Nederduitsch Hervormde Kerk. Cape Town: N.G. Kerkuitgewers, 1976.

Reich, Robert. "The Bankruptcy of Detroit and the Division of America." Reader Supported News, September 6, 2014: http://readersupportednews.org/opinion2/279-82/25725-focus-the-bankruptcy-of-detroit-and-the-division-of-america (accessed September 8, 2014).

"Report on Homosexuality." In *Agenda for Synod: Fifth General Synod of the Uniting Reformed Church, Unity in Diversity, 29 September-05 October, 2008 Hammanskraal.* Wellington: Bible Media, 2008.

Rieger, Joerg. *Christ and Empire: From Paul to Postcolonial Times.* Minneapolis, MN: Fortress Press, 2007.

Rieger, Joerg and Kwok Pui-Lan. *Occupy Religion: Theology of the Multitude*. Lanham, MD: Rowman and Littlefield, 2012.

Ring, Trudy. "Gambian President on Gay Asylum-Seekers: 'I Will Kill Them'." *Advocate*, May 16, 2014: http://www.advocate.com/world/2014/05/16/gambian-president-gay-asylum-seekers-i-will-kill-them

Romero, Oscar. *The Violence of Love: The Pastoral Wisdom of Archbishop Oscar Romero*. James R. Brockman, translator and compiler. New York, NY: Harper & Row, 1988.

Russell, Letty. *Human Liberation in a Feminist Perspective: A Theology*. Philadelphia, PA: Westminster John Knox Press, 1974.

Sacks, Jonathan. *The Dignity of Difference: How to Avoid the Clash of Civilizations*. New York, NY: Continuum, 2006.

Schlingensiepen, Frederich. *Dietrich Bonhoeffer 1906–1945: Martyr, Thinker, Man of Resistance*. Isabel Best, translator. New York, NY: T&T Clark, 2010.

Schotroff, Luise. *The Parables of Jesus*. Linda M. Maloney, translator. Minneapolis, MN: Fortress Press, 2006.

Sharlett, Jeff. *The Family: The Secret Fundamentalism at the Heart of American Power*. New York, NY: HarperCollins, 2008.

Sheppard, Gerald T. "'Enemies' and the Politics of Prayer." In *The Bible and Liberation: Political and Social Hermeneutics*, edited by Norman K. Gottwald and Richard A. Horsley. Maryknoll, NY: Orbis Books, 1993.

Smit, Dirk J. "Kairos Documents." In *Essays in Public Theology: Collected Essays I*, edited by Ernst Conradie and Christo Lombard. UWC Study Guides in Religion and Theology 12. Stellenbosch: Sun Press, 2007.

———. "Reformed Faith, Justice, and the Struggle Against Apartheid." In *Essays in Public Theology: Collected Essays I*, edited by Ernst Conradie and Christo Lomard. UWC Study Guides in Religion and Theology 12. Stellenbosch: Sun Press, 2007.

———. "Resisting 'Lordless Powers'?" In *Prophet from the South: Essays in Honour of Allan Aubrey Boesak*, edited by Prince Dibeela, Puleng Lenkabula, and Vuyani Vellem. Stellenbosch: Sun Press, 2014.

Smith Sr. J. Alfred. *Making Sense of Suffering: A Message to Job's Children: A Guide to Teaching and Preaching the Book of Job*. Progressive National Baptist Convention, Board of Education, 1988.

———. *Speak Until Justice Wakes: Prophetic Reflections from J. Alfred Smith, Sr.* Jini M. Kilgore, editor. Valley Forge, PA: Judson Press, 2006.

Smith Sr., J. Alfred with Harry Louis Williams II. *On the Jericho Road: A Memoir of Racial Justice, Social Action, and Prophetic Ministry*. Valley Forge, PA: Judson Press, 2004.

Snodgrass, Klyne. *Stories with Intent: A Comprehensive Guide to the Parables of Jesus*. Grand Rapids, MI: Wm. B. Eerdmans, 2008.

"South African Teens Die after Alleged Abuse at Reported Gay 'Conversion' Camp." *The Huffington Post*, April 30, 2013: http://www.huffingtonpost.com/2013/04/30/gay-south-africa-conversion-deaths_n_3186820.html

Stroud, Dean G., ed. *Preaching in Hitler's Shadow: Sermons of Resistance in the Third Reich*. Grand Rapids, MI: Wm. B. Eerdmans, 2013.

Stuart, Jeff. "Junkets for Jesus." *Mother Jones* (November–December 2010).
Tan, Sylvia. "Zimbabwe's Mugabe: I 'pity' the Queen Over Britain's 'Gay Habits'": http://www.gaystarnews.com/article/zimbabwes-mugabe-i-pity-queen-over-britains-gay-habits200414
ter Schegget, G. H. *Het Geheim van de Mensenzoon*. Baarn, Netherlands: Wereldvenster, 1972.
That All May Be One: World Alliance of Reformed Churches 24th General Council Proceedings. Geneva: WARC, 2005.
Thomas, M. M. "Issues Concerning the Life and Work of the Church in a Revolutionary World." In *Unity of Mankind*, edited by A. H. van den Heuvel. Geneva: World Council of Churches, 1969.
Tin, Louis-Georges. *The Dictionary of Homophobia: A Global History of Gay and Lesbian Experience*. Mark Redburn with Alice Michaud and Kyle Mathers, translators. Vancouver: Arsenal Pulp Press, 2008.
Tooley, Mark D. "Archbishop Tutu Shuns Tony Blair." *Frontpage Mag*, August 30, 2012: http://www.frontpagemag.com/2012/mark-d-tooley/archbishop-tutu-shuns-tony-blair/
Turley, Melissa. "South Africa: The Fight for Acceptance in the Rainbow Nation." *Global Post*, October 18, 2012: http://www.globalpost.com/dispatches/globalpost-blogs/rights/South-Africa-lesbians-violence-lgbt (accessed June 4, 2013).
Van Eck, E. "When Neighbours Are not Neighbours: A Social-Scientific Reading of the Parable of the Friend at Midnight (Lk. 11:5–8)." *HTS Teologiese Studies/Theological Studies* 67, no. 1.
van Selms, A. *Genesis I: Prediking van het Oude Testament*. Nijkerk, Netherlands: G.F. Callenbach, 1967.
Villa-Vicencio, Charles. "An All-Pervading Heresy: Racism and the English-Speaking Churches." In *Apartheid Is a Heresy*, edited by Charles Villa-Vicencio and John De Gruchy. Cape Town: David Philip, 1982.
———. "Quo Vadis?: The Dangerous Memory of the Gospel." *The Link* 47, no. 2 (April–May 2014). 3–10.
———. *Trapped in Apartheid: A Socio-Theological History of the English-Speaking Churches*. Maryknoll, NY: Orbis Books, 1988.
Villa-Vicencio, Charles and John De Gruchy, eds. *Apartheid Is a Heresy*. Grand Rapids, MI: Wm. B. Eerdmans, 1982.
Vellem, Vuyani S. *The Symbol of Liberation in South African Public Life: A Black Theological Perspective*. Unpublished PhD. thesis. University of Pretoria, 2007.
Walsh, Jerome T. *1 Kings*. Berit Olam: Studies in Hebrew Narrative and Poetry, David S. Cotter, editor. Collegeville, MN: Liturgical Press, 1996.
Walzer, Michael. *The Revolution of the Saints: A Study in the Origins of Radical Politics*. London, UK: Weidenfeld & Nicolson, 1966.
West, Cornel. *Democracy Matters: Winning the Fight Against Imperialism*. New York, NY: Penguin Press, 2007.
West, Gerald O. "Explicating Domination and Resistance: A Dialogue between James C. Scott and Biblical Scholars." In *Hidden Transcripts and the Arts of Resistance: Applying the Work of James C. Scott to Jesus and Paul*, edited

by Richard A. Horsley. Society of Biblical Literature, Semeia Studies, No. 48. Atlanta: Society of Biblical Literature, 2004.

———. "People's Theology, Prophetic Theology, and Public Theology in Post-Liberation South Africa." Unpublished paper. Ujamaa Centre, School of Religion, Philosophy, and Classics, University of KwaZulu-Natal.

Westermann, Claus. *Genesis 1–11: A Commentary*. John J. Scullion, translator. Minneapolis, MN: Augsburg Publishing, 1974.

Williams, Reggie L. *Bonhoeffer's Black Jesus: Harlem Renaissance Theology and an Ethic of Resistance*. Waco, TX: Baylor University Press, 2014.

Wind, Renate. *Dietrich Bonhoeffer: A Spoke in the Wheel*. John Bowden, translator. Grand Rapids, MI: Wm. B. Eerdmans, 1991.

Witte, John. *The Reformation of Rights: Law, Religion, and Human Rights in Early Modern Calvinism*. New York, NY: Cambridge University Press, 2007.

Wolterstorff, Nicholas. *Hearing the Call: Liturgy, Justice, Church, and World*. Mark R. Gornik and Greg Thompson, editors. Grand Rapids, MI: Wm. B. Eerdmans, 2011.

———. *Journey Toward Justice: Personal Encounters in the Global South*. Grand Rapids, MI: Baker Academic, 2013.

———. *Justice: Rights and Wrongs*. Princeton, NJ: Princeton University Press, 2008.

———. *The Mighty and the Almighty: An Essay in Political Theology*. New York, NY: Oxford University Press, 2011.

———. "Seeking Justice as Hope." In *Hearing the Call: Liturgy, Justice, Church, and World*. Mark R. Gornik and Greg Thompson, editors. Grand Rapids, MI: Wm. B. Eerdmans, 2011.

———. *Until Justice and Peace Embrace: The Kuyper Lectures for 1981, Delivered at the Free University of Amsterdam*. Grand Rapids, MI: Wm. B. Eerdmans, 1983.

———. "The Wounds of God: Calvin's Theology of Social Justice." In *Hearing the Call: Liturgy, Justice, Church, and World* by Nicholas Wolterstorff, edited by Mark R. Gornik and Gregory Thompson. Grand Rapids, MI: Wm. B. Eerdmans, 2011.

Zunes, Stephen. "California State Assembly Seeks to Stifle Debate on Israel." *The Huffington Post*, August 30, 2012: http://www.huffingtonpost.com/stephen-zunes/california-state-assembly_b_1842841.html

———. "Supporting Nonviolence in Syria." *Truthout*, January 8, 2013: http://truth-out.org/news/item/13774-supporting-non-violence-in-syria

Index

absolutization, 108–10
Abyssinian Baptist Church, 73, 90, 234n57
Accra Confession, 64, 91, 101, 104, 240n30
Ackermann, Denise, 81, 86
Acts of the Apostles, 57, 61, 77, 167
African National Congress (ANC)
  chaplain general, 13
  Christianity and, 203–11
  Kairos Southern Africa and, 88, 233n49
  Luthuli and, 182–4, 186, 251n34
  Mbeki and, 254n14
  Naudé and, 222n3
  prayer and, 200–1
  Umkhonto we Sizwe, 76
  violence and, 182–4, 188–9, 192, 251n30
Afrikanerdom, 46, 74, 82, 89, 131
Ahab (biblical figure), 143–8, 154–6
Allen Temple Baptist Church, 7, 169
Amos (biblical figure), 4, 16, 128, 135, 143, 157–62, 220n55
Anderson, Cheryl B., 96, 220n54
Arab Spring, 20, 23
Arendse, Aunt Maria, 40, 43
Arrison, Edwin, 9
Aryan Paragraph, 131
Asmal, Kader, 199–211
Assman, Hugo, 29
Ateek, Naim Stifan, 13, 32–3
Baartman, Francis, 54
Baldwin, James, 104, 170
Bantustan, 77–8
Barmen Declaration, 103, 113, 235, 239n25
Barth, Karl, 100, 147, 201, 228n71, 239n25
Belydende Kring (the Confessing Circle), 51
Bethge, Eberhard, 70
Beyers Naudé, Christiaan Frederick, 5, 7, 40–1, 50–1, 54, 71–2, 74–5, 77, 80–2, 85–91, 98, 131
Beza, Theodore, 55–6, 227n61
Biko, Steve, 16, 40, 42, 59, 63, 89–90, 129
bin Laden, Osama, 246n22
Black Consciousness, 41, 79, 89, 234n55
Blair, Tony, 144, 149–53, 245n21, 246n22, 246n24, 246n26
Bond, Patrick, 214n4
Bonhoeffer, Dietrich, 4–5, 7, 23–4, 29, 36–7, 64, 69–75, 81–7, 90–1, 132–3, 135, 139, 143, 147–8, 181–2, 191, 201
Book of Kings, 143, 156, 158
Botha, David, 223n11
Botha, P. W., 78, 199, 231n22
Broederbond, 222n3
Broederkring, 50
Brueggemann, Walter, 16, 45, 163–4
Bush, George W., 133, 144, 149–51, 153

Calata, John, 54
Call for the End to Unjust Rule, 6
Calvin, John, 4, 11–13, 39–68, 94, 100, 106, 111, 119, 122–3, 125, 128–9, 157–9, 163, 204
Canons of Dordt, 104
Cardonnel, Jean, 180–1, 190
casus confessionis, 106
charity, 50, 60, 86, 176–7, 180, 193, 197
Cheney, Dick, 150
Chikane, Frank, 245n21, 246n24
Chomsky, Noam, 130
Christian Institute, 40, 74, 82, 230n13, 239n25
Cilliers, Johan, 131
Clingan, Ralph Garlin, 234n57
Cloete, Gerhard D., 97, 236n2
Cole, Juan, 151
colonialism, 26, 28, 34, 44–6, 91
Colossians, 73, 109
Comaroff, Jean and John, 135
Cone, James, 22–3
Confession of Belhar, 5, 26, 47, 93–117
conscience, 51, 64–8
Constantine, 18, 27
Cooey, Paula M., 85
Cottesloe Declaration, 44, 76–8, 86, 222n4
counter-violence, 80
Couper, Scott, 182–5, 188–9
Crossan, John Dominic, 177, 218n31, 249n10

Dalit-Bahujan, 14
De Gruchy, John, 7, 25, 43, 201, 214n6, 219n42
De Klerk, F. W., 149
De La Torre, Miguel, 96, 234n57
de Vos, Pierre, 238n14
decision, kairos and, 69–75
Defiance Campaign, 26, 76
defining presence, 103–5
Democratic Republic of the Congo, 19, 238n15
DeYoung, Curtiss Paul, 7, 172
Dibeela, Prince, 223n9
dignity, 14, 20, 22–3, 25, 30–1, 42, 46, 51, 54, 64–5, 84, 86, 93–6, 98, 108–12
diversity, 108–12
divine obedience, 40, 50–4, 57, 60
Durand, Jaap, 97–100, 102, 117
Dutch Reformed Church in Africa, 4, 39–41, 44, 46, 49–50, 77, 82, 102–3, 113, 131, 162
Dutch Reformed Mission Church (DMRC), 98–100, 109, 236n2, 241n43

ecumenism, 40
Egypt, 60, 96, 124, 141
Eisenhower, Dwight, 97, 253n6
El Salvador, 142, 216n19
Elijah, 4–5, 16, 35, 37, 143–4, 154
Elphick, Richard, 44, 219n44
Engelhardt, Tom, 20
Equality Court, 95

Family, The, 97
Fanon, Frantz, 42
Felder, Cain Hope, 172
feminist, 27–8, 30
Ferguson, Missouri, 3
Finkenwalde, 69
Fiorenza, Elizabeth Schüssler, 20
First Table of the Decalogue, 59
Fraser, Giles, 149–53, 245n21

Gaza, 13, 215n1
General Synod of 2008, 93, 105, 113
  see also Uniting Reformed Church in South Africa
Genesis, 83–4, 141, 162–3, 166–7, 202
Gleichschaltung, 131
Goebbels, Joseph, 131

Gollwitzer, Helmut, 42–3, 65
Gospels
apartheid and, 41, 111–12
Belhar and, 103–4, 107
Bonhoeffer and, 69, 71
Calvin and, 61–2
combative love and, 178–9
inclusiveness and, 115
integrity of, 17
liberation theology and, 28
Luke, 167, 172–3
Matthew, 4, 33
Nazism and, 131–2
Reformed tradition and, 41, 46, 98, 101
revolution and, 21–2
South Africa and, 41, 44, 46–7, 77, 148, 152, 178
Gott mitt Uns, 131, 139
Gourevitch, Philip, 166, 248n57
Graaff-Reinet church, 44
Greenwald, Glenn, 134, 243n30
Group Areas Act (1950), 40, 43, 222n5
Guevara, Ché, 42

Handel, Georg, 137
Harding, Vincent, 177
Hedges, Chris, 134
Hendricks, Obery M. Jr., 179
Herbert, T. Walter, 133, 141, 151
heresy, 2, 4, 17, 26, 49, 88, 93–4, 98, 104, 106, 111–13
Herzog, William R., 169, 179
Hitler, Adolf, 5, 70–1, 73, 81, 121, 131–2, 139, 147–8, 182
HIV/AIDS, 196, 204
Horsley, Richard, 6, 60
HR35, 134
Huguenots, 55–6
human rights, 3, 55, 67, 86, 112, 114, 134
Human Rights Day, 200, 206, 209
Hussein, Saddam, 149, 151

idolatry, 31, 103, 111, 207
imperialism, 172–3, 195
"in the wilderness," 135–9
inclusion, 6–7, 20, 30–1, 49, 85, 95–7, 108–17
India, 14, 19, 78
Institutes (Calvin), 52–3, 55–7, 60–1, 106
Iraq War, 133, 141, 144, 149–53, 166
Is a Confession Really Necessary? (Durand), 98
Isaiah, 5, 35, 59, 136–7, 147, 161, 163–4
Israel, 3, 6, 13, 29, 32, 57–8, 60, 126, 134–5, 143, 154–9, 161, 163, 165, 173, 179, 202, 207

Jammeh, Yahya, 114
Jeremiah, 16, 35, 37, 123–4, 132–3, 139, 143, 155, 202
Jericho Road, 21, 170–82, 193, 196–7
Jewish Question, 69, 81–2, 181
Jezebel (biblical figure), 143
John the Baptist, 4–5, 34, 152
Johnson, Krista, 204
Johnson, William Stacy, 67

kairos
consciousness and, 9–19
consequences of confession and, 97–102
crisis and, 141–7
decision and, 69–75
end of words and, 119–30
Jericho Road and, 175–80
liberation and, 93–7
prophetic ministry and, 169–71
rhetoric of barricades and, 130–5
rivers of justice and, 157–62
theology, 25–33
Kairos Document, 1–2, 4, 9–10, 12–13, 15, 17–19, 25–6, 32–3, 88, 153, 203

Kampala, Uganda, 97
Kato, David, 95, 97
Kenya, 149, 220n55
Kenyatta, Uhuru, 149
Khoi-Khoi, 44–6
King, Martin Luther Jr., 4, 11, 23, 137, 177, 184–5, 251n33
King, Mary Elizabeth, 24
King Francis I, 52
King Herod, 34–5, 63, 152, 179
"King of kings," God as, 54, 56, 58, 65, 226n46
Kings
 see Book of Kings
Klein, Naomi, 134
Kliptown, 26, 76
Kuyper, Abraham, 47, 50, 66, 225n40
kyriarchy, 20

Land Acts (1913 and 1936), 77, 222n5
Landeskirchen, 131
Le Bruyns, Clint, 25, 27, 31–3, 172, 215n1, 220n61
Lehman, Paul, 12, 24, 66
Lenin, Vladimir, 42, 208
LGBTI, 5, 23, 84, 91, 93–9, 105, 108–16, 196
liberation theology, 4, 6, 13, 25–33, 43, 51, 100, 110
Lischer, Richard, 6, 119–22, 241n1
loyalty and lesser loyalties, 85–90
Lutheranism, 67
Luthuli, Albert, 4, 26, 54, 63, 77–80, 182–92

Mahati, David, 97
Malcolm X, 23
Mandela, Nelson, 23, 40, 63, 76, 80, 149, 182–5, 187–92, 203, 207–8
martyria, 73–4, 81, 87
Marx, Karl, 42, 208
Massey, James, 14
Matthews, Z. K., 26
Mays, James Luther, 158
Mbeki, Thabo, 6, 199, 204, 214n4, 246n24, 254n14
McClaren, Brian, 18
Metaxas, Eric, 201
Micah, 5, 123–9, 151, 158, 161
Mighty and the Almighty, The (Wolsterstorff), 59
Moment of Truth, A (Cloete and Smit), 97
Mugabe, Robert, 114, 153, 241n40
Museveni, Yoweri, 5, 237n12

National Defense Authorization Act, 134
National Prayer Breakfasts, 97
National Security Agency (NSA), 134
nationalism, 41, 46, 50, 70, 83, 100, 132, 144, 183
Nazism, 24, 27, 36, 71, 73, 85–6, 103, 120–1, 131, 139, 181, 191
Niemöller, Martin, 132
Ntsikana, John, 178–9

Obama, Barack, 134, 242n15
Oduyoye, Mercy, 136
"opposition by evasion," 91
Other, 6, 10, 65, 67, 74, 87, 94, 103, 108–9, 111–12

Palestine *Kairos* Document, 9, 19, 23, 27, 32–3, 57
Pan Africanist Congress, 75, 183
Pass Laws, 75
peace question, 82
Plaatjie, Sol, 26, 54
"possession of God," 105
poverty, 49–50, 64, 91, 101, 105, 122, 157, 196–7, 204
Powell, Adam Clayton, 90, 234n57
Preaching in Hitler's Shadow (Stroud), 121
Premawardhana, Shanta, 247n45

Prince Antoinne of Navarre, 55
Pro Veritate magazine, 74
Programme to Combat Racism (PCR), 75
propaganda, 13, 46, 119–21, 131, 135, 151, 161
prophetic theology, 1, 13, 15, 25–6, 31–2, 123
Psalm, 44–5, 50, 202
public theology, 26, 32, 66, 169, 220n61, 229n94

Qwelane, Jon, 95

racism, 2, 10, 22, 24, 39, 41–2, 48–50, 62–4, 75, 86, 94, 96, 101–12, 120, 131, 169, 188–9, 196–7, 208–9
Ramaphosa, Cyril, 13
Reformed tradition
  costly discipleship, 55–64
  divine obedience, 50–4
  giving voice to voiceless, 43–8
  making choices, 39–43
  tenderness of conscience, 64–8
  wounds of God, 48–50
repression, 63, 76, 180
rhetoric of the barricades, 119–20, 130–5, 154, 157
Rieger, Joerg, 217n29
righteous calling, 65–6
righteous choices
  kairos and decision, 69–75
  loyalty and lesser agonies, 85–90
  parting of the ways, 75–82
  serpent question, 82–5
  turning words into deeds, 90–2
Rivonia trial, 40, 76
Rizpah, 4, 150, 246n23
Robben Island, 76
Roman Catholic Church, 55, 206, 219n42
Roman Empire, 14, 18, 34, 52, 63, 152–3, 167, 173, 177, 179, 195
Romero, Oscar, 142
Russell, Letty, 28

Sanhedrin, 57, 61
Scalia, Antonin, 114
Schlebusch, Alwyn, 51, 199
Schlingensiepen, Ferdinand, 231n29
Schneider, Paul, 121
Schotroff, Luise, 176, 250n13
serpent question, 82–5, 91
sexism, 30, 105, 197
Sharpeville massacre, 40, 75–6, 78–9, 82, 86, 166, 182, 200, 202, 222n3, 230n13, 233n42
Sheppard, Gerald D., 202
"shock and horror," 81
Sisulu, Albertina, 54
Sisulu, Walter, 182
sizwe, 12, 123
skandalon, 104
slave revolts, 26, 45
slavery, 2, 6, 28–9, 32, 41, 43–6, 58, 64, 124, 165, 177–8, 194–5, 202, 207
Smit, Dirk J., 31, 97, 101
Smith, J. Alfred, 7, 169–72, 175, 193, 196–7
Snowden, Edward, 134, 243n30
sola Scriptura, 40
South African Council of Churches, 47, 51, 75, 199, 233n49
sovereignty, 52, 54, 57, 66
Soweto uprisings, 26, 63, 166, 199–202
St. Paul, 52–4, 194, 211
Stroud, Dean, 121, 131
Swart, Ignatius, 233n49
synods, 51, 53, 93, 95, 97, 101–2, 105, 113, 116, 131–2

Tambo, Oliver, 63, 184, 203–4
Taylor, Charles, 149–50
Ten Commandments, 60
terrorism, 134, 190

theology
  church, 15, 20, 217n20
  feminist, 28, 30
  incarcerated, 32–3
  liberation, 4, 6, 13, 25–33, 43, 51, 100, 110
  prophetic, 1, 13, 15, 25–6, 31–2, 123
  public, 26, 32, 66, 169, 220n61, 229n94
  state, 13, 15
Thomas, M. M., 19, 21–3
Tooley, Mark, 246n22
Tower of Babel, 141, 143, 162, 166
Treason trial of 1956–1961, 40, 76
"true liberation," 90, 202
Turley, Melissa, 238n14
Tutu, Desmond, 149–53, 169, 199, 246n21–2, 246n26
tyranny, 12, 42, 52–6, 58–9, 63–4, 66, 80, 114, 121

ubuntu, 90, 111, 173, 196
Uganda, 5, 95, 97, 237n7, 238n15
Umkhonto we Sizwe, 76, 182
United Democratic Front, 78, 231n22, 251n30, 253n11
Uniting Reformed Church in South Africa (URCSA), 95, 98–9, 102–3, 105, 107, 113–16, 235, 241n43
  see also General Synod of 2008

Valls, Manuel, 213n3
van der Kemp, Johannes Theodorus, 44, 219n44
van Selms, A., 163
Vellem, Vuyani, 7, 27
verbastering, 40–1
Verwoerd, Hendrik, 77
Vietnam War, 135, 177
Villa-Vicencio, Charles, 6–7, 27, 82, 202, 233n49
Volksromantik, 41
Vorster, John, 199
Vorster, Koot, 40–1, 43

Walsh, Jerome, 144
Walzer, Michael, 224n30
West, Cornel, 17
West, Gerald, 6, 215n1, 217n20
Westermann, Claus, 163
Western theology, 22, 30, 60
Williams, Reggie L., 235n57
Wind, Renate, 232n29
Witte, John, 59
Wittenberg, Gunther, 6
Wolf, Naomi, 134
Wolterstorff, Nicholas, 7, 47–8, 53, 59, 61–2, 65, 201, 225n30
Women's March on Pretoria (1956), 76
World Alliance of Reformed Churches, 64, 101, 106, 222n2, 225n34
World Council of Churches (WCC), 76, 80–1, 232n31

Yeats, William Butler, 119

Zimbabwe, 114, 149, 153
Zuma, Jacob, 52
Zunes, Stephen, 134

Made in the USA
Monee, IL
03 January 2024

51071084R00157